About t...

Stefanie London is a *USA Today* Bestselling author of contemporary romance. Her books have been called 'genuinely entertaining and memorable' by Booklist, and her writing praised as 'elegant, descriptive and delectable' by *RT Magazine*. Originally from Australia, she now lives in Toronto with her very own hero and is doing her best to travel the world. She frequently indulges her passions for lipstick, good coffee, books and anything zombie related.

Writing romance for Mills & Boon is truly a dream come true for **Soraya Lane**. An avid book reader and writer since her childhood, Soraya describes becoming a published author as 'the best job in the world'. Soraya lives with her own real life hero and son on a small farm in New Zealand, surrounded by animals and with an office overlooking a field where their horses graze. Visit Soraya at sorayalane.com

Michelle Smart is a Publishers Weekly bestselling author with a slight-to-severe coffee addiction. A book worm since birth, Michelle can usually be found hiding behind a paperback, or if it's an author she really loves, a hardback. Michelle lives in rural Northamptonshire in England with her husband and two young Smarties. When not reading or pretending to do the housework she loves nothing more than creating worlds of her own. Preferably with lots of coffee on tap. Visit michelle-smart.com

Sports Romance

December 2024
On The Stage

January 2025
On The Ice

February 2025
In The End Zone

March 2025
In The Saddle

April 2025
On The Pitch

May 2025
On The Track

Sports Romance:
On The Stage

STEFANIE LONDON

SORAYA LANE

MICHELLE SMART

MILLS & BOON

First Published in Great Britain 2024
by Mills & Boon, an imprint of HarperCollins*Publishers* Ltd,
1 London Bridge Street, London, SE1 9GF

www.harpercollins.co.uk

HarperCollins*Publishers*
Macken House, 39/40 Mayor Street Upper,
Dublin 1, D01 C9W8, Ireland

ISBN: 978-0-263-39772-7

MIX
Paper | Supporting
responsible forestry
FSC™ C007454

Printed and Bound in the UK using 100% Renewable Electricity
at CPI Group (UK) Ltd, Croydon, CR0 4YY

ONLY THE BRAVE TRY BALLET

STEFANIE LONDON

To Nan and Nonno for teaching me what
it means to be brave.

To my amazing husband for his endless supply of
love and support (and for always doing the dishes
when I was stuck in the revision cave).

To my family for never thinking my dreams were
crazy, or loving me enough not to say so.

To my editor, Flo, for seeing past the rough edges of
my first submission and taking a chance on this story.

CHAPTER ONE

WHAT DO A ballerina and a football player have in common? It was the question Jasmine Bell pondered as she watched the footballer in front of her struggling to master a *plié*. Discounting a need for flexible hamstrings... they have nothing in common. Absolutely nothing. Yet here they were.

She stood in the middle of the studio, wearing her usual uniform of a black leotard, tights and ballet shoes. These items were like a second skin to a dancer, but tonight she couldn't have felt more exposed than if she were standing there butt-naked. She folded her arms tight across her chest.

'Let's take it from the top. Keep those shoulders down,' she said, forcing a calming breath. She loosened her shoulders, rounded her arms into first position and turned her feet out to match. 'Prepare...left hand on the *barre* and *plié*—one, two, three, four...'

The man in front of her smirked as he followed her instructions with a lazy swagger. Everything about Grant Farley got under her skin, from the cocky grin on his face to the way his thick blond brows rose at her when she spoke. He was a man designed to destroy a woman's concentration.

Keeping her distance, she watched his movements and provided assistance verbally. Usually she helped her students by guiding them with her hands, but there was something about him that made her mind scream *Look but don't touch.* Maybe it was because he moved with a self-assurance that she envied, or maybe it was because after her six months of celibacy he looked good enough to eat.

Much to her chagrin he was a quick learner, and rapidly gained ground despite his insistence on goofing around.

'You're doing well,' Jasmine said as they paused between repetitions. She was determined to be the consummate professional, even if it was harder to pull off than the *pas de deux* from *Don Quixote,* Act Three. 'I can see improvements already and it's only your first lesson.'

'It's not exactly difficult,' he responded, his blue eyes meeting hers and sending a chill down her spine. His tone dismissed her praise. 'I'm bending up and down on the spot. A two-year-old could master that.'

Jasmine bristled. Only a beef-head Aussie Rules footballer would fail to see the importance of the step she'd taught him.

She pursed her lips. 'That's an over-simplification, don't you think?'

'Not really.' He crossed his arms and leant back against the *barre,* appraising her. 'You can give it a fancy French name if you want, but it's just bending your knees.'

'Well, I never thought a career could be made out of chasing a little red ball.' She tilted her chin up at him. 'But there you go.'

'Our balls *aren't* little,' he drawled, a smile tugging at the corners of his lips.

Her cheeks flamed. She ignored the innuendo and started the music, preparing herself to repeat the exercise facing him.

'Once more from the top.'

As the music started he followed her lead, bending with his feet in first position. The teacher in her couldn't ignore the fault of his technique, as he bent his hips moved out of alignment and his feet rolled inwards. She instinctively reached out to correct the error but retracted her hand when her brain kicked into gear.

'I don't bite.'

His wolfish grin seemed at odds with the promise of safety, but Jasmine wasn't going to let some arrogant joker mess with her head. *She* was the teacher; *she* was the one in charge here.

'You need to keep your hips steady.' She stepped forwards and placed a hand on each hip. His muscles were tight and flame-hot beneath her palms. He bent down into *plié* once more and she guided him, ignoring the frisson of electricity that shot through her.

'Make sure your core is pulled in. It will increase balance and stop you rocking forwards.'

'Like this?' He grabbed her hand and placed her palm against his stomach. She could feel the ripple of each muscle through his T-shirt. His sports tights moulded every curve of his muscle, every bulge...

Jasmine gulped, her blood pounding as though she'd run a marathon. *Get it together.*

'Yes, like that.' She withdrew her hand, the heat of him still burning her fingertips.

She was going to strangle Elise, her soon to be former best friend, for roping her into this disaster waiting to happen. She was going to—

'Earth to Bun-Head.' Grant waved a hand in front of her face, chuckling when she returned her focus to him. 'I don't see how this is helping my hamstring. Shouldn't we be stretching or something? We need to speed up this flexibility thing. I've got an important game coming up.'

He shook his leg and rubbed at the muscle.

'Flexibility is a slow process. You can't turn up to one ballet lesson and expect to be a contortionist. It takes time.'

'I'd settle for being injury-free,' he replied. 'But if you want to show me how you can put your ankles behind your head then be my guest.'

'This is *not* Cirque du Soleil.' Jasmine bit each word out through gritted teeth.

'It might as well be.' He checked the clock above them. 'Though, shocking as it might seem, I'm not here for the laughs. I want to fix my hamstring and get back to spending my time on *real* training.'

Jasmine wasn't ready to let him have the last word. Sure, she had her motivations for agreeing to take Grant on as a student, but that didn't give him licence to be rude. 'I'm not exactly here for enjoyment either.'

'If you loosened up you might find some aspects of it enjoyable.'

She sucked in a breath and willed herself not to respond. Glancing at the clock, she held in a sigh of relief as the hand neared 8:00 p.m. Their hour together had hardly been successful. In fact she could chalk it up as her most frustrating lesson ever…and this was only the beginning.

'Is it that time already?'

His amused tone set fire to Jasmine's resolve to play cool, calm and collected. She wanted to slap the mocking look right off his ruggedly handsome face. He raised an eyebrow, as if to punctuate his question.

This was going to be her life two nights a week for the next six months, and she wasn't looking forward to it one bit! Unfortunately these lessons weren't about the ideal way to spend her free time. No, it all came down to dollars and cents. Once again she was in a position where she needed to play up to some arrogant guy who thought he owned the world to be able to pay her bills.

'I think we can *finally* call it a night,' she said.

'Don't sound *too* upset to be rid of me.' He uncrossed

his arms and leant forwards, his broad shoulders casting a shadow over her.

'The lessons are for one hour, Mr Farley.' Her voice was tight and her lungs were arid and devoid of air. 'If you want more time you'll have to arrange it with the studio owner.'

'One hour is plenty, *Ms* Bell,' he teased, and raked a hand through his thick blond hair.

Why did he have to be so damn attractive? Her insides flipped as his hair sprang back into place. She headed towards the door to the waiting room and he walked with her, a little too close for comfort. The scent of his aftershave found its way to her nostrils and filled her head with unwanted though not unpleasant images. She shut her eyes for a moment, pushing away the desire that flared like the lighting of a match.

He wasn't good-looking in the traditional, clean-cut way she preferred. But there was something about his rough-around-the-edges look that drew her in. He had a strong jaw and razor-sharp cheekbones; his nose was crooked, as though it had been broken at some point and hadn't healed properly. She had a strange, powerful urge to run her fingertips over the bump, to confirm her suspicions.

She bit down on her lip. There was no way in hell she would let herself fall for a guy like him. Egotistical, cocky guys were a thing of her past, and she intended to keep it that way. It was strictly business, and after he paid her for the lesson she could go home and forget she was selling out. Forget that her dream had been reduced to this BS.

Grant walked over to his duffel bag and rifled through it, withdrawing a thick envelope. He thrust it in her direction.

'This should cover me,' he said. 'Coach thought it'd be easier to pay up front since you only take cash.'

The rewarding heaviness of the envelope sat in Jasmine's hands. It would cover her rent and bills for the next month or two, and give her a little breathing space. Relief coursed through her, immediately followed by a wave of shame as she tucked the envelope into her handbag. She didn't bother to count it. A guy who earned more than a million a year, if you believed the papers, was hardly likely to scrimp on a couple of hundred dollars for ballet lessons.

'Thanks,' she muttered without looking at him, dropping onto one of the couches and peeling off her leg warmers.

'Just so we're clear, this is something I have to do to tick a box. I don't have any secret dreams of wearing a tutu and getting up on stage. So don't take it personally if I don't crave your feedback.'

Self-important, arrogant, egotistical...

'Fine.' Untying her ballet shoes, she reached for her fleece-lined black leather boots. Her body was cooling down and her ankle ached. Grimacing, Jasmine rubbed at the soreness, feeling the rippled skin of her scar underneath her tights before sliding the boot on. 'You're here to tick a box. I'm here for the money.'

If he wanted to play it like that, then he could expect an equal response from her. Hopefully the weeks would pass quickly and then she could move on to figuring out what to do with her life.

As he pulled a pair of tracksuit pants from his bag Grant's leg muscles flexed and bulged through his leave-nothing-to-the-imagination sports tights. She'd spent the whole hour forcing her eyes up and away from the tight fabric that stretched over his thighs and...well, everything.

Heat crawled up the back of her neck and pooled in her cheeks. She pulled her eyes away as he stood and turned to her, staring at the ground as she pulled on her boots.

'See something you like?' he asked, his smile indicating it was a rhetorical question.

Dammit.

* * *

He regretted the words as they came out of his mouth, but Jasmine Bell stirred something in him that made him want to bait her. She had this prickly demeanour that he found both frustrating and fascinating.

He was used to swatting the football groupies away with a metaphorical stick. But Jasmine...well, she was a different breed entirely. All long limbs and straight lines, she was sexy as hell in spite of her don't-mess-with-me attitude. Or maybe that was *exactly* what he liked about her.

She glared at him as though she were mentally setting his head on fire. Her slender arms were crossed in front of her, as if trying to hide the lithe figure beneath. She wasn't going to give him the satisfaction of answering his question. There was a small part of him that enjoyed the power struggle; it was a game he liked to play. Moreover, it was a game he liked to win.

Now he'd ticked her off royally, and that was fine by him. He needed to keep his distance. Women were not a permanent fixture in his life...*people* were not a permanent fixture in his life. The fewer people he saw outside his footy team, the fewer people had the opportunity to use him. So he kept his distance, and he would do the same with her.

'Did becoming famous cause you to forget your manners, or is that the way you were raised?'

She smiled sweetly, her sarcastic expression stinging him as much as the intentional barb in her words. The tilt in her chin issued a challenge.

'All I wanted was to play footy; the fame is an unfortunate by-product,' he said, surprised by his own honesty. Her small rosebud mouth pursed, and her dark brows creased above a button nose. 'As are the ballet lessons.'

'Isn't that what they call a first-world problem?' She hoisted her bag over her shoulder and walked to the front door. He followed, holding back an amused smile. 'Like *Boo-hoo, I'm famous and it's such a tough life.'*

'I'd be happy to swap for a day so you can experience it first-hand.'

'As much as I'd love to see you in here, trying to wrangle a bunch of toddlers, you couldn't handle my job.' She held the door open for him, and offered another saccharine smile. 'Besides, I have the *most* annoying student to teach.'

Grant couldn't help it—a hearty laugh burst free. She was prickly, all right, but hot damn if he didn't enjoy it. 'Sucks to be you?'

He waited while she locked up, and then they walked to their respective cars. The lights on his Mercedes flashed as he pressed the unlock button. Inside the car was chilly, and the windows took a moment to clear.

By then Jasmine was gone. Within minutes Grant was zipping along the freeway, the street lights blurring orange outside his window as the car tore down the open road. It was late and the city had long cleared its peak hour congestion. He massaged his injured hamstring, the muscle aching under the pressure of his fingers.

Who would have thought something as prissy as ballet would be such a workout? Not that he would dare admit it to Jasmine *or* any of his team-mates.

His phone buzzed in the mobile-phone holder attached to his windscreen. The goofy face of fellow Victoria Harbour Jaguars player Dennis Porter flashed up. He swiped the answer button.

'Den.'

'How are the ballet lessons going?' Even through the phone line Dennis's mischievous tone was obvious. 'I wanted to see if your masculinity is slipping away by the minute.'

Ballet lessons were far from Grant's idea of fun, but a persistent hamstring injury meant the need for increased flexibility training, and who better to help with that than a ballerina? His physiotherapist had made it sound good in theory, but the reality was proving to be much more irritating—especially since it gave his team-mates more than enough fodder for locker room jokes.

'Ha!' Grant scoffed. 'Even if it was you wouldn't be in with a chance. You're not my type.'

'Yeah, yeah. That's what all the ladies say. So tell me that at least your teacher is hot?'

'*Hot* doesn't even begin to cover it.'

He'd been expecting someone older, more severe... maybe with a Russian accent. He'd had to keep his mouth firmly shut when a willowy beauty with a long black pony-tail and porcelain skin greeted him at the studio.

'Maybe I'll have to pop in to one of your lessons.'

A surprising jolt of emotion raced through Grant's veins at the thought of letting Den anywhere near Jasmine. He shook off the strange protective urge and forced his mind back to the present. 'I know you want to see me in action.'

'The whole country wants to see you in action. It's going to be a good season. I can feel it.'

'Me too.'

A drawn-out pause made Grant hold his breath.

'Do you think all that other stuff is behind you now?' Den asked.

Part of him wanted to answer truthfully. He didn't know if it would ever be behind him. How could you forget the moment you almost flushed your life's work down the toilet? Considering football was all he had, it was a damn scary thought. But Den was only a buddy, a mate...and as one of the more junior guys in the team he was not some-one to whom Grant could show weakness.

'Of course. You know me—I'm practically invincible.'

He hung up the phone and allowed his mind to drift back to Jasmine. She was a curious case, seemingly unaffected by him in the way other women were. How much did she know about his past? Was that why she eyed him with such wariness?

Regret coiled in his stomach. Gritting his teeth, Grant turned up the stereo and shook his head. The beat thundered in his chest and made his eardrums ache, yet he couldn't drown out the thoughts swimming like sharks in his head. Around and around they circled, occupying the space—scaring off any semblance of peace.

He slammed his palm against the sturdy leather-covered steering wheel. He wasn't looking forward to the rest of his ballet lessons, even with a teacher who was a walking fantasy. He had better things to do with his time…like figuring out how he was going to get his team to victory.

Given his not-too-distant fall from grace, he had a lot to prove and a reputation to rebuild. In particular he had to convince his coach, his team and the fans that he was at the top of his game again. The last thing he needed was to be distracted by a woman. If it were any other girl he'd simply scratch the itch and move on, but that wasn't going to be possible given the ongoing nature of their lessons.

Groaning, he pressed his head back against the headrest. He had a bad feeling about her; there was something about her that set his body alight in a way he hadn't felt for a long time. And the way she'd been staring at him after the lesson…talk about an invitation to sin. Warning bells were going off left, right and centre.

He couldn't do it—not now that he was finally making progress in clearing the mud from his name. This was going to be *his* season. Nothing was going to distract him; nothing was going to stand in his way.

'No!'

Grant sat bolt upright, rigid as though a steel rod had replaced his spine. Perspiration dripped down the side of his neck, his face, along the length of his spine. He felt around in the dark. The sweat-drenched sheets were bunched in his fists as he held on for dear life.

He was alone.

His breath shook; each gasp was fire in his lungs. His chest heaved as he sucked the air in greedily. More. More.

His eyes adjusted to the dark and he could make out the lines of the furniture around him. City light filtered through the slats of his blinds, creating a pattern on his bed. The apartment was silent; the rest of the world was sleeping while he shook.

Slowly his heartbeat resumed its normal rhythm. The tremors would take a while longer to go away—he knew that from experience. It was only a dream. *The* dream. The one he had over and over and over—the one that woke him with a fright every single time.

Flashbulbs disorientated him, microphones were shoved in his face.

'Grant! Grant! Is it true you put a man in hospital? Is it true you beat him to a pulp?'

Shaking his head, he disentangled himself from the bed-sheets and strode out to the living room. Starlight streamed in through the window and the city twinkled a silent tune. It was a surreal feeling to be in close proximity to thousands of people and yet be completely and utterly alone.

Opening the lid of his laptop, he settled onto the couch. His personal email showed the same sad scene it did every day: zero new messages. Even Dennis, the closest thing he had to a friend, hadn't sent him anything...not even a stupid Lolcats photo. He clicked on the folder marked 'family' and sighed at the measly three emails that he couldn't bear to delete. The last one was dated over six months ago.

He checked the spam folder, wondering if—hoping that—maybe a message had got caught in the filter, that maybe someone had reached out to him. No luck. The folder was empty.

He'd never regretted leaving the small country town where he'd grown up to pursue football and success in the big smoke, despite the verbal smack-down he'd got from his father. He could remember with clarity the vein bulging in his father's forehead as his voice boomed through their modest country property. Those three little words: *How could you?* How could he desert them? How could he abandon the family business? How could he put a pipe dream before his father and sister?

Those wounds had only started healing, with the tentative phone calls and texts increasing between him and his sister. The old bonds had been there, frayed and worn but not completely broken. Not completely beyond repair. Even his father had provided a gruff enquiry as to Grant's life in the city.

But all that was gone now. Those fragile threads of reconciliation had been ripped apart when he'd brought shame to the family name. They were his father's words but he couldn't dispute them. He didn't have the right to be mad. He was alone because of his own actions, because of the mess he'd made. And, knowing his father, he wouldn't get a second chance.

All the more reason to make sure the Jaguars were on top this year. If his career was all he had left he'd give it everything. He would *not* fail.

Slamming the lid of the laptop shut, he abandoned the couch to grab a drink from the fridge. If sleep was going to be elusive he might as well do something to pass the time.

CHAPTER TWO

'DAMMIT,' JASMINE MUTTERED as she battled with her large pink umbrella. The blustery weather meant it was virtually useless to ward off the sideways rain as it pelted her in the face and soaked her jeans.

Her hair streaked around her, the dark strands blocking her vision as she wrestled it into submission. She dashed across the busy street, feet sliding on the slick pavement. Panting, she hitched her bag up higher on her shoulder and ducked under the shelter of the doctor's clinic. She shook the umbrella, flicking droplets of water all around her, and walked through the automatic doors to the clinic's reception.

'Hi, Jasmine.' The receptionist greeted her with a familiar smile. 'Dr Wilson will be with you momentarily.'

Jasmine sank into a chair and wound her rain-drenched ponytail into a bun. Water dripped down the back of her neck and her ankle throbbed inside her boot, a constant reminder that the accident was not yet behind her.

Another one of the staff members gave her a friendly wave as they walked through the reception area. She was practically part of the furniture here.

After a brief check-up and lecture from her doctor Jasmine left, a fresh prescription in her hand since she'd fed the last one to her shredder. She hated taking the painkillers he'd prescribed; along with her inability to heal, they felt like another sign of weakness.

The doctor had again broached the topic of her seeing a psychologist…as though her problems were all in her head. But they weren't—they were real. Her ankle would never again be strong enough to sustain her *en pointe,* and without ballet she had nothing…*was* nothing. She wrapped her arms around herself as she made her way to the reception desk.

God she missed it—the glitter of stage lights reflecting off sequins, the thunder of the audience's applause, the thrill of mastering a new part. What could she do with her life now that all those things were gone? Every time she tried to think about it her mind went blank. There was nothing else in her heart except ballet, nothing else she was passionate about. It was ballet or bust…and she was definitely going bust.

Rain thundered outside the clinic and a bright flash lit up the windows, signalling that the storm was raging on. She regretted catching public transport; there was no way she'd get home dry. Stupidly, she'd come without the car she sometimes borrowed from Elise's mother, thinking perhaps she could save money if she stuck to buses and trams. In hindsight it was a doomed plan, given that Melbourne's public transport system was prone to failure when the weather turned. But without the cash for her own set of wheels she'd be rocking the drowned rat look on a more frequent basis.

Cursing, she signed the appointment form and paid with the notes from the envelope in her bag. It had her name scrawled across the front in Grant's chicken-scratch handwriting.

'Jasmine?'

A familiar voice demanded her attention. *Speak of the devil.*

Grant stood in the centre of the waiting room, dressed in his training gear. He looked infinitely more relaxed than the last time she'd seen him, his face open, though he hadn't lost any of the arrogance in his swagger. People in the clinic—mainly women—admired him openly and whispered to one another behind their hands.

'Fancy seeing you here.' She kept her voice professional, pushing aside the prickle of irritation left over from their first lesson together.

'The club gets remedial massage here.' He signed his own form with a scrawl. 'These tight calves are giving me hell.'

She couldn't stop the spread of an evil smile across her lips. Her calf exercises were notorious for punishing new students and she felt a small tingle of satisfaction that he was no different.

'Cry-baby,' she said, wrapping a fluffy orange scarf around her neck and preparing for the onslaught of the rain.

He chuckled. It was a sound designed to make a woman's stomach flutter, and hers did…right on cue. She cursed her body for its mindless response.

He walked beside her, and a frosty blast of air hit them as the automatic doors slid open to reveal a wet and miserable winter's day. 'What are you here for?'

'An old injury.' She paused under the awning of the clinic. She undid the clasp on her umbrella and opened it against the wind, wincing as the material flapped in protest. Turning to walk away from the car park, she waved. 'Well, I'd better run.'

Grant raised an eyebrow and cocked his head. 'You didn't drive?'

She couldn't blame him for thinking she was mad—even she was thinking she might have gone loopy. Who would choose to give up a car with seat warmers on a day like this? Her bones were already chilled to their core, and a five-minute walk to the bus stop was only going to make things worse.

She shook her head.

'I'll give you a lift. You can't walk in the rain.'

Grant set off towards the car park without waiting for her to accept his offer. She paused, her brows furrowing. Another blast of cold air made her shiver as she followed him. Indignation at his demanding tone wasn't going to force her to give up a free ride today.

Grant's long strides made quick work of the car park. He walked with his head bent to the wind, not looking to see if she'd followed him. She quickened her pace, her boots splashing through puddles as she jogged. The car's lights flashed as it was unlocked and Jasmine scampered around to the passenger side, eager to get out of the wet.

Slamming the door behind her, she shivered. Droplets of water had flicked all over the pristine leather seats, and the windows fogged from their breathing. Grant turned over the engine and flicked on the demister. They waited while the glass returned to its normal transparent state.

His eyes were on her.

Her pale skin was flushed from the cold. A strawberry colour stained her cheeks and, even as dishevelled and rain-soaked as she was, Jasmine was still the most stunning woman Grant had ever encountered.

'Where am I taking you?' He started the engine and let the car idle while it warmed up.

'To the ballet studio.' Blowing on her hands, she rubbed them together and shivered in her seat. 'Please.'

Grant turned up the heater, flicking the centre vent so that it blew in her direction. He could smell the combination of perfume and rain on her skin. Water droplets slid down her neck, disappearing beneath her scarf. For some reason he found that indescribably erotic.

'So you're dealing with an injury?' He forced his mind onto another topic. Injuries were safe, unsexy. 'From dancing?'

'Yeah.' Her voice sounded tight and she didn't elaborate.

He stole a glance at her profile as he turned to the rear window, easing the car out of its spot. She shot him a rueful smile, a dimple forming in her cheek. His eyes flickered over her small but full-lipped mouth.

'I bet you get more injuries in football, though—like a broken nose, perhaps?' Her voice held a slight sense of mischief.

Most girls wouldn't be so quick to point out that he had a crooked nose. But, then again, he could see she was different in every way from the women he met on the football circuit. She wasn't fake tanned and bleached to the hilt. She didn't have that artificial look that was the uniform of the WAGs. She was an authentic beauty—a rarity. Her long black hair was wound into a neat bun, and the only skin that showed was on her hands and face. She had a certain primness about her that Grant found appealing—a polished elegance that made her look every bit the perfect prima ballerina. And she gave him attitude left, right and centre.

'Yes to the broken nose, but it didn't happen on the footy field,' Grant said, returning his eyes to the front. 'I had a fight when I'd barely turned eighteen. It was my first night out drinking and I got into a fight at a bar.'

At one point that memory would have filled Grant with a sense of macho pride, as though it were a rite of passage for a young male. Now it made him queasy, with memories bubbling to the surface. Many women liked the whole 'bad boy' thing—hell, he'd used it to his advantage time and time again—but those days were well and truly over. Not that anyone believed him.

'That was a *long* time ago.'

He kept the mood light, but Jasmine wasn't letting him get away that easily.

'I don't understand why guys fight.' She shook her head. 'You don't need to beat your chest to attract the ladies, you know.'

'It wasn't like that.'

'What *was* it like?'

'I was young, thought I had to prove something.' He forced a hand through his hair. 'I wasn't always this way.'

'What do you mean?'

He was at a loss for words. People usually didn't ask personal questions—well, not those beyond what his bank balance was. They never showed any interest in him as a person, never cared about who he was…where he came from.

He shrugged, grappling for a response. 'In charge.'

'I have no doubt that you can take care of yourself,' she said, a soft smile on her lips. 'But being macho isn't the way to go about it.'

Perhaps she'd seen the media fuss that had erupted after the incident. There had been an awful paparazzi shot of him doing the rounds on the internet for months afterwards. Luckily the media moved on quickly. Sports stars behaving badly were a dime a dozen. Grant had experienced a sense of guilt when it died down so quickly, though the story still popped up on gossip sites whenever there was a slow news day.

'You don't get ahead in AFL by being a softy.'

'I don't know. I reckon you might be a big softy on the inside.' She laughed, poking him in the ribs. 'You're like one of those mean-looking dogs that rolls over for a tummy scratch.'

'I'm at the top of my profession, sweetheart.' He wanted to come across as controlled, but the words sounded hollow to his own ears. Defensive. 'I'm not in it for the belly scratches.'

'So what *are* you in it for?'

'I'm in it for the game.'

'You like to win?'

'Hell, yeah, I like to win.' He laughed. 'Don't you?'

'Depends on your definition of winning, I guess.'

A dark shadow passed over her face and for a moment he caught a glimpse of something beneath the surface of her warm brown eyes.

She moved on before he could probe deeper. 'Why weren't you always in charge?'

Of course she'd latched on to *that* little statement. Memories flickered at the edge of his consciousness. He didn't want to talk about this. He'd never told anyone about what he'd left behind, about the guilt that racked him for abandoning his family only a year after his mother had passed away.

'Let's just say I was a late bloomer.'

'And now?'

'Like I said, I'm at the top of my game.' His eyes flickered over to her. 'Belly scratches not required.'

There was no way she'd understand. Her face was neutral, giving nothing away. She kept her gaze trained on the front window, her hands folded primly in her lap.

'If you're at the top of your game then why are you concerned with my opinion?'

'What exactly *is* your opinion?' He steered the car around a corner and forced his eyes to stay on the road. He wanted to see her expression, watch for a hint of how she really felt.

Why did he even care?

'Like you said to me the other night—don't take it personally... I don't understand why football is such a big deal. I mean, you chase a ball around a field until some-one kicks it between two posts. It's not rocket science.'

'We live the life of a dedicated athlete, we give up the things regular people take for granted.'

'I'm sure keeping up with the constant partying and bedding groupies is a *real* sacrifice.'

'Yeah, it's hard to keep up with the groupies, but I try my best.' He winked at her while they were stopped at a red light. 'It's good for building stamina.'

'You're unbelievable.' She rolled her eyes.

'So I've been told.'

Deflecting her away from the personal stuff with OTT arrogance wasn't his finest hour, but it had steered her away from the dark parts of him and it had made her laugh. As far as he was concerned it was a win.

She huffed and shook her head. Grant couldn't help but notice the pink flush that had spread from her cheeks down her neck, and she squirmed under his gaze.

He drove the car down the street that led to the ballet studio. Automatically he felt his shoulders tense as they drew closer. The feeling of dread that he experienced each time he came to the studio kicked in as he pulled into the car park. It was as if his body associated the studio with the pressure he was putting on himself—a manifestation of the fine line he walked with each game this season.

'Thanks for the lift.' Jasmine gathered her bag and um-brella from beneath her feet. 'That rain would have been awful to travel in.'

'No problem.' He tried to keep his eyes forwards, but he couldn't help stealing a glance as she stepped out of the car. The clingy fabric of her pants showed off one mag-nificently tight, toned ass. He gulped.

'See you tomorrow.'

Jasmine practically bounced from the car to the studio, her pink sports bag swinging against her hip while her pert behind wiggled enticingly. Grant gave himself a moment to let his breath settle before he peeled out of the car park.

Don't even think about it.

A quiet studio was not what Jasmine needed right now. The silence encouraged thinking, and sifting through the questions in her head was not productive...not when she had to focus on work. She stood at the *barre,* rolling her ankle around in a slow circle. The joint protested, the tendons tugging sharply as she pushed herself to flex or point a little more. If only she could push it a little farther each time...

Years of stretching had given her a perfect curve *en pointe,* but now she could barely rise up onto the balls of her feet. They refused to stretch, refused to flex and curve as they once had.

Gritting her teeth, she attempted a few moves from an old routine. Her feet thumped against the floor, clumsy in their poor imitation of how she had once danced. She wanted so badly to be able to go back to the way she'd been before the accident, before she'd stranded herself in this horrible place known as dancer's limbo—where you were too broken to move forwards, too proud to go backwards and too engrained to go anywhere else.

She missed dancing with an ache that felt as if it split her chest wide open every time she failed to flex her feet properly. There were times when she feared that her soul might wither up and die if she went much longer without dance.

Voices from the waiting room pulled her out of her dark thoughts; she whipped her head around.

Grant stood in the waiting room, talking to her best friend and owner of the studio, Elise Johnson, but his eyes were undeniably on Jasmine. Even from a distance she could see the fire burning in their ice-blue depths. He nodded in response to something Elise said but he didn't tear his gaze from her…not even for a second. Stomach fluttering, she crossed the studio. Their muffled voices became clearer as Jasmine reached the waiting room.

'How come your girlfriend doesn't come and watch you practise?'

Elise batted her eyelashes at Grant as Jasmine poked her head into the waiting room. She bit down on her lip to stop herself from groaning; the girl was as subtle as a sledgehammer.

'No girlfriend.' Grant shook his head, catching Jasmine's eye and winking.

'Wife?'

'Definitely not.'

'Interesting.' Elise cocked her head to one side and smiled at Jasmine conspiratorially as she turned to grab her coat and bag. 'Well, I'm off. Enjoy your lesson.'

Her smile was sweet as a cupcake piled high with frosting. Jasmine stifled a laugh at Grant's get-me-out-of-here expression. Elise was full-strength girlie—none of that watered-down diet stuff. As Grant came forwards Elise shot Jasmine a thumbs-up behind his back. Her face sparkled.

Despite the fact that Elise was single herself, she'd made it her mission to try and set Jasmine up, no matter how many times she protested.

She held open the door to the waiting room. 'Shall we get lesson number two over with?'

'It's going to feel even longer if you count down every single lesson,' Grant said, walking past her, close enough that she could smell the faint aftershave on his skin.

'You were the one who wanted to speed up the results,' she said, focusing her attention on the mirrored wall as they walked over to the *barre*. Each breath had to be forced in and out of her lungs, as though she might forget to breathe if she were near him for too long.

'Do I need to wear these stupid things every lesson?' He pulled at the fabric of his sports tights and allowed it to snap against his thigh. 'At least at footy I can wear shorts over the top.'

'Are you worried about your modesty?' She raised an eyebrow.

'It's not *me* I'm worried about.'

She put on her most serious teacher voice. 'I need to see how your muscles work while we're going through the exercises.'

Heat crawled up her neck and she forced her eyes to stay on his face. She would not look down. She would *not* look down.

'My muscles? Right.' He drew the last word out, barely containing his laughter.

'I think you should consider taking these lessons a little more seriously, Grant. Preventing injury is no laughing manner.'

'God, you sound like an insurance commercial.'

He was pushing her on purpose, and he seemed to be getting an immense amount of pleasure out of it. Since this was *her* lesson, she could pay him back.

'Why don't we get started with some calf raises?'

He rolled his eyes and groaned, as though she'd told him he needed to climb a mountain with one hand.

'Suck it up, Grant. If there's one thing you should know about people who've studied ballet it's that we have discipline beyond anything you could imagine.' She sounded smug, sure, but he totally deserved it.

He shook his head and laughed. 'You're not selling the ballet ideal very well.'

'You don't think you've got what it takes?' She cursed herself. She shouldn't be baiting him. No doubt he'd be the kind of guy to enjoy a little verbal sparring. But the words had slipped out before she could stop them. It was too... *fun*. And she needed a little fun right now.

He grinned at her, confirming her fears. 'If I want something, there ain't a force in the world that will stop me from having it.'

Jasmine gulped. His pointed look sent liquid fire through her veins. There was no doubt in her mind that she was on his list of things to want. She had to remind herself that this was business and—fun as it might be, she was only after a pay cheque. But that grin...the crooked, self-assured way he smiled...it was like a fist through her stomach.

No, this would *not* work on her. She wasn't another airhead groupie, ready to fall at his feet.

'You can't have everything you want. That's not how the world works.' And didn't she know it.

He raked his eyes over her. 'Watch me.'

Awareness tingled on her skin. She could feel his gaze so keenly that it might as well have been the brush of his fingertips or the rasp of his tongue for what it was doing to her insides. She bit down on her lip, trying unsuccessfully to blank out the flickering reel of R-rated images in her mind.

'Since you're so strong of mind, why don't you focus some of that energy on this lesson?'

After Grant had made his way through the warm-up she moved them on to a new exercise, facing him at the *barre*.

'We'll start the *tendu à terre* in first position. Watch me.' She extended her right leg forwards until only the tips of her pointed toes touched the ground.

Looking as out of place as one would expect from a footballer in a ballet studio, Grant struck an angled version of first position with his working arm, his shoulders bunched up around his neck.

Jasmine rested her hand on the tense muscle. 'You

have to loosen up from here or you'll never relax into it,' she said, running her hands down his arm and shaping it into the proper position. Her fingertips brushed his hard, curved biceps. Her breath quickened while her heart bounded like an over-excited puppy. 'Now, extend your working leg forwards slowly. Point your foot and keep it on the ground.'

He shifted as he moved his leg forwards, tipping his hips out of alignment. Her hands automatically went down to put them back into place. Her fingers fluttered involuntarily against his hipbone. Through the thin fabric of his running tights his muscular thighs were perfectly visible. The fitted garment didn't leave much to the imagination... and, speaking of imagination, hers was running wild.

From the sharp intake of his breath and the flare of his pupils he must have felt it too. And the jolt of electricity that made her whole body feel like a live wire—could he feel that as well?

She stepped back and instructed him to complete the exercise on his own. Using her remote, she played classical music so he had timing to work with. He fought to keep his posture straight and Jasmine clasped her hands in front of her to stop herself from reaching out to touch him again.

'That's looking good. If we can get those hips to stay square, then you'll master this in no time. The *tendu* leads on to a lot of other steps in ballet.'

She was babbling—a side-effect from the onslaught of lust. God, it had been far too long since she'd been with a man, it must be the hormones making her crazy. That's all it was, a perfectly reasonable and natural response...absolutely nothing to do with him. She needed a break. Now.

'Why don't you grab a drink?' She walked to the front of the studio where her water bottle sat next to the MP3 player and her mobile phone. 'We'll get started again in a few minutes.'

They had another half an hour to go—how was she going to keep herself in check for that long? She took a swig of her water and relished the cool liquid sliding down the back of her throat.

'Did you ever think about going pro with your dancing?' His voice caught her off guard and she stiffened.

Busying herself with the MP3 player, she grappled for a response. She tried to swallow, her mouth suddenly dry.

'I'm not sure if any ballerinas would refer to it as "going pro."'

'Picking on my slang is an excellent way to avoid the question,' he said. 'But I'll rephrase. Did you ever think about dancing professionally?'

'Yes.' Not a lie, but not an invitation either.

'And?'

She bit her lip and sighed. The last thing she needed was for him to pity her...or, worse, want to help in some way. She always dealt with problems by herself; she preferred it that way. Dealing with things on her own meant there was no one pushing their ideas on her, no one convincing her to do something outside her comfort zone and no one controlling her.

But how could she get around this topic for the rest of their time together? At some point it would come up again and she'd have the same dilemma: lie or expose herself.

'I was a soloist with the Australian Ballet.' She kept her voice even, unemotional. 'I trained in ballet my whole life and have wanted to be a professional ballerina ever since I was eight years old.'

'Then why did you quit?'

'I didn't quit.' The word tasted dirty in her mouth. She would *never* have stopped dancing if her hand hadn't been forced. 'I was injured in a car accident and now I don't have full movement in my foot and ankle. I can't dance *en pointe* anymore.'

She opened her mouth to continue but the words died in her throat. Her lips were parched and her tongue was heavy, as if physically resisting the truth. She couldn't mention the constant pain. The mental torment. The shame of how it had happened.

She couldn't talk to anyone about that—not even her best friend.

Grant was silent, lines forming at the centre of his forehead. His thick brows were knitted together. Out of nowhere his left hand reached out and clasped hers. Jasmine jumped at the unexpected touch. Her hand was tiny in his grip. Fragile.

CHAPTER THREE

HE CLASPED THE fragility of her hand between his fingers, her bones feeling tiny and delicate and perfect. She gasped, her lips opening and closing, before she clenched her jaw. She'd been hurt before, and she wore it like a warning sign that read Stay the Hell Away.

She frowned, her rich brown eyes narrowing at him as she withdrew her hand from his grip. He wasn't even sure why he'd touched her, but something stirred deep within him. Everything about her was restrained, from her not-a-hair-out-of-place bun to her neatly filed pink fingernails. She had a carefully constructed veneer that held him at arm's length, and while he had no interest in getting closer she looked as though she could use the comfort. Yeah, he was comforting her…it had nothing to do with the strange ache in his chest.

'I'm sorry to hear that.'

'Not as sorry as I was…. You're here to work on your flexibility, remember?' Her voice wobbled slightly but she retained control. 'You're here to work.'

The way her eyes glittered and her cheeks were stained pink told him he'd unintentionally hit a nerve. How interesting. A woman with a mystery was his personal weakness, and there was a hell of a lot more to her story than she was letting on. He was drawn in by the opportunity to uncover her secrets, to peel away the layers of complexity that shrouded her. He would pick his moment, when she wasn't so raw, so exposed. He would find out what had hurt her more than a shattered dream.

'I mean it.' She walked towards him and stopped barely inches from where he stood. 'Back to work.'

The air between them sizzled. Grant's heart thudded an erratic beat in his chest. Her power seemed to come from nowhere. She'd frozen him on the spot with a single look. Her eyes blackened, pupils engulfing the ring of warm brown around it. She stood in front of him, close enough to touch. He could feel every damn millimetre between them and he wanted desperately to close the gap, to draw her to him with force.

But she was playing the same game he was. Testing the boundaries. Pushing to see how far they could go.

She returned to the *barre,* seemingly unperturbed. 'Let's keep working on your *tendu* for now.'

Jasmine settled her body into the starting position and waited while Grant did the same. She demonstrated where the turn-out should be coming from by touching the tops of her thighs where they connected to her hips, her hands inches from the place he wished his own hands were…or maybe his mouth.

Grant swallowed. She looked at him through her thick curly lashes as though she was completely aware of how difficult he was finding it not to stare. Damn her, she was doing it on purpose.

'Extend forwards.' She completed the move facing him, so that their feet met in the centre.

Her words counted out the beats of the music and he trained his eyes on her legs, making a poor imitation of her movements. He should leave her well alone, but something kept pulling him in. Something in the way she held him at arm's length made his blood pulse harder and hotter in his veins.

'Try again.'

She started the music—the same strains he'd listened to over and over that lesson. His feet moved in time, the steps less foreign to him now.

Neither of them spoke while he completed the exercise. She stood stock-still, observing him. There was something strangely sensual about the complete silence except for the whisper of their feet against the floor. The air crackled between them.

Her eyes flicked over his body. Was she assessing or admiring?

'You need to rotate your turn-out more,' she said, walking to him. She placed her hands on his upper thighs, smoothing the muscles outwards. 'Otherwise you're putting a lot of strain on the knees.'

Her hands lingered on his thighs, all too close to where his body cried out for her touch. He stirred and bit down on his lip. There was no way he'd be able to hide an erection in these damn tights.

At this distance he could see that her eyes were not merely brown but a medley of chocolate shades: milk, caramel and dark cocoa. Her skin was porcelain-white. She lacked the flaws—freckles and scars—that years on the field had given him. Her lips were rosebud-pink, parted and moistened by the gentle swipe of her tongue.

'If you leave your hands there I take no responsibility for what happens.' He leant in, closing the gap between them.

Her eyes flickered up to him, her lips pursing. God, he wanted to taste her. Was she game?

'Lucky for you I have no problem with taking responsibility,' she said, withdrawing her hands. 'You should try it some time.'

Damn.

As they cooled down and stretched out she kept her distance, eyeing him as one might a large dog that wasn't on a lead. He was momentarily distracted by the sharp pull in his hamstring. Stifling a groan, he leant into the stretch but couldn't get enough from it. This damn injury was affecting his game and it was pissing him off.

'Do you want a hand with that?' She pushed up onto her feet and came closer.

He waggled his eyebrows. 'Yeah, I want a hand—'

'Finish that sentence and you'll get nothing,' she warned.

Jasmine Bell wore the prissy schoolteacher look better than he'd thought possible.

He kept his mouth shut and she knelt down in front of him. 'Lie flat on your back and put your right leg up. I'll give you a little push.'

Was it his imagination or did a subtle flush of pink rise up her neck as she instructed him? She leant her shoulder into the back of his thigh and eased forwards. With her body too close to his, he should have been revelling in the fantasy.

Unfortunately the muscle was so resistant he had to blow out a long breath and focus his energy on allowing it to lengthen. For once he couldn't even voice the innuendo.

Cold fear trickled down the length of his spine. What if his injury couldn't be fixed? What if he couldn't lead the Jaguars to victory? He'd bet everything on his career, and if he lost he'd have nothing at all.

At the time of her next lesson with Grant, Jasmine was in the studio, choreographing a routine for the teachers of the EJ Ballet School. Looking sexy as hell in a leather jacket over his hoodie and jeans, he stood about in the waiting room, watching her through the viewing mirror. He was early...for once.

Instead of heading straight out, Jasmine had the sudden urge to put on a show. She stretched out at the *barre,* determined to show off the best of her flexibility. Inside, her head sensibly protested that he was not the kind of guy to encourage. But the thought that he might up the ante of their teasing sent a shiver down her spine. Their last lesson had thrown her into a spin. His questions, the genuine concern in his voice, the tenderness of his touch...it was enough to make even the most sensible girl fantasise. And *sensible* was Jasmine's middle name.

Her heart fluttered as she stretched, excitement dancing along her nerves. What was *wrong* with her? She shook her head and forced herself to focus. Abandoning the *barre,* she set her shoulders straight and drew a deep breath.

Elise got to Grant before Jasmine made it to the waiting room. She was throwing *all* her charm at him—flipping her wispy blond ponytail and offering him a smile that could power a small city. Something twisted in Jasmine's gut—a strange pang that she hadn't experienced in a long time. She pushed it aside and walked out in time to catch the tail-end of their conversation.

'That would be amazing!' Elise's voice was high-pitched. Buoyant. 'Did you hear that? Grant is going to get us access to the Long Room for Friday's game. We can watch him in action.'

A warm heat flared in Jasmine's chest. Access to the Long Room was more than a couple of general admin tickets. It was a sweet gesture, and for some strange reason it made her tummy flutter. Whether that was from the generosity of his act or the thought of seeing him in his element, she didn't know.

'Isn't that exciting?' Elise nudged Jasmine in the ribs with her elbow, a hint of warning in her voice.

'That's extremely generous,' Jasmine said.

However, as the warm flush of excitement faded she realised what his invitation meant. Access to the Long Room was kind of like an insider event in the art world—filled with people who knew one another, who dressed the same way, who belonged. And she didn't belong with the other halves of football's elite.

Her heart sank. 'Of course I'll have to make sure I don't have anything else on.'

'You *don't* have anything else on,' Elise said pointedly, her elbow once again digging into Jasmine's ribs. 'We'll definitely come and watch.'

Relax, she told herself, *it won't be like the art community. Sport is inclusive, right?* Her stomach pitched. Her ex had dragged her around to all manner of gallery openings, VIP exhibitions and artist previews. She'd never fitted in. Everyone at those events had been able to afford the art hanging on the walls. She'd had more in common with the paintings themselves than the people she'd been paraded in front of.

'Great.' Grant flashed them both a smile. His eyes lingered for longer than necessary on Jasmine. 'Elise has given me your number so I'll text you the details.'

'Great.' Jasmine fought to keep the sarcasm out of her voice. *Of course* Elise had given him her number—why would she expect anything less?

An amused smile played on his lips. The two women watched him walk into the studio, both of them locking on to the way his hips rolled in their lazy, sensual gait.

'I can't believe you gave him my number.' Jasmine glared at her friend as soon as the door swung closed behind him.

'I'm doing you a favour, Jazz,' Elise said, positioning her hands on her hips. 'He's drooling over you during class and you're too chicken to do anything about it.'

'That's *not* true. He's practically a celebrity—he could have any of those red-carpet bimbos by his side.'

'Yes, but he's looking at *you.*' Elise sighed. 'You're too blinded by your own stubbornness to see it.'

'I am not stubborn.' But even as she said it Jasmine knew it was a lie.

'Right.' As if on cue, Elise cocked her head and rolled her eyes. 'You know not every guy is like Kyle. Grant is different. He—'

'Stop it.' Jasmine shut her eyes. 'I don't want to hear any more.'

She loved Elise, but this was crossing the line. She didn't want anyone pushing her towards Grant—especially when she was having a hard time controlling herself around him as it was. There was something about him that drew her like a magnet.

Magnetic attraction or not, she knew a relationship with him would never work because she didn't belong in his world. She'd had her time in a glamorous community filled with extreme wealth, cliques and persistent paparazzi. She'd promised herself she'd never go there again. But something pulled her to Grant—something deep and inexplicable.

She watched him through the viewing window while he warmed up at the *barre*. Against her better judgement, she didn't look away.

The pre-game rush was what had drawn Grant into the world of football back in his childhood. Some guys lived for the relief that came when the siren sounded, others purely for the swell of the crowd's cheer upon victory. But Grant was all about the build-up, the anticipation...and this match had it in spades.

He told himself it was because the Jaguars were playing their fiercest rivals. But deep down he knew the jangling of his nerves was caused by two things: Jasmine, and the niggling sensation in his hamstring. He couldn't let it get the better of him today...not when so much was at stake.

'Bloody hell, you're a space cadet today.' A hand

slapped down onto his back, the sound barely registering above the locker room din.

'Huh?' Grant turned to see his team-mate, Archer, standing beside him, shaking his head. He was a small guy, as rovers tended to be, but he had a larger than life personality. His eyes glittered with mischief.

'You seem light on your feet lately, mate. I should start calling you Twinkle Toes.'

'Now, now…' their coach warned, his voice booming above the noise.

'I thought Grant might be able to share some of his experiences with the team.' Archer looked up at Grant, unperturbed by the half a foot height difference between them. 'How *are* the pirouettes going?'

'You don't want to go there, Arch.' Grant stretched up to his full height. 'Even doing ballet I'm still twice the man you are—mentally *and* physically.'

'Short jokes…clever.' Arch rolled his eyes as he stretched out his quad.

'Nothing wrong with getting in touch with your feminine side, is there Grant?' Another player chimed in.

'Back off.'

'Oh, don't be such a bad sport.' Arch elbowed Grant in the ribs. 'I'd say pink is your colour.'

'You're just jealous, Arch.' Grant felt the frustrations of the past year building, but he remembered the breathing exercises and calming techniques he'd learnt. Unclenching his fists, he let out a slow breath. 'I get one-on-one time with a hottie ballerina and you're going home to your old lady. I know who *I'd* rather be.'

Den Porter came up to the two guys and clapped them both on the back, chuckling at Grant's joke. 'Can't argue with that, can you, Arch?'

Archer muttered a retort but left Grant alone. The locker

room buzzed around them, pre-game jitters filling the air with a crackling, unpredictable energy.

'You *have* been a bit of a space cadet,' Den echoed, taking a long swig from his water bottle.

'I've got things on my mind.' Grant shrugged.

'They'd better be game-related things,' the coach said as he walked past. 'This season is your chance, Grant. An opportunity for redemption.'

'He sounds like a goddamn evangelist,' Grant muttered as the coach disappeared from earshot. 'He's got the memory of an elephant too.'

'Maybe you should have thought of that before you dragged the club into your personal life.' Archer's voice was stony. '*You* cost us that season.'

'If I remember rightly, you didn't score a single goal that game,' Grant said through gritted teeth.

'Who could concentrate, with you stumbling all over the place? You were a mess.'

Grant slammed his locker shut, enjoying the loud crack. He'd been on the straight and narrow for over six months now, but his team would never pass up the opportunity to have a go. They thought he'd cost them a winning season—their *first* winning season—and that his antics had distracted the team.

He'd given up the partying, he'd given up the booze, he'd even given up the groupies. But it wasn't enough; in everyone's mind *he* was the reason for their failure. He could still remember the last call he'd had with his father in the days after the story had hit the media. *'Now you're a deserter* and *a drunk. You're no son of mine.'*

'You whinge like an old woman, mate.' Den rolled his eyes at Arch.

The coach approached Grant, his weathered face drawn into a stony expression. 'Don't forget you promised me this season would be a winner, Farley. When I agreed to give you a second chance you told me you'd give me a winning season.'

'I will.'

'You'd better not have any distractions this time.' Two hard eyes bored into him. 'I make it a rule not to give third chances.'

Message received.

Jasmine and Elise arrived early to the Melbourne Cricket Ground, where all the big AFL games were held, to collect their tickets. As they were gaining access to the most exclusive part of the MCG they hadn't been able to dress down like the rest of the fans who were streaming into the stadium. Amidst the black-and-green Jaguar guernseys, and the occasional fan sporting the red and yellow of the away team, they looked out of place.

The winter air bit right through Jasmine's coat and boots, a fine mist of rain dampening her exposed neck. She shivered and huddled closer to Elise. They moved with the crowd, searching for the 'Members Only' area.

Following the signs, they eventually ended up in the Long Room, with its floor-to-ceiling views of the ground. It was another world. Away from the crowds and coloured flags of the general admission area. Away from the manic cheering, meat pies and scarf waving. Away from the 'real' football experience.

Up here men wore tailored suits and women dressed in all manner of finery, toting handbags that probably cost more than a month's rent. The sound of dramatic air kisses and tinkling laughter rose above quiet conversation.

'It's something else, isn't it?' Elise looked around, dazzled.

Jasmine shifted on the spot and removed her coat, slinging it over one arm. She smoothed her free hand down the front of the vibrant emerald dress she wore over thick black tights and boots. She'd changed a dozen times before leaving, even though she knew she was unlikely to see Grant after the game. Still, she'd fussed over endless combinations until she'd ended up back in the first outfit she'd tried on. Last minute, she'd thrown a long strand of onyx beads around her neck to try and fancy up what essentially was a plain cotton dress.

She looked even more out of place here than she had in the crowd. Elise loved being amongst the rich, but Jasmine hated it. Such wealth flung around, while she could barely scrape together enough money to keep her electricity turned on. She felt frumpy and juvenile next to these elegant swans in their silk dresses and needle-thin heels.

Worse, she'd been here before. The glitz and the glamour of the arts world wasn't so different—though there was a distinct lack of fake tan and fake boobs where ballet and art were concerned.

She'd been on the arm of a wealthy man—the son of a financier—who'd thought his family's bank balance meant that he owned her, that he could control her as he controlled the investments in his portfolio. His family had money equivalent to the GDP of a small nation.

And it had ended badly...*very* badly. Her stomach churned.

'Champagne, miss?' A waiter held out his silver tray, four delicate flutes of bubbling wine catching the light in front of her.

'No, thank you.'

'I will.' Elise reached for a flute and smiled.

The waiter drifted into the crowd and they found a spot to stand in front of the mammoth glass window. Outside the seats were filling up. A sea of black and green engulfed the stadium, and excitement was palpable in the atmosphere. Inside the clinking of champagne flutes and muted chatter filled the air.

'I would have thought you'd be OK to have a drink by now.' Elise took a delicate sip from her flute.

Her blond hair was piled on her head, with wispy strands loose and alluring around her pixie face. A chunky strand of grey pearls offset her steel-coloured eyes. Even Elise looked more as if she belonged than Jasmine did.

'It's not like I'm working hard to resist it,' Jasmine said.

'You're missing out—this is the good stuff.' She winked. 'The *French* stuff.'

'I don't want it.'

Elise watched her, assessing her as she sipped again. Her tongue captured a stray droplet of the fizzing liquid. Jasmine forced a smile; she didn't want to ruin what would be an exciting night for Elise.

'One glass won't kill you,' Elise went on. 'I'm driving, so you don't have to worry about safety.'

'I don't want one.' She couldn't keep the frost out of her voice.

Elise sighed. 'I'm not trying to push you. I'm just saying that it's OK to let your hair down every once in a while. You know—live a little. Maybe act like you're twenty-seven instead of seventy-seven.'

'I'm sure there are seventy-seven-year-olds who are more fun than me.'

Both girls laughed, and Elise hooked her arm through Jasmine's. 'Yeah, I'm going to trade you in at a nursing home on the way back.'

The room filled up around them. A woman in a knee-length indigo shift stood next to them. Jasmine was sure she'd seen her in the society pages, possibly mentioned as the wife of one of the Jaguars players. She was so close the headiness of her perfume made Jasmine breathe deep. The scent was rich. Refined. French to match the red soles of her designer shoes.

Elise nudged Jasmine and pointed out another woman

who'd walked past—a semi-celebrity, famed for the high-profile sports-star boyfriends she turned over frequently. Her tanned skin glowed as though she'd returned from the Maldives that day. She probably had.

'Why don't we sit outside? We can't take Grant's tickets and then stay in here all night.' Jasmine motioned for the door to the balcony. Her chest felt squeezed tight, as though two hands were crushing her ribcage, pushing all the air out of her. She gripped her handbag to her stomach, wishing the swishing sensation would stop.

Mercifully, Elise downed the last of her champagne and they stepped out into the members' balcony area.

The vibe outside was entirely different, and the din that rose up from the crowd was full of excitement and anticipation. Jasmine's heart immediately slowed, the pressure in her chest easing as she located two spare seats. She wrapped her coat around her shoulders and crossed her arms as she sat, popping the collar to protect her neck from the chill.

'You OK?' Elise touched her arm.

Jasmine nodded. Now that she was outside, away from the dismissive glances and claustrophobic atmosphere of the Long Room, she felt marginally better.

Still, she'd prefer to be at home with a blanket, a good book and a cup of hot chocolate. Not here, freezing her butt off in a dress that seemed to be too dressy and yet not dressy enough. But Elise could be a bulldog when she wanted to; sometimes it was easier to give in rather than indulge her Goldilocks complex about her wardrobe.

More members piled out of the Long Room and into the balcony seats. They were mostly men in suits; the women seemed to be staying inside, except for a group of younger girls with extra-long hair extensions and too-short dresses. They occupied the front row, giggling and pointing as the players took to the field.

It was match time, and the fans were chomping at the bit. The Jaguars had won the coin toss and the players now jogged into position. The noise level in the stadium swelled. Even Jasmine couldn't help but get caught up in the rush...just a little.

For some reason her stomach fluttered at the thought of seeing Grant out there. She jumped as the siren sounded and the game began. A centre bounce set the ball into play and the crowd was on the edge of their seats from the first few seconds.

'It's going to be a close game,' Elise said, her tone serious. 'The Jags lost by a point last time they played the Suns, and only by two or three points the time before that.'

'Since when are you such a football expert?'

'Since there are hot guys in tiny shorts.' She laughed.

Jasmine nodded. 'Where's Grant?'

She scanned the ground, looking for a familiar head of thick blond hair since that was about all she'd be able to see from the balcony. The players were quick, running at full speed as the ball flew from the centre towards the goalposts at one end. There was a mad scramble and the ball went out of play.

'He's the full forward.' Elise pointed to the other end of the field. 'Number eighteen.'

Jasmine spotted Grant's hulking frame, his arms bulging in the sleeveless Jaguars guernsey. His muscles rippled as he moved, tense and ready to spring into action. She noticed one of his shoulders was covered in tattoos— something she hadn't seen beneath the T-shirts he wore to her lessons. His blond hair shone under the stadium lights, and even at such a great distance she could see the focus on his face.

Her stomach clenched.

He was so masculine out there. So powerful. He moved with all the strength and grace of the big cat his team was named after. Each movement was practised and precisely executed. He tracked the other players effortlessly, moving to cover and dodge with incredible agility.

She swallowed, pushing down the attraction humming through her. He was so...*virile*.

The ball hurtled towards Grant. He sprang into action. It bounced, there was a flurry of arms and legs, and then he got his hands on it. He kicked. The ball sailed into the air, straight through the goalposts in a single graceful arc.

Around her the crowd roared; flags and scarves waved in a blur of black and green. She jumped to her feet and cheered. The air rushed out of her lungs as she shouted his name.

The players clapped one another on the back and Grant looked up towards the members' area. Jasmine was certain he was looking straight at her. OK, so maybe she *did* get the appeal of the footballer...

CHAPTER FOUR

GRANT'S MUSCLES WERE FREED, tired and a little bruised—just the way he liked it after a good massage. Most of the guys in his team booked their treatments around the schedule of a pretty brunette masseuse, but Grant much preferred the stout, middle-aged woman with knuckles of steel.

He gave his shoulders a tentative roll. They moved better than they had an hour ago, but he was tender to the touch. The game against the Suns had done a number on him. He'd pushed himself harder than ever, stretching himself beyond where he'd thought his limits were.

And all because he'd known Jasmine was watching.

Pushing thoughts of her from his mind, he walked into the reception area. People huddled at the front door, waiting for a break in the weather before they made a dash out to the car park. Rain pelted against the glass doors and lightning flashed amongst heavy clouds, illuminating the small patches of sky peeking through.

He smiled at the receptionist as she handed him a form to sign, her eyes inviting him to linger. He didn't bother. He was far too preoccupied to engage in flirtation.

His mind was on other things—namely the fact that he couldn't get a certain ballet teacher out of his head. It had been years since he'd felt genuine attraction to a woman—years since he'd had the urge to pursue a woman for something other than sex…though sex would definitely be involved.

When his ex-fiancée, Chelsea, had left him, abandoning their five-year relationship, it had felt like losing his family all over again. Since then he'd reassessed his approach to women. She'd departed with nothing but a scrawled note. He'd responded by limiting himself to a string of football groupies who were more about scratching an itch than genuine attraction. If he didn't invest in a relationship then he couldn't have it thrown back in his face. They all wanted to use him for something, so he kept them at a distance. He kept *everyone* at a distance.

Grant glanced back to the group of people waiting at the door and noticed a slender figure with a long black ponytail. *Jasmine.*

He scrawled his name on the form with haste and handed it back to the receptionist. He walked to the front of the room and slipped into the group until he stood directly behind her. She titled her head to the side and her ponytail swished against her back like a thick band of silk.

'Don't tell me you walked today.' He leant forwards, his lips all but brushing her ear. The flowery scent of her perfume immediately made his stomach flip.

She turned. Her cheeks were flushed and a black smudge ran across her upper cheek.

'I learned my lesson last time.' She managed a smile, but it didn't crinkle the corners of her eyes as it usually did. Her arms were crossed tight across her chest, though it was stuffy and warm inside the waiting room. Her mouth was a harsh line, the corners downturned slightly.

'Is everything OK?'

'I'm fine.'

Grant didn't miss the way her body stiffened next to his.

'Somehow I don't believe you.' Something within Grant

shifted as Jasmine looked at him, her face a mask of forced composure.

'Great game, by the way.' The catch in her words made him want to wrap his arms around her. He fought back the urge and shoved his hands into his pockets. 'You killed it out there.'

'The Suns didn't stand a chance.' He grinned, puffing his chest out. 'And nice attempt at changing the subject.' He nudged her in the ribcage with his elbow.

'Am I that transparent?'

'Yeah.' He reached out and ran his thumb along the black line on her cheek. 'Plus you have a little smudge on your face.'

'I'm fine.' Her eyes were wide, cheekbones flushed where he'd touched her a moment ago. Her breath hitched.

'Don't tell me you're fine when you're clearly not.'

She shook her head, looking towards the doors. He had the feeling that if he didn't grab on to her then she might bolt through the clinic's entrance into the rain. Usually it was he who had the itch to run, but not now.

He slung an arm around her shoulders as though they were old friends. The gesture should have felt platonic, safe...but the way she automatically pressed into his side felt anything but safe.

'Let me take you for a coffee. It'll make you feel better.'

Her faced tilted up to his. 'That's very sweet, but I'm OK. Honestly, I don't need your help.'

'You know you're only supposed to say "honestly" if you're telling the truth, right?'

She poked her tongue out at him.

'Just coffee, then, and I won't try to help.' He grinned. 'In fact I'll be actively unhelpful if that makes you feel better.'

'Persistent, aren't you?' She rolled her eyes at him, but she couldn't hide the smile tugging at her lips.

'Yes.'

'Is there any chance you'll take no for an answer?'

'Never.'

'I *guess* I could use the caffeine.'

He took the opportunity and linked his arm through hers. 'Let's make a break for it. We'll go in my car.'

Pushing forwards, he opened the doors against the raging wind and held Jasmine close. She shrieked as the rain hit them head-on, and they rushed down the pavement towards the car park. The ground was slippery and he held her tight so that her body bumped against him as they sprinted.

'Quickly!' she cried, her black hair whipping around her face like wet ebony ribbons.

He pulled her towards the second row of cars and fumbled with his keys. Jasmine let go of him, dashing around to the passenger side. The doors slammed loudly as they fell into the car in a rush, their breathing fogging up the windows of the Mercedes. Jasmine's laugh was a punch to his gut; even drenched and puffing she was a vision.

'Bloody Melbourne!' Grant rolled down the driver's windows and backed the car out of its spot. 'I can't see a damn thing!'

'It's freezing.' Jasmine rubbed her hands together, breathing on them. 'I swear it's going to snow this winter.'

'Fat chance.' Grant pulled the car out onto the street. 'I've never seen snow in the burbs.'

'Are you always so literal?' Her voice was teasing and Grant glanced at her sideways. A smirk passed over her face.

'Men are wired that way.' He laughed. 'Simple creatures, we are.'

'Yeah, you *are* pretty simple.'

He gave her a mock wounded expression. 'I'll have you know I'm a man of many skills.'

'Such as?'

'I solved a Rubik's cube once.'

'Really?' She raised an eyebrow at him.

'Yeah. I may have peeled off some of the colours and stuck them back down so the sides matched...'

'That's resourceful.'

'I was four.'

'I'm surprised your parents didn't get you admitted to Mensa with skills like that.'

'Who says they didn't?'

'You're a clown.' Her laughter was like bells tinkling. 'And here I was, thinking that all footballers were big oafs with more brawn than brains.'

'That's a bit judgmental.' Grant pulled the car in front of a café. 'I'm rethinking this offer.'

It was an idle threat; no way was he giving up the opportunity to get into Jasmine's head. She was too much of a puzzle for him not to have a go. He wanted to see what she was all about underneath the defensive exterior.

'Too late.' She grinned at him and leapt out of the car.

The café was one of those too-trendy-for-their-own-good places, with a coffee menu that had more options than a pizza joint had toppings. Grant normally avoided them like the plague, but he couldn't deny how amazing the coffee was. Besides, a small part of him wanted Jasmine to be impressed with his taste. Outside the studio he had the opportunity to be her equal rather than her student.

'Oh, I've been meaning to come here,' she said, shrugging off her coat and unwinding her scarf.

Grant bit back the desire to touch her as she exposed delicate ivory skin. She was utterly sensual even when doing the most mundane thing.

'It gets great reviews on a bunch of coffee blogs.'

The smooth porcelain of her neck begged to be touched, to be marked with the hunger of his kiss.

'It's good.' Grant signalled to the waiter that they wanted a table for two. 'If you can put up with the hipster vibe.'

The café was filled with people in skinny jeans and ironic T-shirts, sporting all manner of moustaches and thick-framed glasses. It certainly wasn't somewhere where he'd fit in, but he'd put up with the pretentious patrons for a decent macchiato. Plus, he was unlikely to be recognised somewhere like this—somewhere where football wasn't the religion of choice. The last thing he wanted was anyone interrupting them.

'I might not be able to read the menu.' She followed him to an empty table by the window. 'Can't say I've ever heard of *syphon* coffee before.'

'It's lighter than regular espresso 'cause the beans are roasted at a lower temperature—it's good stuff.'

'Wow.' Jasmine looked impressed. 'You should have gone with the coffee facts instead of the Rubik's cube story.'

'I stand by my choice.'

An awkward silence descended on the table. He rubbed a hand along his jaw, feeling the scratch of stubble against his palm. The café buzzed around them, full of people escaping the weather. Their table had a view of the empty rain-drenched street, and tucked away in the back he could pretend it was just the two of them.

Jasmine toyed with the single flower that sat in a jar in front of them. Her fingers brushed the blood-red blossom and the petals sprang back into position as she moved her hand away.

'Are you going to tell me what's wrong?' The words came out of Grant's mouth before he could stop them. She looked out of the window, her eyes shadowed.

'I thought you said you weren't going to help.' She

turned back to him with a small smile. 'I distinctly remember the words "actively unhelpful" being uttered.'

'I *did* say that.'

'I don't want to talk about it.' Jasmine quietened as the waiter took their orders. 'It's not something you can help with, so I don't see the point of going over it.'

'Try me.'

He couldn't tell if she was annoyed or if he was finally breaking through. Her eyebrows were knitted together and she tapped her fingernails against the edge of the table. Each nail was a glimmering pale pink. *Perfection right down to her damn fingernails.*

She was getting to him, making him want to see what secret she kept so close to her chest, what pain she hid from the world. He was drawn to her in some primal, uncontrollable way. But there was nothing he could do to sate that desire—not unless he wanted to cross a line he'd promised himself he wouldn't. Jasmine was complex. She played her cards close to her chest and she hadn't asked him for a single thing. That put her in a special category all of her own, and that meant he couldn't treat her the way he treated others.

'You *are* persistent, aren't you?' she said.

'It's one of my many qualities.'

Her dark lashes fluttered as two dots of pink formed on her cheeks. 'I am familiar with your other qualities.'

'What have you got to lose?'

Would she put up a wall between them and close him out? He wanted so desperately to delve beneath the surface, to see past the barrier she put between them. Most of all he wanted to see how far down that feminine blush of hers went. Grant fiddled with the hem of his jumper.

'Why are you so curious?'

'Why are you so guarded?'

Jasmine had to laugh. If there was one thing she could

say about Grant it was that he was like a dog with a bone. The waiter set two coffees down in front of them and she eagerly reached for hers, wrapping her hands around the warm terracotta-coloured cup.

The familiar clutches of grief tugged at her chest, closing their cold hands around her heart and lungs—making it difficult to breathe.

'Remember how I told you that I'd been in an accident?'

'Yeah.' He nodded.

'I caused it. I'd had a few drinks and argued with my boyfriend. It was stupid. I shouldn't have been driving.'

She remembered the swirl of her silk gown as she'd rushed to the car. The tears and champagne blurring her vision. The world as it tilted around her when the car rolled. The pain as she'd tried to drag herself to freedom through the driver's window.

'I don't know what to do.' Her voice was devoid of emotion. 'I can't stand the sight of alcohol anymore and I can't even take painkillers because I'm afraid to lose control.'

She held her breath, waiting to see if he would miraculously provide the solution to her problems. He didn't.

'Why do you think that taking painkillers will make you lose control?'

'You know, I'm not actually sure.' She shook her head. 'I think it started as a little game for myself when I was first recovering. I tried to wean myself off, thinking that if I could do without the painkillers then it meant I was better and I'd be able to dance again.'

'But it didn't work.' His face softened, blond lashes dropping to cover his eyes for a moment before he looked back up at her.

'No. I tried to tough it out for six months at the ballet company before I gave up. That was the worst six months of my life. I had to watch someone else dance the part I'd been given the day before the accident. It was my first lead role—a small contemporary ballet—but it was a sign… a sign that my career was going in the right direction. A sign that maybe I could make it all the way to Principal.'

'Is ballet out of the question now?'

'Yeah.' She traced the opening of her coffee cup with the pad of her finger. The smooth edges were soothing against her skin. 'My ankle is stuffed. There was a lot of damage to the tendons and the strength hasn't fully returned. I can't even stretch up on my toes properly, let alone dance *en pointe*.'

'That sucks.' His hand reached over the table and clasped hers.

The unexpected and tender gesture shocked her, while the heat from his palm filled her body with irresistible warmth. It spread through her, heating her chest, colouring her cheeks and stirring the butterflies in her stomach.

'It's my fault.' Disappointment surged through her. 'It's my issue to deal with—and one that I need a psychologist for, apparently.'

For once his face showed nothing. His glacial blue eyes were fixed on her, his blond lashes still as he looked at her as though he were seeing past her exterior. She shifted in her seat. She didn't want people to look at her like that… as if they could see the darkness inside.

'Maybe seeing a psychologist wouldn't be such a bad thing. At least he'd be trained to listen and help you work through the problem.'

'The problem is not in my head,' she said, her teeth grinding together. Her white-knuckled grip shook the coffee cup in her hands. 'The problem is my leg, not my brain. I don't need to see a psychologist. This is what I've been saying.'

She couldn't believe he was agreeing with the doctor. Could no one see where the real issue was? She wasn't crazy, or delusional, or incapable of understanding what had happened. The problem was in her leg. End of story.

'Has it occurred to you that perhaps you can have pain in two places at once?'

Grant leant forwards and locked his eyes on Jasmine. His raw power stopped her in the midst of her tirade. 'Life would be a lot easier if we only ever had to deal with the physical, but unfortunately it's not that simple. You need to get over those narrow-minded notions and start dealing with the problem from all angles.'

Her eyes widened at the roughness of his voice. Each word was like silk over gravel: luxurious, rugged.

'Quite the bossy-boots, aren't you?' She spoke down to her coffee cup.

The intensity in his words belied the calm mask he wore. Passion simmered in the depths of his eyes, and his hand was gripping hers like a vice. Jasmine removed her hand and sipped her drink, using the time to think up a response to Grant's argument. Well, something other than calling him a bossy-boots.

His reaction shocked her. It had been a long time since someone had told her to get over herself. In fact she couldn't remember a time where anyone in her life had said something even remotely similar to her. Even Elise had gone easy on the whole recovery subject.

They were usually too busy walking on eggshells around her to be honest. Grant spoke his mind. She liked that about him. His humorous, carefree nature was a bit of a farce. Deep down he was a fiery person, opinionated and caring. Much more than his cocky demeanour had led her to expect, and definitely more than the football stereo-type would suggest.

She'd underestimated him.

Shaking her head, she looked up. His thick brows were crinkled, his eyes trained on hers. He looked so sincere she wanted to grab his face and kiss the worry away. Her lips tingled with anticipation as she fought back the urge to lean over the table and press her mouth against his. Every cell in her body craved his touch, tingling so that she couldn't ignore the effect he had on her.

Fighting back the powerful wave of attraction, she asked, 'Have you ever done something so stupid that you wished every day you could take it back?'

'Some thing*s*,' he said, stressing the *s*. 'I've made every mistake in the book.'

'Really?' She tilted her head, watching the way his large hands toyed with the small espresso cup.

For a moment she was lost in wondering what those hands would feel like on her, cradling the curve of her neck, smoothing down the length of her back, stroking her hair. Heat swelled in her, causing her to shift in her seat for a different reason this time. He was not the person she'd predicted when he'd walked into her studio that first day.

'Yeah, you take a boy out of the country and drop him smack-bang in the middle of city life and it's bound to make him go crazy. Add to that the lack of parenting, the money, the girls, the parties... Hell, I wanted to try it all at once.'

'That's understandable.'

'It's understandable to want to *try* it all.' He offered up a rueful smile. 'It's another thing to actually do it.'

'Isn't it just part of being a footballer?' she asked. 'Aren't you all known for your antics?'

'I'd rather be known for playing good footy.'

'I'm pretty sure you're known for that already.' She wanted to comfort him, the same way he had done for her, but she didn't know where to start. Her hand fluttered in her lap.

'It wouldn't be so bad if it weren't so damn public. Everyone makes mistakes, but ours are documented by the media. And once it's out there you can't ever erase it.'

His face darkened when he mentioned the media, and for the first time Jasmine felt as if she might be on exactly the same plane as Grant. Her family and friends had brought her magazines and newspapers to keep her busy while she was in hospital, and one day she'd seen a picture of her ex with a new woman on his arm. Another ballerina—a girl she'd known since she was a child. It wasn't the media's fault, sure, but if they didn't report on every single little happening in people's lives she might have been spared that gut-wrenching pain for a while longer.

'So tell me about football,' she said, eager to change the topic and see Grant's face return to its normal unstressed state. 'Do you think you'll make finals this year?'

'That's certainly the plan. Some guys don't like to call it early, in case they jinx it, but I don't think it's possible to get out of bed and train as hard as we do if you don't believe you can get there.'

Oh, how she envied his confidence. She'd been like that once.

'I'm sure it's the same with dancing. The physical aspect is only one part. These things are as much about the mental game as they are about the training and the practice.'

'Looks like we're not so different after all.' She smiled, trying to keep the tone light, but it struck her how similar their lives were once you got past the superficial differences.

He drained the last of his coffee and set the cup down on the table, the smile back on his face. 'Another?'

'I should probably get you to take me back to my car.' She shook her head. 'I appreciate your honesty, by the way—a lot of people are too busy pitying me to give me a kick up the butt when I need it.'

She detected a hint of uncertainty as he smiled back at

her—there was definitely something going on behind those glacial blue eyes of his—but he managed to keep himself behind a wall even while he coaxed her to let her own guard down. She wanted to know more, but it had been so long since she'd had a man in her life who wanted anything from her aside from the physical that she wasn't quite sure how to ask the questions that swirled inside her head.

'My pleasure.' He stood and manoeuvred his hulking frame between the crammed tables of the café. 'Buttkicking is a speciality of mine.'

'Cheating a Rubik's cube, random coffee facts and buttkicking…it's an unusual skill set, I'll give you that.'

As they made their way to the counter to pay for their coffees an icy breeze blew in from the street. The rain had calmed, but the temperature was still low enough to slice straight to the bone. She huddled instinctively against Grant, seeking out warmth and protection. He wrapped an arm around her shoulders and pulled her closer while he fixed up the bill. She felt good nestled against him—as if nothing could get to her. The unexpected familiarity of his embrace made her mouth run dry.

'Time to brave the cold.'

He moved his hand down to her lower back and pressed gently as they walked out into the street. They hurried to the car, their faces bowed against the wind, and Jasmine stayed close to Grant right until they reached the passenger door.

Once inside the car she was acutely aware of their proximity, of the way his jeans hugged his strong thighs and stretched across his hips. The car was hot as a sauna.

Heat pulsed between her legs as her mind gave way to the salacious fantasy of him taking her in the back seat of the Mercedes. It had occupied her ever since he'd first given her a lift.

Seemingly unaware of her erotic thoughts, Grant navigated the car onto the main road and headed in the direction of the doctor's clinic. She allowed her eyes to slip downwards, over his broad chest and down...

'See something you like down there?'

His voice caused Jasmine to snap her head back up to the windscreen. Her cheeks flamed as she realised she'd been caught in the act. *Jasmine Bell, your mother would be ashamed!*

His gravelly laugh set fire to her belly, the embarrassment and desire mingling into one confused knot of emotion. He was cocky—but with that kind of intense sexual power she couldn't blame him. Her eyes flickered up to his face. His lips were parted with hunger but his eyes were focused on the road ahead, although he glanced at her whenever they stopped at a red light.

She'd seen something else today: the tenderness in the way he'd covered her hand with his. He'd cared for her, even if only for a split second. Like the bump in his nose, there was a crack in the image he presented—a softness beneath the tough outer shell and she'd glimpsed it today. Part of her wanted to reach in and pull him apart, to see what he was made of. The other part of her knew what his life would be like—glamour, paparazzi, wealth. And she couldn't go there...not again.

CHAPTER FIVE

JASMINE THREW HERSELF into the choreography for the EJ Ballet School's annual Winter Performance. It was something to focus her energy on—something other than fighting off the pulse-racing thoughts of Grant interrupting her day. She needed a project, a reason to wake up in the morning, something to pour her heart and soul into.

The routine was coming together well, and she'd finished her first lesson with the four teachers who would be performing it.

'How come you're not dancing with us?' one of the teachers asked, snapping Jasmine's attention back to the present.

'Jasmine has an injury,' Elise said, steering the teacher towards the exit of the studio. 'I made her promise that she'd get better before she put any pressure on herself to perform.'

Details of her accident had been kept quiet when Elise had brought her onto the teaching staff. Not because she necessarily had anything to hide but because she was still recovering emotionally and physically. Not much had changed in six months.

The teachers gave Jasmine a wave as they left the studio. She followed them out to the waiting room so she could relax before Grant arrived. Dropping down to one knee, she sighed as she rifled through her sports bag. Her fingertips brushed the roughened satin of her *pointe* shoes and she pulled one out. They were the shoes from her first professional performance as a member of the *corps de ballet* all those years ago. The satin had split and frayed around the shoe's box, and the shank was broken, but she hadn't been able to throw them away. Elise had signed the soles in her flowery cursive, and Jasmine had done the same to Elise's first shoes.

It was days like this that made her wonder if she should give it up all together. She loved choreography but the wounds were still wide open. It hurt so damn much not to join in as the teachers danced her steps. Once again she was sitting on the sidelines, wasting all the sacrifices her parents had made to help her get where she was.

A sudden impulse made her put the shoes on; she lovingly tied the ribbons around her ankle and stood. They felt comfortable, and since she wouldn't be able to rise up *en pointe* anyway the broken shank didn't matter. She twirled on the spot, practising the steps from her new routine. Her body warmed and the glow she always felt when she danced spread through her. The world seemed more beautiful when she danced; her troubles evaporated and she was at peace.

'That's pretty damn good.'

Grant's voice came from behind her. She'd been so lost in the movement she hadn't even heard him come in. 'I bet you say that to all the girls.'

'I don't have to say anything.' He grinned that delicious crooked grin of his. 'The girls usually drop to my feet as I walk past.'

Jasmine rolled her eyes. It bothered her that despite his sarcasm it was probably the truth. And why *wouldn't* girls drop at his feet? Football players were practically the *crème de la crème* of Australian society. Many women craved the spotlight and the access dating a footballer would provide...but not her. For a moment she wished he was an ordinary guy, rather than a famous athlete. Why couldn't he be someone who could walk down the street unnoticed?

'You'd better be careful—if your head gets much bigger you won't be able to get out of the building.' She dropped to the ground and removed the *pointe* shoes, slipping her feet back into her soft split-soles.

'These are like proper ballet shoes, aren't they?' Grant picked up one of the *pointe* shoes and examined it as though it were a piece of an alien spacecraft. 'The real deal.'

Jasmine nodded. 'They are the real deal indeed.'

'You miss it a lot, don't you?' He turned the shoe in his hand, touching it as though it were the most precious thing in the world.

Her stomach flipped. 'Yeah, I do.'

'And you can't go back?'

The studio hummed in the midst of their silence, a broken light flickering overhead. She held out her hand and he handed over the shoe. The familiar shape of it in her palm caused her breath to hitch. She packed it away safely in her bag and forced a smile.

'You didn't come here to talk about this.' She motioned for him to follow her into the studio. 'Let's get to work.'

He opened his mouth but then closed it again, a curious expression on his face. She gave herself a little shake to bring her back to the present. She didn't want his pity, and he wasn't here to listen to her sob story. Again.

'Today I'm going to teach you a new step,' she said, focusing her attention on business. 'The *relevé* is a position with the feet together at the ankles, heels lifted from the ground.'

Jasmine rose up onto her toes, her ankles crossed. She wasn't able to rise as high as she'd used to, but it was enough to show the intention of the step. Her ankle groaned under the position, warning her not to push too far.

He followed along, but wobbled before he could fully stretch up. She stepped closer and put her hand on the flat of his stomach.

'You have to activate your core muscles,' she said. His abs flexed under her touch as he stabilised himself, sending a frisson of excitement racing through her. 'You're strong here. You need to keep your body centred otherwise you won't be able to balance.'

He smirked and heat flooded her cheeks. It was impossible for her to forget what he looked like on the field, his body primed and masculine. Her every nerve-ending fired with need, betraying the sensible restrictions her mind enforced.

'Try again,' she said, doing her best to sound professional.

But she couldn't draw her hand from his stomach. It was stuck there, as though forced by some invisible magnetic energy.

As Grant worked to keep himself stable he rose taller and stretched so that he could look clean over the top of her head.

'Much better.'

'Show me one more time?'

Grant's eyes were locked on her; her skin tingled everywhere they travelled.

'Of course.' Jasmine pulled her shoulders back and relaxed her body into a perfect turn-out. Bending down, she extended her knees outwards and brought her feet into *relevé,* her ankles crossed as she balanced without a tremor of unsteadiness.

Grant stepped forwards, his hand reaching out to touch her stomach in the same way she had touched his. His full lips parted as he stepped close to her. 'Yes, very stable.'

They stood frozen—neither bold enough to make the next move. Jasmine held her breath. She didn't want to move in case he might withdraw his hand and break the spell, yet she trembled at the thought of what she would do if he didn't pull back.

Grant moved his hand down to her waist, tilting his

body into hers so that their faces were only inches apart. She could smell the spice of his aftershave and the subtle mint on his breath. She could easily give in, draw her hand up to his chest and submit.

There was something utterly disarming about him. The combination of his strong jaw and the slightly crooked, freckle-smattered nose enchanted her. He was real and unabashedly male, unlike many of the effeminate boys she'd grown up with.

'Are you ready to do it on your own?' Jasmine dropped down from the position so she was an inch or two below eye level with Grant. She tried to unscramble her senses, to focus on the lesson.

'I can.' His voice was low, predatory. 'But don't you think it's much more fun when we do it together?'

The air between them was thick with electricity, its gravitational pull unravelling her sensibilities. She so desperately wanted to touch him. Her mouth was dry, anticipation making her pulse race.

He placed his hands over hers and Jasmine jumped at the way her blood pulsed harder and harder.

'Why so jumpy? Are you uncomfortable being alone with me?'

'No,' she whispered.

The problem was she was far too comfortable as he stood close to her. All she wanted to do was melt against him. She envisaged herself pressing against his broad chest and sturdy thighs. Her entire body crackled with excitement as they stood, merely inches apart, in the empty ballet studio.

Why was she feeling like this? He was out of her league— in a league she never wanted to be a part of again. Ever, *ever* again.

He reached his hands up to her face, cupping the sides of her cheeks in his palms. It was the wrong thing to do;

she shouldn't be going down this path. But desire raced through her veins and filled her with irresistible warmth, overpowering logic. He was intoxicating.

Up close, she felt the pull of his hypnotic stare. The endless blue of his eyes made the rest of the world fall away. It made sense and reason evaporate. Her lips parted.

Grant drew Jasmine's face to his in a swift and practised movement. Her eyes fluttered closed as his mouth came down. The soft fullness of his lips pressed hungrily against hers, his tongue hot and probing. Jasmine sighed into him. It had been so long since she'd been kissed, and a lifetime since she'd been kissed in a way that made her weak in the knees.

Grant moved one hand from her face, down the length of her arm, and snaked it around her waist, drawing her closer to him. Every inch of her burned as their bodies fused together, the thinness of their workout clothes mimicking the deliciousness of skin on skin. Her hands found their way into the wavy depths of his golden-blond hair. It was thick and silken against her palms. Her fingers gripped tightly as he dipped her, demanding deeper access to her mouth.

His breath was hot on her face as his lips moved down her jawline to the slender column of her neck, each kiss searing her skin. He backed her up until she pressed against the wall of the studio, crushed between plaster and the hardness of him.

He worked back to her mouth, tugging at her lower lip and flicking his tongue against hers. He tasted of mint, smelled of spices and earthy maleness. Blood coursed through her, hot and thick, as he devoured her. His hand skimmed her hips, reaching around to curve against her ass. He pressed her to him, the thick length of his arousal digging into her belly. She moved her hips against him, dragging a guttural plea from his lips.

'You taste so good,' he murmured against her mouth, drawing out the syllables of the last word. '*Feel* so good.'

Her tongue traced the sharp angle of his jaw. The golden hairs of his stubble were rough against her. She wanted to lick every inch of him...every single inch. She clamped her eyes shut and lost herself.

His thigh nudged her legs open and she gasped. His hand smoothed up the side of her, traversing over her ribcage and palming her breast. Her nipples pebbled in response, desperate for skin-to-skin contact. His thumb brushed the hardened peak, pushing her further into oblivion. This was the most pleasure she had allowed herself since the accident.

Visions of them flooded her...their bodies slick with sweat, limbs entwined. Panting. Writhing. Aching. She'd never wanted something with such desperation in all her life.

She could envisage how breathtaking he would be when he was naked, but it was the image of herself naked that jolted her out of her reverie.

Her leg.

Picturing the mangled piece of flesh she called her right leg halted her thoughts. The long snakelike red scar would stand out angrily against her paleness. The skin itself was ruined, never again to be smooth and supple like the rest of her. There was no way he'd find her attractive after that—how could he?

She looked like a freak show.

Pressure mounted in her chest as she brought her two palms flat against his chest and pushed hard. Grant stumbled backwards, a look of utter shock and surprise on his face—his blue eyes swam with confusion.

'I'm—I'm sorry,' she stammered. 'I can't—'

Pushing past him, Jasmine sprinted from the room, only stopping to scoop up her bag as she bolted for the exit.

* * *

'I ran out of there like an idiot.' Jasmine shook her head as she raised a jumbo coffee cup to her lips. 'Tragic.'

Elise stared at Jasmine—wide-eyed and open-mouthed—while her coffee sat on the table, untouched. Her grey eyes were unblinking as she processed this new information. 'Let me get this straight. The Football Hunk had you pinned up against a wall and you bailed? What's wrong with you?'

The café around them buzzed with activity. They'd managed to get a table that was off to one side, giving them a semblance of privacy, though Jasmine still lowered her voice.

'I think I'm broken.' She nursed the steaming coffee in both hands.

Elise patted her arm across the small round table. 'You're not broken.'

Elise had called at her house at the crack of dawn because she'd found Jasmine's mobile phone and boots in the studio. Elise's conclusion upon finding the items—perhaps not logical, though not unusual for Elise—was that Jasmine had been kidnapped. So her tale of failed seduction was a welcome alternative.

'You know what freaked me out the most?' Jasmine said as she traced her finger around the rim of her coffee cup, forehead creased. 'All I could think about was my leg. What would happen if he saw it? How would he react?'

Her voice wavered. For so long her body had been a source of success and pleasure—she'd *never* despised the way she looked. Sure, she'd wished at times that her boobs had developed past an A cup, but a flat chest was something that went with being a ballerina. She'd never felt the crippling wash of shame that she had last night. Jasmine put her cup down and dropped her chin into her hands.

'At some point you're going to have to get past that...

unless you plan on being a spinster and filling your house with stray cats, of course.'

A smile twitched on Jasmine's lips. The one thing she loved about Elise was her strength of character. She looked soft and sweet as a marshmallow, but there was an iron will packed into that petite package. She was often the only one who could give Jasmine the straight-up truth. Her parents, her friends at the ballet company and even her teachers had sugar-coated the news from the doctors. They'd instilled a false sense of hope while she recovered. It had been born out of love, sure, but sometimes she needed the cold, hard truth delivered with an empathetic smile and a pat on the back.

'I know.' Jasmine brought the cup to her lips, inhaling the comforting coffee scent before taking a sip. 'I get that I have to move past it. But how can I expect any man to look past it when I can't even do that myself?'

'That's my point exactly.' Elise grabbed her hand, wrapping her slender fingers around Jasmine's palm and squeezing. 'Maybe what you need is to realise the world won't implode if you get naked. It's not going to get all apocalyptic if someone sees your leg. Perhaps getting this guy into bed is exactly what you need to move on? If you can see that it's not a big deal to the other person then maybe it won't be such a big deal to you.'

'Sex as therapy?' Jasmine tilted her head. 'Is that a thing?'

'No idea.' Elise took a big gulp from her latte. 'What's the worst it can do? You have a little no-strings fun, enjoy yourself, and if you're still having issues over the leg thing then maybe we need to get you some professional help.'

'I am *not* seeing a shrink.' Jasmine glared. Elise was pushing her buttons on purpose.

Going to a psychologist would be like admitting that she'd fallen apart and didn't have the ability to fix the problem herself. It was the ultimate sign of weakness. No, there was no way she was doing that. Sex as therapy seemed like a much more enjoyable way to deal with it—not to mention it wouldn't send her broke.

'What have you got to lose?'

'My dignity?' Jasmine shook her head.

There was no way she could proposition Grant. What if he laughed at her?

'Did he initiate the kiss last night?'

'Well, yes, but—'

'No buts.' Elise slapped her palm down on the table and the coffee cups clattered against their saucers. 'Do you want to be a crazy cat lady?'

People at the nearby tables looked over, not even bothering to hide their curiosity. Jasmine let out a laugh.

'I'll think about it.'

'How long has it been, anyway?'

Only Elise would ask such a personal question in the middle of a café.

'Too long.' *Too damn long.*

The idea of propositioning Grant was making her sweat. It was well outside the realm of her fairly limited experience. She hadn't had sex since she'd broken off her relationship with Kyle Waterhouse, and before him there had only been one other awkward experience with a boy she'd had a crush on at school.

Sex had certainly taken a back seat while she was dancing. Her focus had always been; ballet first, boys second. Her nickname 'Queen Bun-Head' had been well earned.

Needless to say she'd never openly propositioned anyone before...let alone for a one-night stand with a psychological agenda.

Elise seemed satisfied that Jasmine was at least willing to give her plan some thought, though Jasmine had no idea how she would approach Grant. Would he even want to be around her after she'd run off like a crazy person last night?

Probably not.

Fear, excitement and doubt knotted in her stomach, each emotion fighting to overtake the others. Jasmine tapped her nails against the hard wood of the café table while she played the situation out in her head.

'Don't be nervous,' Elise said, waving her hand dismissively. 'If he tries to say no—and I highly doubt he will—remind him how flexible ballerinas are. That should do the trick!'

'You might be on to something there.' Jasmine laughed. 'But I haven't committed to anything, remember?'

'Sure, sure.' Elise waved her hand as if to dismiss Jasmine's comment. She picked up her cup and drained the last of her coffee. 'I need to head off.' Elise stood, bundling up her trench coat and handbag. 'I've got a date with the costume designer to talk through the final alterations for our swans.'

'Have fun with that.' Jasmine finished her coffee and joined Elise.

'You'd better give me an update on Operation Hunky Footballer Seduction,' Elise said as they left the bustling café, squeezing their way through the crowd and onto the street. 'I want details!'

'Is that what we're calling it now?'

'Has a good ring to it, I think.' Elise giggled and waved as she headed off in the opposite direction to Jasmine.

'I said I'd think about it,' Jasmine called after her as she headed off towards the car, with excitement putting a spring in her step.

CHAPTER SIX

GRANT SAT IN his car, his body defiantly rooted to the driver's seat of the Mercedes. Since his close encounter with Jasmine he'd been unable to think of anything else. Her glossy black hair and those enormous sparkly brown eyes filled his every waking moment.

Never before had a woman left him high and dry like that. Hell, one of the main perks of being a football player was that the girls lined up for him. But Jasmine Bell was a lady unlike any of the women he usually fell into bed with. She was a breath of fresh air and a thorn in his side. She'd responded to his advances with surprising gusto and then she'd run without explanation.

What the hell?

Drumming his fingers on the dash, Grant let out a long breath and forced himself out of the driver's seat and towards the studio. Inside it was quiet. Elise was chatting to a student and acknowledged him with a smile as he dropped his bag onto the waiting room couch. Jasmine was in the studio, stepping out the choreography he'd seen her practising the other night.

If she hadn't told him about her injury he would never have known from watching her. She seemed perfectly steady on her feet as she danced. It was like peering into a very private part of her world—in some ways like watching her undress. It couldn't have been further from his initial impression that ballet was stilted and boring. She moved with an effortless grace, swanlike in her fluid yet precise movement.

Each move was filled with raw passion and sensuality. He couldn't have looked away even if his life had depended on it. It was a crime that she couldn't perform; he could only imagine how incredible she would have looked on a stage. Was there nothing she could do? He wondered what he would have done if his mistakes had ruined his career instead of just his reputation.

She paused to study the piece of paper in one hand. Concentration narrowed her eyes, and her focus was reflected in the wall-to-wall mirror. As she worked through a problem she melted into the movement.

Remember the rule: no attachment. They all want something.

It was true; all the people he allowed into his life were after something. Distant acquaintances wanted members' tickets, the women he bedded wanted access to VIP lounges, old friends wanted money for a snippet of his history and Chelsea... All she'd wanted was a stepping stone to the next big thing. Even his best friend had sold out for a chance at the spotlight, flipping on him and leaving him alone at the worst possible moment. Funny that when he needed their help these people were nowhere to be found.

Grant closed his eyes to shut out the painful memories. Tempting as Jasmine was, history had taught him that commitment was dangerous, and something deep down told him that one taste of Jasmine wouldn't be enough. That was if his reactions to date were anything to go on.

The kiss had been a slip-up, confirming that she was definitely in the look-but-don't-touch-because-its-too-damn-tempting basket. He couldn't afford to let anything take his mind off football—not when his career and reputation were hanging in the balance.

Even now, as he steeled himself with resolve, the thought of having her for even one night filled him with an indescribable heat. A silent, familiar voice urged him on—just one taste.

He hadn't experienced urges like that in quite a while— the urges to consume, to lose himself in pleasure, to blank out the loneliness.

He shook his head. He couldn't give in because it was that same voice that told him it was OK to have another drink, another night on the town, another nameless woman in his bed. He couldn't trust that voice.

Jasmine held herself straight, struggling to keep her breathing steady. With each lesson it was becoming harder to maintain control, to preserve the distance between her and Grant. Elise's suggestion weighed down on her, luring her with the possibility of revisiting that intoxicating kiss. The memory of his palms pressing her against the studio wall sent delicious shivers down her spine.

Now, as he watched her through the window, she couldn't help the spiral of delight that shot through her. Her body tingled when he entered the studio, crossing the large space in a handful of long-legged strides, his broad shoulders a magnet for her attention. She was pretty sure it should be illegal to be that good-looking.

'Ready to get those muscles moving?' she chirped, surprised when he didn't return her smile.

'I'm ready to get on with it.' His tone was dry. Different.

She wrinkled her brow and tilted her head to one side. Something was amiss. His frosty eyes were calm. Like a perfectly still lake, they reflected the outside in order to mask what lay beneath.

'Right.' She turned and walked to the *barre,* frowning. What had turned him from the man who'd pinned her up against a wall to this impersonal lump? Or perhaps that was it? He'd taken her running as a sign to stay the hell away, that she wasn't woman enough to handle one steamy kiss.

Jasmine drew a deep breath and shook her head to dislodge the negative thoughts. She was being paranoid. But a cold lump of steel wedged in her belly anyway.

As the lesson progressed he remained withdrawn, avoiding eye contact and providing single-word responses to her questions. She searched his face for a hint of warmth, but he was as cold as the winter outside.

Soon it was time to cool down and work on Grant's flexibility problems.

They sat in the middle of the floor, stretching out their hamstrings while facing one another. A flicker of pain crossed his face as he leant forwards, trying to elongate his injured muscle. He usually appeared tense when they stretched, which was strange since most people looked relieved after a ballet class. Stretching was supposed to be the enjoyable bit, but his brows were knitted together and he often gritted his teeth. Perhaps his injury was more painful than he let on?

'Is something wrong?' she asked.

He didn't make eye contact, instead focusing on the ground ahead of him. 'No.'

'You've barely said two words to me all evening.'

For someone who had been so persistent in getting her to talk, he sure was giving her the silent treatment.

'Nothing's wrong.'

Grant rolled onto his back, lifting his injured leg in the air and reaching up towards his foot. The muscle was so resistant he couldn't even get into the proper position. Without asking if he wanted help, Jasmine knelt between his legs to administer an assisted stretch. His calf rested against her shoulder and she pressed forwards slowly, feeling his hamstring muscle release.

'Is it about the kiss?'

His eyes were still frosted over. They were like two chips of ice: cold, hard-edged and unyielding. 'I'd prefer if we didn't talk about that while you're practically on top of me.'

'Don't be such a baby. I'm only helping you stretch.' She tried to ignore the fact that a few items of flimsy clothing were all that prevented them from being a *Karma Sutra* illustration.

'The kiss was a mistake.'

Jasmine swallowed, sitting back and motioning him to switch legs. 'Why?'

'Because I...I shouldn't have done it.'

'That's not an answer.' She pressed into the stretch, one hand braced on the ground next to his arm, the other holding his active leg. 'Besides, it takes two to tango.'

'If we must talk, can't it be about something else?'

'Such as?' She peered down at him while she pushed on his leg.

'How about your dancing?' He sighed, closing his eyes for a moment as Jasmine pressed slowly.

'What about it?' She leant back and motioned for him to switch legs again.

'Why are you teaching here? It's clear you've got too much talent to be teaching toddlers.'

'Why do you care?' She didn't want to get into it; her pain was not his concern.

He didn't answer. Instead, he stared at her wordlessly until she felt as if she might burn up on the spot.

'You don't want to talk about a simple kiss, but you're quite happy to talk about my personal trauma?'

He paused. 'I think you should give dancing another shot.'

'It's not that easy.' She sighed. Why did everyone think

it was as simple as that? If it were, wouldn't she have gone back by now?

'I know you can do it.'

'I want to talk about the kiss instead.' She pursed her lips.

'Why? You were the one who ran off like...like...' He grappled for words. 'I can't talk about this while you're... there.'

'This is a perfectly legitimate cool-down activity.' Maybe if she said it enough times she'd convince herself it was all for his benefit...and not because she felt compelled to be close to him.

'I should have stopped it.'

'It's not a big deal.'

'Yes, it is. I'm not looking for a relationship and I don't have the time nor the interest to have anyone in my life.' His voice was low, guarded. He was censoring himself, barricading his true feelings behind the commanding tone and blank stare. 'It was a momentary lapse of judgement.'

Jasmine sat back, startled by the complete one-hundred-and-eighty-degree turn that had taken place. It was as if she was speaking to a different person.

'I'm not looking for a relationship either.' *Hell, that's the last thing I need.*

'Trust me,' he said, standing up and dusting off his tights. His eyes raked over her, calculating and cold as he observed her reaction. 'It's for your own good.'

Heat spread from Jasmine's neck to her face. She was sure her cheeks burned red as tomatoes.

It's for your own good.

She'd heard that phrase many times in her failed relationship with Kyle Waterhouse. Her ex had been the possessive type, controlling. That had been his catchphrase. The one he'd tried on every time she rebelled against his commands. When she hadn't been allowed to wear a short dress it had been for her own good. When he'd prevented her from going out with her friends it had been for her own good. When he'd embarrassed her in front of his family by telling her she shouldn't be eating anything fattening it had been for her own good.

The statement hung thick and heavy over them, sucking the air from her lungs. She was about to lose it—about to let go of the rage that was a tight, flaming knot in her stomach.

She lowered Grant's leg to the floor and rocked back onto her heels. She rose slowly.

'What is "for my own good" is none of your concern. I take care of myself. So do us both a favour and don't tell me what to do.'

Mustering her composure, she turned and walked to the door. Heart pounding, she grabbed her coat and bag and headed out of the building. It was incredible how four little words could fill her with a boiling pot of blinding, white-hot emotion.

Wincing as the night air slapped her in the face, she tried to feel satisfaction as the door slammed shut behind her, the bang resonating out into the empty parking lot. Logically she knew that he couldn't understand the effect those words had on her, but hearing them made her want to run. Made her want to put as much distance between them as possible.

Lungs burning, she continued at pace towards Elise's car. She fumbled in her bag, hands shaking as she looked frantically for the keys—praying that he wouldn't come after her.

She'd deluded herself, tricked herself into reading something into his kiss…into the way he'd touched her hand in the café. Her insides tumbled as she realised what a fool she must look, expecting something from him that she shouldn't. Lusting after him like some starstruck teen.

Idiot, idiot, idiot!

How could she have been so naive? Was she so desperate after Kyle that she thought the next guy to kiss her was something special? Elise was right—crazy cat lady status was cemented in her future.

Heat burned her cheeks. Her vision was blurred by the puffs of white smoke that billowed up as her hot breath connected with the chilly night air. Mercifully she located the car keys and hit the unlock button. Sliding inside the car, she turned the engine over and pressed her foot to the ground. The car's tyres screeched as she raced from the car park.

He was just like the rest of them.

The EJ Ballet School's big day had arrived. Its annual Winter Performance was a matinee showcase of all the routines due to appear in the upcoming competition season. It would be Jasmine's first time back in a theatre since she left the Australian Ballet.

Her footsteps echoed, and even though she was indoors condensation billowed from her mouth as she hurried down the aisle to the first row of seats. The theatre's heating system had just kicked in, and it would take a while for the chill to wear off. Memories flooded her, and the old thrill of adrenaline that came before a performance lit up her senses.

She could see the back of Elise's head, her flaxen hair already slicked into a bun and affixed with a glittering headpiece.

Jasmine slumped down next to her. Shivering, she brought a takeaway cup to her lips. The coffee inside was strong and piping hot, exactly the way she liked it.

'Morning.' Elise was sewing a string of sequins around the hem of a costume, her golden brows knitted together while her tongue stuck out from the side of her lips.

The past few days had been like wading through sludge and the way things had been left with Grant weighed on Jasmine. She shouldn't care. It had only been a kiss. But as far as kisses went…it had been the motherload.

'Do you want to talk about it?' Elise said without looking up.

'Talk about what?'

'Why you've been moping around like a kid who's lost her puppy.' Elise continued to focus on her costume, pushing the needle through the fabric and pulling it out the other side. She threaded a sequin, then a bead, and drove the needle back down.

'I have not.'

'Don't lie to me, Jazz.' Elise paused to give her friend a withering stare. 'I can't take your denial before breakfast.'

Jasmine presented the coffee and bagel she'd picked up for Elise on her way in and let out a chuckle at the look of complete adoration that washed over her friend's face. 'No, I don't want to talk about it.'

'I think you *should* talk about it.' Elise looked up after taking a long swig of her coffee. 'Did you pitch the sex as therapy idea?'

'I didn't even get that far,' Jasmine replied, frowning.

'How come?'

'Because he back-pedalled on the whole thing. Apparently the kiss was a mistake.'

'He said that?'

'Verbatim.' Jasmine rolled her eyes. 'Then he told me he was protecting me—that he was backing off for my own good.'

Elise winced. 'I can imagine how *that* went down.'

'It was just a kiss…we're both adults…I don't see why he's got his knickers in a knot about it.'

'You were the one who bailed after you kissed.' Trust

Elise to flip it on her. 'Do you think he freaked out because of that?'

'No idea. He's hot one minute…hotter than hot…and then freezing cold the next.' Jasmine sipped on her coffee. 'I can't keep my head straight, watching him bounce back and forth.'

Both girls paused when the sound of the theatre door opening caught their attention. Missy, a long-time friend and fellow dance teacher, made her way to the girls at the front. Her skin held a sickly green tinge.

'What the hell is wrong with you?' Elise asked.

'Stomach bug,' Missy replied, and her bleary eyes showed how many times she'd got up in the middle of the night. 'I'm OK. I just need a minute—'

Her eyes bulged and she shot up from her seat, racing towards the front exit where the toilets were. Elise and Jasmine looked at one another.

'Crap.' Elise dropped her head into her hands. 'There's no way she's going to be able to pirouette without barfing on the stage. What a disaster!'

Missy was one of the quartet dancing in the teachers' routine Jasmine had choreographed. They'd been working towards this performance for weeks, and with several of the scouts from the Australian Ballet School attending everything needed to run like clockwork.

They waited until Missy returned. She curled up into a ball next to Jasmine, her teeth chattering, her skin glowing with a clammy sheen.

'We can do the dance with three people instead of four. I'll re-choreograph the partnering in the middle.'

'I'm fine,' Missy protested weakly.

Students filed into the theatre, excited voices chattering, oblivious to the problems their teachers were dealing with.

'We can't change the choreography now.' Elise shook

her head, ignoring Missy's feeble protest. 'That's way too much pressure.'

'But no one else knows the steps.'

Jasmine massaged her temples. She knew exactly what was coming.

'You do.'

The statement hung in the air, eclipsed by the sound of blood rushing in Jasmine's ears. There was no way she could step in now. She hadn't been on stage in so long and she wasn't ready for her first time to be in front of an entire ballet school's worth of family and friends.

No. No way in hell.

'I can't do it.'

'I'm sorry, Jazz.' Missy shot up from her seat again and raced through the exit.

'Yes, you *can*,' Elise implored her. 'I know you can.'

'I'm not a dancer anymore.' Jasmine's voice broke as the pressure overwhelmed her.

She jumped up and walked out of the theatre, through the foyer and into the chilly morning air. The sky was grey, storm clouds looming like a prediction of the future. Her stomach churned with guilt. She was letting Elise and the others down. But she couldn't get back out there. Not yet. Not now. No amount of puppy-dog eyes from Elise would make her do it. What if she fell? What if she'd lost all of her talent and she looked like a fool beside Elise and the other teachers? She couldn't risk that.

Damn it!

Elise had worked so hard at pulling the Winter Performance together and this wasn't fair. She deserved a better friend than Jasmine—someone who could get past her own problems and step up. But she couldn't do it. She was too broken.

'What are you going to do?'

The voice startled Jasmine and she spun around. *Grant.*

'What are you doing here?' she asked.

He was perched on the handrail that led from the theatre door to the valet area. Thigh-hugging jeans and a leather jacket that looked soft as butter clung to his frame in all the right places. His jaw was freshly shaven and his thick blond hair was mussed into a peak.

He looked hot as sin.

'I bought a ticket.' He shrugged. 'You know...supporting the community and all that.'

Jasmine couldn't stop the corners of her mouth twitching into a smile. 'Very big of you.'

'So what are you going to do?' He cocked his head to one side, waiting for her answer.

'About what?'

'If I read the situation correctly your routine is one dancer short.' He paused. 'I saw her coming out of the ladies' room...I don't think I've ever seen a person who was literally green before.'

Jasmine let out a rush of air. They were screwed. 'I don't know what we're going to do, but it's not something you need to worry about. The show must go on, as they say.'

'So you're not going to step up?'

His question sucked the breath from her. It was one thing to hear it from Elise, but it was another thing entirely for Grant to get involved. Especially since he'd made it clear the little intimacy they'd shared was something he didn't wish to repeat.

'It's not a matter of stepping up.' Jasmine folded her arms across her chest. 'I'm not a dancer anymore.'

'Yes, you are. I've seen you in that studio.'

'You don't know what it's like, Grant.'

'You crave it. You feel incomplete without it.' He stood and stepped towards her. 'Does that sound about right?'

She bit down on her lip. OK, so maybe he *did* know what she was feeling. That didn't change the situation.

'Don't you think I would have done it by now if it were that easy?' She tightened her arms, partly to warm her and partly to quell the tiny flicker of hope in her chest.

She wasn't ready. Her body wasn't ready, nor her mind… Hell, she didn't even have her ballet shoes with her.

'Nothing worth having is easy.'

'What motivation poster did you steal *that* from?' Sarcasm dripped from her voice. It was a natural defence, and right now pushing him away was easier than dealing with any of it.

She couldn't take him and his confusing hot/cold actions. She couldn't take this pressure, the competing desire and fear that somersaulted in her stomach. It was too much, too soon.

He caught her shoulders between his hands. His jaw was clenched, his eyes burning into hers. 'If you don't do it now you might not ever have the guts to perform again.'

'You don't know that.' She looked away. The cold was seeping through her clothes and into her bones. 'Why do you even care?'

'Because I've been there. I've stood on that edge, wondering whether to play it safe or take the plunge.'

'And?' She held her breath, frozen by the intensity that radiated from him and rooted her to the ground.

'It's worth it. It's worth the fear and the sacrifices you've already made to be who you need to be. You need to try again.'

Were they still talking about her dancing? Memories swirled up and shimmered before her. She'd been happy once…before she'd gambled everything on a career that had crashed and burned. What did she have to show for those years of hard work?

'I can't.'

'I thought about giving up football, you know.' He scuffed the ground with the edge of one heavy black boot.

'I dragged my team's name through the mud when I went off the rails. I remember going to training the morning after a huge blow-up and hovering at the entrance to the ground. I wasn't sure I could face them all. I wasn't sure I could risk them rejecting me.'

'This is different.' She tried to keep the surge of empathy out of her voice—this wasn't the same situation. 'I'm not hesitating because I'm worried I can't do it. I *know* I can't.'

'Yes,' he said roughly, 'you can.'

'Please don't pretend you know me.' Her voice shook, the weight of her decision crushing down on her chest. 'Or what I'm capable of.'

'For God's sake, Jasmine!' He threw his hands up in the air. 'Don't you know how brilliant you are? You're *so* talented. And you're ready to throw it all away because why? Because you're scared? That's not good enough.'

She wanted to slap him and kiss him and be held by him. Emotion rose up within her, choking the words before they could reach her lips.

'You're better than that,' he whispered. 'Don't let your fear get the better of you.'

'Says the man who's afraid of a kiss.'

She tipped her nose up at him, forcing away the desire to lean in and kiss him. She wanted so badly for someone to comfort her. She wanted *him* to comfort her. But he'd already put that barrier firmly in place.

'Says the girl who ran away.'

CHAPTER SEVEN

A SENSE OF déjà vu washed over Jasmine as the dancers prepared for the show. She rolled her good foot around in circles, testing its flexibility, before switching to her injured ankle. It creaked under the movement but no pain materialised.

Perhaps with a little stretching she would be OK to dance the teachers' piece, especially since none of them danced *en pointe* anymore. A tiny bud of hope flickered like a flame struggling to stay alight in a draft.

What if she did dance again? Would she be able to dance outside the EJ Ballet School? Dancing *en pointe* was out of the question because her ankle was far too fragile; it was the reason her career was over. But she could move on to something else, try something new. Grant's words swirled in her head: *If you don't do it now you might not ever have the guts to perform again.*

Her palms were slick as she balled them into fists.

Could she do it? Could she step back out there and risk humiliation in front of all those people?

The first strains of the opening scene set the dancers into motion, their graceful forms taking the music and interpreting it into lyrical movement. Elise appeared beside her and patted her arm.

What if this was her last chance? The finality of such a concept made her blood run cold. What if she never danced again? She wouldn't know herself anymore. Fear lodged in her throat, its cold grip restricting her air.

You need to try again. This was the edge he'd talked about—the one where she could jump off and deal with the consequences. Or she could turn away and risk never finding her way back.

'I'm going to do it,' Jasmine whispered.

Elise grabbed her hand and squeezed. 'I knew you would.'

Intermission came and Jasmine changed into Missy's costume. She was relieved that life after ballet hadn't meant her putting on a huge amount of weight, as she'd predicted, though Missy's costume *was* still pinching her in areas. The arms and legs were too short, exposing several inches above her ankles and wrists. But it zipped up, and she could move around enough to accommodate the choreography.

If she was being honest it wasn't an ill-fitting costume that would be holding her back...

Making her way through the crowded change room, she weaved through the throng of ballet students up to the side of the stage where the teachers were waiting for her. A quick run-through of the steps would cement her decision to dance or send her into a downwards spiral of self-doubt. Either of those options was better than the purgatory of indecision that had been her life the last few months.

Elise grabbed her hand as she walked up to the wings and led her onto the stage, where the teachers were waiting. The steps came easily to her, since she'd created them, but her feet weren't as responsive as they'd used to be. A droplet of sweat ran from her hairline down the back of her neck and between her shoulderblades. She was working harder than ever before to keep up with the music. Doubt pooled in her stomach as she toiled over the repetitive *pas de chat* steps that dominated the routine.

'Stop stressing.' Elise smiled at Jasmine as she made her way off stage so the opening act of the second half could assemble. 'You created this. The rest will come naturally once you get out there.'

'I hope so.' A quiver ran through her voice. Fear was spiking her heartbeat. She rubbed the slickness of her palms down her thighs; the moisture collected a fine layer of glitter that stuck to her hands.

As the first scene of the second half played out on stage Jasmine watched with her heart in her throat. The desire to run flooded her, making her head pound and her palms itch, but she stood rooted to the ground. She wouldn't let Elise down—it was now or never.

The teachers took their place in the wings, hands interlocked across one another's bodies. Elise's hand squeezed hers as they waited. Jasmine's throat clenched as her lungs screamed for air. The dancers on stage took their finishing poses and there was silence for a brief moment before music boomed from the speakers above. She was sure everyone in the audience could hear the shaking of her breath in those few seconds.

Before she knew it she was on stage, her feet gliding in time with the music. The glare of the stage lights overwhelmed her, blinding her momentarily, until the audience came into focus. Then there was nothing but the gentle thumping of their steps as they unfolded the story. Her feet flexed and pointed, aching under the movements they were no longer used to, but she was free. With each movement a sense of abandon filled her body, running at high-speed through her veins.

As she turned the stage was a blur of shimmering particles. She had to remember to mark her spot, so she wouldn't get dizzy, but the world tilted around her in a haze of glorious fragmented light. It was unlike anything she'd felt in a long time.

They built to the climax of their performance, stepping forwards into a line of identical *arabesques*. Then the ground rushed up far too quickly. Someone gasped as Jasmine's foot released from *demi-pointe* and she fell hard into the final position. The audience applauded and the curtain dropped, but Jasmine could barely see or hear for the blinding white pain that rocketed through her.

Her ankle was on fire.

Elise lifted Jasmine's other arm over her shoulder and they carried her off stage. She put some of her weight onto her right foot and bit down on her lip, her eyes clamped shut.

'Girls, we have to keep going.' Elise shooed a startled group of dancers onto the stage in preparation for the next scene. 'Come on—we have a show to deliver.'

Jasmine limped to a chair, supported by her friends. Her ankle was already swelling and her skin had taken on a bluish hue. Her chest felt as though someone had stomped on it with a stiletto.

'Something snapped...' Her voice wavered and she swore under her breath. *No, no, no, no, no.*

'It's OK, it's probably a sprain.' Elise soothed her, her voice the epitome of cool, calm and collected. 'We need to get it elevated. Someone bring the first-aid kit.'

Jasmine clamped her eyes down in an effort to quell the pain. The commotion of the performance was a dull roar around her. Only when she heard a familiar deep baritone did she open her eyes.

'What happened?' Grant peered down at her, his brow furrowed.

'What does it look like?' she said, wincing as she tried to move her ankle. 'I proved my point.'

A group of young dancers walked past, concern for

their teacher momentarily forgotten in the presence of a footballer. Wide-eyed, they tittered behind their hands and were promptly shushed by one of the older dancers.

'What point?'

'The point where I said I couldn't dance anymore.' She sighed, closing her eyes again. 'Please go.'

'Forget it.' He crossed his arms.

She'd rather have been left alone. It was embarrassing enough that she'd injured herself on stage. She could only hope the audience hadn't noticed how hard she'd landed into the final position—perhaps they hadn't known any different. But having *him* see her at what was possibly her most vulnerable moment... Ugh, that made it a hundred times worse.

'I'm fine. Go and watch the show.' Jasmine accepted an ice pack from Elise and tried to ignore the raised eyebrows her friend was giving her. 'Honestly, I don't need any help.'

'Actually,' Elise replied, 'you probably could use Grant's help getting home. You need to keep that ankle elevated and we can't have you sitting on a rickety chair the whole night.'

Oh, no, she didn't.

'Of course,' Grant said, reaching out to Jasmine. 'I'll give you a lift.'

'No.' Jasmine swatted his hand away, mortification seeping through her as the young dancers watched the exchange. She lowered her voice. 'You've paid for your ticket; enjoy the show. Elise will take me home afterwards.'

She shot Elise a warning glance. However, she knew that once the seed of a devious idea had been planted in her best friend's mind there would be no getting away from it.

Grant knelt down in front of her and reached for the ribbons on her borrowed ballet shoe, his large hands holding her ankle as though it were a newborn duckling. His fingertips seared her skin, each delicate brush causing sensation to bloom within her.

'What are you doing?'

'There's some swelling.' He looked up at her, his cool blue eyes locked onto hers, and her stomach fluttered. He gently moved the foot, inspecting the joint for signs of a break. 'I think you'll live.'

'Of course I'll live.' She rolled her eyes and bit the words out through the pain. 'Like I said, I'm fine.'

'Jazz, you're distracting the dancers,' Elise said in a stage whisper. 'It would be best if you let Grant take you home.'

'But—'

'Go home.' Elise handed Jasmine her handbag and shooed them both, barely containing a grin. 'I'll bring your dance kit and your other bits and pieces with me later.'

A cheeky smile pulled up the edges of Grant's lips, but he kept his mouth shut. He tucked his shoulder under Jasmine's arm and helped her to her feet.

She tested pressure on her ankle and dots of white light flashed in front of her eyes.

'Ow!' A strained cry escaped her. She bit down on the fleshy part of her lower lip as pain pulsed in her ankle. The joint was on fire. Queasiness swelled in her stomach until she slumped against him, unsteady.

Jasmine hobbled out of the backstage area with Grant walking slowly beside her. Even through the pain the closeness of his body distracted her. Each slow step caused their bodies to bump against one another.

Once they were out in the hallway, and they could talk more freely, she tried to release herself from his grip. 'I can do this on my own.'

'Let me help you.'

He held her tight, but she tugged her arm from his grip. Hopping on one foot, she lifted her chin and squared her shoulders. The effect was ruined by the fact that she could only hop on her good foot.

'No.'

Letting out an exasperated sigh, he swooped down and scooped her up in his arms.

With a surprised squeak she twisted and writhed. 'Let me go!'

'Don't wriggle.'

Her face was pushed up against the hard muscle of his shoulder, her legs dangled over one of his arms and her back was cradled in the other. Every nerve-ending in her body fired warning signals. Her blood was thick and hot in her veins.

'This is absolutely ridiculous,' she muttered.

He pushed open the backstage exit with one hand and easily held her with the other. Kicking the door wide, he stepped through, making sure she didn't bump her shoulders as they exited. She'd have been impressed if she weren't so mortified.

His booming laughter filled the air, causing a few of the dance students to poke their heads out of the change room and watch as he carried her out of the building. She clutched her handbag to her chest, debating how much it would hurt if he dropped her when she brained him with it.

'This is *so* not funny.'

'No, the situation is not funny.' He made his way across the car park. 'But your cheeks are as red as tomatoes right now.'

'Way to take advantage of my predicament...'

'Trust me, if I were taking advantage of this situation you would know about it.'

If she'd been red before then what was she now? Crimson, perhaps? Her skin sizzled where it touched him, which in her current position was pretty much everywhere.

'Put me down. I can walk on my own.'

'Why can't you accept a little help?'

'Can't I be independent?' she argued. 'I don't need anyone to look after me.'

'I'd say your current situation begs to differ.'

She was losing the argument, but avoiding the question was a whole lot easier than explaining why accepting help was so painful. The moment she'd realised how much her ballet tuition was costing her parents she'd worked her ass off trying to ease their burden. But even then she'd had to do it by getting a scholarship to study at the Australian Ballet School...which was just another form of help, really.

She'd vowed as a fourteen-year-old that she would earn everything in life through her own blood, sweat and tears. She'd never be a burden on anyone ever again. But how could you say that to a guy who wanted to play big, strong rescuer?

'How far is this going to go?' she said, changing tactic.

'Don't argue with me,' he said. 'I'm taking you home.'

He didn't mean it like that, but the words sent a roaring heat to her centre all the same. Being tucked up against his broad chest with her face tilted to his neck, her lips inches from him, was oh, so tempting. She could lean in and press against the soft skin there, run her tongue along its length to see what the reaction was. To see how he tasted.

No. No, no, no. This couldn't be happening.

It had been the wrong thing to say. *I'm taking you home.*

As soon as he'd uttered the words it had been as if the floodgates had opened and in had poured all the images he'd suppressed since kissing her. Jasmine naked on top of him, under him, against the wall of the studio, laid out on the back seat of his Mercedes...

'How do you think you're going to get me home?' She interrupted his thoughts, her confidence belied by the tiniest tremor in her voice.

'I'm going to drive.' He held her tight as she wriggled in his grip once more. Though she wasn't exactly a short woman she was light as a feather, and easy to bundle up in his arms. 'Obviously. How else would I take you home?'

'You don't know where I live.'

'You're going to tell me.'

'How do I know you're not going to take advantage of my vulnerable position?' She was stalling, the provocative question designed to make him focus on it rather than the task at hand.

However, he knew his intentions were good, and all he cared about was getting her home safely. There was nothing wrong in indulging in a little fantasy so long as he didn't act it out. The thought surprised him. It had been a long time since he'd ignored his attraction to someone. It had been longer still since he'd felt attracted enough to worry about what the other party might think.

'I'm going to set you down now.'

He stopped, lowering her gently to the ground, keeping one arm around her back so that she could lean on him and keep her weight off the injured ankle. He unlocked the car and opened the passenger-side door for her, brushing off the glitter that had transferred from her costume to his T-shirt.

She balanced on one foot, hopping away from him. 'You didn't answer my question.'

'You're in safe hands, Bun-head.' He grinned at her. 'Promise.'

'I don't know...'

She folded her arms across her chest. Her costume sparkled like a beacon under the lamps of the parking lot. She wore a funny construction in her hair that tinkled as she shook her head back and forth.

'I'm not sure I can trust you.'

He reached out and brushed his fingers through the dangling beads on her headpiece. 'Let me take you home. You have my word that I won't try to do anything untoward.'

'OK, but no judgement on my place.' She looked from the building to him and back again. 'I'm sure it's not anywhere near as fancy as yours.'

He frowned and opened his mouth to protest her lack of faith in him, but she was already hobbling towards the car. He helped her into the low bucket seat and she gave him her address to programme into his GPS.

The drive was short—a straight run down the main road from the theatre—but it was the longest fifteen minutes of his life. Being cooped up next to Jasmine and having to concentrate on the road was no mean feat. She was wound tighter than a spring by the time they pulled to a stop. Yet she'd said nothing—not even looked his way.

The trip had passed in silence. He stole a glance at her profile, illuminated in flickers by the passing street lights, but her eyes remained fixed on the road ahead.

Outside her unit, the street was quiet. No cars driving past, not a soul outside. Jasmine pushed open the door and stepped out onto the nature strip. She steadied herself on the rain-slicked ground. Grant came around the front of the car and wrapped his arms around her, hoisting her into the air as though she weighed no more than a bag of marshmallows.

'Hey, what about our deal?'

'I said I'd get you home.'

He spoke as though he had some kind of responsibility for her, provoking a sensation that felt foreign and not entirely bad.

'I *am* home.'

They made their way to her front door while she protested about how she could take care of herself. She wriggled in his grip.

'OK, OK. I'm putting you down.' He set her on the porch and she reached into her bag.

Unlocking the door, she balanced on one foot. The door swung open and she limped inside, flicking on a light. He followed her without waiting for an invitation and closed the door behind him.

'Yes, please *do* come in.'

Her voice held a hint of sarcasm that he chose to ignore. She hopped into the lounge room, her hand smoothing along the wall as she went.

'You need to get that leg up.' He followed her, making no move to leave her alone. Her face had the don't-mess-with-me look down pat, eyes narrowed.

'I'm fine,' she protested.

'Don't make me pick you up again.'

The threat hung between them, sizzling with underlying intention. Part of him was tempted to push her buttons, to see how far she would let him go. The other part—the part that smelled trouble—won over.

'Now, dinner...'

'I'm not hungry.' She hovered by the couch, running a hand over her costume to see how much glitter would transfer if she were to sit down. When her palm sparkled she remained standing. 'What I need is to get changed.'

'You need to eat. I'll order takeaway.' Pulling his mobile from the pocket of his jeans, he brought it to his ear.

She tested the back of her costume, her hands reaching behind her. Grant pretended to search for a pizza joint on his phone while watching her struggle from the corner of his eye. She switched hands and tried again.

Huffing, she conceded. 'Can you help me with this zip?'

Putting the phone down, he walked to her and she spun around, balancing on one foot. There was a long zip that ran the length of her back; she'd managed to get it down to just above where her shoulderblades were. He took the tiny puller in his hands and slowly slid it down, revealing inch after inch of flawless porcelain skin.

'Thank you,' she whispered.

A powerful urge to touch his fingertips to the subtle jut of her spine overwhelmed him. He wanted to see if she felt as silken as she looked.

Clearing his throat, he stepped back. 'No problem.'

She could hear Grant on the phone, ordering their dinner, as she hobbled to her bedroom. She felt about a million degrees in her costume, with the Lycra clinging to her body like a second, oppressive skin.

When he'd undone her zipper she'd barely been able to breathe. Her skin had cried out to have his hands brush over her, but he'd performed only his gentlemanly duties.

Sighing, she peeled the costume from her body, leaning on her bed to help keep the pressure off her injured ankle. The throbbing had quietened, and she knew from experience it wasn't a serious injury. Still, she'd learned her lesson about returning to the stage. That dream would go back into the dark recesses of her heart for a while...at least until she'd forgotten the sting of humiliation enough to contemplate trying again.

She changed into sweat pants and a T-shirt, making certain to pick the ones that hugged her closely without looking as if she'd chosen them on purpose. She made her way back out to the main room in time to hear Grant in the kitchen.

'What are you looking for?' And why was he going through her cupboards? He was certainly acting familiar for someone who had entered her home for this first time.

Grant came back to the lounge with a tall glass of water. 'I've got some anti-inflammatories in my bag if you want?'

'No, thank you.' She reached for the water and sipped, watching him warily as he dropped down onto the couch opposite her. His legs were too long for the crowded space of her unit; he bent his knees and let them fall apart. The position was unabashedly male, and Jasmine had to divert her eyes or else she'd be staring straight at his crotch.

By the time the pizza arrived she was starving. Though she wouldn't admit it to Grant, the thought of hot melted cheese and carbs was far better than anything she could have whipped up in her ill-equipped kitchen. He answered the door and paid for their dinner. The steaming box was making her stomach churn in anticipation.

She shuffled over on the couch to make room, so that they could share the pizza from the same box.

'Are you going to get back on the horse?'

'You don't beat around the bush, do you?'

She rolled her eyes, swiping a slice from the box and biting into it. Tangy parmesan cheese melded with salty olives and spicy salami on her tongue. It wasn't ordinary pizza—this was the good stuff…the proper Italian stuff. She stifled a moan of pleasure. The man knew his food.

'It's a waste of time. If I have a question, I ask it.' He chewed. 'Simple.'

'I don't know…sometimes I think maybe I should take the hint.'

'What hint?'

'That it's over—that part of my life, I mean.' She shrugged. Now that she'd got home and her ankle had eased she'd calmed down. But the thought of getting back out on stage was, for the moment, stuck in the 'crap to deal with another day' basket.

'You shouldn't give up.'

'Ah, well, if it's that simple, then…'

'It is.' He reached for another slice and closed the lid of the pizza box. 'If you're passionate about it then you put up with the bad bits.'

'Do you ever think about doing anything else aside from footy?'

'Not really.' He looked thoughtful. 'Well, I studied psychology at university, but I haven't done anything with it.'

Jasmine couldn't help the quirk of her eyebrows.

'Don't look so shocked,' he said, frowning at her. 'We're not all dumb jocks, you know.'

'No judgement here.' She reached for another slice. 'I just figured that it seemed unlikely that you were lucky enough to be a professional athlete, look the way you do and be smart as well. You have to admit that's kind of lucky.'

'Have you forgotten the Rubik's cube story already?' He grinned, a small spot of tomato sauce clinging to the corner of his lip. 'And what do you mean by "look the way you do"?'

She sucked in a breath; the words had tumbled out uncensored. Clearly her guard had dropped while she'd been stuffing her face with pizza.

'Well, at the moment you look like a bit of a grub,' she said, her belly curling anxiously.

He swiped his tongue along the edge of his lip, catching the sauce and grinning, as though he knew exactly how hot she was burning inside.

'I want you to promise me something.' His tone changed, and his brow narrowed above an intent stare. 'Don't let this beat you.'

She wasn't ready to go there yet. She wasn't ready to have this conversation…especially not with him.

'Grant…' Her voice issued a warning, but he would not be deterred.

'I meant everything I said before you stepped out on that stage.' He swallowed. 'This is a stumbling block, not the end of the road. Your ankle will be fine in a week or so, and I want you to keep trying.'

'I don't want to talk about this.' She felt hot, angry tears pricking at her eyes. She would not break down in front of him. This was *her* pain. Hers alone.

'You need to talk.' His hand was on her arm, stroking the length from her shoulder to her elbow in deep, reassuring lines. 'It'll help you get past it.'

'Is that your psychology degree talking?'

'It's someone who cares talking.'

'Why do you care?'

She wasn't sure she wanted to know the answer. The feelings that had been bubbling below the surface—the attraction, the desire and the inkling of something more—were things she didn't have room for...or, more truthfully, didn't have the guts for.

'Because you're crazy-talented, and smart and...different.' Something flickered across his face—realisation, perhaps?

'*Different* is usually a synonym for something negative,' she pointed out, trying to lighten the mood.

'But you *are* different—to me at least. Do you know this is the most conversation I've exchanged with a woman in...God, I can't even remember.'

'Are you usually too busy getting to business with most women?'

He raked a hand through his hair, the gold strands catching the soft glow of the lamp. 'Something like that.'

'Don't you talk to your mum?' She tilted her head, suddenly curious beyond belief about this secretive man in front of her.

'Actually, no. Mum hasn't been with us for some time.'

'I'm so sorry.' She bit her lip.

'The whole family thing is...strained.' His mouth drew into a flat line. 'I guess some families aren't meant to be close.'

Her mind flashed to her mother and father. It had been

a while since she'd seen them. Facing them was harder these days. The worry on her mother's face or in her tone on the voice mails she left made her chest ache. Guilt was an ugly, dirty, painful emotion.

'Are you close with your folks?' Grant peered at her as though trying to see exactly what was going on in her head.

'Not as much as I should be.'

'Are they far away?'

'About forty-five minutes.' She smiled ruefully. 'Not far enough for me to claim it as an excuse. I haven't seen them much since the accident.'

'Why?'

'It's hard. They sacrificed a lot to enable me to dance, and look what I've done with it...'

'I'm sure they don't blame you.'

'They don't.'

They'd been by her side all through the surgery, the re-habilitation, her return to the company... It had only been after she'd quit her position with the Australian Ballet that it had become hard to look them in the eye.

'But you still feel guilty?'

'Ashamed is probably more accurate.' She sighed. 'I call my mum every week, but I have to force myself to do it. Sometimes I'd rather curl up in a corner and ignore the world.'

'You have *nothing* to be ashamed of.'

'I poured every cent they spent on my ballet tuition down the drain when I crashed that car. I guess it's lucky that I managed to get a scholarship when I started training seriously, so at least I didn't send them completely broke in the process.'

Hands shaking, she reached for another slice of pizza, determined to give her mouth something to do instead of spilling out her skeletons to Grant. He did the same and they ate in silence.

'You don't have to throw it all away,' he said. 'You *can* dance again. Maybe not ballet, but I'm sure there are other types of dance that you could do. Surely your training would help?'

'Why do you believe that I'm such a great dancer? You've never seen what I was like before...'

'I've seen your eyes when you dance, your face. That tells me enough.'

He had another droplet of sauce on the corner of his mouth. She reached her hand to his lips and wiped the spot, her fingertips grazing his skin.

He caught her wrist in his hand, bringing it to his mouth and slowly drawing her in. As he wrapped his lips around her finger and sucked Jasmine's heart stilled. The gentle pressure made her throb, and a jolt of arousal ran through her.

As he released her their wide-eyed gazes mirrored one another. She drew her hand back, holding it to her chest as the finger burned where he'd tasted her. Neither of them moved.

The silence between them was thick, heavy. Grant's eyes were clouded, his pupils dilated with the lust he held back. Silent tension pushed and pulled, threatening to shatter their restraint.

'I should go.'

His voice was heavy, each word rough with desire as he leant back, creating more distance between them...as if that would help.

'Why don't you stay?'

Was she doing this? Her voice had been the merest of whispers, barely audible above the sound of her fluttering heart.

Torment seeped into his features. His mouth pulled into a firm line and he looked at her.

'I shouldn't...'

And yet he lingered. He was inches from her; she could reach out and touch him, reach out and shatter those last shards of control with a gentle brush of her fingertips. She knew she had it in her to be sensual again, to use her body for pleasure.

She placed her hand on his denim-clad thigh and smoothed the fabric beneath her fingertips. Hard muscle flexed beneath her touch and she could swear all his breath rushed out into the air between them. She leant forwards, her lips parted.

Two solid hands eased her back against the couch, and when the pressure of his body didn't follow Jasmine's eyes snapped open. Grant was on his feet, looking down to where she sat.

'I'm not starting something that neither of us will be able to stop.'

'What if I don't want to stop it?' Humiliation burned beneath her skin but she had to ask—she had to know how he felt.

'That's exactly what I'm trying to avoid.'

She didn't move her gaze from the floor until the front door clicked behind him. Only then did she let herself dissolve.

CHAPTER EIGHT

GRANT WOKE UP with grit in his eyes. Yet another night of inadequate sleep, though this time it hadn't been due to the nightmares. This time his mind had been occupied with dreams of another kind.

Dreams of Jasmine sprawled beneath him on her couch, pressed up against the railing of his balcony, on her coffee table… The list went on. He was finding it harder and harder to resist her charms, and when she'd reached for him last night—when she'd asked him to stay—it had taken every last morsel of will to keep from ravishing her on the spot.

He thumped the tiled wall of the shower, releasing a fraction of his pent-up frustration. It wouldn't do. He'd had a cold shower as soon as he'd arrived home last night and yet he'd still woken up with a raging hard-on and a head full of fantasies. She'd dug herself so far under his skin that he didn't know left from right. Even when he promised himself he'd leave her alone, he couldn't stay away!

The hot water rushed over him as he pressed his forehead against the tiles so the back of his neck was under the strongest part of the stream. He rolled his shoulders and groaned. No matter what he did, no matter how he rationalised away his attraction to Jasmine, she managed to throw it all out of the window with a single look.

'Dammit,' he growled against the wall.

With a flick of his wrist he shut down the hot water and flinched as an icy stream hit him dead-on. The cold water stung his body but it would quash his excitement... for now. At least until the next time he saw her.

Grant stepped out of the shower and wrapped himself in a big fluffy towel. He wandered into the lounge room and turned on the TV. While he fired up his coffee machine he heard someone saying his name. He turned in time to catch the daytime entertainment reporter for Channel 9.

'It's been a while since we've seen footy players behaving *this* badly.' Her exaggerated facial expressions made him curl his lip into a sneer. 'But I'm sure you'll all remember when Grant Farley, full forward for the Vic Harbour Jaguars, had a *very* public fall from grace last year.'

His photo flashed up onto the screen. He had a fat lip, from the one punch he hadn't been able to dodge, and his eyes were bloodshot beyond recognition. He was barely standing.

'After spending the night in prison he was charged for starting a brawl that landed two men in hospital. Luckily for Grant the assault charges were dropped shortly after. I guess that's what happens when you're one of the highest earners in the AFL.'

Her perky voice dipped an octave as she leant in close to the camera, the screen capturing her ample cleavage.

'Now, this week's mugshot comes from star—'

Grant switched off the TV, his blood boiling. It had been a year. A whole damn year and they were still feeding off his photo like a pack of vultures. Shame washed over him, as it did every time he was reminded of when he'd hit rock bottom.

His partying had got steadily worse through his mid-twenties, and then he'd started blacking out and getting into trouble.

The night it had all come to a head he'd drunk so much

that he hadn't been able to do more than throw the first punch before his friends had jumped in and he'd stumbled off. The pub's security system had shown clearly that he hadn't thrown any of the blows that landed the two men in hospital. Still, he'd been the only famous one there, and he had deep pockets.

Grant had never felt lower than when he'd signed that cheque to make it all go away. He'd taken voluntarily leave from the club so they didn't get dragged down with him. He'd disappeared overseas for a few months, cleared his head and come back with the strongest commitment of his life—the commitment to do right by his club and his fans.

It had been a whole year, he hadn't gone clubbing once, and his career was back on track. He'd also ditched the so-called best friend who had leaked the photo to the media, making a promise to himself that no one would ever use him again.

However, the media loved to tell his story over and over. He wondered how long it would be before they forgot about it—if they ever did. What if he could never clear the mud from his name?

He cringed; the Farley name had been an honourable one once. The rural veterinary and farming business his father ran had had a good, solid reputation in their community… Now they were known as the family whose son had gone off the rails. It was an inerasable mistake—one that had cost him dearly.

Maybe if he could get one win this season he could prove he was back on track. At least then he'd have the respect of the fans and of his team. That would be a step in the right direction.

Jasmine had been cooped up inside for days since her fall. Her ankle was looking better: the swelling had reduced and the bruises had shifted from purple to a yellowish-brown. It wasn't a pretty sight, but it was a far cry from what she'd feared.

She knew the drill—take it easy, give the strain time to heal, keep the ankle elevated. But she was bored, bored, *bored*.

The drivel they featured on daytime TV didn't hold her interest and she'd devoured three books from cover to cover before exhausting her supply of new reading material. She needed something to distract her—anything to take her mind off the shambles that Grant Farley had made of her senses.

Jasmine huffed, resting against the side of her couch while she looked around, desperate for something to do. All she could think about was how close she'd come to letting him in, to baring herself and all her flaws to a man she barely knew. It was stupid. Reckless.

The last time she'd trusted a man she'd flushed her career down the toilet. Kyle hadn't come to visit her once after her surgery, though she'd heard reports that he'd used his social rank—and the donations his family had made to the hospital—to check in with her doctor as to the status of her injuries. It had been concluded that she wouldn't be dancing for a very long time, if ever again.

After that there had been a brief note delivered by one of the hospital staff. His elegant handwriting had told her that their relationship wouldn't work out. And that had been that. She'd never seen him again.

The humiliation still burned in her throat every time she thought of the absolute car crash—no pun intended—that had been her relationship with Kyle Waterhouse. Not only had he treated her as the ultimate asset—something to show off to his mates as a sign of his status—but he'd viewed her very much in the same way as the projects and stocks he funded. She was something to throw money at, to control and shape as he pleased. He had not cared about her beyond potential returns. And when she'd no longer been valuable he'd cut his losses.

Tears prickled behind her eyelids, hot and angry. She couldn't stay cooped up in this house any longer, lest she send herself around the twist. Though she wasn't supposed to drive, Elise's mother's car was automatic and her good foot was the only one she needed. Surely a little trip to the ballet studio wouldn't hurt? It wasn't far from home and the fresh air would do her good.

Besides, she wanted to find out how the rest of the performance had gone and to see if any of her students had been approached by the scouts. Feeling justified, she stood and limped to the car.

By the time Jasmine pulled the car into the studio's parking lot her ankle was burning. She pushed herself from the seat, balancing on her good leg. The walk to the studio door seemed to take for ever as she alternated between limping and hopping. All the while she cursed herself for not bringing the crutches Dr Wilson had lent her.

'What are you doing here?' Elise abandoned her choreography midstep to admonish Jasmine as she hobbled into the studio.

'I couldn't stay at home, El. I was going crazy.' She hopped in a pitiful little circle. 'See? I'm fine.'

Elise shook her head but she didn't argue. 'I'll get you a chair.'

Dragging one from the reception desk, she placed it at the front of the studio. Grateful, Jasmine dropped down and settled in to watch the class.

As they were wrapping up Jasmine noticed Grant had arrived for his lesson. Given her state of relative immobility—not that she was allowing herself to be confined by it—Elise had offered to cover her lessons for the week without taking any money. Lucky, since Jasmine was walking a fine line between making ends meet and having her phone cut off.

Grant walked into the studio and came straight up to Jasmine. Lines creased his forehead and his strong jaw was set into a forbidding angle.

'You're supposed to be resting.' He stood over her, arms folded across his chest so that his biceps bulged beneath his T-shirt. His full lips pursed into a shape far more appealing than it should have been, given he was admonishing her as one might a child.

Jasmine shrugged. 'It's boring.'

He tilted his head to one side and gave her an impatient look. 'That's a pretty weak excuse.'

'Consider yourself lucky you got one at all.'

He sighed. 'You should be resting.'

'You said that already.'

They stared at one another, the air crackling between them. Part of Jasmine knew he was right, but the other part wanted to give him a kick in the shins for being so bossy. Since he'd rejected her advance the other night she knew the smart move would be to push him away.

'When you two are done I'll start the lesson.' Elise stood in the middle of the studio with her hands on her hips.

She pulled a stern face but Jasmine could see the amused smile twitching on the edge of her lips.

'Wait around and I'll take you home afterwards.' He turned to meet Elise.

'My car is here,' she protested. 'I don't need you to chauffeur me around.'

'It wasn't a question.'

Grant knew he was pushing the boundaries with Jasmine, but the girl didn't seem to want to take care of herself. She had a self-destructive streak that unnerved him—

probably because he'd seen that same capacity in himself. And learning she was the one who'd caused her accident had only made him more certain she needed someone to look after her. Elise seemed to keep an eye out, but he doubted that was enough.

When he'd gone through the kitchen cupboards at her house he'd noticed how bare they were: a whole lot of tea and coffee, a few muesli bars and some limp-looking fruit and veggies in her fridge. Not the kind of nutrition required for someone who had a physical job like she did.

She sighed, but didn't make a move to leave. Instead she stayed in the chair and watched as Elise began her instruction.

He was finding it difficult to concentrate on Elise's voice because his mind kept wandering to Jasmine. She watched them with an open interest, and he felt the weight of her stare on his shoulders. He was messing up the steps and growing increasingly frustrated with the exercises.

The lesson was a disaster. In truth, he was completely over the ballet treatment thing, but something urged him to continue…and it wasn't the benefits his hamstring was seeing.

'Tough lesson?' Jasmine asked as he came up to her afterwards. Her head tilted to the side, sending dark, glossy hair slipping over her shoulder. She looked delectable, even free of make-up and dressed in jeans and a grey sweater.

'Tough when you were staring me down.'

'I wasn't staring you down.' She laughed, pushing up onto her good leg. 'You seem to get off on the knight in shining armour thing, so I'll let you take me home tonight but that's it. Tomorrow I go back to looking after myself, OK?'

'We'll see,' he grumbled. He wrapped his arm around her waist and pulled her to him so he could help her to the door.

'I *am* going to remind you that this is completely unnec-essary,' she said, looking up at him. 'I drove myself here.'

'Just because you did doesn't mean you should have.'

Her body fitted perfectly against his, and it was tough for him not to notice that as she made a lame attempt to get rid of him. As she hopped her shoulder bumped against him, her hand tightening around his lower back. It was all he needed to imagine where else he'd like those hands to be on him…smoothing over his chest, cupping his ass and—

'Good night, you two.'

Elise's sing-song voice caused Jasmine to turn around and glare at her friend. Her cheeks coloured to a faint pink, making his pulse race even more.

'You know I'm going to have to come back here in the morning and collect the car.' Jasmine sighed as he helped her out of the studio and towards the Mercedes.

'I'll have it brought to your unit.' He wasn't going to let her make her way home on her own—not with an injured foot on these icy roads. If something happened to her he would never forgive himself.

Grant frowned. He wasn't sure what it was about Jas-mine that was stirring all these protective instincts. The only woman he'd ever cared to protect had been Chelsea, and look how that had turned out.

'OK, fine.'

He held the door open for her and she slid awkwardly into his car. When he was satisfied she was OK he walked around to the driver's side and got in. Firing up the engine, he let the car warm up before backing it out.

'So what's the deal with you wanting to look after me?' Jasmine watched him closely as she questioned him, her eyes narrowed slighly. 'Do you have some compelling need to protect women you barely know?'

'I know you.'

She paused for a moment. 'No, you don't.'

'Yes, I do.' He glanced sideways at her. 'I know you're a great dancer who's trapped because of a stupid mistake.'

'I don't know if my most recent performance would allow anyone to classify me as a great dancer.' She bit down on her lower lip.

'I know you like to be in control and you hate asking for help. I know that Elise is pretty much the only person you have in your life.'

Jasmine blinked, her eyebrows arched. 'OK, so maybe you know me a bit.'

'I studied psychology at university, remember? I can read people.'

'So what are you reading now?'

'You're testing me, although I'm not sure why.' Grant forced away a smile at her open-mouthed surprise, though he could hardly claim much achievement in accurately assessing her—reading her face was as easy as reading a book.

'OK, that's kind of freaky.'

'Why don't you fill in the blanks, then?'

'I don't know why I'd do that,' she said, her voice small. She was looking out of the window, avoiding him. 'I'm not ready for this. But I can't seem to push you away... I don't think I want to.'

The honesty of her statement was a fist to his stomach. She felt the same way he did. They were two people who knew better, who were smart, who protected themselves from all the crap that life threw at them. Yet neither of them could resist the gravitational pull when they were together. It relieved him to know that she felt it too.

'I don't know what I'm doing,' she continued. 'But I can't stop wanting to touch you, wanting to taste you.'

His lips ran dry at her last statement, his tongue heavy in his mouth as he steadied his breath. His blood seemed to pulse twice as fast as he looked at her, his flickering glance capturing the flush of her pale skin under the streetlamps. The arousal he'd been fighting pooled in his groin and desire wrenched inside him.

'It's strange, I haven't felt this kind of attraction to anyone in a long time...not since the accident.'

'Why are you telling me all this?'

'I thought you wanted to know.'

The uncertainty in her voice almost broke him in two. He wanted to hold her and tell her everything would be OK.

'I do.'

'It must be your psychology voodoo.'

'Yeah, that must be it.'

He laughed and she offered up a small smile. It was like a peek of sunshine through storm clouds—a sliver of hope against the grey backdrop of her fear.

Neither of them spoke while they lost themselves in their thoughts. They were both damaged goods, victims of broken hearts, and casualties of laying yourself bare to another human being.

He'd promised himself he would never go there again, but it was getting harder and harder to ignore the way she awakened him. She stirred the old Grant—the one who loved without fear. He felt a spark of his former self, the wide-eyed kid from the country who'd wanted to study psychology because he had a burning to desire to help people, to know more about them, to unravel them until he understood what made them tick. It was a part of him long dead and buried.

Now he pushed people away as a default. But she made him want to reach out again. She made him want to crawl out of his cave.

'What happened wasn't your fault.' His voice cracked as he tried to console her.

'Yes, it was.' She nodded, the look of resignation on

her face one he suspected she'd worn many times before. 'I drank the champagne, I got into the car and I hit the accelerator. That makes it my fault.'

'I don't mean that.' He shook his head. 'I mean the way he treated you. *That* wasn't your fault.'

'I used him as much as he used me.' She laughed, the sound hollow and sharp in his ears. 'He used me because he liked having a pretty thing on his arm, and I liked him because he got me more face-time with directors.'

'I'm sure you didn't need it.'

'I didn't,' she said, her voice wavering. 'But I was so insecure back then, and I didn't realise he'd been feeding me lies to keep me close to him. He made me believe that I wasn't able to make it on my own, that I wouldn't succeed without his help.'

Her mouth drew into a grim line. Her regret was palpable in the air.

Grant pulled up in front of her house and turned off the engine. She wouldn't meet his eyes, looking down so that all he could see were the tops of the dark curly lashes that framed them. In a moment of impulse he reached out and cupped her cheeks with his hands. They seemed so large in comparison to her small, delicate features.

'Look at me,' he commanded.

Her eyes flickered up and they sat there for a moment, unmoving in the darkness of the car. He knew he shouldn't, he knew it was the wrong thing to do by her...by them both...but that didn't stop the intensity with which he brought his lips down to hers.

There was nothing tentative about his kiss, no gentle exploring of her. It was hungry and raw. It took her a moment to respond, but when she did it was with equal fervour. Her small rosebud mouth opened up to him, her tongue meeting his. He could taste the honeyed sweetness of her, smell the faded soap on her skin.

His senses sparked and flared as he drank her in: taste, smell, touch…and sound. A small moan escaped her mouth when he ran his hand down from her face to her shoulders, down her arms, grazing her breasts as he went. The soft fabric of her sweater showed no resistance to his touch.

Outside the car a dog barked and the lights of a lone car passing by broke them apart. The car was cooling down and Jasmine shivered next to him.

'Let me get you inside.' His voice was hoarse, barely recognisable through the haze of lust that roughened its edges.

Jasmine nodded. Her lips were puffy from the roughness of his kiss, her cheeks pink, her eyes wide. She opened the door but waited for him to help her, for once. He darted around to the passenger side and reached down to help her out of the car. She gripped his arm and steadied herself on her good foot as she rose slowly from the low seat on the passenger side.

Sliding an arm around her waist, he leant down and kissed her again. Her back pressed against the car, his hips pinning her down. He found her mouth, hot and ready for him this time. Hands came to his hair; her fingers tangling in the lengths of it, tugging it. Showing him that he wasn't in charge.

Though she came close to matching him in height, she still felt tiny next to him. Her long, slender arms and graceful dancer's legs were easily pinned down by his strength, though as she pressed against him now he knew that she wouldn't be delicate in bed.

He swallowed and pulled away, looking down at her soulful brown eyes as they glowed at him from under the streetlamp. Her lips were parted and she dragged her bottom lip between her teeth. He knew where this was going.

This was his last chance; he could turn away now and protect her. He could protect his heart from being shattered again. He felt as if time was standing still as he deliberated, his head pulling him away and his body pushing him closer.

He should leave. She deserved someone who could take better care of her than he could…

'Grant…' she whispered, and his name sounded like a plea on her lips. 'Take me inside. Please.'

And with that the very last scraps of his resolve were shattered. He scooped her up and she immediately wound her arms around his neck—no protest this time. In a few strides he crossed the front yard and set her down so that she could open the front door. He hugged her from behind while she fiddled with the lock, his hands slipping under the hem of her jumper to find the bare skin of her belly. It was smooth and flat, her skin hot to the touch despite the cold outside.

The door finally opened and she limped inside with him close behind her, pulling the door shut. The unit was cold. Jasmine turned on the heater from a panel in the entrance.

'We don't need that,' he said, coming up behind her and bringing his lips down to her neck.

She simmered beneath him, her hips tilting backwards so that she could press her ass against him.

'It's going to get hot in here.'

CHAPTER NINE

GRANT REACHED FOR Jasmine and scooped her up. She felt slightly ridiculous, with him carrying her everywhere, but as his mouth met hers again she lost herself in the velvet warmth of his kiss.

'Which way?' He murmured his question against her lips.

She motioned to the bedroom, her response muffled against him. He nudged the door open with his foot, carrying her through before setting her gently down in front of him. She balanced on one foot and encircled his neck with her arms, dragging him down for another searing kiss.

A snake-like sensation twisted and turned in her gut. It had been so long since she'd had sex—not since breaking up with Kyle, though his frequent infidelities had meant their sex life had died a while before that fateful night.

What if she'd forgotten how to seduce? How to pleasure? How to enjoy her body?

She ignored the fluttering of her heart and the prickling of her palms. She needed this—she needed to be loved in a physical sense. She'd been deprived for so long and there would be no fighting it.

Leaning down to plant a soft kiss on his mouth, she sucked in a breath. Her tongue brushed over his lower lip in a sweet, tentative stroke, eliciting a groan. She had him right where she wanted him, so hungry with desire he was unlikely to notice or care about her leg.

He grasped the hem of her sweater and pulled it up slowly. Her T-shirt followed and then she was wearing only her jeans and the lacy blush-pink bra she'd thought nothing of wearing that morning. It looked sensual against her skin; she'd always had a thing for beautiful lingerie and her drawers were filled with a rainbow of lacy, frilly French things. It seemed he too enjoyed them—his eyes drank her in as though she were the proverbial glass of water on a hot summer's day.

'I don't expect anything out of this.' Her voice shook as he traced the scalloped edge of the bra with his fingertip.

'Me neither.'

'I mean, I'm not looking for anything permanent right now.'

He dragged his gaze away from her breasts, the endless depths of his sky-blue eyes drawing her in and yet telling her nothing. His face was unreadable except for the arousal that widened his pupils, simmering below the surface.

'Nor am I.'

'One night only,' she whispered, knowing full well that words alone couldn't protect her. She was in too deep and her heart was desperately trying to maintain the distance that her body was unable to. But the words were hollow. Meaningless. He was under her skin and one night would never be enough.

'No one gets hurt.' He brushed the edge of her jaw with his hand, tilting her face.

'No one gets hurt,' she echoed.

Grant's hands dropped to her waist, undoing the zip on her jeans, and then he was bending down, dragging the denim with him as he went. Her French knickers in baby-blue cotton were trimmed with the same blush-pink lace as her bra.

He sighed, and the slow whoosh of breath tickled the exposed skin of her thighs. He traced a line of kisses along the edge of her underwear, sending goosebumps rippling across her skin. She removed her sneakers and leant on him, stepping out of her jeans gingerly to avoid putting too much pressure on her sprained ankle. He reached for the top of the knee-high white cotton socks she wore to keep her legs warm...and to hide the scars.

'Don't,' she whispered. 'Leave them on.'

She couldn't do it. No matter how hungry he got he wouldn't be able to ignore the puckered flesh and shades of red. She knew that.

Distract him—quickly!

She loosened her hair from the tie that held it in place so that the dark strands tumbled over her shoulders and bust. She tossed the tie to one side, not even looking to see where it landed. Giving her head a little shake, she felt her hair fall about her.

'Holy hell.' His mouth formed an appreciative O. 'I can honestly say I've never seen a more exciting sight in all my life.'

'Is that so?' She cocked her head to the side, allowing her hair to brush over her hardened nipples as they pressed against the lacy fabric that contained them. A tight clenching sensation in her stomach sent heat spiralling down to the juncture of her thighs.

'You've knocked finals off the top of the list.'

He reached for her, drawing her waist to him with one hand and using his other to gather her hair and pull it over her shoulders. It slipped down her back, the ends tickling the bare patch of skin above the waistband of her French knickers.

'No other woman has ever come close to that.'

'I'm sure I'm not like the girls you're used to,' she said, her voice raspy and low.

She was shaking on the inside. His reaction excited and terrified her. She knew he would be a practised lover, far more experienced than her, and she could only hope it wouldn't show.

He ran a fingertip over her collarbone before dropping his hand to cup her breast, his thumb and forefinger gently rolling a taut nipple through the thin fabric. 'You're nothing like anything I've ever experienced before.'

Jasmine's head rolled back as pleasure shot through her veins, heating every inch of her body in rapid succession. Grant's touch was equal parts gentle and insistent, his expert movements slowly eroding her fear. If she didn't have him soon she'd burst.

She reached for the hem on his jumper and pulled it off—along with his T-shirt—in one swift movement. He was the perfect specimen of male health, muscular and lean. She ran her hands down the front of his chest, admiring the freckles that scattered across his skin to where his tattoos finished. The colourful intricate lines spread up towards his shoulder and down over the top of his arm. She traced the outline of the psi symbol woven into the design. Running her hands down his chest, she brushed her finger over his nipples and continued down to the waistband of his pants.

Hovering, her hands trembled above the tell-tale bulge of his excitement. She hooked a finger under the waistband of his pants and brushed the taut skin there. A shudder rippled through him as her hands continued their exploration, coaxing him gently as she went.

'Good Lord, you're a tease.' A frustrated growl rumbled low in his throat. He pulled her to him, cupping her buttocks with both hands so that she was pressed against him as hard as possible. And hard he was, the thick length of him digging into her lower belly.

Without warning Grant leant forwards and scooped

Jasmine up, her legs dangling over one of his arms as she wound her own arms around his neck for support. Their lips met as he walked to her bed, and her hands found themselves once again amidst the thick mass of his golden hair. His mouth was urgent now, lips rough and probing against hers.

Dropping her to the bed, Grant stripped completely to reveal the full extent of his arousal. Reaching for him, she felt her breath catch in her throat. Her fingertips brushed the silky strength of his erection. He was magnificent. Hotter than anything she could have dreamed up on the nights she spent alone in this very bed.

'I need you, Grant,' she whispered, grabbing his hips and pulling him down to her. 'I need you inside me.'

'Not yet.' His lips skimmed over hers and found their resting place around a tight, sensitive nipple. He pushed the strap of her bra down so that he could remove her breast from its delicate confines. Jasmine's back arched at the sudden intensity of pleasure that pooled within her. His tongue flicked against the sensitive bud, heightening her excitement so that behind her closed lids all she could focus on was the heat of his mouth on her.

His hand trailed down the plane of her stomach, dancing lightly over the lacy knickers to her bare knee above one of her socks. He smoothed his hand back up, letting his fingers skirt the edge of her underwear. He let out a throaty laugh against her breast as she squirmed beneath him.

'Who's the tease now?' she panted, gripping the bedspread and bunching the thick material in her hands.

With continued gentleness he kissed his way to her other breast and removed her bra altogether. Discarding the scrap of lace with one hand, he toyed with the scalloped edge of her knickers near her inner thigh. Jasmine gasped as his fingers brushed over her sex. She'd reached boiling point, her blood simmering while he stoked the fire within her. He touched her with an unhurried enjoyment, each stroke, kiss, lick doled out with a lazy sensuality that made her head spin.

He peeled back the waistband of her kickers and removed them slowly, all the while watching as he revealed her inch by inch.

'Stunning,' he murmured.

As he lay down beside her Grant possessed her mouth, leaving her dizzy through lack of air. He dipped a finger into her core, rubbing his thumb gently across the tight bud at her centre. Jasmine let out a cry. His teasing had wound her tighter than she'd ever experienced. Tighter than she'd thought possible. Her body ascended slowly to climax and she revelled in the exquisite torture of pleasure a hair's breadth out of reach.

'Please, Grant.' She grabbed his face with her hands, forcing him to look at her. 'Don't make me wait.'

Jasmine reached over to the drawer in her nightstand and fished around for a condom. There had to be one in there—surely she hadn't thrown them all out. Her fingers moved about the drawer as the sound of their breathing filled the air.

Please.

Mercifully, her fingers brushed the crinkled edges of a condom packet. She handed it to Grant and he tore it open. Lying back, Jasmine felt her stomach flutter with anticipation as he took care of their protection. He paused before slowly lowering himself to her, nudging her legs apart with his thighs.

His hands were on either side of her, his face hovering above hers. At this angle his golden hair flopped forwards, the too-long ends brushing his forehead. She'd never wanted a man so badly as she wanted him right now.

She bit down on her lower lip as he filled her completely, the sensation sucking the air from her lungs. She adjusted to the thickness of him and his face burrowed against her neck. The weight of him pressing her into the bed was exquisite—terrifying and all-consuming.

'Jasmine...' he groaned. 'You're so damn...'

He trailed off as he moved inside her, slowly at first, giving her time to adjust. His hands roamed her, stroking up and down the lengths of her arms, tangling themselves in her hair, cupping the sides of her face as he kissed her. Gathering speed, he bucked his hips against her hot, wet centre. She tilted to meet his thrusts, giving him greater access. Complete access.

He slipped one arm beneath her lower back, drawing her body to his as he pushed back onto his knees and pulled her up so that she straddled him. He bore the weight of her and she moved her leg so that there was no pressure on her ankle.

Upright, Jasmine was exposed as she met him eye to eye. From her vantage point she could watch everything about their lovemaking, from the stark contrast of his tanned, freckled skin against the porcelain of hers to the way his shoulders tensed as she rode him. His eyes were half open, heavy-lidded with desire, and his thick lashes fluttered as she moved her hips in a circular motion.

She lowered her head and pressed her lips to his shoulder as she leant against him, her breasts flattened against his chest. They were fused, moving with a harmony she'd never experienced before. Perhaps this was the way it felt when there was no agenda other than lust.

He ran his hands up and down her sock-covered legs. Her breath caught as his fingers brushed over where her scars were hidden beneath nylon and cotton. She studied his face for any change but he appeared not to have noticed. Relaxing, she brought her face to his and planted a hot, open-mouthed kiss on his lips. He tasted mildly salty from where a thin sheen of sweat coated his upper lip. Responding immediately, he kissed her back with force until her lips were bruised and puffy.

He shifted to be properly beneath her, while she writhed on top of him. She felt incredible, with the blatant adoration in his eyes urging her on, urging her to open up to him. She ran her palms over her body while she continued circling her hips, brushing her hands over her own breasts and flicking her hair over her shoulder so that it dropped down to where his legs extended underneath her.

The tension rose. He gripped her, urging an increase in speed. She held him back, teasing him until the last possible moment, dangling the possibility of release over him like a taunt.

But it seemed Grant had other plans. He slipped a hand between them and a sharp jolt of pleasure ripped through her as his thumb connected with her clitoris. He massaged the swollen bud until she was panting. Her breath came in short bursts as she climbed higher and higher. She clenched around him as waves of pleasure rolled through her.

Her climax came hard and fast, causing her to clamp her eyes shut. It felt as if she was bursting apart at the seams. Her whole body shuddered with release and she gripped him so hard she thought she might break him in two. She opened her eyes to stare straight into Grant's, pushing her hair from her face as she smiled at him.

'That was...' she said, still catching her breath. 'Something else.' She pressed her lips to his neck, grazing her teeth along the roped muscles. He smelled faintly of aftershave—something woody and earthy. She breathed it in as she murmured, 'Come for me.'

The words pushed Grant over the edge; he gripped her hips and increased their rhythm so that he could tip himself into oblivion. He cried out her name as he came, his face contorted with ecstasy, and then he fell back against the pillow, sated.

Jasmine watched Grant, and instead of removing herself from him lay down so her body was flat against his. His heart thudded against her chest and the deepness of his breath blew warm on her ear. He let out a mumble of enjoyment as he pressed his lips to her temple.

'*You're* something else.' Their faces were so close that his eyelashes brushed her cheek.

Jasmine's chest contracted and pleasure tugged in response to his praise. She'd never felt like this after sex— she'd never felt this deep bonding and connection with another. It was as though she was safe, as if she was even and equal with him.

One night only—that was the deal.

She couldn't deny the comfort of lying on top of Grant now, and nor could she deny the way her body sang out when he wrapped his strong, thick arms around her. His fingertips traced the lines of her back, causing little ripples of pleasure to run through her.

Against her better judgement, Jasmine wished that time would stand still so she could savour her body against his.

What a day. He'd gone from ignoring thoughts of the lithe ballet teacher to experiencing her first-hand. Pushing guilty thoughts from his mind, he watched the flutter of her heavy-lidded eyes and the curl of a contented smile on her lips.

Lying back against her bed with her slender body curled up on top of his was the stuff fantasies were made of. He ran his hand down her back, over her pert buttocks, and allowed his fingertips to skim the tops of her knee-highs. *So hot… She was like a naughty schoolgirl.*

The whole thing had escalated so quickly. He'd had no intention of taking her to bed when he'd offered her a ride home. He'd been noble in his desire to make sure she was safe. But seeing her open up had flicked some kind of switch. She was so incredibly beautiful when she was vulnerable—something he suspected she hated to be.

He'd wanted nothing more than to make her pain go away. Still, part of him worried that he'd taken advantage of her weakness.

She shifted on top of him, rubbing against his lower body and causing him to stir. Hell, they'd barely finished and he was ready to go again. It had been a long time since he'd had sex sober, let alone with someone who wasn't a random football groupie. She was different in every possible way from what he was used to, and he'd enjoyed it far more than he wanted to. He wasn't supposed to feel this way.

He buried his face against her neck to block out the confusing thoughts.

'Once not enough for you?' Jasmine asked, her voice low and gravelly in his ear. She circled her hips against him.

Groaning, he pressed up against her heat while his lips found hers. Her rosebud lips were pink and puffy, her taste delectable.

'I get the impression it would never be enough with you,' Grant said.

Her face hovered inches over him, her lips brushing his cheeks and nose. Grant looked up into her warm brown eyes and lost himself for a moment.

After sex he wanted to run, to put as much distance as possible between him and the woman he'd slept with. He needed to reclaim his space, his privacy. It happened every single time...except now. The usual twitching of his muscles and the restlessness in his hands seemed far away. His eyes weren't roaming the room; his mind wasn't formulating an exit strategy. He'd never needed to specify a 'one night only' rule before—it was his MO—but the whole concept seemed ridiculous with Jasmine. There was no way one night would be enough.

Now he wanted to revel in the feeling of her. It scared the hell out of him. A sigh escaped him as her thighs pressed up against his sides and he watched the way her thick lashes touched each time she blinked. Through the twinges of guilt he was hyperaware of her presence, as though he could notice every miniscule movement. Every breath, every strand of hair as it fell about her.

'I'm guessing this is a first,' he said, gripping her slim waist and shifting so they lay side by side. He brought his lips down to her neck and she muttered her enjoyment. 'Considering I'm a student and all.'

'You're the only legal male I teach.' Her lips gave a small teasing smile. 'So, yes. Though it's…it's been a while for me.'

'Me too.'

He wasn't sure why she'd told him that, and he was even less sure of why he'd responded. Part of proving himself to be the reformed and focused athlete he was had meant giving up the partying…and that had meant giving up the girls—at least for the most part. Staying away from relationships had been easy; he didn't need to be burned twice. But staying away from physical intimacy had been difficult when at first he'd wanted to fill the void of loneliness with something. But being with Jasmine was so much more than scratching an itch.

Part of him wanted to talk to her—to divulge all his troubles and faults, to strip himself bare. But it couldn't happen. Besides, they'd made a pact.

'Two peas.'

She looked at him, her eyes shining. But there was something tentative about the way she touched him, something careful in her movements, and that told him she was as unsure as he was.

He pressed his lips together for fear that he might spill out more than he wanted to. There was something powerful about Jasmine—something that made him feel he might finally be able to open up.

Thoughts like that were both dangerous and stupid. He'd done enough damage to his life without baring his sins to someone he had no reason to trust. For an AFL player, or anyone in the limelight, that was practically asking for a front-page news headline: Secret Lover Tells All. And unfortunately there was no statute of limitations on sports gossip. He'd borne the brunt of that before, and he was never going back there again.

Hooking her leg around his, she wrapped her foot around his calf and shimmied closer. The soft touch of her fingertips slid over his chest and down towards his stomach. Closing his eyes, he pushed the worry from his mind. Now was a time for pleasure—pure and unadulterated pleasure. As her hand dipped lower it became easier for him to focus on the steady path she drew around his bellybutton towards his growing erection.

'I think you've taught me a thing or two already.' Grant brought his hands up to her hair, pushing his fingers through the thick glossy strands until he cupped the curve of her head. 'I'm sure those *plié* things will come in handy at some point.'

'You'll be thanking me when your Achilles' tendons are strong and flexible.'

'Flexibility is certainly a plus.' He struggled to get the words out as Jasmine pressed against him.

'It *does* come in handy.'

His body lurched with the image of Jasmine bent in two and he growled in appreciation. 'I know this is a one-time thing, but I don't think once will do it justice.'

'It's like you read my mind…'

He pulled her beneath him, leaning down to kiss a trail

from the gentle sweep of her small breasts to her stomach. He couldn't help but smile as she giggled when his lips brushed over her most ticklish parts. He continued down to the smooth skin of her sex, his senses sparking at the sharp intake of breath when he pressed his lips gently to the most private part of her. She tasted sweet and feminine and carnal.

Her body opened to his touch, porcelain thighs falling apart and welcoming him. Her hands found their way to his head, fingers tangling in his hair as she gripped him. He traced the line of her with his tongue, enjoying the way she arched to his mouth with such wanton need. She was slick with desire, her body primed for him.

He found the sensitive bud of her clitoris and concentrated his energy there. Her hands were curled into the fabric of the bedspread as she bucked against him, seeking the release he held out of reach. When he paused momentarily she cried out.

'Don't stop...' Her voice was strangled. 'Please.'

'I've only got one night, remember?' He rested his chin on her lower belly. 'Don't rush me.'

He ran his hands up and down her legs, toying with the edges of her knee-highs. He hooked his fingers underneath the elastic and went to peel one from her.

She gasped. 'No!'

'It's OK,' he soothed, his voice low and quiet, as though he were convincing a frightened animal not to run from him.

'No.'

She shook her head, and the tremble of her lip almost undid him. She was far from the writhing, sensual beauty of a minute ago. Her pale face and sad eyes sliced away at his composure. He remembered the shame in her eyes as she'd talked about her accident, the self-loathing he understood with a painful acuity.

'Let me see you,' he said, reaching up to clasp her hands. Her delicate wrists were fragile in his grip, trembling beneath his fingertips. 'Please.'

'It's ugly.' She squeezed her eyes shut, her head angled away from him.

'Jasmine, open your eyes.' He was firm, determined to be strong for her. 'Open them for me.'

She did as he asked, her eyes shimmering beneath heavy lashes. She let out a shaky breath as he brought his hands back down to her calves.

'You're stunning.' His voice was rough, emotional. 'Scars or no scars.'

She gave a slight nod of her head, the most minimal of movements, but he wasn't going to proceed until he got her consent. His lips pressed against her knee and followed the line of her shin as he peeled her sock away from the skin. The room was heavy with silence; she was holding her breath so that all that could be heard was the thundering of his heart. The ankle she'd injured recently had yellow patches discolouring the skin. The swelling had gone down, but the marks on her skin would remain awhile longer.

He moved to the other sock and revealed the leg injured in her accident. The scar was bright red against her fair skin; it snaked up the side of her leg and finished a few inches under her knee. He looked up and saw that she had her eyes clamped shut again, her bottom lip between her teeth. His heart burst at her fear.

'I tried to warn you.' Her voice quivered.

Grant pushed up from his position on the bed; locking his eyes on hers. 'I don't care that you have scars.'

His fingertips gently traced the length of her injured leg. He treated it as though it were as precious and beautiful as the rest of her...because it was. He pressed himself against her, pushing her body into the soft depths of the bed.

'We all have scars…even if you can't see anything on the outside.' His lips trailed the length of her jaw until he reached her ear. 'If you think even for a second that I'm bothered, then I'll stop right now.'

She stared up at him, uncertainty flickering across her face. Each second felt like hours as Grant held himself there, waiting for her to call the next move.

'Don't stop.' Her voice was the barest whisper.

He brought his hands to the insides of her thighs and lowered himself down her body. He ran his tongue up the delicate join of her hip, working his way back to her centre. A moan—soft and delicate—urged him on.

Something within him shattered as her eyes fluttered shut. She pressed another condom into his hand and he sheathed himself before entering her with a single, smooth thrust. Jasmine clenched instinctively around him, her body responding to his as though they were made for each other.

The tension had melted from her face and her wide eyes glimmered up at him. Her full lips were parted, a pink flush warming her cheeks. She was stunning.

She lifted her hips so that he could hook his arms underneath her thighs and drive deeper into her. Each thrust sent pleasure shooting through him. His entire body was alight with the feeling of her. She lifted her legs higher, draping her ankles over his shoulders, and giggled at the delight on his face.

'Being a dancer does have its perks.' She smiled up at him, the confidence blossoming on her face once more.

'No kidding.' He ran his hands up and down her legs, taking care to be gentle over her scars but not wanting to leave any part of her out of his worship. 'Your body is amazing—every goddamn inch of it.'

His careful strokes were aimed at putting pressure in the spot where she needed it most; she clenched around him as her pleasure mounted. It was all he could do to control himself, to stop himself from ravishing her.

'I need it now...' Jasmine tipped her head back, exposing the delicate white skin of her neck. Grant kissed her there, she shivered and a soft moan escaped her lips.

He moved harder and faster, pushing her towards release with each thrust, until her fingers dug into his back, her nails scratching at his skin as she peaked. The sound of her crying out his name brought him to a sudden and powerful climax.

Exhausted, he fell forwards. His face was cradled in the sweet curve of her neck, where she smelled of pleasure and satisfaction and wonder. The room was silent as they clung to one another as if their lives depended on it.

CHAPTER TEN

GRANT HAD BEEN tempted to slip out of Jasmine's apartment when the sky had not yet encountered the pink whisper of dawn. After they'd ravaged one another for a second time Jasmine had fallen asleep curled into his side, her French knickers hanging from the post at the end of the bed.

The temptation of her lithe body tucked into his had been far too much. The way she slept—with her hair fanned out over the pillow and a small smile on her lips—had made Grant want to stare at her until the image was permanently embedded in his mind. He'd known he should get out before she decided to wake and go for round number three...as good as that sounded.

But he hadn't been able to bring himself to do it. Thinking about leaving her had caused his heart to clench. What would she make of a silent departure?

She said herself it was a one-time thing. Though his logic was faultless, he couldn't help but worry that she might conclude that he viewed her as a one-night stand—nothing more.

So he'd stayed, savouring her body against his. His mind swirled with confusion. This girl was going to bring him undone.

One slender arm draped over his midsection. Her nails were painted baby pink and in the pale morning light they shimmered like pearls. Everything about her was graceful and dainty, yet she'd turned out to be a tightly wound bundle of sexual heat.

His coach's voice echoed in his head: *Don't replace one crutch with another*. He had to make sure that this thing with Jasmine—whatever it was—remained casual. He couldn't afford to fall into anything serious...not while his reputation was hanging in the balance. He needed a big win this season to get his career back on track.

Even as he warned himself he ached at the thought of leaving her. He was in trouble...big trouble.

Jasmine shifted, her sleepy movement causing her small naked breasts to rub against him. He felt himself stiffen beneath the cotton bedsheet and he had to contain the guttural groan that threatened to burst forth. She had the most *incredible* effect on him.

Her eyes fluttered open, dark lashes blinking as a shy smile spread across her lips. 'Well, that escalated, didn't it?'

Grant chuckled and pulled Jasmine closer to him. Her hair swept over her, the glossy lengths giving her a goddesslike appearance. He ran his hands through the gleaming strands, enjoying the silken sensation against his palms.

'No regrets?' He searched her face.

'We didn't do anything to regret.' Her face was buried into his side, her lashes tickling his ribcage as she blinked.

'You should be able to look me in the eye, then.'

She peered up, her cheeks pink. 'No regrets. I promise.'

Silence settled over them until all that could be heard were the sounds of normal life occurring outside. Inside, life was anything but normal. They'd crossed a line that could not be uncrossed, no matter how they tried to rationalise it away.

Jasmine rolled onto her back, eyes locked onto the ceiling. 'So...'

'So?'

They looked at one another and laughed. 'This is...'

'It's only awkward if we let it be awkward.' He rolled onto his side to face her. 'I know our one night is over, but I propose coffee.'

Her eyes lit up at the suggestion of coffee—it was like a moment of pure sunshine. 'I never say no to coffee.'

She hadn't been sure of how Grant would react the morning after, though part of her was relieved he hadn't made some lame excuse to run away. Or, worse still, made a sneaky exit in the middle of the night. Her fragile self-esteem wouldn't have been able to take it. However, what it now meant was that they were standing awkwardly in her kitchen, making small talk.

In some ways that was worse than nursing a bruised ego. She should never have gone down this path in the first place. You didn't have to force conversation with a fantasy—nor did you have to make it a cappuccino.

She folded her arms across her chest, pulling her baggy sweater closer around her. Her feet were bare, and the cold of the tiles seeped into her bones. She'd thrown on a pair of leggings to cover up her scars—not that it made much difference at this point.

How had she allowed him to see so much of her last night? Was she that desperate for affection that she let him take over? He'd been tender beyond what she'd expected, his gentle handling of her more visible flaws better than she could have hoped for. But the dark part of her mind—the blackened recess where Kyle had once burried his claws—told her that he was secretly disgusted.

How could he not be?

She turned to the coffee machine, hoping he couldn't hear the shame that roared within her at full force. She let out a breath, forcing herself to be silent as the machine whirred to life. She twisted the too-long sleeves of her jumper, covering her hands completely as though it might protect her.

'About last night—' he started.

'If you say *How was it for you?* I'm going to brain you with this mug.' She waved a coffee mug at him as if to illustrate her point.

'What?' A sly smile spread over his lips as he leant against the breakfast bar. 'You got a problem with giving positive reinforcement?'

She poked her tongue out at him.

'No matter—I'll take the fact that you screamed the house down to mean I did a good job.'

'Do you want this coffee or not?' Her cheeks flamed, but she couldn't prevent a smile twitching at her lips. He was cocky, but then again, when you were that good....

She held his cup under the coffee machine and filled it with steaming dark liquid. The scent filled the room. Usually it was the most comforting scent in the world—reminiscent of early-morning ballet rehearsals and catch-ups with Elise—but today it did nothing to quell her morning-after jitters. Weren't people supposed to feel anxious *before* sex, not after?

'I've heard of love 'em and leave 'em, but never love 'em and cease all conversation,' he teased.

'We don't need to cease *all* conversations.'

'Just ones pertaining to sex?'

'Yes.' She filled her own mug and brought it close to her face. Inhaling deep, she willed the curling tendrils of steam to work their magic, but her shoulders remained bunched, her hands in a death-grip around the mug's handle.

'So...how about that local sports team?' He drummed his fingers against the countertop.

'That would be you.'

'Right.' Grant took a sip of his coffee and paused for a moment. 'Why don't you like talking about sex?'

'Don't pull your psychology voodoo on me.' Getting psychoanalysed was the *last* thing she needed right now. She was having a hard time dealing with her own thoughts without someone else picking them apart.

'I'm only asking—'

'Sex is for doing, not for talking about.'

'Only if you're repressed,' he muttered.

'Based on what you saw last night, do you think I'm repressed?' she asked, but as he opened his mouth to answer she cut him off. 'It's a rhetorical question. I don't see why we need to make a big deal out of it. It was one night between two consenting adults...who never need to speak about it again.'

'Point taken,' he said.

Jasmine experienced a strange twinge of emptiness when Grant left, though she had no right whatsoever to feel that way. After all, she was the one who'd enforced the 'one night only' rule and made it clear commitment wasn't on the agenda. She tried to focus on other things as soon as the door closed behind him, and knew she was in trouble when she waited by the door until the sound of his car vanished down the street. Yeah, she was in trouble, all right.

So it turned out that Grant Farley wasn't just an ace football player, but he also had some other—more carnal—skills at his disposal. He'd rocked her world in a way that had surprised her, and she couldn't help reliving the night in her head.

Over and over and *over*.

'Earth to Jasmine.' Elise waved a hand in front of her face. 'Anyone home?'

'Huh?' Jasmine shook her head and focused on her friend. 'Sorry, I drifted off then.'

'I'll say.' Elise eyed her suspiciously. 'And judging by

the expression on your face I'd say you drifted somewhere muscular.'

Jasmine gave Elise a light punch in the arm, but the smile that refused to leave her lips revealed enough. Elise's eyes widened until they looked as though they might pop right out of her pretty little head.

'You *didn't?*' She grabbed Jasmine's face and examined it. Jasmine twisted away, but Elise was stronger than her petite frame would suggest. 'You *did!*'

'Fine.' Jasmine batted her friend away. 'Twice, if you must know.'

Elise's mouth opened and closed in shock. Eventually she let out a surprised laugh.

'The goldfish look isn't good on you,' Jasmine said, rolling her eyes.

'I'm just surprised.' Elise picked up a costume from the bag on the table and commenced sewing a row of sequins. 'I'm guessing it went well, otherwise you wouldn't be grinning like a court jester...'

'It did go well.' Jasmine sewed a matching costume, her hands practised in the simple up and down threading motion. 'In fact I could say I haven't experienced anything that good in a long time. If ever.'

Jasmine had forgotten all about her promise to assist Elise with the costumes for an upcoming dance competition. When Elise had arrived with enough sequins to make a small nation sparkle Jasmine had had no choice but to hope that she didn't look as loved up and dishevelled as she felt.

'I guess football players have a lot of practice.' Elise propped her chin in one hand, her face alight.

'He was...' Jasmine paused, thinking of the best way to describe him. 'I don't know...more tender than I expected. More considerate.'

Elise raised an eyebrow.

'Don't get me wrong, it was still hot as hell, but he wasn't as self-focused as I expected. He seemed to get a kick out of pleasuring me.'

'Good.' Elise nodded her approval and went back to her sewing. 'I won't stand for you dating any more selfish bastards—you've had your share.'

Jasmine nodded. Though her dating experience was minimal, she did seem to have a type—heartless bastards with more money than feelings. If it had only been Kyle she could have chalked it up to bad luck. One was a mistake; three was a trend.

She yawned. A night of passionate lovemaking might have been good for the soul, but it wasn't great for her energy levels. She was in desperate need of another coffee and a blanket.

'So how did you go?' Elise abandoned her sewing and went to the coffee machine, as if reading Jasmine's mind. 'With the whole leg…thing…'

'That wasn't easy. I tried to keep my socks on, but he wasn't having a bar of that.'

'You tried to keep your socks on while you were having sex?' Elise seemed unsure of whether Jasmine was joking or not, and her delicate features pulled into a frown. 'You're not an old married couple.'

'It wasn't like that—they were knee-highs and it was kind of sexy…a bit of a naughty schoolgirl thing.'

'Well, that's OK.' She came back to the table with two coffees. 'But still…*socks?*'

Jasmine laughed, her mind wandering back to the way he'd peeled those socks from her. It had been the single most petrifying thing she'd ever experienced. Give her a packed house at State Theatre over that any day of the week.

Damn him for leaving her so unsettled. The whole idea of sleeping with him had been to get it out of her system.

But she was thinking about him more than ever. Damn, damn, *damn*.

'Have you looked him up on the internet yet?' Elise's eyes lit up. She had on her scary I've-got-a-wild-and-crazy-plan face. Jasmine had seen that face before.

It never ended well.

'No,' she replied, drawing the sound out slowly. She wasn't the most tech-savvy of people, and the internet stalking habits of her generation confused her. What was wrong with a little mystery?

'Oh, this is happening!' Elise jumped up from her seat, snatched her coffee from the table and made a break for the study.

'Dear God...' Jasmine started after her, her limp preventing speedy mobility.

The study—which was more of a glorified broom closet than a legitimate working room—was already alive with the sounds of Elise's hands flying across the keyboard. She typed like a woman possessed.

Elise jumped out of the desk chair, allowing Jasmine to sit, but retained control of the mouse. The search engine spat out a seemingly endless amount of 'Grant Farley' links. The images that popped up showed shots of Grant in action on the football pitch, as well as a younger Grant with a bounty of beautiful girls on his arm—she recognised two of them as Australian models on the rise.

Seeing photos of famous men and their trophy women made her stomach churn. It was a little too close to home.

'Did you see that?' Elise leaned in, clicking on one of the photos.

Red carpet shots from the previous year's Brownlow Medal sent shivers down Jasmine's spine. The man certainly scrubbed up well in a suit. One blonde woman came up with him repeatedly—captions identified her as Chelsea Aims, fiancée of Grant Farley.

Jasmine raised an eyebrow. This was the first she'd heard of him having a fiancée. Looking more closely at the pictures, she could see the photos featuring Chelsea were old. Grant's face showed the youthful glow of a young man in his prime. He lacked the serious, square-jawed look he now wore permanently, and he seemed lighter...happier.

When the photos of Chelsea stopped there were a few of Grant suited up with a brooding stare—much closer to the way he looked today—standing alone on the red carpet.

Elise flicked over the articles section of the search engine. There was a link to the official Jaguars website, and a few articles referencing him when the Jaguars merger had taken place. But one headline stood out in particular: Jaguars Star Grant Farley Falls from Grace.

'Oooh, what's this?' Elise clicked on the link and both girls waited with bated breath.

As a picture of a very bleary-eyed Grant appeared on the screen, Jasmine sucked in a breath. Holding his hand up in an attempt to cover his face, though doing a poor job of it, Grant appeared to be stumbling, and there was a smear of something red across his fitted white T-shirt.

Farther down there was another picture of him, looking very sombre, wearing a dark suit and an open-necked shirt. The caption read: 'Grant Farley leaves court in Melbourne after pleading not guilty to assault charges.'

The article detailed the incident: a bar fight that had ended up with two men being hospitalised. It mentioned that the assault charges had been dropped after the matter had been settled out of court, which could only be code for using his money to make his problems go away.

'That doesn't sound like him at all.'

Jasmine couldn't keep the quiver out of her voice. The article showed a person very different from the tender, passionate man she'd come to know. Sure, he was a typical football player—headstrong and iron-willed—but she couldn't imagine him beating two men to a pulp and then paying them off.

It didn't sound right. Yet she couldn't deny the heaviness that settled in the pit of her stomach like lead. Perhaps it was a good thing they had decided on a one-night-only rule. She'd already been with a man who thought he could buy his way out of anything, and he'd ended up treating her like another investment.

With the end of the football season looming, Grant was more focused than ever. This was his opportunity to put the past behind him. He'd cleaned himself up, kept off the partying and was playing the best footy of his life. As much as he hated to admit it, the ballet was doing him a world of good...and not only due to the magical touch of one very sexy ballet teacher.

The weeks since he'd slept with Jasmine had gone by in a blur. He'd missed a few lessons as the preparation for footy finals increased. It was the last week of August and they were only a month out from Grand Final. The Jaguars had been hovering around the top of the ladder for the last three rounds—not a first in the club's history but certainly a first in the past few years.

He wanted to be a part of them making the Grand Final for the first time in the past decade, and he knew it was his moment to show the team and the fans that he was a changed man. That he'd moved on from his mistakes and that he could be the player they all wanted him to be. He was so close he could taste it.

Jasmine had been distracted too. She seemed absent during their lessons but he assumed she was as focused on recovering from her injury and other ballet stuff as he was on his footy. Though it hadn't stopped him thinking about revisiting their fantasy-provoking scorcher of a night together.

Today he watched as she wrapped up her lesson with some of her older students, her beautiful face pulled into the look of concentration he now knew well. She clapped her hands together and gave a pep talk to the group.

'Well done, ladies,' he said as he entered the studio, passing the students on their way out.

One winked at him and the other women tittered amongst themselves, blushing under his praise. At one point he would have enjoyed the blatant adoration, but now his tastes seemed to run more to the snarky sting of a former ballerina with a soft, sensual centre.

'Your effect on women is sickening,' Jasmine drawled, standing with her hands on her hips.

That's more like it. His heart kicked up a notch and his lips were unable to resist a smile.

'I don't do it on purpose,' he replied, leaning against the *barre* and cocking his head to one side.

She rolled her eyes. 'Tell me you don't love it. You relish the sex-symbol status.'

Ha! She made it sound as if he was one of those vain sportsmen who supplemented their incomes by modelling jocks or something ridiculous like that. He'd even turned down a spot in a Most Eligible Bachelor competition because he hated all the attention. These days if people were paying attention to him he wanted it to be because of his footy. Nothing else.

'I'm a country boy.' He thrust a hand through his hair, his fingers pushing the strands away from his face. 'I *don't* see myself as a sex symbol.'

The words sounded weird coming from his mouth— unnatural. In his experience girls were after more than looks. What mattered were important three-letter acronyms like VIP and MVP, and *lots* of zeros on your bank statement. Looks were a bonus.

'But you are,' she replied, her tone cool. 'A quick internet search will tell you that.'

'Have you been stalking me?' He laughed. The thought of her poring over images of him online seemed ridiculous.

Never mind the fact that he'd done *exactly* the same thing. He'd trawled through photos of her dancing *en pointe* and even found a video of one of her Australian Ballet performances and watched it, enraptured.

'It's not stalking if you're looking up someone famous.'

His heart stilled. What had she been looking for? A mask of calm slipped over his face. As he'd said to her before, fame was an unfortunate by-product of his career. A necessary evil. Something he put up with because it was part of the deal.

In truth, after the paparazzi hell he'd endured as part of the court proceedings he'd be happy never to see another camera again. But life didn't work that way, and sometimes you had to slap a smile on your face even when you wanted to drop an F-bomb. Swallowing, he forced himself to relax. This was Jasmine, not some fame-hungry groupie.

'You *know* I'd prefer to play footy without the added extras.' He walked over to the *barre* and got himself ready for their warm-up. 'Although there are some perks to the celebrity aspect.'

'Like what?'

'Like the fact that I get to take dates along to fancy functions,' he said, keeping his tone even. 'You should come along to one.'

He hadn't planned on using the invitation as a test to see what her intentions were, but when she'd said she'd been looking him up online a funny feeling had settled in his stomach. He wanted so desperately for her to be the woman he'd come to know—for her to be so very different from all the women he'd been with before.

'Excuse me?' Her eyes widened.

'The Brownlow is coming up.' He leant forwards, watching her intently. 'I want you to come with me.'

Jasmine stood there, her mouth agape. He'd gone stag in the past, but it had usually ended up with the other WAGs pairing him with one of their friends/sisters/cousins. They were seldom good company and *always* in it for the chance to get their picture in the papers. Taking Jasmine would mean having a shield against those annoying matchmaking offers, *and* he'd have the pleasure of seeing her dressed up to the nines. Something told him that she'd outshine every other woman there by a mile.

Yeah, he wanted this firecracker with her smart mouth and gorgeous smile by his side all night. He could only hope that she'd want to be by his side for the person he was—not for the other reasons people usually gravitated towards him.

'I don't think so.' She shook her head, her dark brows pulling together. 'I'm not the red-carpet type.'

He stepped forwards, closing the space between them. 'It's all very glamorous.'

Mixed emotions churned in his gut. On one hand the fact that she hadn't jumped at the invitation meant she wasn't after the limelight. On the other hand he hadn't expected her to decline his invitation flat-out.

Wasn't it every girl's dream to frock up and walk down a red carpet? He'd even called in a favour with an old acquaintance who was a designer. The gown was wrapped up in a huge box hidden in his linen closet with a note he'd written himself. *That* was a first—notes and cards and gifts were way out of his MO.

Usually the girl would ask for something before he'd even had the chance to offer. Perhaps Jasmine *was* perfect for him. He frowned to himself.

'Why don't you take someone from your family?'

Her voice brought him back to the present.

'I want *you*.'

She drew her lower lip between her teeth. She could block him out with a lowering of her thick dark lashes if she liked, but he'd seen the heat that flared bright and brilliant. He'd seen the black of her pupils expand at his words *I want you*.

'Jasmine, I could take anyone. I bet if I asked any of the teachers from this ballet school they would come with me at the drop of a hat—Elise included.'

She frowned. 'Your point?'

'I don't want anyone else.' He brushed his hand down the length of her arm, sucking in a breath at the way goosebumps rippled along her skin at his touch. 'I want you to come with me. I plan to win, and when I do I want you to help me celebrate. Think about it.'

'Fine.' She smiled stiffly, the curve of her lips a mismatch with the guarded expression in her eyes.

She crossed her arms on her chest, guarding herself. Something was amiss. What was going on with Jasmine Bell?

CHAPTER ELEVEN

JASMINE WAS STUNNED, he'd asked her—no, *told* her—she should be his date to the Brownlow. This wasn't in line with their one-night-only rule, and frankly the idea of having cameras shoved in her face while they posed on the red carpet turned her stomach. The Brownlow was the biggest off-field football event of the year, and even as a complete sports dunce she was well aware of the event's prestige.

Did he want her as arm candy? She'd been there, done that. Having Kyle parade her around like a piece of designer luggage had been bad enough, but at least back then there had been something in it for her—a chance to further her career. Now Grant wanted her to do the same thing. Why? Surely he had his pick of the pretty young things who normally attended those events. They were the type of girls who craved attention, with their hair extensions and fake tans, the ones happy to have their photo taken.

Girls *not* like her.

There was no way she'd accept his offer. She'd figure out a way to let him down gently, and until then she'd keep it one hundred per cent professional between them. There had been a tiny part of her that had entertained the idea of seeing Grant again, but his world was too different from hers. It had all the hallmarks of what she'd hated about her former life.

They stood at the *barre,* their bodies close as they

worked through the warm-up. Jasmine had been keeping her distance from Grant, yet every time she was near him her body rebelled. The tips of her fingers tingled with the need to touch, to explore. Her blood pulsed harder when he was around, and her heart fluttered at the mere signal of his presence.

But she knew it was the wrong path for her. She'd promised herself when she left the Australian Ballet that her days of being someone else's puppet were over. She wasn't sure what it was that incited men to try to control her, tell her what to do. That was why it was easier to stay away.

Then she could speak for herself. She could be her own person. Unfortunately it also meant she couldn't be a part of Grant's world.

'I read an interesting article about you,' she said.

'There's a lot of stuff on the internet.' He shrugged.

She could tell that beneath the blasé gesture he was hiding his true emotions and immediately jumping on the defensive. The relaxed stance didn't match the hard set of his jaw, nor the acute focus of his light blue eyes.

'Was it anything of particular interest?' he asked.

She paused for a second. Why was she even bringing this up? She knew that the majority of news relating to famous people was pure fiction. Did she believe that Grant was the person the gossip site had made him out to be?

No, she didn't believe it. But something deep within her compelled her to find out the truth. She *had* to know. Perhaps if she had another reason to push him away she'd be able to keep her distance. Lord knew she needed help in that department.

'The one about you paying off those guys you got in a fight with.' She knew the moment she saw him stiffen that she'd hit a sore spot.

'Excuse me?'

'I saw the pictures of you leaving court...'

Fire blazed in his eyes and she thought for a moment that he might scream at her. But his voice came out deadly calm.

'And?'

'I want to know your side of the story.'

He raked a hand through his hair and stared through her. He had asked so many questions of her, pressed her about her dancing. Didn't she deserve to know him too?

The studio was so silent she could hear the cars driving on the rain-slicked road outside.

'Why?'

'Do I need a reason? I don't believe the things they said—'

'I paid them off.' The words were sharper than a blade. 'I did it.'

She shook her head. 'There's more to it than that.'

'How would you know?' He seemed to sneer at her, his features fixed into a frightening mask of calm.

'Because I know you, Grant. You're not like that.'

His Adam's apple bobbed in his throat as he choked the words out. 'I did it.'

'You hit them?'

'No.' The mask was slipping, cracks showing through to the vulnerability he'd no doubt become accustomed to hiding. 'I was too drunk out of my mind to even get past the first swing in that fight.'

'I knew it.'

'But I did pay them.'

'Why did you pay them if you didn't hit them?' She shook her head. 'That doesn't make sense.'

'Because the club wanted it to go away as quickly as possible. We couldn't take the bad press —not when we'd struggled through the past few years. We were losing sponsors...'

Jasmine's stomach pitched from side to side.

He continued. 'They'd rather let me appear to be the guilty party than risk damage to the club. There's a good chance I would have been cleared, based on the witness accounts and footage from the pub security cameras, but they didn't want to risk the media crawling all over us during the court case if it dragged on.'

He glowered at her, his mouth pulled tight into a line. Had she pushed too far? No, she deserved to know. They were friends...sort of.

'I'm not perfect—far from it. But I'm not violent.'

'I know.'

'Then why did you ask?' His expression softened, the defences slipping from him as his body relaxed.

'I wanted to hear the truth. I wanted to...get to know you.' She bit down on her lip, confused by the emotions running around in her.

'You *do* know me.' He uncrossed his arms.

'Not really,' she said. 'I know *about* you, but you seem to do all the asking when we're together. I feel like you know me but I don't know you. I wanted to know the real you.'

'Fame is hard work,' he said with a sad smile. 'It makes you wary of anyone asking questions. I guess I've become a little more defensive than I realised.'

'I can understand that.'

'I imagine it's the same with ballet,' he said, taking a step towards her. 'Didn't you want to dance and forget about everything else?'

'Yeah.' She nodded.

Her whole body tingled with awareness as he closed the gap between them. On their first ballet lesson she'd seen a beef-head football player who thought he was a god. Now she saw a complex, intelligent, misunderstood man. No god, just a man.

'I was a simple kid from the country who loved playing footy.'

'You were dazzled by the big smoke?'

'Damn straight.' He reached for her, his large hand wrapping around her smaller one. 'I was dazzled by all the beautiful girls.'

'You're full of it,' she whispered.

Energy crackled between them. The rest of the world fell away as he pulled her to him.

'I left my family behind. I left a quiet, dull life full of expectation and burden. Everything here was exciting and I was like a kid in a candy store.'

'And you ate too much candy.' She could feel it. The ease with which he'd been swept up by his success was believable and forgivable.

'I gorged myself on it until I was sick.' He brought his lips down to hers, cupping her face in his hands. 'And speaking of things I want to gorge myself on...'

She blew out a breath, knowing exactly where he was going. What she didn't know was if she could stop it.

'Are you reconsidering your one-night rule?' Grant asked, nuzzling her neck. 'You're looking at me like I'm dinner.'

'You're quite sure of yourself, aren't you?' Jasmine tilted her chin up at him, studying his features. There was something utterly disarming about him. The combination of his strong jaw and the slightly crooked, freckle-smattered nose enchanted her.

His voice was low, predatory. 'I'm not asking you to stop.'

In one swift movement Grant had pulled Jasmine to him and pressed her up against the *barre,* his hands gripping the wooden rail on either side of her hips so that she was trapped. He pressed urgently against her, and she arched to him with equal candour. She ran her hands up the sides of his thighs, skimming the tight curve of his behind until her hands reached his back.

'You're getting there...' she said, her voice catching. With each second that passed Jasmine's resistance was falling harder.

'I want you to wrap those incredibly flexible legs around me so I can make you scream.' His eyes were hooded, his voice coarse with lust. 'Again.'

Before he could say anything else she pressed up against him, her mouth hungry for more. Grant's arms wrapped around her, encircling her waist as he lifted her up so that she could wrap herself around him. Grant carried her weight seemingly without effort as she pressed against him, her breasts hard against his chest.

'Not here,' she whispered.

Jasmine fidgeted in the car, her hands unwilling to be still as Grant drove them back to his apartment. She was out of control. The fearful voice inside her told her she was crazy. She didn't *do* reckless, and this was pretty damn reckless.

There were rules and boundaries that she needed to adhere to. Jasmine liked those things. There was a reason she loved ballet enough to make it her life. Ballet was all about rules, about precision. These things made her comfortable. But this...this was something else entirely.

Her 'one night only' was turning into a spontaneous night number two, and she was powerless to stop it.

'Penny for your thoughts, Miss Bell?' Grant's voice was teasing, and he watched her as he held the car straight along the freeway.

'Not a penny's worth.' She sank down lower in the comfy leather seat. 'I'm just admiring the view.'

The city was drawing closer. The ethereal orange glow that encompassed the tall buildings of Melbourne's CBD grew nearer with each minute. Jasmine loved the city. The lights had fascinated her as a child—she'd always wondered how something could exist for so long without ever sleeping.

'The view will get a lot better than this.' His eyes raked her slouched form. 'I promise.'

'Are you always so smooth with the ladies?' Jasmine propped herself up on one arm and watched him as he laughed, the sound rumbling deep within him. It curled her insides.

'Hardly.' His lips turned up into a sardonic smile. 'The sad fact is footy players don't need to be much of anything to have the girls lined up.'

Jasmine screwed up her nose at him. The thought of a gaggle of screaming girls surrounding Grant made her stomach churn. 'So you've become lazy?'

'I haven't become anything,' he said, frowning at her insinuation. 'Those girls aren't my style. I like 'em feisty... like you.'

'Flattery won't get you anywhere.' She gave his arm a playful shove.

'Correct me if I'm wrong, but I've already got somewhere.' His eyes glinted in the reflection of the streetlights. 'You are in my car, on your way to my apartment, are you not?'

'Details...' She waved her hand, dismissing his argument.

'Have you thought any more about the dancing thing?'

'No,' she lied. She'd been thinking about it constantly... or rather trying *not* to think about it constantly.

'I asked you to promise me that you wouldn't stop trying.'

'I remember you asking, but I don't remember making such a promise.'

Grant pulled the car into the parking lot and killed the engine. 'I'd give anything to see you back up on a stage.'

'Why?' She unbuckled her seatbelt and turned to him.

'Because you're magnificent.' He leant over and crushed his mouth to hers.

He tasted faintly of mint and the scent of him invaded her nostrils, making her dizzy with lust. If he kept kissing her like that she might promise him anything.

They walked hand in hand to the building entrance and Jasmine marvelled at how luxurious it was inside. Her attention was diverted from him momentarily as they stepped into the Art Deco elevator, but he didn't give her long to marvel at the stylish design before he pulled her to him.

As the reflection of their embrace filled the ornate floor-to-ceiling mirrors she rested her body against the hard wall of his chest, enjoying the way he immediately curled his arms around her. His hands rested against her behind, pressing her against him so that she could feel his erection straining between them. She slipped her hand down to cup the bulge in his pants, enjoying the unrestrained groan that escaped his lips as she massaged him.

'Straight to business?'

'Yep.' She sucked at the curve of his neck. 'I find it stops you from asking questions.'

'Suits me fine.' He wound his hand through the length of her ponytail and gave a gentle tug, pulling her face up towards him. He landed a possessive kiss on her lips and she melted under him.

The elevator doors slid silently open. The hallway was empty. Tasteful watercolour paintings dotted the pale walls and grey carpet was soft underfoot. Their steps quickened with anticipation and heat shot through her arm where his hand wound tightly around hers, his fingers interlaced with her own.

Grant opened the door to his apartment and held it aside. She brushed past him, allowing her fingers to graze his hardness. A shiver ran down her spine; anticipation and excitement pooled in her belly.

The apartment was stark, a bachelor pad, with a large flat-screen TV as the focal point rather than the stunning view that filled the mammoth windows running the length of the room. The city lights dazzled against an inky winter sky and she lost her breath.

Grant took her hand again. 'It's better from the balcony.'

As he pushed open the sliding door the chilly air enveloped them. Jasmine stood against the railing, her hands gripping the bar tightly at her waist, and leaned over to look down on the city below. Noise from the remnants of city traffic, from people going about their evening and from the dinging of passing trams floated up to them. The scent of rain hung in the air. Grant stood behind her, pressing her against the protective balustrade, his lips on her neck.

'It's amazing,' she breathed, arching back against him. Her neck burned where he brushed his lips against the sensitive skin there. 'You're so lucky.'

'I am now.'

He squeezed, his hand trailing down her stomach until it brushed against the juncture of her thighs. She murmured as his hands slipped between her legs and stroked her heat. She was still in her leotard and tights with only a thick woollen coat to protect her from the cold. The thin fabric of the leotard provided little resistance to his hand, and she quivered as his fingers increased their pressure.

Turning around, Jasmine parted her legs so that Grant could press himself between them. She tilted her head back, enjoying the chilly rush of air across her face while her body burned beneath her coat. Feeling more than a little daring, she felt for his waistband and pulled down his pants, exposing his hardness to the night air.

She lapped up the surprise in Grant's eyes as she slid

down to a kneeling position in front of him and pressed her lips gently to the tip of him. He gripped the railing of the balustrade above her head.

Jasmine parted her lips and wrapped them around the head of his cock, sucking gently at first. He tasted salty. She brushed her tongue against his length, feeling him tremble against her. She slid him slowly out and then back in again, hearing him groan from above her as one hand clasped the back of her head.

'If you keep that up—' he warned, his voice strangled.

She drew back and looked up at him. His hand brushed her cheekbone as she stood in front of him. 'Then take me inside.'

They stumbled through the door into the living room and Grant tugged her along into his bedroom. A huge king-size bed dominated the room, covered in a simple navy bedspread that looked soft as a cloud.

There were no personal photos on the walls—nothing that gave away any clues about anyone in his life. She recalled him saying his relationship with his family was strained, but she hadn't expected to find an apartment devoid of *any* personal photos. The room was simply furnished and utilitarian. Only one picture hung on the wall—a large signed photograph of a football player that looked as though it might be from the seventies. She removed her coat and draped it over the back of a tub chair.

'Enough looking around.' Grant sat on the bed and drew her to him so that she was standing between his legs. He'd kicked off his pants and was sitting in his jumper. Reaching down, she pulled his jumper and T-shirt off with a single smooth movement.

'I'm looking at you now,' she whispered, climbing onto his lap so that she faced him with her legs straddling his waist.

Grant pulled down one of the straps on her leotard,

baring a small breast. His lips took in the sensitive bud of her nipple, causing a wave of pleasure to rush through her. Heat throbbed incessantly as his tongue flickered against her. A long drawn-out moan came out of her lips as her head lolled backwards.

He pulled on the other strap of her leotard and helped her arms out before he continued his attention to her breasts. Pushing away from him, Jasmine peeled off the leotard and let it drop to the floor around her ankles. Her tights and underwear followed, leaving a pool of nylon and cotton at her feet.

Grant ran his hands up the flat plane of Jasmine's stomach until they rested on her breasts. His fingers honed in on her erect nipples, rolling the rosy buds between his thumbs and forefingers, wringing a sharp cry of pleasure from her. Beneath his hands the worries of her world slipped away, her fears about her future, the pain of her loss...gone.

One hand came to dance over the smooth patch between her thighs, his fingers teasing apart the slick folds of flesh to find the tight bundle of nerves at her centre. Jasmine clenched tightly as his thumb found her and started its slow assault on her senses. She spasmed as waves of intense pleasure rolled over her until she reached breaking point. Orgasm shattered through her and light flared behind her shuttered eyes, her cries echoing off the walls of Grant's bedroom.

Spent, she collapsed against him and pressed a kiss to his cheek, feeling the roughness of his stubble against her tender lips. She felt safer than she had in a long time—as though the enclosure of his arms could protect her from the world.

CHAPTER TWELVE

SOME TIME LATER they lay tangled in the sheets of his bed, limbless with satisfaction and exhausted. Sex with Jasmine put to shame any of the workouts in his training regime. Grant took pride in the fact that she was limp and murmuring incoherent pleasure sounds against the crook of his neck. He'd be happy to listen to that sound for the rest of his life.

He rolled the thought around in his head. The rest of his life was a long time, considering he was generally fed up with someone after twenty-four hours. To go from a day to forever seemed…crazy. But the more time he spent with Jasmine the more he wanted. She'd become part of his life without him realising it, and going without her would be like going without air or food or any other life-giving necessity.

When had it happened?

'Grant?' His name was stretched out, half yawn, half groan. 'Am I dead?'

'Why do I feel like this is the start of a cheesy pick-up line?'

'It's a little too late for that, don't you think?' She laughed and stretched her legs out.

'Especially considering we broke the one-night-only rule,' he pointed out.

She traced her fingertip over his shoulder, outlining

the curves of his tattoo. 'That rule was put in place so no one got hurt. Therefore, if we don't hurt one another we should be OK.'

'Sounds good in theory.'

'And in practice?' She stilled beside him, her face tilted up.

'I'd like it to work in practice too.'

Like most things that sounded good in theory, reality was a little more complicated. But that didn't stop him wanting—for the first time in years—to see where reality could take them.

She reached up and pulled his face to her, kissing the corners of his lips, the tip of his nose. 'Sounds good to me.'

'So you'll come to the Brownlow with me, then?'

And just like that the post-sex glow was sucked out of the air. Jasmine's body tensed, her hand withdrawing from his face.

'I *said* I'd think about it.'

'What is there to think about?'

It figured that the one time he opened himself up he chose a woman who didn't want anything to do with his lifestyle. After a decade of people using him it was both a shock and a relief.

'Unless that's your way of stalling before you say no?' he added.

She sighed. 'I can't come to the Brownlow with you.'

'Why?'

'Do I need a reason?' She sat up on the bed and turned away from him.

'Call me curious.'

'I don't do the whole gala thing.' She raked her hands through her hair, twisting it and feeling around on the bed until she located her hair tie. 'I had to put up with it when I was with the Australian Ballet. Now I have a choice I choose *not* go to those things.'

'Sounds like there's some history behind that.'

'This is not a couch and I'm *not* your patient.' She tied her hair up and turned back to him, crossing her legs under her. 'You're a frustrated psychologist.'

'I'm observant,' he corrected. 'Not that I need to be…'

'Excuse me?'

'Anyone would be able to read you, Jasmine.'

'What's that supposed to mean?'

'You're an open book.' He reached out to place a hand on her knee. 'You might think you're good at hiding your emotions, but you're not.'

She pursed her lips. 'And?'

'I would rather have you on my arm than any of those other girls.' He sighed. 'You're not like them. That's what I like about you.'

'Really?' Her face softened and she traced the back of his hand with one delicate fingertip.

The sensation sent a ripple of awareness through him, though how his body could stir to life after what they'd done tonight was a complete mystery.

'I've been with those women before. I was engaged to one of them before she decided that I wasn't high enough up the food chain.' He swallowed the memories. That had been a long time ago and he was a different person now. 'I drank and partied myself into a hole, and I've been clawing my way out for twelve months. Something in my gut told me you were different.'

'I *am* different.' She lowered her eyes to her hands, wrapped into a neat ball in her lap. 'I'm *too* different—that's the problem.'

'That's crazy.'

'Is it? You said yourself I was nothing like the girls on the scene.' She paused. 'A life in the spotlight isn't what I want. My ex loved it—he dragged me to party after party so he could show me off. But that's all he wanted. It was never about me.'

'He was an idiot.'

'Yeah, he was.' She traced her fingertip over the pattern on the bed. 'But it put me off that kind of life. I don't want the whole world scrutinising me. I promised myself I wouldn't put myself in that position again. You understand that's why this can't be anything more than casual?'

Her face implored him and he wanted nothing more than to hold her until the past melted away. His chest ached. Could he offer her a life without public scrutiny? It seemed impossible, but something deep inside told him not to let her go. Maybe he could find a way to make it work. If he could keep her close until he built up enough trust, maybe then he could show her that he was different too. That he didn't want to show her off like some possession.

Even thinking the word made his blood boil. What he felt for Jasmine had nothing to do with possession. It was deeper than that. It was basic, fundamental.

'Fine.' He sighed and held his hands out, and when she took them he tugged her forwards so that she crawled onto him. 'Let's stick to what we have in common for the moment.'

'Deal.'

He would change her mind—he had no doubt about it.

Jasmine woke the next morning when the sunlight peeked through the wooden blinds on his window. Pale light filtered through the slats, indicating a rare showing of sun that was uncharacteristic for winter.

She was curled up on her side, Grant's body wrapped protectively around her. The hardness of his thighs pressed under hers, the hairs tickling her skin. One arm was slung over her midsection, heavy and comforting. As the haze of sleep cleared her vision she looked around the room.

She'd never seen a more impersonal sight in her life. It was far neater and more organised than she'd expected, but the distinct lack of personal effects was startling. A memory flickered in Jasmine's mind—something Grant had said last night before they'd argued about her going to the Brownlow with him. He'd once told her that his family life was strained. She'd thought nothing of it at the time—didn't everyone have a little strain in their family life? But she couldn't recall a single instance when he'd mentioned another person other than his coach and his ex-fiancée.

Then there was the lack of photos in his house, and he'd never taken a phone call or a text during their time together. Surely it wasn't possible that someone who was a household name had not a single person to call his friend?

She rolled over, watching as he stirred into wakefulness. A sleepy smile passed over his lips as he blinked, the lure of slumber pulling his eyes closed.

'Good morning.'

'*Very* good morning,' he replied, ducking a hand under the sheets and finding her naked breast.

'You're an animal.' She laughed, swatting away his hand and shrieking when he rolled on top of her.

'I prefer finely tuned athletic machine.'

His grin all but melted her bones, and she could feel him growing excited again.

'Can I be the one to propose coffee this time?' she asked.

'Don't think I'm going to forget about this.' He pushed up, giving her space to wriggle out of the bed. 'I'm dragging you back in here after breakfast.'

'Deal.'

Though her limbs were aching, and the memory of his touch still burned brightly, the thought of coming back to bed with Grant was no less thrilling. She looked around for something to wear. Her leotard and tights were still in a pile where she'd stripped them off last night.

'Here.' He pulled a T-shirt from his drawer and tossed it to her.

Grateful, she slipped the fresh cotton over her head. The hem skimmed the underside of her bottom and the fabric swam around her.

'Now, *that's* a sight to wake up to.'

They wandered out to the lounge room and Jasmine made herself at home on a bar stool while Grant fired up his coffee machine. The scent of freshly brewed coffee filled the apartment, combined with his scent on her skin and the clean cotton of his T-shirt. She was in heaven. Cosy, new relationship heaven.

She frowned. This was *supposed* to be casual. She'd been the one to label it such last night... It felt anything but casual. Could she possibly trust him to see if there was anything more between them? Anything deeper?

Blowing a stray stand of hair out of her eyes, Jasmine pushed the confusing questions from her mind and watched as he moved effortlessly around the kitchen. He made the coffee on a big, fancy machine that had probably cost more than she'd be able to spend on a car.

'So you could afford the swanky apartment but not a decorator?' she asked, accepting a coffee cup and blowing on the steam.

'Ouch.' Grant chuckled. 'You sure know how to hurt a guy's feelings.'

'I only ask because it's so plain. No photos or anything.'

'I have a fruit bowl.' Grant gestured lamely to the single apple that looked lost in the giant metal bowl. 'I don't have any pictures to put up.'

'None at all? No family pictures? None of you goofing around with mates at footy training?'

'I'm a bit camera-shy.' He shrugged.

His face was expressionless but she'd learned to watch out for the tell-tale tightening of his shoulders. He gripped his coffee mug a little too tightly.

'That's sad.'

Silence descended on the kitchen.

'The papers do their best to take lots of photos. I don't need to do it as well.' He took a gulp of his black coffee. 'I get a bit sick of being in the spotlight, to be honest.'

A sad smile played across her lips. 'I don't think I'd ever get sick of the sound of an audience applauding.'

'An audience applauding and the paparazzi harassing you while you're trying to have a night out are two different things.'

'Aren't your family upset when they come here and see you've got no photos of them up?' It was a loaded question, but she couldn't keep herself from wanting to confirm her suspicions.

'Like I said before, our relationship is a bit strained.' He shrugged. 'They've never been here.'

'Never?'

'No.' He shook his head and attempted a smile, but emotion flickered close to the surface. 'My family lives a long way away. It's too far for them to visit.'

'Do you go and visit them?'

'What's with the *Dr Phil* act?' He pushed a few buttons on the coffee machine and filled up another cup.

'I figured since you're so interested in my future with dancing that maybe I could help *you* with something.'

'You have helped me with something.' He blew on the steam curling from his cup. 'My hamstring is in the best shape it's ever been, thanks to you. I might finish the season without injuring it again.'

A satisfied smile curved Jasmine's lips. 'Good. So the next thing you need to work on is the family stuff.'

He didn't need to respond—the guilt on his face was

response enough. She wasn't exactly the best person to offer advice on this kind of thing—she hadn't seen her folks in a while either, but she was planning on mending that, along with making another visit to her physio to see if her ankle had made any progress.

Still, she wrote emails and called her parents once a week, and they knew better than to ask about her injuries. It would take time for her guilt to ease, but at least she was on the right path. Grant, however, was a different story. Her heart clenched for him.

This can't just be casual sex...not with feelings like this.

'Jasmine, I...' He trailed off, looking down to his coffee cup.

'You should call them some time, before it's too late.'

'I wish it were that simple.'

'Isn't it?' They couldn't possibly blame him for what had happened with the court case. 'Surely they know you didn't hit those men?'

'It's not about that.' He shook his head, his eyes focused away from her.

'Talk to me, Grant.'

He hesitated. 'I had a huge fight with them when I left to come to Melbourne to play footy. I never managed to fix it.'

'What was the fight about?'

She waited, biting back the urge to say anything else. It was a trick she'd learned a long time ago: the less you said the more others would want to fill the silence.

'Well, my father wasn't exactly supportive of my decision. He'd always thought I'd go into the family farming and veterinary business. I had the brains to do it but I just wasn't passionate about it.'

'That's fair enough.'

'Not in his eyes.' Grant sighed. 'Mum was always the supportive one—the buffer between Dad and me. After she died and I decided to give footy a go…it all fell apart. He said that I had a choice. I could choose football or my family, but I couldn't have both. My sister was left to pick up the pieces. She gave up her dreams of being a model to stay with Dad and help out with the business. I think she's always blamed me for it.'

'That's not fair.'

'No, it's not.' He shook his head, playing with his coffee cup.

'Did you ever try to make amends after you moved here?'

'Yeah, things were getting better at one stage. I'd reached out to Annabel and she was starting to come around. We were close growing up and she missed me. She'd even started working on Dad—we spoke a few times when he picked up the phone at their office.'

She sensed the 'but' before he had a chance to say it.

'But then everything turned to crap after I started drinking again and those charges made the news. He said I'd dragged the family name through the mud, that I was a bad egg and a poor example to my nephew. Even Annabel turned her back on me. She said she didn't want her son growing up to be like me. She said I'd hurt Dad too many times for her to forgive me.'

When he didn't continue she asked, 'And that was it?'

'Yep. Haven't heard from them in over six months.' He drained his espresso and set the cup down on the bench with a loud clink. 'Country men don't do so well with sharing their feelings.'

'You seem to be doing a good job.'

He gave her a rueful smile. 'I guess that's what happens when you've bottled things up for so long. It has to come out some time.'

'Then maybe your father is feeling exactly the same way,' she pointed out. 'Have you tried calling them?'

'They made it clear they want nothing to do with me.'

The pinch of his brows and the faraway look in his eyes almost broke her in two. His hands were white-knuckled on the edge of the breakfast bar, and there was a slight shake in his grip.

'You should try, Grant. What if something were to happen?'

'I *said* they don't want anything to do with me.'

Jasmine leant over the breakfast bar, almost knocking her coffee over in the process, so she could plant a kiss right on Grant's lips. Somehow she thought it might actually be possible to kiss his problems away.

He met her hungrily, his teeth nipping at her lips as she braced herself against the countertop.

'I'm going to stop this now.' He eased her back gently. 'Otherwise I won't have the will power to leave and get us breakfast.'

'Be quick.' She slid back onto the bar stool. 'Actually, I would love to take a shower.'

'Towels are in the cupboard by my bedroom.' He came around the side of the bench and planted a kiss on her forehead. 'I won't be long.'

When he left the apartment she was engulfed by the silence. What was she *doing?* The whole thing with Grant had spiralled so quickly out of control and now she was here, in his place, feeling far too much as if she wanted to hang around, knowing far too much about who he was. She was thinking things she had no right to be thinking... feeling things she had no right to be feeling...things that indicated something more than what they'd agreed upon.

Abandoning her coffee cup, Jasmine went in search of towels. She found the linen closet in the hallway, where Grant has said it would be. The shelves were stacked with all manner of football equipment—guernseys, footy boots—and there was a single shelf dedicated to towels.

A gold box sat on the lowest shelf, its ribbon sparkling and drawing her eye. Curious, she bent down and slid it from the shelf, her breath catching in her throat when she saw her name in his handwriting. It was light, and the packaging was free of any branding. The box itself was smooth and expensive-looking, with large gold swirls embossed on the thick cardboard.

A small card was tucked into a fold of the ribbon. It read simply: 'Jasmine, come to the Brownlow with me. Grant.' She slipped the lid off and placed it next to her. Inside there was something wrapped in fine apricot tissue paper.

It was a dress—possibly the most divine dress Jasmine had ever seen off a mannequin. She lifted it up, treating it as though it were made of delicate crystal.

It was long—floor-sweepingly long—and made of pale pink silk the exact colour of ballet shoes. The neckline was intricate—a refined tangle of plaited silk and tulle strands embroidered with tiny seed pearls.

For a moment she couldn't breathe. It looked as though a designer had deconstructed a tutu and turned it into an elegant gown. The body itself was plain, simplistic, but the attention to detail in the neckline elevated it to a piece of art.

It was so perfectly *her*.

Jasmine's head pounded. She hadn't even said yes and he'd bought her a dress, given his written command. *Come to the Brownlow with me.*

It was an instruction, not an invitation. There was no question—as though he assumed she could not possibly refuse him. Her cheeks heated as she placed the gown back in the box, folding the tissue paper gently over it, tucking the card neatly back in its place.

She carried the box to the kitchen table, her hands shaking. This was precisely why they couldn't be together—he couldn't take no for an answer. While she was sure his intentions to take her to the Brownlow were good, the fact that he couldn't accept her refusal was *not*.

Whatever this thing was between them, it had to stop. She'd promised herself long ago that she wouldn't be anyone's arm candy. She was done with that. Memories of her accident came flooding back. Her gown had been beautiful that night too. They'd had to cut it from her, and the bloodied silk had ended up in a trash can as a sickening symbol of the life she'd ruined.

She looked around the apartment, her stomach somersaulting as she decided what to do. She knew her feelings for Grant had grown, but it wasn't enough to make her backflip on her promise to herself. If she said yes this time who knew where it would end? It had started out the same way with Kyle, and a little persistence and persuasion had ended with her being a living, breathing trophy.

Grabbing the envelope with her name on it, she flipped it over and borrowed a pen from the kitchen bench. Scrawling a note to Grant, she fought back the rise of bile in her throat. She couldn't go on pretending they had something when she wanted nothing to do with such a large part of his life...the *largest* part of his life.

She had to end it before it had even started.

CHAPTER THIRTEEN

GRANT ROLLED HIS shoulders back and stretched his arms out in front of him. He stood outside the ballet studio, mixed emotions flowing through him hot and fast. The thought of seeing Jasmine was setting him on edge, and he fought the urge to turn around and leave her behind.

He'd raged when he'd come back to find a note telling him she didn't want the dress and she didn't want him. The rejection had stung—not only because he'd thought there was something between them, but because she'd left him in *exactly* the same way as his ex-fiancée.

She had fled by leaving him a note. A goddam *note*. She hadn't even had the guts to say it to his face. Heat flared within him, his fists clenching by his sides. He had to do it—he had to know if this was really the end.

He marched into the ballet studio, channelling all his energy into driving him forwards. This was it. If he couldn't resolve things with Jasmine he was going to swear off women for ever.

The building was deserted, and she was packing her bag in the front room. At the sound of his unceremonious entrance she snapped her head up, eyes opening wide. She sucked in a breath.

'You weren't going to wait for our lesson?' he asked, gesturing to her packed bag.

'I didn't think you'd be coming.' Her voice was steady

but she looked poised to make a break for it—like a spring forced down, ready to release at any second.

'I can't leave things with a note.' He sat down on the couch and folded his hands in front of him. 'I need an explanation.'

'I don't have to explain anything.'

'No, you don't. But tell me you don't think I *deserve* an explanation.'

Silence. She assessed him, her eyes roaming up and down as though she expected him to lash out at her. He didn't want to think about her being so badly treated she couldn't even have a conversation without expecting the worst.

'I promised myself that I wouldn't let another man own me, and I'm sticking to it.' Her face was full of false bravado. 'Now, will you leave me alone?'

'Only if you tell me what the deal-breaker was.'

'You wanted to parade me around at some stupid footy function and when I said I'd think about it you took that as a sign to give me a dress that probably cost more than my entire savings. You can't buy me.'

'I wasn't trying to buy you.' Her accusation settled in his gut. He was *not* that kind of guy.

'Then explain the dress.'

'I wanted you to be my date to the Brownlow. It's one of the most important events in my career and I wanted you by my side.' He couldn't help the wave of emotion that rose within him. He threw his hands up in the air. 'God, so many women would kill to be in your shoes right now.'

He knew it was the wrong thing to say as soon as the words left his mouth.

'Listen to you,' she said, getting to her feet and planting her hands on her hips. 'I'm not *so many women,* Grant. I'm me. And I don't want to go to the Brownlow or any other stupid event. No dress will make me change my mind, and if you can't understand that then I guess it's a good thing we didn't try to make it work between us. Why don't you just take someone else?'

'Judging by the look on your face, I'm going to assume you don't mean that.'

Her brows were pinched, her lips were drawn into a flat line and her skin was lacking its usual lustre.

'I do mean it. This thing—whatever it is—it's over.'

'How can you be such a coward?'

The words scythed through her with an intensity that almost made Jasmine lose her legs. She couldn't believe that he'd arrived here demanding an explanation and then had the audacity to call her names when she didn't comply. It was *exactly* the reason they shouldn't be together. Why, then, did she want to curl up into a ball and cry?

'Coward?' She jabbed a finger in Grant's direction, cheeks aflame and eyes unblinking. 'You have absolutely no right to come here and call me a coward. *You* are the one who can't get up the guts to reconcile things with your father and you call *me* a coward?'

'You don't want to bring my family into this.'

She wondered for a second if his eyes might actually set her ablaze. They were almost electric with fury, but his voice was icy and calm. He rose slowly from the couch, his sheer size dwarfing her by comparison.

'But I do, Grant.' She stuck her chin out. 'You come here to my place of work and call me a coward. Were you expecting me to accept that? You're so goddamn stubborn that you can't even see past your own pain to what really matters. Call your father. You've hurt him as much as he's hurt you. You'd see that if you stopped focusing on yourself for a few seconds.'

She'd hit a nerve. His lips pressed together and he pulled his shoulders back, but she couldn't miss the hurt simmering close to the surface. She wanted to grab his shoulders and shake him until he could see what he was throwing away.

A little voice hinted that she might be doing exactly the same thing, but she pushed it aside.

'That's none of your business,' he said.

'Just like my reason for not wanting to go to the Brownlow is none of yours.'

'You're putting me in the same box as your ex, and I'm not like him. You know that.'

Grant stepped forwards, sending Jasmine's nerves on high alert.

'I'm not trying to use you. I'm not trying to parade you around. I just want to be with you and I know you want to be with me.'

'You want to be with me on *your* terms.' She stepped back, desperate to put distance between them because she could feel herself breaking. 'And that's not good enough for me. I won't change myself to suit you.'

'I'm not asking you to change. I'm asking you to trust me.'

'You're *telling* me.'

His voice was deep and low, his disbelief palpable in the air between them. 'How can you be so frightened of giving us a chance?'

'Because I know what happens when I go against my better judgement.'

As soon as she said it she felt regret seep through her like a poison. Her heart hammered out of control. What had she done?

The barriers shot up around him so quickly Jasmine felt as though a door had been slammed shut in her face. He was slipping away and she was letting it happen.

His nostrils flared as he drew a long, deep breath. 'And being with me is going against your better judgement, is it?'

'Yes.' It was a whisper so powerful it sliced right through the thick, heady air between them.

'Then you're right. There is nothing between us.'

Hearing the words from his mouth was even more painful than hearing them in her own head. Somehow when he said it was over it suddenly felt real. *Over before it had even started...*

'I know I'm right.'

The lie tasted sour in her mouth. She'd never been so uncertain of a decision in her entire life. Her head was pushing her to run, but her heart was already crying out at the loss of him. He was dangerous—she'd known that from the outset—only now she realised just how much he had the ability to split her in two.

The echo of the door slamming behind him seemed to stretch on for ever. Jasmine sat on the ground, wondering if she'd just made the biggest mistake of her life.

Spring had dissolved the chill from the air and there was even a little sunshine peeking through the clouds. The Grand Final was looming and with each passing week the Jaguars inched closer to success.

Painful as it was, Grant put Jasmine out of his mind. it was necessary for both their sakes. Still, her parting words had affected him more than he'd ever admit.

Her swipe about him being too cowardly to make up with his father had caused many a sleepless night, and he'd thought long and hard about his family. About the way he'd grown up, the way he'd been treated, and the way he'd treated his father and sister. He could go on clinging to the bad memories as an excuse not to see them. He could use his father's lack of communication as a shield. Or he could make the first steps in putting it all behind him. His relationship with his father would take work, but it would be worth the effort. He could see that now.

Despite the fact that Grant had not been able to convince Jasmine to give their relationship a chance, he still
owed her a lot. Talking to her had lifted a great weight
from his shoulders and her comments on his reluctance to
make amends had given him a new perspective. It was an
angle he'd not been able to see on his own, and since he'd
been living as a veritable hermit for the past year she'd
been the first person to see past the façade he presented
to the outside world.

She'd helped him see that he was as much a party to
the problems as his father was. That he'd done some of the
hurting along the way.

A deep ache in his chest had started up as he'd left the
ballet studio that night, darkening his world until he'd felt
that he might not be able to face daylight again. But he
had to. This time he wouldn't take the coward's way out.
He would face his problems and he *would* rebuild his life.

Step one was contacting his father. He'd tried calling
home a few times so far, typing the number into his phone
and planning out what to say. Each time he'd chickened
out—but he wasn't giving up...not by a long shot.

He typed the number into his phone again and pressed
the call button before he could back out. His fingers hovered over the cancel button, but the call was answered on
the first ring.

'Hi, Dad. I know it's been a while...'

The desire to dance scratched at her senses, burrowing
deep in her skin and prickling at her so she couldn't ignore it. Even after her not-so-successful return at the Winter Performance she couldn't supress the desire. In those
moments before she'd fallen the world had made sense.
Sure, she'd tried to jump in at the deep end, but watching
the playback tape of the concert had shown her that the
majority of the audience wouldn't have noticed a thing...

and she'd looked good. She still danced like a pro, even if she couldn't pull her *pointe* shoes out of the closet yet.

She'd started practising in her living room, where no one could see. She'd moved the couch and turned up the music to test out new moves and see how far she could push her ankle. One night it had resulted in a bag of frozen peas being wrapped around her foot, but she'd recovered. Quickly.

She had to keep busy. Sitting around thinking about Grant and dancing was killing her.

Grabbing her coat from the stand in the entranceway, she headed for the front door. As she stepped outside a smile spread across her face. The sun was out and bright light filtered through fluffy clouds. Spring was making its first proper appearance, even though it was nearing the end of September. She tilted her face to the sky, enjoying the mild air as it brushed over her cheeks and nose. It smelled of last night's rain and the orange-blossom tree in her neighbour's yard.

It was the scent of happiness.

As she was about to leave her driveway she noticed the mail sticking out of her letterbox. The handwriting on one letter caught her eye. She'd seen that chicken-scratch scrawl before.

Grant.

Unceremoniously she snatched the letter and tore it open, leaving the edges jagged in her haste. A flyer for a dance company, a business card and a brief handwritten note.

Jasmine,
I've done some research. The director of the Melbourne Contemporary Dance Company is a huge Jaguars fan. I've traded membership for a meeting. Call him to arrange a time.
Grant.

A lump lodged in her throat as she stood rooted to her driveway, a light breeze fluttering the leaflets in her hand. She'd done her utmost not to think about Grant in the weeks since their argument. She'd rationalised away the curling need in her belly and the ache in her chest. She'd talked herself through all of the reasons they couldn't be together, chanting them like a mantra.

Yet he was constantly in her dreams, and in the moments where her concentration slipped and her mind wandered to better times. His touch haunted her; his smile was forever etched into her memory. She couldn't forget how she'd felt with him—how she'd blossomed and come alive again under his kiss. In her weak moments she'd thought about calling him…she'd fantasised about how she could make it better between them. But then she'd wonder what they'd say, and if he'd even be interested in talking to her.

It usually ended with her tucking into a tub of ice cream and then going on a brisk walk to burn the calories.

She missed him. She missed him so badly sometimes that she couldn't sleep for the cavity in her chest that felt as if it would swallow her whole. Being without him was like trying to be half a person. He'd burrowed into her life without her even realising it, and she felt his absence as keenly as she would feel the loss of a dear friend.

Jasmine flipped the envelope over; it was postmarked within the past week. He was still thinking about her. She'd made it clear that there was nothing between them, and yet he'd gone ahead and done something thoughtful for her. Why? Was he hoping the goodwill gesture would win her over?

She bit down on her lip and carried the mail to her room. She tucked the leaflets and his note into her lingerie drawer and closed it with a slam. The note didn't change anything. It didn't change who he was, or his lifestyle. Nor did it change her or her ideals.

She'd made her bed and now she had to lie in it.

* * *

Spring had well and truly arrived in Melbourne, and with the Grand Final less than a week away the city was hoping the weather would hold. Jasmine, on the other hand, had taken to torturing herself with the excessive media coverage of finals fever.

Now she was sitting on her bed, watching the pre-Brownlow hype. In a short while the players and their partners would take to the red carpet for a media feeding frenzy. Would Grant have someone on his arm? Was he even missing her?

God, why did she even care? It was over and it was at her hands. But the thought that he'd be there with someone else was killing her, causing her stomach to tumble around. Clamping her eyes down, she shoved the taunting images from her mind. It was useless. She was miserable without him but she couldn't be *with* him...or at least it had seemed that way at the time.

Next to her bed, the brochure for the Melbourne Contemporary Dance Company was on her nightstand; the director's business card was tucked into her notebook. She'd been putting off making the call, but something was pushing her.

She wanted that feeling: the incredible elation that came from doing something you'd always dreamed of. But she was procrastinating.

First it had been because she'd needed clearance from her doctor. She'd wanted to be doubly sure, so she'd seen her physiotherapist as well...and her old mentor from the Australian Ballet.

She'd then taken her doctor's advice and set up an appointment with someone to help her work through the emotional issues associated with her accident and the sudden end to her career.

Turning the brochure over in her hands, she ran her fingertips across the pictures of the dancers in their modern costumes. It would be a different world, but one where she might be able to relinquish some of the control she so desperately craved. The shrink had said it was a mechanism for her to deal with what she'd lost and the years of emotional abuse inflicted on her in her relationship with her ex. She'd shrugged; there was no way she'd give him the satisfaction of confirming that he was right...though that in itself was telling enough.

Taking a deep breath, she tapped in the number on the business card as quickly as she could before she lost her nerve.

'Hello?' The voice on the other end was rich, cultured.

'Mr Antonio? This is Jasmine Bell. I was given your number by Grant Farley, regarding a meeting with you.'

'Ah, Miss Bell,' he said, his tone lightening with recognition. 'I've been waiting for your call. I was starting to wonder if you hadn't received my number.'

'It's been a busy few weeks. I'm teaching at the moment, and we've started competition season.'

'Yes, Mr Farley has told me all about you. He promised me you would take my breath away. Those are some big words to live up to, my dear.'

'I know.' Butterflies swarmed in her stomach. The kindness of Grant's words was making her insides ache.

'I would love to meet you. We're always on the lookout for new talent, and Mr Farley told me that you were a soloist with the Australian Ballet.'

'That's right.'

'And you can't dance *en pointe* anymore?'

'Yes, sir.'

'We can work with that. Have you been cleared to train?'

'Yes.' By three separate people with more degrees than she could possibly comprehend.

'Perfect. Why don't you come by the office next week? Call my assistant to make an appointment, her number is on my business card.'

'I certainly will.'

'I look forward to meeting you, Miss Bell.'

'You too.'

She stood in the centre of her room, her heart fluttering like a butterfly trapped in a cage. Making sure the call had been disconnected, Jasmine let out a scream. The noise echoed off the walls of her unit as she shook her head and danced about in a circle, expelling her pent-up energy.

Nerves flooded her body. The thought of training and performing again for a living was too much to contain. She let out an exhilarated laugh, and clamped her hands over her mouth.

He promised me you would take my breath away...

The words swirled in her blood, making it rush and pound and sending desire and giddiness all through her. She was turning her life around and it was all thanks to Grant. Without his belief she might not ever have been able to contemplate dancing again. While everyone else had walked on eggshells around her he'd been able to call it as it was. Unbiased honesty—it was perhaps the best gift he could have given her.

God, she missed him. Her gut told her she'd made a huge mistake in pushing him away. He was nothing like Kyle. Her ex had abandoned her instead of encouraging her to dance again. He'd never once opened up about himself the way Grant had that day she'd run away. The memory still stung. The note she'd left him *had* been cowardly. What if she'd stayed to face him? Might they still be together now? Perhaps they would have worked through it... But she'd seen red at the time, with memories clouding her judgement.

She should have stayed.

Grant was exactly the kind of man she wanted in her life and she'd let him go.

Something flickered and caught her eye where she sat. A thin beam of light peeked through her blinds and reflected off something shiny. She walked over to the closet and saw amongst the conservative pants, jeans and long skirts that had become her camouflage that there was a peek of something beautiful.

She pulled out a floor-length gown of indigo silk. It was scalloped at the bottom, and the elegant cowl neck was decorated with the tiniest, most fragile black glass beads.

A few months after she'd quit the Australian Ballet money had been so tight that she'd sold all of the gowns and cocktail dresses that had been her after-hours uniform back in those days. The money had helped her survive a few more months and she'd also cleaned out the items that had embodied her bad memories.

All except this dress. It was the only one she'd bought with her own money, because she'd wanted to wear something of her own choosing. The tiniest of rebellions, but it had meant the world to her at the time.

She held it against her in front of the mirror. The deep-coloured silk made her skin look even more translucent than it usually did. She was white as porcelain by comparison. The heavy silk was like liquid beauty against her palms.

Could she...?

The players would be arriving at the red carpet half an hour from now. If she called a cab she *might* make it.

The face in the mirror was from the past, the hopeful sparkle in her eyes unfamiliar. She bit down on her lip. Her mind was telling her to slow down and think about her actions but for once she pushed her fear aside; it had got her nowhere in the past year except to make her life as lonely as a *pointe* shoe without someone to dance in it.

She grabbed her phone, ordered a cab and stripped on the spot. She was going to get her life back on track, and that meant making new rules.

The dress flowed over her body like a caress, every delicate curve highlighted by the glistening fabric. The neckline sat perfectly, the beads catching the light so that it looked like a piece of night sky.

Outside the cab honked its horn and Jasmine rushed out, teetering on a pair of high heels she'd plucked from the depths of her cupboard. Her hair was loose and it fluttered behind her as she ran.

'To the city, please,' she said breathlessly as she slid into the cab. 'Whiteman street.'

'You know you won't be able to get in there?' the cabbie said, looking at her in the rearview mirror with a look that said *Beware—crazy woman on board*. 'It's the Brownlow tonight.'

'That's where I'm going.'

CHAPTER FOURTEEN

SHE PULLED A mirror from her purse and checked her face. Her cheeks were flushed pink from the cold and the excitement in her eyes made up for a lack of mascara.

'Don't they usually send fancy cars?' The driver eyed her through the rearview mirror. 'Why are you getting a cab?'

'It's a last-minute thing.'

The cab slowed as they approached the city, the traffic thickening and blocking their way. Jasmine bounced in the back seat, nerves settling in now she had nothing to do put ponder what she was going to say to Grant.

What *could* she say? That she'd been wrong to push him away? That he'd helped her trust again?

She sighed. If only she'd known at the time what revealing her scars to him—inside and out—had meant.

What if she said all of those things and he rejected her? A heavy ball of nerves rocked in her stomach, causing her to press her hand against her belly. If he did, she would have to deal with it…but she didn't want to live without trying. She wouldn't allow fear to rule her life anymore.

The cab was now stuck in traffic on Spencer Street. A line of limos rounded the corner several blocks ahead; they would take their turn at dropping the players off at the entrance to the red carpet. How would she even find Grant?

All of the limos were identical—or at least they looked

so from this distance. She would have to check every last one. And then what? What if he had a date with him? Was she going to accost him right in front of the paparazzi?

Her head pounded. She hadn't though the plan out beyond putting on her dress and getting herself into the city. This could very well be a disaster.

But she couldn't stop—not now. Now that she was here…now that he could be around that corner. The very thought of seeing him twisted her stomach into knots. She'd shielded her heart for so long that she didn't know what it was like to be free. What if she'd realised too late?

Exhilaration coursed through her veins as she imagined falling into his arms, pressing her lips to his and telling him that she loved him. *Whoa! Where had that come from?*

As she said those three terrifying words in her head warmth spread through her, thick and sweet and comforting. A weight lifted from her chest and she could breathe again. She took in great mouthfuls of air as the realisation dawned on her.

She loved Grant.

She loved his crooked smile, the bump on his nose, and the way he did things for her even when she didn't want him to. She loved his secret tenderness and the way he made her feel as if she was the only person in the room. She loved the way he accepted her, scars and all.

She loved him.

The cab was chugging along Spencer Street, with the traffic thick and heavy as the limos clogged up the road. Jasmine checked her phone. The first players would already be walking the red carpet.

'I have to get out of here.' She fished in her purse for money to pay the driver.

'But we're not at Whiteman Street, miss.'

'It doesn't matter.'

She threw a twenty over the seat. It was more than

she had to pay, but she couldn't afford to wait for change. Those precious minutes could mean the difference between finding Grant and losing him to the blinding glitter of the red carpet.

Possibly for ever.

She pushed open the door and stepped out of the cab into the wind and cool air. Her hair swirled around her as she ran, and goosebumps rippled across her arms and chest.

The thin straps of her heels bit into her feet as she ran. Stumbling, she turned the corner onto Whiteman Street, to where the limos were lined up. Her heart pounded with adrenaline; her blood pulsed as she searched for him. She bent down to the first one and startled the dark-haired player and his very pregnant partner.

Not here.

She searched the next limo, and the next. Grant was nowhere to be seen.

Staff lined the street: security guards with their don't-mess-with-me expressions and event organisers carrying clipboards.

'Ma'am?'

A woman with an official-looking lanyard approached her. Her brow crinkled. It could have been in concern, though Jasmine suspected that it might have been in wariness. She must look like a crazy person, with her hair in disarray and her dress flowing behind her as she jogged in a pair of most unsuitable shoes.

'Can I help you?'

'I'm looking for Grant Farley.' Her voice would barely work above the thundering of her heart and the heaving of her chest. Nerves had stolen her breath, and the crisp spring air seeped right through her dress, making her shiver. 'He plays for the Jaguars, he should be here.'

'Are you on the guest list?' The woman eyed her suspiciously as she glanced down at the paper on her clipboard.

'Jasmine?'

She turned towards the voice.

Grant hung out of the window of one of the limos, his mouth agape.

'Grant!'

She dashed away from the clipboard lady and towards the black limo. He pushed open the door and stepped out on the street, moving as easily in the inky black tux as he did in his sports gear.

Her heart almost stopped at the sight of him. He suited up well. His thick blond hair was mussed just so; his black bow tie nestled perfectly at his throat. His eyes widened as he drank her in, his gaze smoothing over her dress.

'I thought you didn't do galas.' He shook his head at her.

'I don't.' She stepped forwards, her clutch pressed to her stomach as though the barrier might save her from his rejection.

'I thought you didn't want to be paraded around like a piece of meat?' He stepped closer, so that there was only her bag between them.

Something flickered within the depths of his eyes—something passionate beneath the icy surface of that unwavering blue.

'I don't want that.'

'Then what *do* you want?' His voice was rich but jagged, like silk roughened by stone.

'Dancing,' she said, her voice catching in her throat. 'And dinner…and sex…lots of flexible, mind-blowing sex. I want *you*.'

'You left me without even saying goodbye.' He shook his head, his fingers pressing against his temple. 'You left me a *note*.'

'I know.' She bit down on her lip, pleading with her

body to stop shaking. 'I was trying to protect myself from history repeating itself.'

'You freaked.'

He didn't want to understand. He wanted to be angry. He wanted to protect himself too.

'Yeah, I freaked.'

Her deep brown eyes were wide as saucers. She wasn't wearing a scrap of make-up and her hair was loose and flowing around her shoulders—untamed and just-slept-in. She was a fresh rose among poor imitations.

'Then why are you here?'

'I had to see you.'

Her chest heaved beneath her dress and his heart clenched. How could he trust her? At the first sign of trouble she'd fled.

The thing was, after their conversation he'd decided not to give her the dress—he'd decided to respect her wishes. But he hadn't even had the chance to do the right thing.

He hadn't had the chance to explain.

'I...' He shook his head, disorientated by the emotions that swelled in him. 'I can't do this now.'

'Please don't walk away.'

At that moment his date walked up to them. 'Is everything OK, Grant?'

Jasmine's eyes widened and she looked from him to the tall blonde and back again. He expected her to retreat, to step back and run. His stomach churned. What she did now could very well make or break them.

'Excuse me.' She turned her attention to his date. 'I'm Jasmine.'

The woman looked at Grant with a what-the-hell-is-going-on? expression.

'I am so sorry to interrupt your date, but it's important that you know I love this man. I only realised it today on my way here.' Her face was alight, cheeks pink and eyes sparkling. 'But I love him and I can't let him go. So I hope you haven't got any thoughts about getting serious with him.'

'Jasmine,' Grant said, stifling a smile. 'I'd like you to meet Annabel Farley. My *sister*.'

Her mouth formed a shocked O and she blinked. 'You called them?'

'Yeah, I called them…before it was too late.' He sighed, the fight leaving his body. 'I got some very wise advice recently and I decided to make a few changes.'

'You know, now that you mention it, the family resemblance is quite strong.' She pressed a hand to her forehead, her cheeks reddening to an attractive shade of hot pink.

'I'll give you two some privacy,' Annabel said, skipping off to chat to one of the other football players.

'I'm so sorry.' She shook her head, her mouth opening and closing with a failed explanation.

'So you love me, eh?' he teased.

He had to give it to her: she'd done something gutsy, coming here and laying it all out. 'So what else do you want—apart from the flexible, mind-blowing sex?'

'Commitment,' she said, her eyes glittering as she spoke. 'I will do what I need to do to show you that I'm not going to run again.'

'Does that include red carpets?'

'It might do. It might include photos and media. It will definitely include cheering you on at every single game you play until you retire. It will include me wearing your guernsey around the house.'

'Now, *that* sounds like a sight,' he said.

He hovered in front of her, wanting to kiss her but holding back. Could he trust that she wouldn't change her mind about his lifestyle?

'It includes me trusting you…and it means I have a

meeting with the Melbourne Contemporary Dance Company.'

'You called them?' He wanted to grab her and twirl her around, but he needed to be sure she was serious about them. Because he didn't want to meet her halfway—he wanted them to be all the way in. Together.

'I love you, Grant,' she said, her breathing shallow. 'I didn't want to love you, but I do. You've pushed me since the day we met, you've driven me crazy, and I wouldn't have it any other way.'

He laughed. 'Back at you. You're the most dedicated and *difficult* person I have ever known. You didn't give me special treatment because of who I was when the rest of the world was ready to use me for what they could get. You questioned me, argued with me, and I loved every second of it.'

They stood there as the limos crawled past and curious passers-by watched them in the street. But they might as well have been the only two people in the world for all Jasmine cared.

'But what if you wake up one day and decide you can't handle all of this?' He gestured to the fanfare around them—the flashing of the paparazzi's cameras behind him, the limos, the noise and hustle. 'I can't have you leaving me because it gets too much. If you're in, you're in for good.'

'I'm in.' She shook her head and pressed her lips together in determination. 'I'm in all the way.'

'Well, it's a damn good thing we have an extra seat at our table.' He smiled and reached for her, secretly thanking Don's date for pulling out last minute. 'Because I love you too, Jasmine Bell, even if you *are* as stubborn as a bull.'

He crushed his lips to hers, parting them and delving deep for a long kiss that set her pulse racing. Pleasure, desire and love hummed through her body as if she was conducting enough energy to power them both…and the rest of Melbourne.

Lights popped and flashed around them.

'Grant! Grant!' A journalist stuck his microphone towards them. 'Who's the lucky lady?'

'Don't you mean who's the lucky guy?' He held Jasmine close to him and grinned for the cameras. 'That would be me. I'm the luckiest guy in the world.'

* * * * *

MARRIED FOR THEIR
MIRACLE BABY

SORAYA LANE

For my mother, Maureen. Thank you for everything.

CHAPTER ONE

BLAKE GOLDSMITH TOOK a slow sip of whiskey, enjoying the burn of the straight liquor as he swallowed. He wasn't a big drinker, but he'd fast developed a taste for whiskey on the rocks to help get him through the torturous task of attending cocktail parties and gala events. He gazed down at the ice sitting forlorn in the glass. *Darn.* He either had to go without or brave the crowd mingling near the bar again. Neither option appealed to him right now.

Instead he decided to stretch his legs and head outside. If anyone stopped him, he could blame his departure on needing some fresh air. As soon as the auction was over, he was heading home anyway. He craved the solitude of flying, the closeness of being with his unit when he was serving. If he had half the chance, he'd be hightailing it to wherever they were stationed and not coming back. *If only that were an option.*

"Excuse me," he muttered, touching a woman's elbow as he passed, eyes downcast so he didn't have to engage.

After a while, everyone started to look the same—

a sea of black tuxedos and white shirts mixed with elegant women in sparkly dresses. He should have been used to it by now, but playing the black sheep turned good wasn't a part he'd ever wanted, and neither was being part of glittering society parties.

Wow. Blake squared his shoulders, stood a little straighter as he stared across the room. She was standing alone, back to the large windows that overlooked a twinkling New York City below. Her dark red hair was loose and falling over her shoulders, lipstick bright in contrast to her pale skin. She was like a perfectly formed doll, her posture perfect, one hand holding a full glass of champagne, the other clasping a tiny purse. In a room where all the women were starting to look scarily similar with their perfectly coiffed updos and black dresses, she was like the breath of fresh air he'd been so desperately craving only moments before.

Blake didn't waste time. She was alone, which meant she was either waiting for her date to return or actually solo. Either way, he wanted to get to her before anyone else did. He might be avoiding the pressure to settle down, but introducing himself to a beautiful woman would make the night a whole lot more interesting.

He excused himself past a few more people, striding across the room, eyes locked on her. *So much for a boring night out to buy some art and make the company look good.* His evening was looking better by the second. Blake cleared his throat and smiled when dark brown eyes met his.

"I'd ask if you want another drink, but it doesn't look

like you've even touched this one," he said. "Unless you don't like champagne."

The redhead laughed, tipping back a little so her hair tumbled over her shoulders, the unblemished skin of her neck on show. "I love champagne. I'm just…"

Blake laughed. "Bored?"

She grimaced, and it only made him like her more. "Yeah," she said softly. "You could say that."

"I'm Blake," he said, holding out a hand. "Blake Goldsmith."

She reached hers out and he shook it, her skin warm against his. "Saffron Wells."

"So what's a girl like you doing here alone?"

"A bored girl?" she asked.

Blake raised an eyebrow. "No, a beautiful one."

Her smile was sweet. "I promised a friend I'd come, but it's not really my thing." Saffron shrugged. "She's an artist—one of her pieces is being auctioned tonight, so I couldn't really say no. Besides, I don't get out much."

She might feel out of place, but she sure looked the part, as if it was exactly her scene. Blake glanced down when she looked away, eyes traveling over her blue satin dress, admiring her legs. It was short and strapless, and it took every inch of his willpower to stop staring. She was a knockout.

"So what do you do?" he asked.

"I'm having some time out right now," she replied, her smile fading. "I'm just making coffee and…"

Blake cringed, wishing he'd asked something less invasive. He hadn't wanted to put her on the spot or make her uncomfortable. "I love coffee. The barista at my local café is my favorite person in the world."

"How about you?" she asked.

Now Blake was really regretting his line of questioning. He'd walked straight into that one. "Family business. I'm here tonight because no one else would take my place."

"Poor you."

"Yeah, something like that." Blake hated talking about himself, and he liked the fact that this beautiful woman seemed to have no idea who he was. If he read another tabloid or blog article about his most-eligible-bachelor status, he'd lose it. And the lies surrounding his dad's death were driving him to drink. So to chat with a woman like Saffron and not deal with any of that was refreshing to say the least.

A waiter passed and Blake held up a hand, beckoning him over. He smiled and placed his empty whiskey glass on the tray, taking a champagne and putting it into Saffron's hand. He removed her other one, ignoring the look of protest on her face, and then he took another glass for himself.

"I was perfectly happy nursing that," she said.

"Nothing worse than warm champagne," Blake told her. "Want to get some fresh air?"

Saffron's smile was small, but it was there. "Sure. Any excuse to get out of here."

Blake grinned back and touched the small of her back as she turned, guiding her to the only exit he could see. There was a large balcony, which was probably full of smokers, but the room was stifling and he didn't care.

"Excuse me." A loud voice boomed through the speakers, making him turn. "May I have your attention please?"

Blake groaned. Just as he'd been about to escape... "Want to make a run for it?" he murmured, leaning down to whisper into Saffron's ear. Her hair smelled like perfume, and it was soft against his cheek when she tipped her head back.

"I think we need to stay," she whispered in reply, dark brown eyes locked on his for a second. "As much as I'd love to disappear."

Blake shrugged. He would have happily disappeared and made a phone bid, but he wasn't about to leave the most interesting woman he'd seen all evening. Her dark red hair stood out in a sea of bright blondes and raven-haired heads, the color subtle but stunning. And in a room full of slim woman, she seemed even smaller, but not in a skinny way. Blake had noticed the way she was standing when he'd first seen her, her posture perfect, limbs long yet muscled, her body even more sculptured up close than it had appeared from afar. He was intrigued.

"Thank you all for being here tonight to raise funds for underprivileged children right here in New York City," the host said. Blake was tall, so even from the back of the room he could see what was going on, but he doubted Saffron would be able to see a thing. She was almost a head shorter than him. "Funds raised tonight will help to provide a winter assistance package for under-twelve-year-old children who don't have the basics to help them through our harsh colder months.

They will receive a warm coat, shoes, hat, pajamas and other things so many of us take for granted."

Blake glanced down at Saffron. He watched her raise the slender glass to her mouth, taking a sip. He did the same, even though champagne wasn't his usual drink of choice.

"This is my friend's piece," Saffron said, meeting his gaze for a moment. "She's been working on this on and off all year, as part of her latest collection."

Blake pulled the brochure from his inside jacket pocket and stared at the first painting on the crumpled paper. He wasn't the type to get superexcited over art— all he cared about was making a sizable donation to a worthy cause—but he didn't dislike it. The bright swirls of multicolored paint looked interesting enough, and a quick scan over the bio told him the emerging artist could be one to watch. If he got a worthwhile, long-term investment for his donation, he'd be happy.

"We'll open the bidding at five hundred dollars," the auctioneer said, taking over from the host.

Blake raised his hand just high enough for the spotter to see. The bidding quickly moved up to five thousand dollars, and Blake stayed with it, nodding each time now that he was being watched. He didn't like drawing attention to himself, and from the look on Saffron's face when the bidding stopped at just over ten thousand, even she had no idea it was him pushing the price up. He was buying on behalf of the company, so to him it was small change, but he was certain it would be exciting for an emerging artist trying to make a name for herself.

"She'll be thrilled!" Saffron said, eyes bright as she

connected with him. "All the other artists are so well-known, and…" She narrowed her gaze and he laughed.

"What?"

"Why are you smiling like that?" she asked.

Blake grinned. "I bought it," he said simply. "Hopefully she'll be superfamous one day, and I'll have a good story to tell and a decent investment on the wall of my office."

Saffron raised her glass and clinked it to his. "You're crazy."

"No, just in a generous mood." Blake had done his good deed, and now he was ready to go. The auctioneer started all over again, and he placed a hand to the small of Saffron's back. "Meet me outside? I just need to sign for the painting." He'd intended on buying two pieces, but he decided to make a donation with his purchase instead.

He watched as she nodded. "Sure."

Blake paused, hoping she wasn't about to walk out on him, then decided it was a risk he was just going to have to take.

"You never did tell me which café you work at."

She just smiled at him. "No, I don't believe I did."

When she didn't elaborate, Blake walked backward a few steps, not taking his eyes off her before finally moving away. He was used to women throwing themselves at him, wanting his money, being so obvious with their intentions. Saffron was different, and he liked it. There was no desperation in her eyes, no look as though she wanted to dig her claws in and catch him, and it only made him want to get to know her all the more. If she genuinely didn't know who he was right now, then he could be himself, and that was a role he hadn't been able to play in a very long time.

Saffron watched Blake from across the room. She'd been dreading coming out, not looking forward to making small talk and having people ask about her injury, but so far no one had really bothered her. Until Blake. She had no idea who he was or if she was supposed to know who he was, but he'd purchased Claire's painting as if it were no big deal, so he either had money or worked for a company that had told him to spend up. Either way she didn't care, but she was definitely curious.

The night air was cool when she moved out, but the large balcony was virtually empty. There was a couple kissing in the corner, obscured by the shadows, so Saffy walked closer to the edge, admiring the view. She'd never tire of New York. The vibrant atmosphere, the twinkling lights, the fact the city never seemed to sleep. It had a vibe about it that she'd never known anywhere else in the world, and for the first time in her life she felt as if she belonged, as though she was where she was supposed to be.

"Am I interrupting?"

The deep rumble of a voice behind her pulled her from her thoughts and made her turn. Blake was standing a few feet away, his champagne glass hanging from one hand and almost empty, his bow tie no longer perfectly placed against his shirt. The black satin tie was messed up, his top button undone and his jacket open.

Saffy thought he looked sexy and so much more inter-esting than the rest of the suits she'd seen inside.

"Not at all. I was just admiring the city."

"You're not from here, are you?" he asked, moving closer and standing beside her, gazing down at the city as she glanced at him.

"Is my accent still that obvious?" Saffron frowned. She'd lived in New York for almost ten years now, since she was sixteen, and to her own ears she sounded more like a local than a girl from a small town in Kentucky.

"It's just a little twang every now and again. I can't quite put my finger on it, but…" Blake laughed. "Small town?"

Saffy gave him a stare she hoped looked evil before bursting out laughing. "A little place called Maysville, in Kentucky. But I haven't even been back in—" she sighed "—forever. You can take the girl out of the small town, but not the town out of the girl, right?"

Blake leaned against the railing and stared at her, his smile slow and steady as it spread across his face. She should have shrunk away from his stare, from his attention, but instead she bravely faced him. All the years she'd focused on her career, dancing from her childhood through her teens and then through almost all her twenties, she hadn't had time for boyfriends. But flirting with Blake felt good, and it wasn't as if she had anywhere else she needed to be or anything else she should be doing.

"So what's a girl from Maysville doing in New York?" he asked.

Saffy raised her glass and took a sip, wondering how much or little to tell him. "It's a long story."

His grin was infectious, the way it lit up his dark eyes and made a crease form at each side of his mouth. The man was gorgeous, textbook handsome with his dark hair and even darker features, his golden skin sexy against the white of his shirt.

"It just so happens," he said in his deep, raspy voice, "that I have all night."

"I'd rather hear about you," Saffy said, clearing her throat and trying not to become lost in his stare, hypnotized by his gold-flecked dark eyes.

"I'm guessing you want to open up about yourself about as much as I like talking about *myself*," Blake said with a chuckle.

Saffron raised her glass again, realizing she was drinking way more than usual. She was usually too busy training to drink or socialize. Unless it had been with other dancers, she'd hardly seen anyone else, and she'd had to be so careful with her calorie count and her energy levels to waste on alcohol. She felt good tonight, though—alive and buzzing, even if it was due to the champagne and the smooth talker charming her.

"How about we agree to no personal questions then? I don't want to talk about work or my life," she admitted. She'd lived her work all her life as a ballerina, but every night she flexed her leg, only to be rewarded by ongoing shoots of pain, and she was reminded of what had happened. How little time she had left in the city she loved, and how quickly her dream had ended.

"It just so happens that I don't want to talk about

work, either," Blake said. "Want to go somewhere less…" His voice trailed off.

"Dull?" she suggested.

"Yeah, dull," he agreed, knocking back the rest of his champagne. "I hate these kinds of parties."

"I always thought it would be incredible to be asked to amazing parties, rubbing shoulders with the city's elite," Saffron admitted. "But I quickly realized that the part I liked was getting all dressed up. The parties weren't exactly as amazing as they looked from the outside once I'd attended a few."

"So you'd rather be somewhere more fun?" he asked with a chuckle.

"Ah, yes. I guess you could say that."

Saffron passed Blake her glass, not bothering to drink any more. She liked to stay in control, and if she was going somewhere with a man she hardly knew, she wasn't going to get drunk. Blake took it, turning his back for a moment as he found somewhere to leave them. She quickly pulled out her phone to text Claire.

Hey, you did great tonight. I'm heading out with the guy who bought your painting! If you haven't heard from me in the morning…

Saffy grinned as she hit Send. Claire would flip out, or maybe she'd just cheer her on. Her friend was always telling her to have more fun and stop taking life so seriously, but she wasn't the one in danger of having to pack her bags and go back to Maysville if she didn't get her job back. Saffron was serious because her job had demanded it, and she'd been happy to make it her life.

Her phone pinged back almost instantly.

Have fun. I'll track him down if I need to. xoxo

"Shall we go?"

Saffron put her phone back into her purse. "Sure thing."

Blake held out his arm and she slipped her hand through, laughing to herself about how absurd the evening had turned out. She wasn't the girl who went on dates with strangers or disappeared with men and left her friends at a party. But nothing about the past month had gone according to plan, so she had nothing to lose.

"Do you like dancing?" Blake asked as they walked around the back of the crowd. He was leading her around the room, and she could feel eyes on them. Either because they were leaving too early or because of who he was. Or maybe she was just being overly sensitive and imagining it.

Dancing. When in her life hadn't she loved dancing? "Sometimes." If her leg didn't hurt like hell when she tried to dance, she'd love to.

"I was hoping you were going to say no."

Saffron laughed. This guy was hilarious. "It's a no. For tonight, anyway."

"Then why don't we go back to my place?" He must have seen the hesitation written all over her face, because he stopped walking and stared down at her. "Sorry, that came out all wrong."

"It's not that I don't want to…" Saffron actually didn't know what she thought, but she wasn't about to jump into bed with him. Maybe that's what he was used to? She hoped she hadn't read the situation wrong.

"I just meant that if we don't want to dance and we're bored here, it might be nice to just chill with a drink. Or we could find a nice quiet bar somewhere. It wasn't supposed to sound like that."

Saffy looked deep into his dark eyes, didn't see a flicker of anything that alarmed her. "Why should I trust you?" she asked.

He cleared his throat. "United States Army Officer Blake Goldsmith," Blake said, giving her a quick salute. "One of the only things I'm good at in life is keeping people safe, and that's about the only good reason I can give you."

She was more shocked that he was an officer than the fact he'd asked her back to his place so fast. "You're in the army?"

"Was." Blake grimaced. "So much for not talking about my work life, huh? But yeah, you can trust me."

Saffron knew that just because he was a former officer didn't make him trustworthy on its own, but she wasn't actually worried about Blake. She felt as though she could take him at face value. What worried her was how he was making her feel, how desperate she suddenly was to know what it was like to meet a man and go home with him. Not that she could actually go through with a one-night stand, but the thought was making her tingle all over.

"So what do you say?" Blake asked. "I have a car

waiting, so we can either jump in and head to my place or duck into a nearby bar."

Saffron passed a number over and collected her coat, snuggling into it before they stepped out into the chilly night air. On the balcony she'd been so busy admiring the view that she'd hardly noticed it, but now she was feeling the cold.

"Yours," she finally said. "It had better be warm, though."

Blake was holding a black scarf, and he tucked it around her neck, his hand falling to her back as they walked. "I promise."

She walked until he pointed out a black town car, and within seconds he was opening the door for her and ushering her inside.

"Tell me—how does a former soldier end up at a glitzy charity gala with a plush town car at his beck and call?" she asked, curious.

"Goldsmith Air," Blake said, pulling the door shut as he slid in beside her, his thigh hard to hers. "Family business, one I tried to steer clear of but somehow ended up right in the thick of."

Saffron knew what that felt like. "Sorry, I know we promised no work questions."

They only seemed to travel for a few blocks before they were outside a pretty brick building that looked old but had been renovated and kept immaculate. A huge glass frontage showed off a contemporary-looking café inside, the lights still on but the signs pulled in. She guessed he lived upstairs.

"So this is your local coffee place?" Saffron asked.

"I wake up to the smell of their coffee brewing, and by eight I've usually ordered my second cup for the day."

"They deliver to you?"

Blake gave her a guilty look before pushing the door open. "One of the perks of being landlord."

She didn't show her surprise. He was definitely not your average US Army veteran! Saffron stepped out and followed Blake as he signaled his driver to leave before taking her in through a locked security door that required him to punch a code in. They went in, and it locked behind them before he was punching in another code and ushering her into an elevator. Saffy admired the old-fashioned metal doors he pulled across, and within moments they were on the second floor.

"Wow." They stepped out into one of the hugest loft-style apartments Saffron had ever seen. Interior brickwork was paired with high-gloss timber floors, a stainless steel industrial-type kitchen taking center stage. She had to fight to stop her jaw from hitting the floor.

"So this is home?" she asked.

Blake shrugged. "For now."

He closed the door behind them and touched her shoulders, slipping her coat off and throwing it over the arm of a huge L-shaped sofa. Saffy spun around to ask him something and ended up almost against him. He must have moved forward, his arms instantly circling her, steadying her. She stared up at him, touched his arm, her fingers clasping over his tuxedo jacket as she became hypnotized by his stare.

Blake was handsome and strong and intriguing… all of the things that sparked her interest and made her want to run in the opposite direction but at the same time want to throw herself hard up against him.

"Are you okay?" he asked, the deep timbre of his voice sending a shiver down her spine.

Saffron nodded. "Uh-huh," she managed, still not pulling away, not letting go.

Blake watched her back, his eyes never leaving hers, and just when she thought she was going to step back, his face suddenly moved closer to her, *dangerously close*. Saffron's breath halted in her throat; her heart started to race. What was she even doing? In this man's apartment? In his arms? She barely even knew his name!

"Can I kiss you?" he murmured, his whisper barely audible, his mouth so near.

Saffy felt herself nodding even though she knew she shouldn't. But he clearly wasn't going to ask her twice. Blake's lips connected with hers, just a gentle, soft caress at first, his mouth warm to hers, unbearably gentle. She lifted her arms and tucked them around his neck as Blake deepened their kiss, his lips moving back and forth across hers as his hands skimmed down her back.

"I think we should get that drink," he muttered, barely pulling his lips from hers.

"Me, too," she whispered back. But her body had other ideas, pressed tight to him as he cupped her even tighter against him. Saffron had never been with a man she didn't know, her only experience from the one relationship she'd had with a dancer she'd performed alongside. But right now she wanted Blake, and no amount of willpower was going to let her move away.

Blake's groan was deep as he scooped her up, lifting her heels clean off the ground and walking her backward to the closest sofa. She only had a second to gaze up at him, a bare moment to wonder what the heck she was doing as he ripped off his tie and discarded it, staring down at her, his big body looming above.

And then he was covering her, his body over hers. Saffy lifted her mouth up to his, met his lips and hungrily kissed him back. She knew it was all types of wrong, but tonight she was going to be bad. If this was one of her last weekends in New York, then she was going to make the most of it. Her career might be over, but it didn't mean her life had to be.

CHAPTER TWO

SAFFRON OPENED HER eyes and quickly closed them. She groaned and pulled the covers over her head. She'd never had firsthand experience with what to do the morning after, and nothing clever was springing to mind. What had she been thinking?

"Morning."

She took a deep breath and slowly slipped the covers down, clutching them tight to her chest as she sat up. Blake was standing in the doorway, looking just as chiseled and sexy and gorgeous as he had the night before. No wonder she'd ended up in his bed. He crossed the room and sat on the bed beside her.

"Ah, morning," she finally stammered, clearing her throat and trying to pull herself together. She didn't usually lack in confidence, but then again she didn't usually have to deal with handsome men so early in the morning. Saffron ran her tongue over her teeth, wishing she could have had ten minutes in the bathroom before having to face Blake.

"So I need to show you something," he said, eyebrows drawn together as he leaned closer.

It was only then she realized he was holding an iPad. Curious, she reached for it.

"What is it?"

"You know how we didn't want to talk about our personal lives or our work?"

Saffy nodded. She didn't understand what he was trying to tell her. Until she looked at the screen.

"Oh," she blurted.

"I think we probably *should* have had that conversation," Blake muttered. "Maybe we could have taken a back exit and made sure no one saw us."

Saffy kept hold of the covers with one hand and swiped through the photos with the other. There was Blake with his hand to her back, Blake laughing, her laughing with her head tipped back and her eyes locked on his, and there was them getting into his town car. Paired with headlines screaming that Blake was one of the city's most eligible bachelors and naming her as one of ballet's finest forgotten stars. The description stung.

She swallowed away the emotion in her throat, the familiar burn behind her eyes that always hit when she thought about her career. When she passed the iPad back and glanced up at Blake, she wished she hadn't.

"Hey, it's not so bad," he said, discarding the iPad and leaning over. He reached for her hand and lifted it, kissing the soft skin on the inside of her arm.

Saffy smiled. *This* was how she'd ended up in his bed! He was so smooth yet seemed so genuine at the same time, although hearing that he was such a prized bachelor only made her wonder if he'd expertly played her to get her into bed.

"You're really upset about it, aren't you? I was hoping you wouldn't think it was that big a deal being papped."

She shrugged. "I don't care about being seen with you, or the photos. It's the headlines that sting," Saffy admitted.

Blake looked confused. "I'm not sure I'm following. You do realize that the whole bachelor thing has been completely blown out of proportion, right? It's rubbish."

Saffy shook her head. "It hurts to read that I'm a washed-up former ballerina. Sometimes the truth stings more than we realize."

Blake kept hold of her hand, staring into her eyes. "You look far too young to be washed up, surely."

"I'll give you points for being kind, but I'm not too young, not in the ballet world. My body broke down on me, so I'm out."

He chuckled. "By out, you mean injured, right? Taking some time out? From what I've read this morning, you're pretty incredible."

Now it was Saffy chuckling. "You've been googling me?"

He shrugged. "Yeah. I'm an early riser. I saw this, and I've been reading up about you ever since."

She liked that he was at least honest. He could have lied and not admitted to it, but he was obviously curious about who he'd spent the night with. And if she was honest, she was starting to get pretty intrigued about him, too.

"What did it say?" Saffy wasn't clutching the sheet quite so tightly now, not as concerned as she had been about him seeing her.

"From what I've read, you came to New York as a teenager, wowed all the right people and eventually landed your dream role as lead in *Swan Lake* last year."

Saffron smiled. "Sounds about right." She wasn't sure she wanted to talk about it, not anymore. For years ballet had been her life, since she was a little girl in love with the idea of being a pretty dancer to a determined teenager and a dedicated adult. She'd lived and breathed her dream all her life, which was why she was at such a loss now. How did anyone move on if they'd lost the one thing that meant more to them than anything else?

Blake surprised her by stroking her face, his thumb caressing her cheek as he stared into her eyes. "I know the feeling."

She smiled, but it was forced. There was no way he knew how she was feeling. "You don't happen to have coffee, do you?" she asked, hoping he'd say *yes* then go and make her a cup so she had a little privacy.

"Sure do." Blake pulled back then rose, and the moment was over. He looked down at her, his height imposing. He was already dressed, barefoot but wearing dark jeans and a plain white tee.

Saffy waited for him to go then quickly scanned for her clothes. She hardly even remembered how they'd gotten to the bedroom. From what she could recall, her dress was in the living room wherever he'd thrown it, but her underwear was somewhere in the bedroom. She jumped up, taking the sheet with her. It wasn't until she had her underwear back on that she relaxed. Saffy looked around the room but he didn't have any clothes scattered, so she opened his closet and grabbed a sweat-shirt. It was fleecy on the inside with a zipper, and given the size on her, she had to zip it all the way just to cover her body. Then she dashed into his bathroom, splashed some water on her face and ran her fingers through her hair to tame it. Given the fact she'd just woken and didn't have all her usual things with her, she didn't think she looked too terrible.

"So I—" Blake's deep voice cut off. "You look cute in my hoodie."

"Sorry." Saffron spun around, feeling guilty. "I should have asked first, but I didn't want to walk out half-naked."

Blake's laugh made her smile. He waved her toward him and turned, and she followed him out to the living area. He had music playing softly, just audible, and she tried not to gape at the apartment all over again. It was incredible, and it oozed money. He pointed to the coffee machine.

"I can make an okay black coffee, but if you want something fancy, I'll call downstairs."

Saffron shook her head. "I don't need fancy café coffee. Just give it to me however it comes, with a heaped teaspoon of sugar."

"Not what I expected from a ballerina. I thought all dancers would think of sugar as the devil and have eating disorders." Blake turned straight around then, his face full of apology. "Sorry, that was in bad taste. I didn't mean it."

She was used to it. "It's fine, and it's kind of true. There are plenty of dancers with problems."

"Yeah, still. Bad form. Want to tell me what happened?" he asked, pushing a big mug of steaming coffee across the counter and shoving his hands into his jean pockets as he stood watching her on the other side. "Sounds to me like you've had a rough year."

"Yeah, you could say that again," Saffy muttered.

"I have waffles and bacon on their way up, so you can tell me over breakfast."

She groaned. "Do I have to?"

His laugh made her smile. "Yeah, you kind of do."

Saffron hated talking about what had happened, didn't want to have to explain what she'd been through and what it meant for her, but breakfast did sound good and she wasn't about to run out. Especially not if there were paparazzi waiting outside to see if she'd spent the night.

"We could talk about what happened last night instead," he suggested, giving her a smile that made her want to slap him.

"Um, how about no?" she quipped straight back, heart racing.

"So let me guess," Blake started, walking away from her when a buzz rang out. She tracked him with her eyes, admired how tall and built he was. His hair was thick and dark, a full mop of it, and whereas last night it had been styled, this morning it was all mussed up. She liked him even better less groomed, although he had looked pretty hot in a suit the night before.

The next thing he was pressing a button. "Just give me a sec," Blake called over his shoulder before disappearing from the apartment.

Saffy let out a breath she hadn't even known she was

holding. She reached for her coffee and took a slow, long sip. It was hot, but the burn felt nice down her throat, helped her to calm down somehow.

She could run. It wouldn't be her stupidest idea, and she could just grab her dress and bolt for it. Make up an excuse and dash past him. Get out of Dodge and never have to see him again or talk about what happened. She could even mail him back his hoodie, forget what she'd done. Only she wasn't sure she wanted to. The last few months, after the worst of her pain had passed, she'd been bored and miserable. She was working on autopilot, making coffee and serving people food, seeing her dreams disappear. It hadn't mattered what she'd done or how hard she'd tried, her leg hadn't healed fast enough, the ligaments badly torn, and with arthritis on top of it making the pain debilitating at best.

Blake had reminded her she was alive. If she hadn't met him, she'd have stayed another hour at the party, chatted with her friend, then gone home alone. Almost all her friends were dancers, and she wasn't in that world anymore.

So she stayed put, only leaving her seat on one of Blake's leather bar stools to retrieve her purse. It was tiny so she didn't have a lot in there, but she did have her foundation stick and some lip gloss, and she was keen to use both to make herself look half-decent. Plus she needed to text Claire.

She laughed. Her friend had already sent her three text messages, first wondering where she was, then asking how fab her night had been after seeing the article on some lame website. Then asking if she needed to send out a search party. Trust Claire to be scanning those types of pages as she ate her breakfast in the morning.

She sent her a quick message back.

I'm fine. He's gorgeous. Do you know anything about him?

The door clicked then, and she shoved her phone back in her purse. She hadn't had time to google him, and not being a native New Yorker, she didn't know the company name he'd mentioned the night before. He didn't strike her as a spoiled rich kid—more like a man who'd made his own money or his own way in the world, and she wanted to know more. Especially how he'd come to be listed as an eligible bachelor worthy of paparazzi.

"Breakfast is served," he announced.

Saffron stood and made her way back to the bar stool. "Mmm, smells delicious." Now she had clothes and some makeup on, she was a lot less self-conscious.

"Waffles with whipped caramel cream and fresh fruit. I went with sweet." His grin was naughty and she laughed at him.

"Can I just set the record straight about last night," she said, cringing at the way the words had come out.

"Sure. But you don't have to explain anything, if that's what you're worried about."

She sighed, taking the plate he held out to her. It did look delicious, the waffles thick and square, with pineapple and blueberries piled beside a swirl of the cream. "I just don't want you to think I do this sort of thing all the time."

He joined her around the other side of the counter, sitting down and passing her a knife and fork. "I kind of got that impression when you were peeking out at me from beneath the covers this morning with a horrified look on your face."

"Really?" She had to give it to him—he hadn't turned out to be a jerk the morning after.

Blake leaned over, smiling before dropping his mouth to hers, not giving her a second to hesitate. His lips were warm and tasted of coffee, his hand soft as he cupped the back of her head. He kissed the breath from her then pulled back, lips hovering as he stared down at her. Saffy felt the burn of heat as it spread up her neck, every inch of her body tingling from the unexpected kiss.

"You're too cute," he said with a grin, digging into breakfast like he hadn't just kissed her as if it was their last kiss on earth.

"And you're too suave for your own good," she muttered, stabbing her waffle with the fork, irate that he'd had such a visceral effect on her. "I'm guessing most of the women you bed are happy to drag you into bed the moment they lock eyes on you."

She had no idea why she was so mad with him when all he'd done was kiss her, but something about his attitude had gotten under her skin.

"Hey," he said, setting down his fork and turning to face her. "I meant it as a compliment, not to get you all fired up."

She went back to her breakfast, ignoring him.

"And I haven't exactly had the chance to meet a whole lot of ladies since I've been back. First I moved back home, then when I finally took over this place, I was spending more hours in the office than anywhere else. I haven't had time for socializing, other than when I've had to for work."

"You mentioned you were in the army," she said, calmed down and not so ready to jump down his throat. She'd seriously overreacted before.

"In another lifetime, yeah," he said, but he looked away as if he wasn't at all interested in talking about that other life. "Anyway, we're supposed to be talking about you. Tell me what happened. Why aren't you dancing now?"

Blake was intrigued. He'd bedded her already, and most of the time that was when his interest stopped, but she was something else. Even before he'd seen the blog post about them leaving the benefit together, which his sister had been so kind as to forward to him with a message that this one sounded a whole lot more promising than the airheads he'd been photographed with other times.

Blake kept eating his waffles, not wanting to stare at her and make her uncomfortable. He believed her that this wasn't her usual scene—she'd looked like a deer in headlights when he'd come back into the bedroom after hearing that she'd woken. His first instinct had been to dive straight back under the covers, until he'd seen her face and changed his mind. He still wanted her—he just wasn't going to be so forward.

Having a late breakfast with her and relaxing for once was making it clear he'd been way too focused on work the last few months. He'd become so determined not to buckle under the pressure and settle down, just because it would be good for business, but he was starting to realize he'd been missing out.

Saffron's red hair looked darker in the morning. Maybe it was the lack of bright lights, but it still looked incredible. The richest color against skin the lightest, barely there shade of gold, and dark brown eyes that just kept on drawing him in. He cleared his throat and set down his fork.

"Come on, what happened? Maybe I can help?" He doubted it, but he wanted to hear the story, and if she needed help finding work or someone to assist her with whatever injury she had, he did have helpful contacts.

His phone buzzed and he quickly glanced at it, not wanting to be rude by picking it up. He could read just enough of the text to see it was from his assistant and that the investor he'd been trying to impress had seen the paparazzi story. *Great.* Just when he'd been making some headway, now he was going to be labeled the rich playboy again.

"Nobody can help me," she said in a low voice. "Most dancers get injured and that's it, they're injured. Me, I'm out. Which means my career is over, because soon I'll have to go home with my tail between my legs, the washed-up former ballerina. I don't have enough money to stay here without working, and my physical therapy and specialist bills are crazy."

Blake frowned, forgetting the text and focusing on Saffron. "There's no other way for you to stay here?"

Saffron picked at her food, taking a mouthful that he was sure was a delaying tactic. When she finally looked up at him, her eyes were swimming. Big brown pools of hurt, bathed in unshed tears.

"I had a dream of dancing with the best ballet companies in the world, right from when I was a kid. I used to practice so hard, train my heart out and eventually it paid off." He listened as she blew out a big breath, sending a few tendrils of shorter hair around her face up into the air. "My hours of practicing got me noticed at the Lexington Ballet School in Kentucky, and eventually it turned into a dance scholarship with the New York Ballet Company. I started training there, danced my heart out and eventually went on to be an apprentice by the time I was eighteen."

"Wait, you moved to New York on your own *before* you were even eighteen? How old were you when you got the scholarship?" He knew plenty of models and other creative types started their careers early, but he'd never really thought about teenagers making such a big leap on their own. "Your parents didn't come, too?"

She shook her head. "Nope. Just me. I stayed with a relative for the first few months, then I moved into an apartment with some other dancers. I was only seventeen when I officially went out on my own, but I was so determined and focused on what I was doing that my parents didn't have any other choice. I would have resented them for the rest of my life if they hadn't let me come."

He got that. They'd let her follow her dream, and he admired any parent who encouraged their kids. "And then what? You make it sound like your career has already ended, like there isn't any hope." Blake hated hearing her talk as if it was over. She was doing what she wanted to be doing, and nobody was trying to hold her back, stifle her dreams.

"I tore three ligaments in my leg one night when I was dancing *Swan Lake*. I was finally in the role I wanted, as the lead, and I didn't even dance for an entire season at the top before my accident." She was looking away now, couldn't seem to meet his gaze. Blake wanted to reach for her, but he didn't, *couldn't*. The pain of what he'd lost and left behind was too raw for him, and he was barely coping with it on his own without having to help someone else.

"You could recover from that," he said gently, careful to choose the right words.

"No, I won't. I have a form of arthritis that I've battled for years. It first showed when I was stressed over a big performance, and in the past my doctors have been able to manage it. But from what I've been told, we're past that point now. That's why I'm out, why they wouldn't just let me stay on leave due to injury. They don't ever expect me to make a full recovery."

Blake steeled his jaw, hating that someone had had the nerve to put a damper on her dreams. On anyone's dreams. As far as he was concerned, the fight was worth it until the very last.

"You need to see more specialists, research more treatment, get your body strong again," he told her, wishing his voice didn't sound so raspy and harsh. "You can't take no for an answer when you're so close to living that dream."

Her eyes were angry, glaring when she met his gaze. "Don't you think I've done everything? As much as I could?"

He held up both his hands. "Sorry, I didn't mean to jump down your throat like that. I just…"

"I don't need to be told what to do," she said angrily, still holding his stare. "The only thing that will save me now is winning the lottery or a miracle. Money is the only way I can stay a part of this world, to keep searching for help, trying to keep training. Either money or a new treatment to help me get back on stage." She slumped forward, looked defeated. "Instead I'll be back in Hicksville, the girl who had so much potential and still ended up a nobody."

Blake bunched his fists, wished there was something he could do. He didn't know why her situation made him so angry, but it did.

Just then his phone buzzed and he glanced at it quickly. He read the screen, cursed his sister for wanting to be so involved in his love life.

So? Spill! Is she really a ballerina? She looked gorgeous. Keep this one!

Blake didn't bother replying, not about to engage with his younger sister over anything personal. And then he looked up and found Saffron watching him, her full lips parted, dark eyes trained on his.

She needed a way to stay in New York. He needed a wife.

He pushed his sister from his mind and pulled his bar stool closer to Saffron's, thinking that she was the most intriguing, beautiful woman he'd met in a long time. He didn't want to be married to anyone, but the truth was, he needed to be. That text just before was a slap-in-the-face kind of reminder. He was at the helm of a family business that was worth tens of millions of dollars, and he needed to maintain the right image. They were negotiating for a huge contract, one worth millions over the next two years alone, not to mention the investors he was trying to bring on board to grow the business. But his biggest potential investor had made it beyond clear that he was worried about Blake's playboy status, didn't like the fact that he wasn't settled down and married. They were rich men with strong family values, the kind his own father had always managed to impress. Being married could be the key to finalizing those deals, and no matter how much he'd tried to pretend otherwise, it was true, which meant he had some serious damage control to do.

He reached for his coffee and drained it. Real marriage wasn't something he wanted, hadn't been on his agenda since the day his first love had walked away from him as though what they'd had meant nothing. He could still feel the cool sting of betrayal as if it was yesterday. But if he could package a marriage of convenience into something that could work for both him and Saffron? Now that was something he'd be willing to do.

CHAPTER THREE

BLAKE CONTINUED TO sip his coffee, watching Saffron. She was beautiful. She was talented and accomplished. She was interesting. If he had to pick a wife on paper, she was it.

"So come on, spill," she said, setting her knife and fork down, surprising him by the fact she'd actually finished her entire breakfast. "The more you tell me you don't want to talk about yourself, the more I want to know."

He shook his head. "No."

Saffron's laughter made him smile. "What do I have to do then? To make you tell me?"

Now it was Blake's laughter filling the space between them. "Marry me."

Her smile died faster than it had ignited, falling from her mouth. She stared back at him, eyebrows drawing slightly closer together. "I think I misheard you."

Blake smiled, knew he had to tell her his plan carefully, to sell the idea to her instead of having her run for the door and get a restraining order against him. She was probably thinking he was a nut job, some kind of stalker who was obsessed with her after one night together.

"Look," he said, spreading his hands wide as he watched her. "If you married someone like me, you would have access to the best medical treatments, and you could stay in New York without any worries."

She did a slow nod. "Funnily enough, I've been joking about that with my friends for weeks—that I need to find a wealthy husband. But I'm used to having a successful career and standing on my own two feet."

Blake shrugged. "What if we did it? If we got married so you could stay in New York and get back on your feet, so to speak? I could pay for any specialist treatment you need to get you dancing again."

Her gaze was uncertain, maybe even cool. He couldn't figure out exactly what she thought now that her smile had disappeared. "I know why it would be good for me, I just don't get why you'd want to do it. What's in it for you? Why would you want to help me?"

"Marriage to a beautiful ballerina?" he suggested.

"Blake, I'm serious. Why would you marry me unless there's something in it for you? A hidden catch?"

"Look, plenty of people marry for convenience. Gay men marry women all the time to hide their sexuality if they think it's going to help their career or please their family."

She sighed. "Well, I know you're not gay. Unless you put on the performance of your life last night, that is. And anyway, I know plenty of gay people, and it hasn't hurt their careers at all, to be honest."

"Well, you're a dancer. Corporate America isn't always so accepting, even if they pretend to be."

"Back to you," Saffron said, studying him intensely, her eyes roving over his face. "Tell me now, or I'm walking out that door."

Blake wasn't about to call her bluff. Just because she needed a boost in finances didn't mean she was automatically going to say yes to marrying a stranger.

"Running my father's company was never part of my plan," he told her. "Now I'm CEO of a company that I'm proud of, but not a natural fit for. It's not the role I want to be in, but there's also no way I'm about to let that company fall into the wrong hands. I need to keep growing it, and I'm working on two of the biggest deals in the company's history."

"I hear you, and I'm sorry you don't like what you do, but it doesn't explain why you need a wife. Why you need to marry *me*?"

Blake didn't want to tell her everything, didn't like talking about his past and what he'd lost to anyone, why he didn't want a real wife, to open himself up to someone again. Eventually he'd have to tell her, otherwise she'd end up blindsided and their marriage would be uncovered as a sham, but not right now. Not until he knew he could trust her.

"I'm sick of the whole tabloid thing, the paps following me because some stupid magazine announced that I was one of New York's most eligible men." They'd called him the Billion Dollar Bachelor, the headlines had screamed out that women should be fighting over the former soldier back in the city as a corporate CEO and he hated it. Hated the attention and being known for his family's money after doing everything in his power to prove his own worth, make his own way in the world. But most of all he hated that people he most needed to impress right now read the rubbish being written, viewed him as a playboy, were unsettled by the fact that he *wasn't* settled.

"My dad built up the company as a family business, and our clients like that, especially a large-scale investor I've been working on for months. I don't want them to start thinking the company isn't going to continue to succeed because some loser rich-kid playboy is at the helm, and if I can set the right image now, it won't matter if I'm not married in a few years' time because the deals will be done."

Saffron didn't say anything when he paused, just stared at him.

Blake laughed. "Plus I'd like to get my mother and two sisters off my back. They're driving me crazy, trying to set me up all the time." He stood, pushing his hands into his pockets, watching, waiting for a reaction. He probably shouldn't have added the joke about getting them off his back. "So what do you think?"

"What do I think?" she muttered. "I think you're crazy!"

"We can talk through the details later, but please just think about it."

"Wow," Saffron said, holding up her hand. "I need time to think, to process how absurd this is."

"It's not that absurd," he disagreed.

"This is only-in-the-movies absurd," she fired back. "I'm not saying no, but I can't say yes right now, either."

Blake nodded. "I need to head in to the office. Why don't you stay here a bit, take your time and meet me back here tonight if you decide to say yes. I can get the paperwork and everything sorted out pretty quick, and we can go choose a ring together tomorrow."

Saffron shook her head, smiling then bursting into laughter. "I can't believe you're actually serious, that I'm not just being punked right now."

"Sweetheart, I'm deadly serious."

Blake took a few steps forward, touched her chin gently and tipped her face up, his thumb against her smooth skin. He slowly lowered his head and dropped his lips over hers, plucking softly at her lips.

"So we'd actually be married?" she asked, breathless, when she pulled back, mouth still parted as if she was waiting for more.

"Yes," he said, thinking how cute she looked in his hoodie. "You can set the boundaries, but we need it to look real."

He bent and kissed her again, softly.

Saffron could hardly breathe. She'd been outside for at least ten minutes, but her lungs still felt as though they couldn't pull in enough air. Marry him? How could he have asked her to marry him? They'd spent one night together—but marriage? Did she need rescuing that bad?

She pushed through a crowd of people passing on the street to reach a bench seat, dropping the second she found one. Could she actually marry a man she didn't even know, just to stay in New York? Just to get her career back on track, if that was even possible? She wished she could laugh it off and tell him there was no way she'd accept his proposal, but the truth was that it was the perfect solution for her. If it was the only way to give her recovery one last, real shot... Saffron gulped and turned her attention to the people walking past. Tried to lift her thoughts from Blake and failed.

What she needed was a piece of paper and her laptop. She would do what she always did—make a list of all the pros and cons, just like when she'd been offered the scholarship to dance with the New York Ballet in the first place. When she was sixteen, the list had been heavy on the pros and low on the cons, the only drawbacks coming from her parents, who wanted her to stay and didn't understand how desperately she wanted it. This time her list might be more balanced.

Marriage had always seemed so sacred to her, so special, but... She held her breath then slowly blew it out. Dancing was all she had. It was her life. If getting that back, having the one thing in the world back that meant so much to her, meant having to get married, then she had to consider it. Dancing had been her salvation. Could Blake really help her get that back?

Her phone buzzed and she picked it up, seeing it was Claire. She'd been out of touch with most of her dancing friends for the past couple of months, finding it too hard to hear about ballet and what they were training, the pain like a knife to her heart. But Claire had been there for her, been different and she'd enjoyed being part of her arty world.

"Hey," Saffy said when she answered.

"You're not still there, are you?" Claire giggled. "I still can't believe you did it. You're usually such a prude!"

Saffy laughed. "I am not a prude! Just because you have loose morals."

Now it was Claire in fits of laughter. "I'm not loose, I just don't see the point in saying no to a good time. Obviously my amazing personality has rubbed off on you."

Saffron felt better already after talking to Claire. "He…" Saffy changed her mind, not wanting to tell her. Claire was pretty open-minded, but even she might think it was crazy to consider the proposal.

"What? Tell me what you were going to say! He was amazing, wasn't he? Tell me more!" her friend begged.

Saffy sighed, the weight of her decision hanging heavy. "He was amazing, incredible, but…" Her voice trailed off again. "He wants to meet again tonight."

"Awesome! He's seriously hot stuff. Not to mention he paid up big-time for my painting. I've already had phone calls from buyers asking about my commissions and existing work."

If there hadn't been the whole marriage thing to consider, she would have been more excited. Giddy over being with a man like Blake, a man who'd made her pulse race and her mind forget all about what she'd lost while she'd been with him. She'd have liked the idea of getting to know him better, *dating* him, not marrying him.

"Good, you deserve it. And he was lovely. I'm just not sure about everything."

Silence stretched out between them, just long enough for it to be noticeable. "You're thinking about having to go back home?"

"Yeah." Saffy wasn't lying; she just wasn't telling her everything. Besides, Claire would be the one person to know the truth if it did happen, that she'd only met Blake the night before. She trusted her not to say anything, to keep her secret, but she just wasn't ready to open up about it yet, not when she was still trying to process it herself.

"Do you have any more doctors to see? Any other specialists you could visit or anything?" Claire asked. "Can you afford to keep going for a bit longer?"

Saffy shook her head, even though she knew Claire couldn't see her. This was why she was considering the marriage—this was why she *had* to. "No," she murmured. "I've done everything. There's no one left to see, or at least no one I can afford now, and I'm like damaged goods on the dance scene. If I dance again, there's only one company I want to be with, and that's a firm no right now."

"Fight till the bitter end, Saffy. Don't go quitting until you have no other options left."

Saffron had no intention of giving up until the last; it had been her attitude all her life. But even she had to admit that when it was over, it was over.

"There's one last thing I have to consider," she told Claire. "One last option."

"Give it a go—you owe it to yourself."

"I'm going to go, I have a few jobs to get done," Saffy said, wanting to end the call so she could think some more. She started to walk, the familiar twinge in her knee bearable at a walk when she was wearing heels. Barefoot it was almost unnoticeable. It was when she tried to push herself harder or dance that it really hurt. "Enjoy the weekend."

"You, too. Give me a call tomorrow so I can hear all the juicy details from tonight."

Saffy said goodbye and kept walking, suddenly realizing how terrible she must look. She was wearing her blue satin dress, her hair was tangled, and her heels weren't exactly daytime wear. Thank goodness there had been no cameras flashing when she'd exited out the back of Blake's building, through the café. Her career being over was bad enough—the last thing she needed was for the public to see pictures of her looking like she was right now.

Marriage. No matter how hard she tried to clear her head, Blake's proposal was the only thing on her mind. And she was pretty certain that, like it or not, she was going to have to say yes.

Blake sat in his office, staring out the huge windows that bordered two sides. It was a stunning corner office—luxurious and extravagant—but it didn't feel like his. For two decades it had been his father's office, and he'd been in it numerous times, often when his father was trying to convince him that the company was where he should be. That it should be his dream, as if he should grow up to be a carbon copy of the man who'd raised him. But Blake had never wanted to be his father, had had dreams of his own, dreams that were still with him that he'd been forced to leave behind.

He stood and walked to the window, restless being inside and having to stare at paperwork and sign contracts. The city was alive below him, people milling everywhere, and he wished he could just disappear in the crowd and leave his responsibilities behind. But he'd made the decision to come back, and he wasn't a quitter.

"This is your life, son. You're my eldest, and I expect you to take over the business. To look after your family."

The words had echoed in his mind long before his father had died, but now they were never ending. Every time he wanted to walk away, they haunted him, kept him awake at night. He was the eldest, and he'd always had a sense of responsibility that his younger brother and sisters had never had. But it hadn't stopped his brother from wanting to run the company, to absorb everything their father had to share and teach.

Everything had been going to plan—Blake was doing what he loved, and his brother was shadowing their dad, learning the ropes, prepared to take over the company one day. Until everything had gone horribly wrong.

Blake clenched his teeth together and crossed the room, reaching for the whiskey his father had always kept in the office, filling one of the crystal tumblers he'd seen his father drink from so many times. He poured a small amount into the glass and downed it, liking the burn. *Needing* the burn.

The chill he'd felt when they'd died, when his mother

had phoned him and he'd heard the choke in her voice, knowing the helicopter had gone down. He'd gotten there as fast as he could, been with the rescue team on the ground, seen the wreckage with his own eyes. At that moment, he'd known he had no other choice— he had to step up and take over the business just like his father had always wanted him to do. He'd lost so many good people in his life, but losing his father had never been something he'd thought about until it had happened.

Blake set the glass down again and went back to his desk. There were things he couldn't change, memories that would be with him forever, but the only thing that mattered right now was doing the best, given what life had served him. And Saffron would go a long way to helping make his life easier, making sure he secured the deals and the financial backing he needed to take the company to the next level. He needed a wife at his side, and she was the perfect match to him, could be the perfect, capable woman at his side...because they could enter into the relationship with a contract that gave them both exactly what they wanted.

He checked his phone. He'd half expected her to text or phone him after thinking about it, but then he'd also seen the determined look in her eyes, known that she was a fighter from the moment he'd heard about how she'd risen to the top. A ballerina who'd defied all odds and risen through the ranks to become one of New York's most respected dancers. It wasn't an easy path, and he doubted she would like having to do something she didn't want to do.

It was easy for him because it was a win-win situation. He would have a wife, a beautiful woman by his side who intrigued him, and they'd be divorced within the year. He didn't want a family, didn't want children, and he certainly didn't want an *actual* wife. They were things he'd dreamed of a decade ago, before the only person in his life he'd ever completely opened up to and been himself with had ripped out his heart and torn it to shreds. He wasn't ever going to put himself in that position again, just like he would never deceive a woman into marrying him without clearly setting out his terms.

Blake smiled and sat back down in the plush leather chair. Usually Saturdays were his favorite day to work, when the office was quiet and no one was around to bother him. But today his mind was wandering, and it was a stunning redhead on his mind that he couldn't stop thinking about. Whoever said he couldn't mix a little pleasure with business?

Saffron stared at the list she'd made, chewing on the end of her pen. It was a pretty short list. She leaned back into the sofa. There was no other way. Blake had just given her the perfect way to stay in the city, but being at the beck and call of a man like him was…scary. She shut her eyes, smiled when she thought about the night they'd shared.

She was going to do it. Saffy laughed out loud, feeling kind of crazy. Maybe she'd drunk too much the night before and it was still in her system, or maybe she was actually crazy, but she had to do it. She stood and flexed, grimaced when she tried to push up onto her toes and flex her muscles. The pain was tolerable, barely there compared to the excruciating pain she'd experienced at the time, but it still told her that things weren't right. That without some kind of miracle, she wouldn't be dancing anytime soon. But it didn't mean she couldn't keep her body strong and exercise.

She pulled on her trainers and laced them up, carefully stretching out her muscles just like her physical therapist had showed her. Her body was everything to her, and she had always taken care to stretch and warm up slowly, but now she had to treat it with even more care than ever before. Saffron rose up onto her toes, watched herself in the full-length mirror she had propped against a door. She held her arms out, tucked one leg up, bit down hard on her bottom lip as she flexed, forced herself to take the weight on first her good leg and then her bad.

No more. She released her lip from her teeth, expecting to taste blood she'd been biting so hard. The pain was there, was just as bad, and that meant she had to stop even though she would have loved to have tried to push through it.

Instead she grabbed her iPhone and stuck her earbuds in, planning on walking for an hour. She'd rather be running or dancing, but right now it was either walking and swimming or nothing at all. If she pushed herself too hard before she was ready, she wouldn't have the chance to make the same mistake again.

She checked the time before pulling the door shut behind her. She could walk for an hour or so, grab a coffee, then shower and head to Blake's house. Money was tight, which was another pro on her list, because if she married him then she'd be living with him. If she didn't, it would look like the sham it was, and she knew he wanted to keep it real. Besides, he'd told her as much—that she wouldn't have to worry about finances.

Right away she could cut almost all of her expenses, and her back account was already screaming out in the red after the cash she'd spent on all sorts of alternative therapies in conjunction with the specialist's advice.

Saffron Goldsmith. It sure had a ring to it. She glanced at her finger. Tomorrow there could be a diamond sparkling there, a real ring, a ring that would tell everyone that she was engaged. She hadn't exactly been the type to dream of a wedding when she was a girl—she'd been too focused on her career—but it still seemed weird.

She breathed in the fresh air once she was outside and started walking, slow at first. In a few hours' time she was going to be saying yes to a man she hardly knew, which meant this could very well be her last little glimpse of freedom before she had another human being to answer to.

CHAPTER FOUR

SAFFRON SHUFFLED HER bag from hand to hand, hating that her palms were so sweaty. She usually got nervous only before a performance, and even then it always passed as soon as she stepped on stage. This was a weird kind of nervousness that she hadn't felt before.

She took a big breath and squared her shoulders before pushing the button to Blake's apartment. He didn't say anything through the intercom, but the door clicked and she opened it and let herself in, going up in the elevator. When the metal doors opened, she found him leaning on the doorjamb, eyes searching hers out.

"I see you've brought a bag," he said, not taking his eyes from hers.

She kept her chin up, didn't want to appear weak. She felt like a prey animal having to stand up to a predator, standing her ground and being brave even when all she really wanted to do was cower.

"I have," she said back.

"Well, then, come on in. *Fiancée.*"

Saffy gulped and stepped forward, walking straight past Blake and into the apartment. The apartment she lived in was like a shoe box in comparison, small enough to fit inside his five times over. The sprawling spaces reminded her more of places back home, where space wasn't at a premium.

"We need to establish some ground rules," she said, deciding to start how she wanted things to be, not wanting him to think he could boss her around.

"I'm all ears." His smile made him even more handsome, eyes twinkling as he watched her.

She wasn't going to let him rattle her with his gorgeous face. Or his gorgeous body. Although the way his arms were folded across his chest as he stared at her made his shirt strain across his biceps. Even worse was how chilled out he seemed about the whole thing.

"I want everything in writing," she began, setting down her bag and taking a seat on the same bar stool she'd been perched on earlier in the day. "I need to give up the lease on my place and know that I can live here while we're married, for at least a year. I'll continue to pay for my own personal things, but you need to cover all my medical expenses, including any new specialists I find. I'm doing this only because I think there's a chance I could find someone to help me if I have the funds."

He raised an eyebrow, one side of his mouth kicked up at the sides. "Is that all? Or do you have a full list of ransom details?"

Saffy cracked a smile. "That's it."

He walked toward her, and a shiver ran down her spine. She had the distinct feeling that he was the one in charge, even though he'd just agreed to her terms.

"I agree," he said simply. "In fact, I already have a contract for you to sign."

She laughed. "Your lawyer did up an agreement for you on a Saturday?"

His shrug told her this wasn't out of the ordinary. "We have him on a pretty good retainer."

"So just like that, you agree?" she asked. Once again, it seemed too good to be true. For her, anyway. "To funding me and promising that this will go on for at least a year?"

"Sure. I'll even let you keep the diamond ring as a separation gift when we part ways." He didn't look worried about anything. "I need this *marriage* to exist for at least a year, too, to make sure my investors sign on the dotted line and to ensure it doesn't look like a sham. Once I have everything in place, it won't matter whether I'm married or not."

His smile was wolfish now, and she wasn't sure if he was joking or not. "You actually mean it about the diamond?"

"Yes. We can pick something tomorrow." She watched as he picked up a thick envelope from the coffee table. "This is some light reading for you—sign when you're ready."

She nodded. "Okay."

"I'm going to leave you to read it, give you a bit of space. Maybe a couple of hours for you to look over the paper, sign, and take a walk around the apartment without me being here. Feel free to consult with your own attorney if you want to, but you'll find that there's nothing in there not spelled out in plain English."

"Sure." It all seemed so weird, so formal, but she'd made up her mind and she was going to do it. There was no backing out now, not unless he had something sneaky in the contract that took her by surprise.

"We'll head out to dinner to celebrate," he said, passing her the envelope and reaching for her face, touching a stray tendril of hair and then running his thumb down her cheek.

She stared into his dark eyes, wishing she knew more about the mysterious man she was about to marry.

"My mother is going to love you," he said with a chuckle before stepping backward.

If only he loved her. She quickly pushed the thought away, checked herself. Blake was virtually a stranger—the last thing he'd feel was love for her! Maybe she was suffering from some sort of Cinderella complex, because it felt as if Blake was saving her, had ridden to her rescue and was offering her everything.

The everything part was true, but he was no Prince Charming. She was kidding herself if she saw him as anything other than a man who needed something and was prepared to do whatever he had to in order to make that happen.

"Your mother'd better love me," she finally managed in reply.

"Did I mention I also have two interfering sisters?" he asked as he shrugged into a jacket.

Saffy groaned. "Don't say anything else, or you might find the envelope unopened and me long gone." If only she had the power to do that, wasn't trapped in a corner with no other options. She'd still be interested in getting to know him better, but she sure wouldn't be jumping headfirst into marriage.

Blake just grinned and held up a hand. "See you soon. Anything you don't eat?"

She shook her head. "Not really."

"Good, I'll make us a reservation for seven. See you later on."

She watched him go, sat silently, until he had his hand on the door.

"Wait!" she called.

Blake turned, eyebrows raised in question.

"Why don't you stay? Then we can just talk through the whole thing." She didn't actually want to be left alone, didn't want to sit in silence trying to figure out legal jargon on her own.

Blake's smile made her heart skip a beat. "I thought you'd never ask." He shrugged off his jacket as fast as he'd put it on only moments earlier, dropping down onto the sofa, eyes still on hers. "You read, I'll answer questions."

She slowly ripped the envelope open, scanned a little of the first page before leaning on the bar and looking at Blake.

"So obviously there's a prenup," she said.

"Yep," he said. "Standard terms, including that if there were any children born during our marriage the child would be cared for." He laughed. "Obviously that's not in either of our plans, though, right?"

Saffy laughed straight back. "Have you ever seen a pregnant ballerina?" She definitely wouldn't be getting a penny from Blake, because there was no way she was getting pregnant, no way she *could* get pregnant.

"Which leads to the next clause, to ensure that every precaution is made to ensure no children *can* be conceived, something about blah-blah it not being part of either of our plans."

"Phew. Glad we got that sorted out," she said with a giggle, liking that she made Blake laugh again. His smile lit up his face, and it made her feel more relaxed. "Please tell me you have it in writing that I get to keep whatever rock you put on my finger?"

"Why, yes. The bride may keep the ring after separation or divorce. It'll be all yours once you've done your duty."

"Uh-huh," she said, scanning through a few more pages, seeing that everything he was saying was listed. And then she reached the part about the marriage being real, blushed as she looked up to find Blake watching her.

"We must live as a real husband and wife," she forced herself to say out loud.

"You're so cute when your face goes all pink," he said, rising and crossing the room.

She looked down, hating that she was so reactive when it came to him.

"It only stipulates that we have to live together at all times…that we remain faithful and don't speak to the media." He brushed past her, moving into the kitchen. "Beyond that, it's up to you. I just don't want anyone, from colleagues to housekeepers, not to believe that our marriage is real."

"So there's nothing in here you're trying to hide from me? Everything's as you say?" she asked, scanning though the pages again, pleased it wasn't a long document.

"I'm not trying to deceive you. It goes on to say that all your medical costs, including elective consultations and treatments, are covered. You have my word."

Saffy knew she needed to just sign it, that it was the best thing for her right now. So long as she didn't let herself get emotionally involved. She signed at the end, taking a pen from the kitchen counter that she could reach. Then there was a single document, just one page that fluttered out from beneath. From what she could see it was a separate contract.

This one was stamped confidential. She scanned it, realizing that this was the divorce contract. It was crazy—on the one hand she was signing a prenup, and on the other she was confirming a divorce was to take place when they both agreed it should, but in no longer than three years. She was to file for divorce, stating irreconcilable differences. Saffron hesitated, thinking of how long her own parents had been happily married, but she quickly pushed those thoughts away. This wasn't a real marriage. It was a convenient relationship for both of them, and they were both adults. There were no children involved, which meant that the only people that could be harmed by what they were doing were the two of them. The only thing she would have to be embarrassed about would be lying to her parents, because it wasn't exactly something she could keep from them. She'd never deceived them before about anything, had never lied to anyone she cared for, but this was her one chance to dance again and when it was all over she'd tell them the truth.

Saffy signed the second document, looking up and realizing how silent Blake had been.

"All done."

He exhaled loudly. "Guess it's my turn then." He leaned over her, his musky cologne making her wish she'd held her breath instead of inhaling. And then it was done.

"Take a look around. I'll make us a drink," he said with a wink.

"Mind if I take a shower?" She was dying to stand under hot water, needing some time to think.

"It's your home now. You can do whatever you like."

Saffron gulped and left him in the kitchen, going first into Blake's bedroom, taking a look around the very masculine space. The bed was made—a dove-gray cover paired with white pillows and a smattering of gray cushions against a black leather headboard. She'd already looked in his closet that morning and seen the bathroom, so instead of looking around more, she decided to just jump in the shower. Wash her hair and luxuriate in a bathroom that was bigger than her former bedroom, the floor-to-ceiling tiles reminding her of some of the lovely hotels she'd been fortunate to stay in when she'd been touring a few times. She went back out and got her suitcase, pleased to see that Blake was on the phone so she could just slip straight past him, putting her luggage in the middle of the bedroom.

Saffron stripped down, leaving her clothes in a puddle on the bathroom floor and turning the faucet on. The water was warm almost instantly, but she quickly walked out, naked, to retrieve her cosmetic bag that had her shampoo and conditioner in it. The shower was so good, the nozzle spraying so much water out and the steam feeling so good around her that she didn't want to get out. Instead she just shut her eyes and stood there, wishing she could stay there all day. Her hair was washed, the citrusy smell of her shampoo wafted around her, and all she had to do now was soap up her body...

"You need anything?"

Her eyes popped open and water blurred her gaze. Saffy quickly soaped herself and rinsed. Had he just walked in?

"Saffy? Do you still want that drink?" Blake's deep voice sent shivers down her spine, made her self-conscious with no clothes on.

"Just a sec!" she called back, hoping he'd stay in the bedroom and not actually walk on in.

Saffy turned the faucet off and jumped out, hurriedly reaching for a towel and rubbing it down her body then back up again. She was just about to dry her hair when his voice sounded out a whole lot closer.

"Hey. I wasn't sure if you'd heard me."

She wrapped the towel around herself and flung her hair back. Blake was standing in the doorway, looking straight in at her in the bathroom. Granted, she hadn't closed the door properly, but she hadn't expected him to walk in on her!

"Um, I just..." She stammered, knowing it was stu-pid being so body conscious, given the fact he'd seen her stripped bare less than twenty-four hours earlier, but she couldn't help it.

"Sorry, I didn't think you'd…" Blake was talking to her, but his eyes weren't on hers. They kept drifting down, and she held the towel a little tighter. "I can see this wasn't a good idea. I'll make you that drink."

"Uh, yeah, sure."

Blake was still watching her, but his eyes were trained on her face now. "This is weird, huh?"

She tucked the towel in at her breasts. "Um, yeah. Very weird."

Blake backed up. "I'll give you a minute to get, ah, dressed."

Saffy slipped to the floor in a puddle when he disappeared, her back against the glass of the shower. This was ridiculous! She was craving him, wanted him against her so she could kiss him all night, but at the same time she was a bundle of nerves about him even seeing her bare skin.

Maybe it was just because there was so much at stake now. Or maybe she just didn't want to admit that after being bored for so long after she'd had to quit dancing, she was finally feeling alive again and it scared her.

She picked herself up, dashed into the bedroom to get some clean underwear, and slipped on a big thick white terry cloth robe that she'd seen earlier in Blake's closet. She tied it around herself, liking how snuggly it was. It also covered up her body, which she thought might be a good idea in case Blake came back in. Saffy towel dried her hair, deciding to put on her makeup first and rub some moisturizer into her legs since she wanted to wear a dress out for dinner.

They weren't even married yet, and already she felt as if she'd lost control.

Blake sat on the sofa then jumped up and paced back toward the kitchen. He wasn't used to being so…rattled. Seeing Saffron in his bathroom, knowing exactly what was under the towel she'd had clasped to her slick wet body… He groaned. Maybe the marriage contract had been a bad idea. *A very bad idea.* She was supposed to make his life easier, and instead she was stopping him from thinking about anything else.

He glanced at the paperwork on the counter and then looked back toward his bedroom. It was all signed, which meant all that was left was for him to actually go down on bended knee for real so they had a story to tell everyone about their engagement.

Blake opened a bottle of wine, needing to take his mind off Saffron. There was something easy about what they'd agreed to, but for a man who'd sworn off marriage and family years ago, it was unsettling, too. He'd lived alone all his life unless he'd been working, when he'd been bunked down with his unit, and until Saffy he hadn't even brought a woman back to his apartment. And now he'd gone and broken all his rules, let someone get close to him, even though this time around he was in control of the situation. He was never going to be made a fool of again, never wanted to voluntarily feel hurt like he'd felt in the past, but so long as they both stuck to the rules…

"Dollar for them?"

Blake looked up, pulled from his thoughts. She was standing forlorn in the middle of the room, staring at him. Her hair was still damp, hanging loose and tumbling down over her shoulders, and she was wrapped in his robe. A robe he hardly ever wore, but his nonetheless. It was the second time he'd seen her in his clothes, and he was starting to more than like it.

"Nothing," he said, turning his body to face her. "Nothing important, anyway."

He watched as she shifted, looked uncomfortable. Blake had a feeling he wasn't going to like what she had to say.

"Is everything okay?"

She sighed loud enough for him to hear. "I don't know about you, but this whole thing just seems…"

"Unusual?" he suggested.

"Kind of uncomfortable," she said. "I don't know, I just don't know how to act around you. Last night I was me, or at least a version of me. But now…"

Saffron didn't seem to be able to finish her sentences, as though she was overly nervous. He stood but decided not to walk over to her, to keep some space between them instead of pushing her. The last thing he wanted to do was scare her off now.

"How about you finish getting ready for dinner," Blake said gently, trying his hardest to say the right thing. He had two sisters, so being around women and knowing what to say should be second nature to him, only for some reason it wasn't helping him right now. "Maybe we can take a step back, forget about the contract for a bit. We can pretend this is real if we like. Just actually date and try to ignore the marriage part to make it easier."

He had to fight a grin when her saw her lips kick up into a small smile.

"You really think we can go back? Trick ourselves that this is real?"

Not for a minute, because the only way he would ever propose to a woman was in a situation like this. "Sure we can," he said, trying to sound optimistic. "And if we can't do that, then there's no reason we can't be friends, enjoy the next year or so together." He knew that was a lie, too. Because there were plenty of ways they could enjoy being together, but strictly as friends wasn't what he had in mind right now or probably ever would with her.

Saffron turned and disappeared back into the bedroom, and within minutes he heard her hair dryer going. The beautiful ballerina would no doubt emerge a knockout, just like she'd looked last night.

He could be plenty of things to Saffron without having to open up, though. He had no interest in baring his soul to another human being, or reliving any of his past and opening up about anything. If he was in a real relationship, those things would be nonnegotiable, but with Saffron he could choose how much to divulge, how much of his true self to give. Because no matter what they pretended to the contrary, what they had was a contract. He'd fallen in love before, had his heart broken by someone he'd trusted more than anyone else. Fool him once, but never twice...

Blake took a sip of his wine and stared at the documents sitting in front of him.

It was done. He was officially about to become a married man.

Blake pulled his phone from his pocket and dialed his mother. He wanted to get it over and done with now, and he only had to phone one of the women in his family, because news spread like wildfire between his mom and sisters.

"Hello, darling."

"Mom," he said, clearing his throat. He could still hear Saffron's hair dryer, so he launched into what he had to say. "I know you've seen the pictures from this morning."

"Of course I've seen them. I'm just disappointed you've kept such an interesting woman hidden away from us."

If Saffron was really his fiancée-to-be, he would definitely be keeping her hidden from his family! "Mom, I should have told you, but we've just been lying low, getting to know each other without…"

"You don't have to explain yourself, sweetheart. I'm just happy that you're seeing such a fantastic young woman!"

"The girls have been googling her and showing you the results, haven't they." Blake had no doubt that they'd be all over the internet. There was no way his mother was that tuned in on her own; he'd bet they'd all been gossiping and flicking through web pages together.

"Of course!"

"Mom, I hope you're sitting down, because I have news."

"Blake! What is it?"

"I've asked Saffron to marry me."

"Girls!" His mother's screech forced him to pull the phone from his ear.

"I have to go, Mom. We're going out to dinner to celebrate, and I wanted to share the good news with you before anyone else found out."

"Could we join you? Meet this woman who's going to be my daughter-in-law?"

Blake could hear the excitement in his mother's voice, felt a pang of guilt for deceiving her. His mother got on his nerves at the best of times when it came to his personal life, and his sisters drove him crazy sometimes, but he loved them as fiercely as was humanly possible and lying to them made him feel worse than he'd expected.

"Let me take Saffron out tonight, just the two of us. I promised her something special to celebrate," Blake said. "But we'll see you soon, okay? I won't keep her hidden away forever."

He wondered if his mother would even take the bait, if she'd be instantly suspicious, but then she was used to him keeping his personal life private. And as far as he knew, she'd been shielded from what his dad had done, had never been exposed to the truth of the only serious relationship he'd ever had before. Never known how much pain her eldest son had been in.

When he finally got her off the phone and managed to end the call, he glanced up to see that Saffron was sitting on the sofa. He'd been so engrossed in talking with his mom, staring out the window as day became night, that he hadn't even heard the hair dryer switch off.

"You heard all that?" he asked.

Saffron shrugged, still flipping through a magazine. "Mmm, some of it." She looked up. "Do you feel kind of guilty?"

He nodded. "Yes, but it's for the best."

"I'm going to have to put on the performance of my life for your mother, aren't I?"

Blake didn't want to scare her. "Look, she'll be so excited to meet you that she'll probably do all the talking. The real performance will be when I have you by my side at business functions. That's why I'm marrying you."

She didn't look worried about it.

Blake unbuttoned his shirt and stretched out. "Give me a minute to take a shower."

He could feel her eyes on him as he walked, knew she was watching him. His problem was that he didn't know how to behave, how to act. He wanted to forget everything and just… He steeled his jaw. Sex should be the last thing on his mind. He wasn't doing this for sex—he could get that without being married—but looking at Saffron made him think of one thing and one thing only.

He left her on the sofa and stripped, showering then tucking his towel around his waist when he was finished. He went back into the bedroom adjoining the bath and pulled out a fresh shirt. He dressed quickly, ran his fingers through his hair and put some product in.

When he went back out, Saffron was still sitting on the sofa where he'd left her.

"Ready?" he asked, voice sounding gruff to his own ears.

She stood. "Yep, ready."

He walked ahead, opened the door and stood back for her to follow. Her dress was short, cute and covered in sequins. It showed off her toned, slim legs, and there was plenty of skin for him to admire up top, too. Her top was loose but with a low front, hair flowing down her back. It was the hair that got him more than the skin, though. Because when he'd first woken after their night together, it had been her hair touching his skin, falling over his chest. Her hair that he'd stroked.

"Where are we going?" she asked.

Blake cleared his throat. He was lucky she wasn't a mind reader. "Somewhere close. We can walk."

She shrugged her leather jacket on and they walked side by side, lights twinkling and showing the way along the road.

"I booked us in for Japanese. I'm thinking sushi, sashimi and teppanyaki."

Her smile was so innocent he wanted to reach for her and tug her closer. Maybe that was why he'd been drawn to her in the first place, not just because she was beautiful, but because there was something vulnerable about her. Something so unlike most of the women he met, a fragility that was tempered by how successful she'd been in her career.

"Are we sitting at the teppan table?" Saffron asked, her grin infectious. She was more excited child than grown seductress for a moment.

"We sure are. I thought you might like watching the food cooked in front of us."

She laughed. "You mean you thought it would be a good distraction when we ran out of things to talk about."

Blake held up his hands. "Guilty."

They walked in silence a bit longer.

"This is the weirdest one-night stand I've ever had," Blake confessed. "It's kind of awkward, in a we-wouldn't-usually-see-each-other-again kind of way. It's like extending the morning-after part."

Her laughter was gone but her eyes were still twinkling with humor. "I wasn't lying when I said I hadn't had a one-night stand before. So the whole awkward-morning-after thing is all new to me."

"Well, let me tell you it's normally over really fast and then you forget about it." He chuckled. "Although if I'm honest, you might have taken a little longer to forget about."

"So no serious girlfriends? No ex-wives I should know about?"

The last thing Blake wanted to do was talk about his ex. With anyone. "Let's just say that my mother never thought I'd settle down. I've always made that pretty clear."

"Right," she said as he guided her into a restaurant. It was only a few blocks away, so the walk had been brief. "So you've preferred to be the party bachelor boy all your life?"

He kept his anger in check. The last thing he wanted was for her to think the same way about him that everyone else seemed to in this city. "I was too busy with my career to be the party boy, even though everyone seems to forget how long I was away serving."

Saffron seemed confused when she looked up at him. "I'm getting the feeling that there's someone who broke your heart. Someone you really don't want to talk about."

"So let's not talk about it," Blake ground out. It wasn't as if he had a problem talking about the dates he'd had or the women he'd been with—it was just one particular woman who still made him want to slam his fist into a wall. It wasn't because he still had feelings for her; it was the way she'd hurt him, the way his father had been able to hurt him so easily through her. "I'm starving. You?"

He listened to Saffron sigh, knew the sound and that it meant the conversation wasn't over. His sisters made the same noise all the time. But to her credit she didn't bring it up again.

Saffron stayed silent as they were taken to their table, sitting down and starting to toy with the menu. Blake couldn't stand it.

"Look, I didn't mean to shut you down like that, but there are just some things I don't want to talk about."

"Me, too, but we kind of need to know everything about each other."

"What do you want me to say?" he muttered, keeping his voice low so they weren't overheard. "That I was in love once and she ripped my heart out and tore it to pieces?"

Saffron blinked at him, but the expression on her face hardly changed. "You know what? I think this whole thing was a bad idea."

She stood and pushed back her chair, reaching for her purse.

"Saffron, wait." He jumped up and reached for her, one hand over her arm. "I'm sorry." What was he doing flying off the handle like that?

Her eyes were swimming with what he guessed was hurt or maybe just frustration. "This is crazy. I can't be this desperate," she murmured.

"I'm an idiot, and this isn't crazy. It's…" He shrugged. "Convenient. And it's going to work out just fine for both of us."

She looked unsure still, and he ran his hand down her arm until he could stroke her palm and then link fingers with her. He seriously needed to work on his bedside manner.

"Please. Just give me a chance. I promise I'll be better behaved."

Saffron slowly sat down again. Blake would bet there were eyes watching them, but he didn't care. He quickly ordered them champagne, then turned his full attention to Saffron. He sucked back a breath and forced himself to say the words.

"I was in love once, you were right. With a woman I wanted to spend the rest of my life with," he admitted, knowing that if he didn't do something, he was going to end up losing the woman he needed right now. Talking about his past wasn't something Blake made a habit of, and for ten years he hadn't shared what had happened with another soul. He cleared his throat. "Her name was Bianca, and we'd been together for three years. We met in school, and we were joined at the hip from that day on. I thought it was true love, or as true love as it can be when you're barely eighteen and haven't had a load of experience. I would have done anything for her, she was the love of my life."

Saffron's eyes were wide as she listened. "What happened to her?"

"Well," Blake said, nodding his thanks when their champagne arrived and reaching for the glass stem to worry between his forefinger and thumb, "we were off to college and planning our future, and I proposed to her. She said yes, we had crazy good sex, like we always did, and barely three weeks later she disappeared."

"What do you mean, disappeared?"

Blake held up his glass to clink against hers, taking a long sip. He wasn't big on bubbles, but they were supposed to be celebrating their engagement, and Saffron had seemed to enjoy the Veuve Clicquot the night before.

"She broke my heart," he said simply, still feeling the sting of betrayal. Not so much from her as from his father. "I searched for her. My father looked on, and eventually he admitted that he'd offered her money to leave. To not go through with the engagement."

"Your dad did that to you? You must have hated her for taking it!"

"I hated them both," Blake said honestly. "I already disliked my father, knew the moment I confronted him that it had been his doing. He never thought she was good enough for me—her family was not highly regarded or wealthy enough. But she was my girlfriend, the most important person in my life, the one person I was myself with and loved unconditionally." Blake leaned back. "My dad told me he'd known all along she was using me for our money, and he said all he'd done was prove he was right, that he hadn't actually done anything wrong. His theory was that she'd be knocked up within months just to make sure she had me trapped, well and good." He grunted. "Turns out the old man was right after all, although it didn't make me hate him any less. It was a lesson in love for me, and right then and there I decided it was going to be my last."

Saffron stroked his hand, her arm covering the space between them as she touched him. "Do you still love her?"

Blake laughed, but even to him it sounded cruel, dark. "No, sweetheart, I don't still love her. It was a decade ago now, and all it did was show me that the only person in life I could trust was myself."

"Do you still believe that?" she asked, leaving her hand on his as she sipped her champagne. "After all this time?"

He shifted so their connection was lost, disturbed by how easy their touch was. "I trusted my men when

I was serving and the pilot sitting to my left, but I've never trusted another woman since."

She nodded, as if she understood, but he doubted she could. "I've only had one proper relationship."

"Hard to believe," he joked. "I could imagine you having suitors lined up for you backstage."

Her smile was cute, almost bashful. "It wasn't for lack of interest, but I just haven't had time. Work meant everything to me, right from when I was at high school, so it just never happened. Until I met Raf, a dancer I was paired with..."

Blake lifted his glass and she did the same. He waited for her to continue, not wanting to push. He knew how hard opening up was; he was still wondering what he'd just done by telling her about his past. But if they were going to make this work, make the next twelve months bearable, it had to be done.

"I fell hard for him, thought what we had was special. But he was sleeping with every other dancer behind my back. I felt stupid and ashamed, and when I ended it, he made me feel like I was the problem, not him." She shrugged, but the casual action didn't match the emotion he could see on her face, in her eyes. "I decided then and there I was better on my own, and I haven't let myself even come close to being hurt ever since."

"Here's to keeping our hearts safe," Blake said, holding up his glass.

"I'll drink to that," she agreed.

"You see, we're both proof that what we're doing is for the best."

"Yeah, maybe," Saffron muttered.

Blake wasn't sure he liked the fact he'd been so open, but he'd told her now and it wasn't as if he could take it back.

"Let's order, and no more talking about exes," Saffron said.

Blake couldn't have put it better if he'd tried.

CHAPTER FIVE

"So here we are again."

Saffy shivered, even though the apartment was perfectly warm. She'd already discarded her leather jacket, so her arms were bare, but she felt exposed, as if she was naked. Blake's words were having an effect on her all over again; the only difference was that tonight she'd only had one glass of champagne, so she couldn't even blame the alcohol.

"Blake, can I ask you something?"

She watched as he threw his jacket down over the sofa and crossed the room, reaching for a bottle of whiskey.

"Did you know who I was when we met last night?"

He was frowning when he looked up. "No. I was bored, and you were the most interesting person in the room."

She had no other choice but to believe him. Saffy was about to say something else when he turned with two tumblers and moved toward her. "I want to make it very clear that you deserve someone amazing one day, a man who'll love you like every decent woman deserves to be loved. I'm not that guy to any woman, but I will treat you well while we're under contract."

Even though she'd known exactly what she'd signed up for, had her eyes wide-open, the truth of their agreement still stung when he said it like that. It hurt that she was good enough for sex but not a real relationship, even though she understood his reasons. She was being sensitive, but knowing that didn't make it any easier to deal with.

She took the glass he passed her. "So is this to celebrate our twenty-four-hour anniversary?" she asked.

Blake's smile made his already perfect face appear even more handsome. It softened his features, made her yearn to touch him and be in his arms again.

"Here's to us," he said, voice silky smooth. "I never break a contract, and I never back down on what I say. So I'll put good money on it that you'll be up and dancing again once you've had access to the best specialists money can buy."

She wished she could be as optimistic, but she knew firsthand that no matter how much money she had behind her, it wouldn't be easy. It gave her a better chance, but it didn't guarantee anything.

"And all I have to do is be the model wife, right?" She was only half joking, although she had no intention of giving a Stepford wife a run for her money.

"Don't lie to me, play the part when I need you to and we can coexist happily."

They stood facing each other, and Saffron held up her glass, clinking it to his and sipping when he did. The liquor was like silk in her mouth and fire in her throat, and when she swallowed her eyes burned. She blinked the tears away, not liking how amused Blake looked.

He laughed. "*More* than happily."

"I won't lie to you," she said honestly. "All I want to do is dance, and if you can give me that back, then I'll owe you everything." It was the pure, raw truth. There wasn't much she wouldn't do to get her dream back, and even though she was so close to losing hope, she would not stop fighting until the bitter end.

"Come here," he said gently.

Saffy hesitated, waited, wasn't sure if she wanted to give in to the way she was feeling just yet. Until Blake reached for her. His fingers closed over her arm, then worked their way up, each movement sending shivers through her body that she couldn't control. Her mouth parted as he slid his body forward, moved into her space, his body just grazing hers.

"I don't want to presume anything. I mean, anything we do for real has to be your choice."

Saffy stared up at him, eventually nodded. "Uh-huh," she whispered back. She liked that he wasn't pushing her, that the ball was in her court.

"It's your choice," Blake said softly, his eyes full of concern. "I have a perfectly nice spare bedroom with its own bathroom that I haven't even showed you yet, or you could just move into my room with me. We'd need to keep most of your things in my room, though, because I don't want my housekeeper being suspicious, or anyone else who might come over."

Saffron gulped, her eyes fixed on his mouth, carefully pressing her lips to his when he kissed her again, slipping her free arm around his neck to draw him even closer. He was magnetic and handsome and sexy...and technically he was hers. And she did want to be in his room. Besides, her excuse could be that she didn't think the housekeeper would buy their marriage as real if the sheets in the spare room were always rumpled.

When Blake finally pulled back it was to down the rest of his whiskey and discard his glass, placing it on the coffee table and turning back to her with a smile that made her think of only one thing. For a girl who was always so focused and made the right decisions, she was ready to make a bad one all over again very quickly.

"What do you say, fiancée?" he asked.

Saffron bravely sipped her drink, the burn just as bad this time as the first. "I say I haven't had much to make me smile these last few months. Why not?"

Blake took her hand and led her to his room. They stopped only for him to flick off the lights, bathing the apartment in darkness. The only light was from the bedside lamps in his room.

What she was doing was so out of character, but for some crazy reason it felt all kinds of right. Thankfully the awkwardness of earlier had faded a little.

When they reached the bedroom, Blake stood in front of her, kissing her again before gently slipping the strap on her dress down and covering her bare shoulder with his mouth.

If only it was real. She couldn't help her thoughts, even as she tried to push them away. Part of it was real, surely, but the other part...he might not want to date her, or marry her, but his hands on her body and the look in his eyes told her that his desire for her was definitely real.

"Blake, I…" Saffron groaned, not wanting to ruin the moment but needing to.

"What is it?"

"I just, I need you to know why I said yes."

"Right now?" he asked, eyebrows raised.

She nodded, reaching for his hand. Suddenly she needed to tell him, had to get it off her chest so he understood who she was.

"Talk to me," Blake said, pulling her over to sit beside him.

Saffy sighed. "When I was younger, I had an operation for cervical cancer. I've known since I was nineteen that I couldn't have children, so I want you to know that's something you don't need to worry about with me." It wasn't something she usually shared, except with other women to encourage them to have regular checkups, but she wanted Blake to know. She knew how lucky she was to be alive, and it had been the only other time in her life that she'd had a break from dancing. Although that had been a very short one, and it hadn't had any impact on her career, as she'd simply been declared injured for a month.

"I'd always imagined my future with kids in it, once I'd fulfilled my career ambitions, but since that happened I've focused on dancing being my future. I need to dance, because it's the only part of my future I feel I can have any control over."

"I get it," he said. "I'm sorry for what you went through."

"Thanks," she whispered, dropping her head to his shoulder.

"So you can't ever get pregnant, or it's unlikely?"

"Can't ever," she said. "So you've got no worries with me. Besides, I couldn't ever dance the hours I need to and be a mom, so it's not that big a deal to me anymore." Saffron could joke about it now, but at the time she'd mourned the children she would never have, and even joking about it still stung deep down. She'd been too young at the time to want to be a mother then and there, but when the possibility was taken away it had still cut deep, because it had changed the future she'd imagined for herself. But then she'd simply thrown herself back into ballet and tried never to think about it again.

"Come here," Blake murmured in a low tone that sent a delicious shiver down her spine. He pulled her closer, facing her now.

She loved the gruff way he spoke to her, tugging her hard against him.

"Kiss me again," Saffron whispered, forcing herself to be bolder, to ask for what she wanted. She wanted to forget about everything she'd just told him now she'd gotten it off her chest.

Blake didn't disappoint. His lips crushed her, hands skimming her body as she looped her arms around his neck. As far as forgetting all her troubles, this was exactly what she needed. Short-term, fun, mind-blowing... the perfect interlude while she focused on her body and got back her strength.

As she used her toes to push herself forward, climb

up closer to him, she couldn't help the grin that took over her mouth.

"What?" Blake muttered.

"It didn't hurt," she whispered back, flexing her toes and her legs again.

"What? My kissing you?"

"My leg, stupid." Saffy didn't want to talk about it, but her lack of pain when she'd put that kind of pressure on her pointed toes had sent another kind of thrill through her.

Saffron woke and reached out in the bed. She didn't connect with anything. She sat up and searched in the dark for Blake, but the only thing she saw was a sliver of light coming through the door from the living room.

She stretched and got up, still tired but feeling restless. It was weird waking up in Blake's apartment, feeling like a visitor yet knowing she was here to stay. She pulled on the shirt he'd discarded earlier, wrapping it around herself and padding across the thick carpet. The light that she'd seen was a lamp in the far corner of the living room. The light was bathing part of the apartment in a soft light, and she could see the back of Blake's head. She guessed he might be working, unable to sleep and putting his time to good use, but when she reached him, bending down to run her hands down his bare chest from behind, she saw he was staring at a photograph.

"Oh," she stammered.

Blake jumped, dropping the photo.

"I'm sorry. I thought you'd be working, or reading a book or something. I just…"

Saffy didn't know what to say. She looked away as he brushed his knuckles against his eyes, knew that she'd been right in thinking she'd seen tears glinting there. She'd interrupted what was definitely supposed to be a private moment.

"Are you okay?" she asked.

"No," he ground out, sitting deeper into the buttoned leather armchair again and wearing only his boxers.

"Was that…?" She had been about to ask if it was his dad before his blank look silenced her.

"Go back to bed," he said.

Saffron watched him for a moment, thought about pushing the point, then did as he said. He might appear carefree, as though he was in control of everything in his life, but Blake had demons. She'd just seen them firsthand, sitting there in the dark alone, and she knew there was more to her husband-to-be than met the eye. He was acting the part of the happy bachelor, but she didn't believe it for a second.

And he wasn't alone. Tears pricked her eyes as she closed the bedroom door behind her and flopped back onto the bed, pulling the covers up and wishing it were her room and she wouldn't have to face him again. There was so much she had locked away, hidden so deep within herself that she would never open up to anyone. Only she was better at hiding it than Blake, because she'd just glimpsed his soul and his hurt looked a lot closer to the surface than she would ever let hers be.

She pulled a pillow closer, hugged it tight and buried her face into it. If only she could dance again, then everything would be okay. And she wouldn't have to stay here if things turned weird and she wanted out.

Blake felt terrible. He wanted to roar like a lion, yell about the injustices in the world and smash something. Slam his fist into a wall. But instead he stayed silent, lived with the guilt that was weighing on him like a ton of bricks, pushing down so hard on him that he could hardly breathe. He wasn't the angry type, which was why he was beating himself up so much right now.

It always happened at night. He'd go to sleep, fall into a deep slumber, then wake in the darkness, a tangle of sheets and sweat. If it wasn't his father, the helicopter wreckage, doubling over when he saw his brother's mangled body, it was the carnage he'd seen when serving. And that's why it affected him so badly. When he'd been away, he'd been able to compartmentalize the horrors, put his memories into a little box that he'd mostly managed to keep a lid on. But seeing his father and brother dead, like casualties of war among the pieces of metal covering the grass and strewn through trees, had changed everything. Because now images of war, memories he'd once buried, were merging with fresher ones, morphing into visions that often took hours to push away, if he could at all.

Blake steeled his jaw, glanced over at the whiskey bottle but refused to get up and reach for it. He'd gone to sleep with a beautiful woman in his arms, felt at peace, but when he'd woken, his demons had returned stronger than ever.

He shouldn't have shut her down like that, but then he shouldn't have done a lot of things. Maybe everything was just catching up with him. Maybe he should have found new investors, cashed in the business. He could have left his family in a great financial position, provided more for his mother and sisters than they'd ever need, but he was too loyal, too proud or maybe just too stubborn to give up what his family had built.

He shut his eyes, leaned back. His father had finally managed to turn him into the puppet he'd always wanted him to be, controlling him from the grave. All the years he'd fought with him, hated him, stood up to him, and now he just wished he was back. Then everything could go back to normal. That he could have his brother alive and kicking again. Because that was his biggest regret, falling out with the one person who'd have had his back no matter what, but whom he'd been too pigheaded to apologize to. Just another thing he'd never forgive himself for.

Blake doubted he'd find it easy to get back to sleep, and he also doubted Saffron would want him crawling in beside her. And what would he say to her? How could he even start to explain the way he felt? The things that haunted him were not things he wanted to burden anyone else with. Besides, they'd known each other less than two entire days. He wasn't about to crack his heart open and pour out all his feelings to her. Or to any woman. He'd already told her enough when he'd confessed about his ex.

Trouble was, he liked Saffron. And he hated the way he'd spoken to her. Because behaving like that only made him like his father, and he'd rather jump off a bridge than turn into even a shadow of his dad.

He picked up the photo of his father and brother he'd been holding, stared into his brother's eyes one last time, remembering his smile, how passionate he'd been about helicopters and taking over their dad's corner office one day. How good he'd been at schmoozing clients and smoothing over problems. Problems that peeved Blake, first world issues that drove him nuts. After what he'd seen, the things he'd had to do to protect his country, to serve, they weren't real problems in his eyes. Their clients, who were worth millions, hired and leased Goldsmith's helicopters and private planes. They'd made his family a whole lot of money, and his father had been well-known among New York's elite— *America's* elite. But that man, that smiling face that everyone else saw, wasn't the true man. Which might have been half the reason Blake had never been able to smile himself unless he truly meant it.

He tucked the photo into a book and switched off the lamp, staring out the window for a while. New York was the city that never slept, and he was starting to be the guy who never slept. The fatigue was killing him, but somehow a few strong coffees always seemed to give him enough energy to get through the following day. *Just.*

Saffron had a sick feeling in her stomach when she woke. She kept her eyes shut, this time hoping that Blake wouldn't be there when she slowly slid her fingers across the sheets. She peeked out, breathing a sigh of relief when she found she was alone. Again.

She got up, walked into the bathroom and retrieved the robe she'd left in there, tucking herself up in it. Then she summoned all the bravery she could and walked out, expecting to find Blake asleep on the sofa. Instead, she discovered him standing in the kitchen, bare chested and staring intently at something.

"Morning," she called out, surprised by how normal her voice sounded when she was a bundle of nerves.

Blake was frowning when he looked up, but his face quickly transformed into a smile when he saw her. "Morning."

She wasn't sure what else to say, whether they were just going to pretend nothing had happened or whether she should bring it up.

"I'm trying to make you breakfast," he said. "And for a guy who's used to ordering in, it's not as easy as it sounds."

She relaxed a little. "What are you making over there?"

His smile encouraged her to go a little closer. "Waffles again. I was given this fancy maker and I've never used it, so here goes."

Saffron laughed. "First of all, you don't need to keep feeding me. I'll never be a ballerina again if I keep eating with you." She was going to lean over the counter but decided to go around instead. "Second, you just whisk up the batter and pour it in. It ain't rocket science."

"You've making me feel like an idiot," he said with a chuckle. "I can fly a helicopter, but I can't use a whisk."

"You can?"

He gave her a quick sideways glance. "Yeah. It's what I've been doing most of my life."

Saffron tried to hide her surprise. Instead she leaned over and checked out the batter. "You're doing okay, just keep whisking until the lumps are out and give it a go."

Blake turned his attention to her, and she found it hard to read his expression.

"I'm not good at apologies, but I shouldn't have been such an idiot last night."

She appreciated he was trying to say he was sorry. "It's fine. I didn't mean to sneak up on you. I had no idea…"

He shook his head. "Let's just forget it. Okay?"

She nodded. "Okay."

There was something so magnetic about him, a feeling that pooled in her belly whenever she was with him. And seeing him standing in his jeans, bare chested with all his sinewy muscles on display, only reminded her all over again of how much fun she'd had in his bed. Even if she was still cautious after the way he'd reacted.

It was as though they were playing some silly cat-and-mouse game, only she didn't quite have a grasp of the rules yet.

She decided to make coffee instead of ogling his gorgeous body. "Coffee?" she asked, realizing she had no idea how he liked it.

"Love one. Black with one sugar."

Saffy busied herself, keeping her back turned even though she was still crazy aware of him. She got that he had issues, and she'd been so hurt last night, but they hardly knew each other and they were suddenly living together. It was never going to be easy.

"Here we go," she said, spinning around and just about slamming into him. She hadn't been expecting him to be just standing there.

"Thanks." He held out a hand to steady her, smiled down at her with his dreamy dark eyes. She really needed to get back to work! It wasn't like her to be so taken with a man, and she was blaming it on not having anything else to think about.

Blake didn't pull away immediately, and she held her breath, gazing back at him. She was also starting to blame not getting this sort of thing out of her system on when she was younger. The excitement of what they were doing felt forbidden because it was so different from her usual behavior.

She smelled something that didn't seem quite right. "I think your waffle is burning."

Blake spun around, sloshing his coffee and making her laugh. "All I had to do was wait for the green light to come on. Who could burn a freaking waffle?"

Saffy perched on the bar stool so she could watch him. "Just throw it out. The next one will be perfect."

He muttered something and did what she'd suggested. Her stomach rumbled as he poured more batter in.

"So what would a normal Sunday look like for you?" she asked.

"Honestly?" he said, hands flat on the counter as he leaned forward. "I'd probably be eating breakfast that

I'd ordered from downstairs, then I'd be heading in to the office for a bit. Maybe going to the gym. You?"

She watched as he removed the first waffle and put it on a plate. He pushed it along the counter and passed her the maple syrup.

"If I was dancing, I'd be there around ten. My breakfast would probably be a protein shake instead of something like this, because I'd be being a lot more careful with my weight!"

"So you always worked on a Sunday?" he asked.

She cut into the waffle, slicing the first heart-shaped piece apart. "We only had Mondays off, and even then I'd be doing something work related. Although I always tried to get a massage in the afternoon." A wave of nostalgia hit her, just like it always did when she talked about dancing. "Every other day of the week I'd be in the studio by ten, and I'd be dancing or doing dancing-related things until around seven each night, unless we were performing, and then it'd be closer to eleven."

Blake whistled. "I had no idea the hours were so long."

She grimaced. "It's a killer, especially when you first start, but I love it. I would do it until I was sixty if I could."

"So tell me what happened," he said, voice suddenly a whole lot gentler. "I can see how much it hurts for you to talk about."

"I want to talk about that as much as you want to open up to me," Saffy said honestly.

Blake flipped out another waffle, stayed silent, although it wasn't awkward this time. She ate a few mouthfuls of her waffle, loving the drizzle of maple syrup.

"This is great," she praised him.

He smiled and passed her another, even though she stuck her hand out to protest.

"No more!" she managed when she'd finished her mouthful.

Blake just grinned and kept cooking.

"We were performing *Swan Lake*, and I was the lead. It had been amazing, night after night of great reviews," Saffron told him, suddenly needing to get it all out, to just tell him and get it over with instead of keeping it all bottled up inside. "I've had a lot of problems with a form of arthritis since I was young, and I was probably pushing myself too hard. That night I ripped three ligaments in my leg, which was bad enough without the crippling arthritis in my knee."

Blake looked up at her but didn't say anything, and she didn't want him to. There was nothing he could say that would make it any better.

"When I was in the army, I flew helicopters every day, doing what I loved," he said in a quiet voice, not making eye contact, just staring at the waffle machine. "I'd butted heads with my dad for years, but I wasn't going to back down on doing what I was passionate about. I wanted to make a difference, and I wanted to do something that made me feel great. The types of helicopters I was flying, dropping Navy SEALs into remote locations, being part of the most incredible teams…" He paused. "It was the best job in the world."

Saffron forced herself to keep eating, knowing how

hard it was to share when every word felt so raw. Maybe that was why she was so drawn to Blake, because even though they were so different, they'd both lost what they loved. It wasn't a person they'd lost, but the pain was so real, so true, that Saffy felt every day as if her heart had been ripped out. She got it.

"Last night, you saw me looking at a photo of my dad." She listened to him take a deep, shaky breath. "And my brother."

"You lost them, didn't you?" she asked quietly.

He nodded. "Yeah, I did. And as much as I miss my brother, so bad, I feel like it was just one more way for my dad to force me into what he always wanted me to do. Another way for him to control me. I know it sounds stupid, but in the middle of the night that's all I can think about."

Saffron wanted to reach for him, but she didn't know if it was the right thing to do or not. When he joined her at the counter and poured syrup over his waffles, she turned to face him, coffee cup in hand.

"We just have to cope as best we can, right?" she said. "It's so hard to make a career from doing what you love, and when that gets taken away…"

"It's heartbreaking," he muttered. "But yeah, you've just got to grit your teeth and keep on going. What other choice do we have?"

They sat side by side and finished their breakfast, and Saffron rose to rinse the plates and put them in a dishwasher.

"What do you say we go ring shopping?" Blake asked, taking her by surprise.

She tried to hide her grin. Ring shopping sounded like a lot more fun than her usual Sunday afternoon, and she liked the idea of getting out of the apartment. "Give me an hour. A girl's got to look good for that kind of outing."

"You always look good."

Saffy paused, heard what Blake had muttered. She was going to say something, but her brain was blank. Instead she closed the dishwasher door and headed for the bathroom. When she got there, she did what she always did in the mornings, lifting her right leg high and placing it on the edge of the bathroom cabinetry to stretch out her muscles. The granite in Blake's bathroom was cold against her skin, but it felt nice and she let her body fall down, the burn of her muscles making her feel alive. She lifted up then down again before repeating the stretch on the other side, the movement as natural to her as brushing her teeth.

Once she was finished she stared back at her reflection, checked her posture. She would always be a dancer. Every fiber in her body told her it wasn't over yet, and this morning her determination to listen to that feeling was back tenfold.

CHAPTER SIX

"WHAT DO YOU THINK?" Blake asked as they walked through the door of the antique jeweler his mother had always favored.

Saffron's eyes seemed to twinkle when she looked up at him, holding his hand. He'd linked their fingers as they'd headed through the door, conscious of how they appeared together, and somehow it felt right. He was oddly comfortable around Saffron most of the time, more himself than he probably was around even his family. Maybe because he'd laid it all out on the line with her, been honest from the get-go because of the kind of relationship they were in.

"I was expecting Tiffany's," she said.

"We can go there if you want."

"No," she said, letting go of his hand to peer into a display cabinet. "I didn't say I didn't like it—it's amazing. Besides, beggars can't be choosers, right?"

He laughed and watched as she wandered around, smiling to the assistant when she came over.

"Can I help you?"

"Yes," Blake said. "I'm looking for something for my fiancée here. Something elegant."

They started to look, with the assistant showing them a few engagement rings.

"Sir, is there any price range I need to be mindful of?" she asked in a hushed tone.

Blake smiled, reaching out for Saffron. "No. Whatever she wants."

Saffron shot him a look, and he just raised an eyebrow and smiled back at her. He was enjoying the charade more than he'd expected to.

"How about this one?" Saffron asked, pointing to a solitaire diamond surrounded by smaller ones, with baguette diamonds on each side forming the band.

The ring was beautiful and no doubt expensive, but he admired the fact she hadn't just chosen the largest, since he'd already told her she could keep it when their charade was over.

"Try it on," he instructed.

When the assistant passed it over, he quickly grabbed it, changing his mind. "Let me," he said.

Saffron turned to face him, and he smiled as he dropped to one knee in the store. "Saffron, will you marry me?" he asked, wanting to see her smile, knowing it would make her happy even though they weren't marrying for real.

They had talked about marriage, about what they were doing, but he hadn't actually proposed to her. Until now.

She held out her hand, letting him slip the ring on. "Yes," she whispered, laughing at him.

The shop assistant clapped as Blake rose and dropped a gentle kiss to her lips, liking how soft and warm her mouth was against his. It wasn't as though kissing her was a hardship.

"We'll take it," he said when he finally pulled away, reminding himself that it wasn't real, no matter how good Saffron felt against him.

The lines between fact and fiction were blurring between them, or maybe they'd always been blurred. The attraction between them was real; he just had to remember that it couldn't become—*wouldn't* become—anything more. It wasn't part of his plan, the future he imagined for himself, and there was no way he'd ever want a wife or a family. The example his father had set for him was testament to that. Besides, there would never be a woman he could trust enough with his heart or his money, and if he couldn't truly be himself without trying to protect himself and his family's fortune, then he'd never marry for real.

Once they'd paid for the ring, they left the shop with it on her finger.

"Well, that wasn't too hard," he said as they walked hand in hand down the sidewalk.

"It's beautiful," she said.

"And it's yours," he replied.

Saffron laughed as she leaned into him, still holding his hand. "It feels weird. I'm so girly and excited over the bling, but then this whole thing isn't real. I feel like I'm living someone else's life."

"Ditto," he said. Only he'd felt like that well before Saffron had come along. Every day he felt as if he was playing a role, one that had been destined for his brother, and he hated it. Every single day, he hated it.

"When we get back, I'll give you my planner to take a flick through. Anything marked social you'll need to attend with me, and I'll let you know in advance of any client dinners if I want you to join me."

Saffron looked up from admiring her ring. "Good. And I'll let you know how I do searching for specialists and treatments. There's an acupuncturist who works with celebrities I'd love to get in with, so I might need you to make the appointment!"

"I'll issue you a credit card tomorrow," Blake said, unworried, thinking through the logistics of everything. "That way you can pay for any medical expenses. Sound okay?"

She grasped his hand even tighter, but Blake didn't mind. "You've given me hope again, Blake. Just keep me in New York and I'll be the best wife you could have wished for."

He didn't doubt it.

"Oh, did I mention I want you to quit your job?" He'd forgotten all about telling her, but the last thing he wanted was for her to go back to pouring coffee. She could be a resting ballerina, holed up in his apartment or doing whatever she wanted, but he didn't want her tied to a job that she didn't even care about. If she was his wife, he would keep her and make sure she was available whenever he needed her. Besides, no one would believe in their marriage if he let Saffron work for minimum wage.

"You're serious?" Saffron asked, giving him a look that made him realize she actually thought he was joking.

"Deadly," he replied. "No one would believe you were my wife if I let you slave away nine to five."

He saw a hesitant look pass over her face that made him wonder if she didn't like the idea of him keeping her. "Okay," she said. "I guess if you were my husband that's what you'd want."

Blake nodded, but her words jolted him. It was weird hearing her say the *husband* word, especially when in his mind he could still see his mother sobbing over something his father had done when he was only a child. They weren't blurry memories like so many of his childhood recollections, but a perfect snapshot of his mom crying that the man she'd married didn't deserve to be called her *husband*, the man who slammed the door and left her to cry.

He pushed the thoughts away and smiled down at the gorgeous redhead at his side. All the more reason to have a contract, to be clear up front about what he wanted.

Blake wasn't fit to be a real husband, didn't want that life. But he did want to be the one to step his family business into the future, wanted to make his family proud. Because if he wasn't so honorable, he'd have left and never looked back after the funeral, returning to the life he loved. Selfishly leaving everything behind to pursue his dreams, away from his family name and far away from New York. But that was the past now, and it wasn't something he could get back. *Ever.*

Oddly, he felt happier with Saffron at his side than he had for a long while. Or maybe it was just the promise of having her in his bed every night, and the fact he'd been honest with her about who he truly was.

"So this is the woman who got you all tied up in knots?" An elegant older woman with her hair pulled off her face stepped forward to collect Saffron's hand. Her palm was warm, and even though she screamed old New York money, her smile was genuine.

"Mom, I'd like you to meet Saffron," Blake said, coming to her rescue and slinging an arm around her so he could pull her back.

"It's great to meet you," Saffron said, training a smile. "I've heard so much about you."

His mother's smile was wry, and it reminded Saffron of Blake. "I can't say the same about you. My son has been very tight-lipped about the beautiful woman he's all set to marry."

"Nothing fancy," Blake cautioned, taking Saffy's hand and pulling her toward him. She sat down on the sofa beside him, careful to curl up close, keeping a hand on his thigh. "Just a simple wedding."

He glanced down at her, and she retreated with her hand. The heat in his gaze was making her uncomfortable. This might be fake, but their chemistry wasn't, which was why she wasn't finding it that hard to pretend.

"When you say nothing fancy…?" his mother asked.

"I mean we're heading down to the registry office and signing the paperwork. No big ceremony, no fuss. You can wait until the girls get married for a big wedding, because I want this completely under the radar."

His mother pursed her lips, but Saffron could see she didn't want to argue with him, or maybe she knew from experience that there was just no point.

"Saffron, I don't want to offend you, but I must bring up the delicate subject of a prenuptial agreement."

Blake laughed and Saffron leaned into him. She'd been prepared for this, would have thought it odd if any mother with their kind of fortune hadn't raised an eyebrow at how quickly they were getting married.

"Please, Mrs. Goldsmith, that's not something you have to worry about. I have no intention of taking anything from your son or your family, and we've already organized the paperwork." Saffron chuckled. "But don't think for a moment I'm going to let your son run my life. I intend on having my career back on track very quickly. As soon as I've given my body a chance to rest and recover, I'll be back with the New York Ballet Company."

His mother smiled and looked to Blake. "I like her."

Blake dropped a kiss into her hair. It was just a casual, sweet gesture, but the gentleness of his touch took her by surprise.

"She's the one."

Saffron felt guilty sitting there, smiling away and pretending to dote on this woman's son. She seemed like a nice person, and lying wasn't something that came naturally to her, even if she was putting on a good show of doing exactly that right now. She wondered what it would be like if this were real, if she were actually being welcomed into the family. Saffron could see that she'd enjoy Blake's mother's company, which only made her guilt pangs stronger.

"You do realize the tabloids will stop hounding you. Not to mention it'll be good for business," his mother mused, shrugging into her coat and collecting her purse as they watched. "We should hold an engagement party for our clients, let them see what a family man you're becoming. What do you think?"

Blake stood, and she kept hold of him as she rose, too. "I think that sounds like a great idea. How about you organize it?"

His mother's smile was wide. "Excellent."

"Actually, maybe we should just start an annual party for our guests, and we can announce our marriage at this inaugural one to keep it low-key." He knew whom he wanted to impress, but it wouldn't do any harm to invite all their important clients.

Saffron nodded, listening and playing the part of attentive fiancée. She was used to playing a role as a dancer, to being in character, which was probably why this seemed easy. Or maybe Blake was just easy to be around. If she'd had to pick the kind of man she'd want to marry one day, it could have been him. *Maybe*. Although from what he'd said, he had no intention of ever marrying for real, never wanted to settle down.

And that was fine by her. Once she was dancing again, she'd have no time for a husband anyway. Blake would be a distant memory, and hopefully a pleasant one.

"Please tell me you'll invite me to the ceremony," his mother said as they walked out her door.

"Maybe," Blake answered. "Let's see if Saffron survives meeting my sisters first. She might run for the hills before I get her to sign on the dotted line."

Blake laughed and she forced a chuckle. If only his mother knew that she'd already well and truly signed on the dotted line. She was bound to marry Blake, which meant they were as good as husband and wife already. Besides, they'd already decided that they were going to get married in secret as soon as the license came through.

CHAPTER SEVEN

SAFFRON WAS SMILING, and even though her happiness wasn't forced, she wasn't finding it easy to look happy. What was she doing? Blake was treating her like his actual wife, and aside from when he woke up in hot sweats during the night and didn't want to talk about it, everything seemed…good. *Real.* Not that she was under any illusions, but still, it was weird.

"Come on, let's go," Blake said, kissing her on the lips and holding their joined hands in the air. "You were great tonight."

"You sound like my choreographer," she said with a laugh, still smiling as the crowd watched them. She was well used to being the center of attention, and far from feeling unusual having her every move watched just because she was on a man's arm, she was getting a kick out of it. Usually she basked in the attention, full of pride that so many people were enjoying her creative outlet, a performance she'd put hours of her time, not to mention sweat and sometimes blood, into. This time she felt like an actress, and for some reason it didn't feel any less satisfying. "Or maybe my cheerleader."

"You're brilliant, has anyone ever told you that?"

Blake swept her into his arms and out of the room. She was starting to get the feeling that he was enjoying the performance as much as she'd enjoyed putting it on.

Saffron didn't want their conversation to turn around to her dancing, so she let it go and didn't answer. They headed straight outside and into the waiting town car.

"I think they bought it," she said.

Blake leaned over and kissed her, his lips familiar to her now yet still making her body tingle. It would have been a much easier arrangement if they hadn't started out by being intimate, although given the way her body reacted to him, she was starting to wonder if they could ever have been platonic.

"I have some key accounts that have always referred to my dad every time we met, gone on about the roots of the company being a family business and questioning my commitment, or at least that's what it's seemed like," Blake said, settling back into the leather seat. "I don't know if a rival was trying to get to them and spinning rubbish, or if it was just the reputation they thought I had, but things felt fragile there for a little while. Marrying you has made all that go away, and after tonight, man. You seriously wowed my big investor. I definitely believe you can be my little star for the next while."

"So it's been worth it for you already?" Saffron asked.

He grinned. "Yes. You?"

"You've given me access to medical professionals I'd never have been able to afford to consult with," she said honestly. "And I'm still here. I still have a shot.

So yeah." Saffron laughed. "Marrying you hasn't been half-bad!"

The car ride was only short, and soon they were heading up to their apartment. It already felt like home for Saffron after two short weeks, or as home as anything ever felt to her. She wasn't used to spending a lot of time wherever she lived, and she'd been living out of a suitcase on and off for years. But she had some photos up, Blake had given up half his wardrobe space to her and her perfume lingered when she walked into their room.

"I'm just going to respond to some work emails. I'll be in bed soon."

Saffy undressed and put on a nightie, then padded into the bathroom to take her makeup off. She never took the luxurious space for granted, with its floor-to-ceiling tiles and beautiful fittings, and the oversize fluffy towels were her idea of heaven. Especially since he had the housekeeper come in twice a week, so she didn't even have to lift a finger to keep them that way.

The apartment was silent except for the low hum of the television—she was used to Blake having it on whenever he sat up and worked late, which was most nights. She lowered herself to the ground, relaxed into the splits and dropped her body down low, covering first one leg and then the other. Once she was done stretching, she stood and raised up, on tiptoe, smiling to herself as she leaned to each side, reached up high, before doing a little turn. The acupuncture had definitely helped, and even though she could have kept going until she collapsed, she was going to follow her new specialist's orders and only stretch her muscles like that for five minutes each evening and morning.

Still smiling, she curled up beneath the covers and flicked through a magazine before turning off the bedside lamp and closing her eyes. She was going to wait up for him, but they'd had late night after late night and...

Saffron woke up with a fright, sitting bolt upright, heart racing.

"No!"

She blinked in the darkness, eyes slowly adjusting, realizing that it was Blake who'd woken her. She instinctively pulled back, putting some space between them.

"Blake," she said, loudly, forcing her voice. "Blake!"

He groaned but didn't wake, pulled the sheets tighter around himself, thrashing out.

"Blake!"

His eyes opened, a flash of brightness that scared her for a moment until they locked on her. He sat up, disheveled and disoriented looking.

"Saffy?" His voice was hoarse as he pushed the covers down.

"You were dreaming. Are you okay?" she asked, hesitant. She didn't want to push him—they had a good thing going, and that didn't involve asking too many personal questions, going too deep, unless they had to.

"Same thing every time." Blake sighed. "Every single time."

Saffron tucked her knees up to her chin. "Your dad?" she asked.

Blake flicked his bedside lamp on. "Yeah. Always

him. Always a weird, I don't know, collage of memories, I guess. Just a jumble of things all mashed together."

"Do you still wish you were serving?" she asked. It was a question that had been on her lips all week, wanting to ask but not knowing if he'd want to talk to her. "That you could go back, even though you have these dreams?"

"Yeah," he said, running his fingers through his hair, shutting his eyes as he leaned back into the headboard. "Or maybe I don't. I don't know. All I know is that I miss flying, miss having my own identity that isn't tied to my family. As hard as it was, I still miss it, want it."

"I'm not sure what would be harder—having a dream and never turning it into reality, or the feeling of having that dream snatched away when you've already tasted the reality of it." Saffron reached for Blake, her fingers crawling the space between them until they connected with his. At least they knew what it felt like, understood what the other had been through on a level that no one else could.

"Having it taken away," he replied, squeezing her fingers back. "Definitely having it taken away."

"Or maybe we wouldn't have the same fire burning in us if we hadn't tasted that reality, that dream," she whispered. "Maybe we're still the lucky ones, we just can't see it."

"Maybe." He groaned, and she wasn't sure if it was from pain or the subject matter.

"Tell me what it was like, what you loved about it," she asked, suddenly wide-awake, not wanting to go back to sleep if he wanted to open up to her, to talk.

"One day," he said. "One day I'll tell you all about it. About the kick I got every time I put a Black Hawk up in the air or took a unit to safety in a Chinook. But not right now. I need some rest."

She knew he had issues, that whatever was troubling him needed to be dealt with, but as he kept reminding her, it wasn't her problem. She wasn't his real wife. She was more like a live-in mistress with extra benefits.

His problems were his. Her problems were hers. A year or two of fun. A year or two of great sex and parties. One year or maybe more to get her career back on track and have fun while she tried to find her way back to the top. It sure beat going home to serve coffee for the rest of her life at a diner and wishing for what she didn't have. At least this way, what she'd lost still felt as if it was within arm's reach. What she craved so badly was still a possibility instead of simply a memory of what could have been.

CHAPTER EIGHT

Three months later

SAFFRON SMILED UP at Blake, expertly running her fingers down his dinner jacket–clad arm. It wasn't hard to pretend she adored him, but the weird thing was reminding herself all the time that it wasn't *real*. They slept in the same bed, they went to parties and functions, and they put on a perfect show of being a real couple. Which they kind of were. Pity he was so darn irresistible.

A waiter passed and she took a glass of champagne. She held it for a while, listening to Blake talk business, before raising the glass to her lips. She went to sip but then recoiled as the bubbles hit her tongue.

"Excuse me," she said, stepping away from Blake quickly and scanning for the restroom. Bile rose in her throat, and she forced it down.

"Are you okay?" Blake's dark brown eyes met hers, concern etched on his face. So far she'd never let him down once, but this time she needed to bolt. Fast.

Saffy just nodded and hurried as fast as her high

heels would let her. Thankfully her leg was feeling great
and she hadn't had any problems with her knee, so she
was able to move fast. Otherwise she'd have been vom-
iting in the nearest corner!

She left her glass on a ledge in the bathroom and
only just made it to a stall, holding her hair back as she
threw up into the toilet. Her body felt burning hot then
chilled, sweat beading across her forehead before her
skin turned cold. What on earth had she eaten? Or had
she caught the stomach flu?

"You okay in there, sweetheart?" A kind voice
sounded out.

Saffron hadn't even noticed anyone else. She'd been
so desperate not to be sick out in the open that she'd
just hurried straight on through. "Um, I think so," she
managed to say back, trying to hold down everything
else in her stomach, if there was even anything else left.

"You don't sound drunk, and you didn't look drunk,
so either you've eaten something bad or you've got a
little one on the way. Am I right?"

Saffron laughed. "Has to be bad food." Another wave
of nausea hit, and she leaned forward again, trying hard
to hold it down and failing.

The woman sounded closer this time when she spoke.
"You're sure it's not a baby?"

Saffron sighed and leaned against the wall of the
stall. Usually she was grossed out by any kind of public
toilet, but the cool felt nice against her body when she
pushed back, and it was a pretty posh tiled bathroom
with fancy lights and wallpaper. She hoped it was clean.
Besides, she didn't have any other choice.

"Can't be a baby," she replied with a sigh. "Not for me." Saffron finally opened the door and came face to a face with a nice-looking lady dressed in a beautiful taffeta gown. Her gray hair was pulled up into an elegant do.

"I was sick as a dog when I had my boys. Thin as a whippet so nobody knew I was pregnant, and I threw up for months."

Saffron appreciated her concern, and it was nice to have someone to take her mind off how ill she felt. The nausea had passed now, only returning when she thought about the champagne she'd almost drunk. She usually had a cast-iron stomach, so it seemed strange.

"Saffy, you in here?" Blake's deep voice boomed through the restroom.

She cleared her throat. "Just a sec."

"I'll tell your man you're not well. You take your time."

Saffy pulled herself together, taking a mint from her purse and then walking over to the mirrors to check her face. She looked pale and gaunt, but the sick feeling had passed. After washing her hands, she went to find Blake.

"What's wrong?"

His eyes were searching her face, and she had to look away. The hardest part about being with Blake was trying not to fall in love with the man. They'd felt like a real team when she'd been at his side, meeting his new investor and his wife; when Blake had secured the investment, she'd fist pumped and squealed as if it was her deal that had come together!

"I started feeling all weird, sweats and nausea. I think I ate something bad."

He frowned and put his arm around her as they walked back out. "Let's head home."

"No, you stay," she insisted, looking away when a waiter passed. She couldn't stand the thought of alcohol or food. "Schmooze your clients, do your work and let me go. You don't need me here—they've already seen you're a doting husband if that's what you're worried about."

She'd meant to sound positive, but instead it had come out all wrong.

"Just because this isn't, ah—" he cleared his throat, frowning again "—doesn't mean I don't care about you."

Saffy squeezed his hand. "I know. I just meant that I've already fulfilled my purpose." She felt sick again and held his hand tight, waiting for it to pass. "I really have to go."

Blake let go of her hand and pulled out his phone. "Make your way out. I'll call the driver now and have him waiting for you."

Saffron smiled her thanks and hurried through the throng of people toward the exit. She kept her head down, not wanting to make eye contact and have to talk to anyone. She just wanted to undress and crawl into bed.

As promised the car was there within minutes of her walking outside, although she would have been happy to stand and gulp in the cold air for longer. She got in the vehicle and slumped on the backseat. As they headed for home she stared out the window, her hand resting on her stomach in an effort to calm it. It wasn't working, but she kept it there anyway.

Pregnant. She smiled despite how shaky she felt. There was no way she could be pregnant. The specialist had made it so clear to her, and she'd looked into freezing her eggs before having it done, but the success rates of thawing those frozen eggs hadn't seemed worth it to her, not when she'd been so short of money.

Pregnant. Was there even a slim chance? She'd only been with Blake that one time without protection, and if her chances of getting pregnant were statistically zero, surely it couldn't have happened...

"Pull over, please!" she cried as they passed a convenience store.

The driver did as she asked, pulling over farther up the block when it was safe and there was space to park.

"I'll only be a minute," she said, jumping out and rushing back. She entered the store and found the section with women's things, reaching for the first pregnancy test she could find. There were two types, so she grabbed the other one as well, hands shaking so hard she had to concentrate on getting her card out to pay.

"Thanks," she mumbled as she took her things and raced back to the car. It was only a short drive, but it seemed to take forever. When they pulled up outside she raced in, forgetting how ill she'd been. Saffy headed for the bathroom, not bothering to turn any lights on except the one she needed to. The rest of the apartment was dark, except for a couple of lamps, but she didn't care. All she wanted was to do the test so she could be sure that there was absolutely no chance of her being pregnant.

Saffy hovered above the toilet and held the stick out, counting to three before retrieving it. She put the cap back on it and placed it on the counter, staring at the tiny screen that would show one line if she wasn't pregnant. That line showed, strongly, and as she held her breath another faint line appeared, slowly but surely. *Two blue lines.* Nausea washed over her again, but this time she was sure it was from nerves. She couldn't be pregnant!

She paced around the bathroom for a few minutes then ripped open the wrapper on the other test. This one was more expensive, so she was sure it would be more accurate.

She'd only just been, but she forced herself to go again, to do just enough so that the test would work. And then she played the waiting game again, staring at the slightly bigger screen.

Pregnant. Just one word. One simple word.

And it changed everything.

CHAPTER NINE

SAFFRON CLUTCHED HER bag tight and walked back out onto the street. The day was warm and the sun was hot on her bare arms, but she hardly noticed. She just wanted to get to the studio where she'd been training.

Pregnant. She'd known the two home tests the night before couldn't be wrong, but still. After so many years of believing she could never be a mom, it was almost impossible to comprehend. And what was she going to tell Blake? Saffy groaned and held her bag tighter, scared of what was happening inside her, how much everything was changing.

She felt a vibration against her and realized it was her phone. She pulled it out, glancing at the screen and expecting it to be Blake, not ready to talk to him yet. But it was a number she didn't recognize.

She inhaled and stopped walking. "Hello, Saffron speaking."

"Saffron, it's Benjamin. From NYC Ballet."

Her heart just about stopped beating. "Oh, hi," she stammered.

"I wanted to know how you are. Whether you've had any success with your recovery?"

Saffy flexed her foot, something she always did whenever she thought about her injury or someone asked her about it. She couldn't help but smile when she did it without pain. "I'm doing really well. I've seen some great physical therapists, an acupuncturist and a specialist doctor, and I think I'm ready to ease back into dancing again."

It was a half lie, because the amazing people she'd been seeing had all told her to simply start exercising more, to slowly start dancing ten or so minutes a day after running through a series of stretches and strapping her leg. To try taking a few dance classes but not specifically ballet, and they'd been making her consume all types of natural wonder products in conjunction with the medicines the doctor had prescribed. The specialist had been incredibly helpful, referring her to the almost-impossible-to-get-in-with therapist in the first place. She'd already enrolled in modern dance, just to start using her muscles, but only ballet was going to fill the void she felt every day.

"That's fabulous news, darling," Benjamin said. "We all thought you might have gotten married and forgotten about us."

"Never," Saffron murmured. "Dance will always be the most important thing in my life."

He laughed. "Just don't let your new husband hear you talk like that!"

Saffron felt as though she was walking on ice, just teetering and waiting. Why had he phoned her? She was too scared to ask. There had to be a reason for a call to just come out of the blue after so long with no contact.

"Darling, the purpose of my call is to see if we can book you. It's not for another four months, but it's you we need." He cleared his throat. "Can you be ready by then? Are you planning on making a comeback?"

Saffy went burning hot then freezing cold, as if her body was going into shock. Four months? Her hand went instinctively to her stomach. In four months she was going to have a bump. A *very* big bump. If she had this baby, there was no way she'd be able to dance then, no matter how well her leg was holding out.

"Why me?" she asked.

"It's for Pierre. He's retiring from the company, and he's requested you as the dancer for his final show. It's just a one-off performance for him, to thank him for all the years he's put into our choreography, but it's you and only you he wants."

Saffron gulped. Pierre was the reason she'd been the lead in *Swan Lake*. Pierre had given her that big break, had believed in her and what her future could hold. Pierre was the key to her getting back on stage, because only he would request her and not take no for an answer.

"Can I have some time to think about it?" Saffron said, stalling, not ready to say no when she didn't even know what she was going to do, what the next few months of her life would even look like. "I'll need to talk to my physical therapist and specialist, make sure they don't think it's too soon. I don't want to risk injury again." She shook her head, wondering where the words were coming from. She wasn't even over her old injury yet!

"We love you here, Saffron," he said. "Take the week

to think about it and let me know. If you do this, you'll be officially invited back to join the company. You were one of Pierre's best principal dancers, darling. We want you back home where you belong, and I just don't believe you're done yet."

Tears welled in Saffy's eyes. It was the phone call she'd been dreaming of, her big chance. But even without the baby, she had no idea whether she'd ever be strong enough to be a principal again, not until she started training and saw firsthand if her leg tolerated the punishing hours.

"I'd do anything to be back. Trust me," she said, voice as shaky as her hands as she gripped her phone.

When she hung up, all she felt was emptiness. What she'd wanted was so close she could almost taste it, almost within her grasp. But then once upon a time, being a mother had seemed important, when the idea of being a parent had been taken from her. She'd been horrified at the time that she would never have children, something she'd slowly forgotten about the more she'd progressed in her career. But now… She slid her hand back down over her belly, the action seemingly normal now. She was suddenly protective of the little being growing inside her, even though she wasn't sure how she felt about the whole thing. *She was pregnant.*

She reached the studio and entered, pleased there was only one other dancer there running through a routine. She stripped down to her leotard and tights, carefully putting on her ballet shoes and looking down at her legs. She warmed up by stretching out slowly, trying not to think, trying to just focus on what she was about to do, on dance. She lifted a leg carefully into the air, stretched up, rose up then down, using the barre, feeling her muscles as they pulled then released. When she had both feet back on the ground, she stretched some more before leaving the barre to dance a quick routine, to cross the room once, dancing like she used to, dancing in a way that used to come as naturally as breathing to her.

And it still did. Breathless but not in pain, Saffy stopped, knew she had to. If she had it her way she would dance all day, but she wasn't ready. Not physically.

After warming down, stretching some more, she slipped her yoga pants back on and then her sweater, collecting her bag and heading back out the door. Saffy set off at a walk, heading for the apartment, needing to face reality. Either she told Blake and he would deal with it, let her make her own decision about what to do, or she never let him find out. He didn't want to be a dad—he'd made that clear when they'd signed the marriage contract—and she'd told him outright that her getting pregnant was impossible. He'd just think she was a liar, that she'd purposely deceived him, set out to fool him. This didn't have to be his problem; it was something she could deal with on her own. If she wanted this baby, she could do it. Trouble was, she'd signed a marriage contract, and she knew Blake only had one of the deals together that he'd needed her for, and she doubted he'd want to let her out of the contract so easily. Not until he had what he needed from their arrangement.

She let herself in and went straight for the kitchen,

pouring a big glass of water and drinking it down. Then she peeled a banana and sat in silence, eating.

"Saffy?"

She jumped, choking on her mouthful. What was Blake doing home?

"Blake?" Saffy walked toward the bedroom. "Where are you?"

"In bed. I'm sick," he said.

She peeked in. "I had no idea you were here."

"I think I've got the stomach flu that you had," Blake said, groaning. "Where have you been?"

It was an innocent question, but it felt like an interrogation all of a sudden. Because for once she'd been somewhere she shouldn't have. "Um, just the doctor," she told him, going closer and sitting down on the bed beside him, reaching for his hand. It was warm, his skin comforting against hers. "I've been thinking about going back to the studio some more, actually pushing my leg a little to see how I do, see if I'm ready to go back."

His smile was kind, and he let go of her hand to prop himself up on the pillows. They'd developed a relationship that went way beyond a simple contract, an easiness that she would miss. Blake was complicated yet beautiful, a man who was straight up about what he wanted, but one who was hiding a power load of pain. He'd shared so little with her about how he truly felt, had just scratched the surface and told her the bare bones of his past, but she knew how much he hurt, how hard it was for him to trust. And now she had to figure out how to tell him what had happened, make him believe that she hadn't deceived him.

"What happened?" he asked, staring into her eyes like he always did and making her feel as if she was the only person in the room, as though what they had was genuine. As real as it felt sometimes.

Heat started to rise up her body, flooding her cheeks. This time she had to lie. "I had a phone call. An opportunity."

"To dance again?" he asked.

Saffy nodded. "Yes. In four months' time, if I'm up to it."

"That's great news," Blake said with a smile. "I'd offer to celebrate with you, but…"

She held up her hand and rose. "I'll let you rest."

Saffron was relieved to walk away and not have to talk more, because she had a lot of thinking to do. More than that, she needed to make a decision. The doctor had been very diplomatic in explaining all her options, but the thought of anything other than protecting the growing baby inside her made her want to be physically sick. But what if this was her one and only chance to dance again? What if this was the last time in her life she'd be offered an opportunity like this? What if…

Saffy bit down hard on her lip. *Be a mother.* She collapsed onto the sofa, finding it hard to breathe. *Or be a dancer.*

She dug her nails into the cushion beside her. *Run away from Blake and never look back.*

Right now, it was sounding like the best option. Or maybe it was feeling like her only option. She couldn't give up this baby, which meant she couldn't be a dancer, not now, maybe not ever, because Pierre would be gone and then she'd have to try to impress a new choreographer who didn't know or love her. Besides, the two didn't go hand in hand, not with the hours she'd have to dedicate to dancing again *if* her body ever let her. And there was no way she could dance that punishing routine at all during pregnancy, not a chance.

Blake checked his watch and frowned at the time. It was unusual for Saffron to be so late. He was going to wait another five minutes but changed his mind, leaving a tip on the table and simply walking out. He wasn't that hungry anyway, and he wanted to make sure she was okay.

He dialed her number and it went straight to voice mail. Again.

Blake left a message this time. "Hey Saffy, it's me. We had a dinner reservation at seven—did you forget? I'm on the way home now. We can always order something in. Call me."

It didn't take him long to make it back, and when he let himself in, something felt wrong.

"Saffy?" he called. When she didn't answer he headed straight for the bedroom. Maybe she was in the shower. "Saffron?"

And then he stopped. There was no five-book-high pile on her bedside table, no perfume bottles or jewelry scattered on the buffet beneath the big mirror. He walked faster into the bathroom. No makeup, no hairspray, no deliciously citrus smell.

Blake stopped dead in front of the closet, not hesitating to yank the doors open and stare inside. The empty space hit him like a fist to his gut. What was going on?

Saffy was gone. She was gone as though she'd never existed in the first place, as if she'd been a figment of his imagination.

Just like Bianca. Just like the day he'd found their little apartment empty all those years ago.

He walked backward until his legs touched the bed, and he dropped down on to it, not noticing the cream envelope until he was sitting. He slipped his finger beneath the seal and plucked out the single piece of paper inside, unfolding it and instantly recognizing Saffron's handwriting.

Blake,

I left like this because I didn't want to look you in the eye and tell you the truth myself. The last few months might have been an arrangement, but I feel closer to you than I ever really have to any other person before. And that's why I didn't want to see the distrust in your eyes when you found out that I was pregnant. You deserved to know, but you don't owe me anything. This baby suddenly means the world to me, and I'll do everything I can to make this little person be loved. I'm sorry I left when I was supposed to stay with you as your wife for longer, but staying would have only made things more complicated. You made it clear that you never wanted a family, or a real wife, and the last thing I want to do is trap you into something else you don't want.

I've kept the ring only because you told me it was mine, and it'll help tide me over until I can work again.

I'm sorry things had to end this way, and I want you to know that you'll always hold a special place in my heart. Don't try to find me, just let me go.
Saffron

What the... Blake screwed up the letter into a tight ball and threw it across the room. She was *pregnant*?

He rose and stormed into the kitchen, wrapping his hand around a bottle of whiskey and pouring a big splash into a glass. He knocked it straight back.

Pregnant? How? They'd always used protection. Besides, she'd told him she couldn't have children, that it wasn't possible, that...*one night*. There had been that one night, months ago. Before the contract. Before he'd proposed. Before they'd gotten married.

Maybe this had been her plan all along, to lure him in and have a child, just like countless women had done to rich men in the past. Maybe she'd played him right from that first night. Maybe she was no better than the first woman who'd scorned him.

Damn it! They'd had an agreement, a contract, and he'd be darned if he was going to let her walk out on that and have a baby. A baby that he'd have no choice but to support, to see, to know. A baby he didn't want. A baby that shouldn't even exist. The one thing in life he'd been certain about for the past decade was that he didn't want a woman in his life and he didn't want a family. Ever. The one and only time he'd slipped up, put his trust in someone else... Blake poured himself another nip, swallowing it down fast before pushing the glass away. He'd had enough, needed to keep his head, to stay in control.

Saffron might be able to run, but he wasn't going to let her hide. Not with his baby on board. Not now, and not ever.

He sat in silence, in the dark. She was supposed to be dancing again, or had that been a lie? She was supposed to be in contention for a role that she'd seemed excited about. Or was that just a ruse to throw him off track, not make him suspicious?

Blake picked up his phone and scrolled through some numbers until he found the contact from the art auction. It was late but he didn't care—he'd make a donation large enough to make it count. If he found her friend Claire, he'd find Saffron. And if that didn't work, then he'd start at NYC Ballet. He'd contact the airlines, stop her from flying, do whatever it took. She wasn't leaving him—not with his baby.

CHAPTER TEN

SAFFRON HAD NEVER felt so guilty in her life. The pain was shooting through her chest, making it hard to breathe. But the problem was that guilt wasn't the only thing she was feeling.

Her heart was broken. Saffy gripped her water glass tighter, staring at the slice of lemon floating as she sat at the bar in the hotel. Just like every time she started to doubt herself, she touched her stomach, ran her palm lightly across it, just enough so that she hoped the baby could feel.

She checked the time and stood up, ready to take her taxi to Newark airport. It had been a long night, lying awake, wondering if she was doing the right thing, but she'd made up her mind and it was time to go. Maysville, Kentucky, wasn't New York, but it was an amazing place to raise a child and she had her family there. She could start a dance studio one day, nurture young talent, incorporate what she loved with being a mother. Or at least that was what she was telling herself to deal with the move.

"You're my little blessing," she murmured as she

walked, one hand carrying her bag, the other on her belly still.

She wasn't supposed to have a baby, and the fact that she'd gotten pregnant was a miracle. A miracle that she had no intention of turning her back on. Dancing had been her everything, until her body let her down. Now her body was doing what it was never supposed to do. It might have been a shock, but she could sure see the irony of it.

Saffron spoke to the concierge as she passed through the lobby and was directed to her taxi, getting in and letting them take care of her luggage. She didn't have a lot, just two suitcases. It seemed ironic that after so many years living in New York, she had so little to take home with her. But her mom would be there to welcome her with open arms, even though they hadn't seen each other in a long time. They were like that—could just pick up where they'd left off. Same with her dad. They knew she loved them and vice versa; she'd just spent so many years doing her own thing that they weren't the best at staying in touch.

She rested her head against the window, the cool glass refreshing against her hot skin. The city whizzed past once they'd gotten through the worst of the traffic, and when they finally reached the airport, she almost couldn't open her door. Leaving New York had never been part of her ten-year plan.

"Ma'am," the driver said, looking back over his shoulder.

Saffy smiled and forced a shaky hand up, opened the door and got out. He was nice enough to help her out with her bags, and she paid him the fare plus a decent tip. Then she went in, checked in for her flight and kept only her carry-on bag in her hand. She knew there would be a long wait ahead of her to get through security, so she went to get a coffee first. When she was finally in line, her hands began to shake, and she clutched the takeout cup tighter even though it was starting to burn her palm.

The line moved slowly, and the anxiety she'd started to feel in the taxi compounded so fast she could hardly breathe. What was she doing? How could she leave New York? She should be dancing for Pierre, she should be back as a principal, her leg was better... Saffy took a slow, steady sip of coffee in an attempt to calm herself.

She was having a baby, and that was the most important thing in the world. She was going to be a mother. She was going to have a gorgeous little child to hold in her arms and love. She could go back to ballet.

Couldn't she?

"Saffron!"

Saffy almost dropped the cup. What the...was she hearing things?

"Saffron!"

Saffy turned slowly, sure she was imagining the deep, commanding voice calling out her name above the din of the airport, the noise and bustle of the busy terminal. She was going crazy, actually crazy.

Blake? *Oh my god*, it *was* Blake! Her heart started to pound. Should she push to the front of the line? Get through security and away from him, beg to be let through? She knew that was stupid—Blake was worth a small fortune, and he'd just buy a ticket no matter what the price so he could follow her.

Saffron held her head high, not losing her place in the line as she defiantly met his gaze despite wanting to cower as he glared. She'd done her best to run away and not have to deal with him, to face a confrontation, but he'd found her and she couldn't back down. It had been cowardly of her to leave him a note, but it had seemed like the only way to break free from him.

"You're not getting on that plane."

Saffy gulped. She guessed they weren't exchanging pleasantries. "I'm going home, Blake, and you can't stop me."

His gaze was cool. Unrecognizable. "Oh, yes, I can. You're not abducting my child, Saffron. Not now, not ever."

She didn't know what to say. It was his child, but she'd expected him to want her to abort, to…maybe he still did, and he was just trying to take charge any way he could.

"I'm keeping this baby, Blake," she said, hand to her stomach, not caring who heard.

"You're coming with me. Now," Blake said, reaching for her, hand closing around her arm and holding tight.

"My luggage is already checked and my flight leaves in two hours."

"Saffron, you're not getting on that plane." Blake might have been angry before, but now he was furious.

"Let go of me," she hissed, tears welling in her eyes, her resolve fading fast, no longer feeling brave. "You can't just make me."

He didn't look like a man about to take no for an answer. "Sweetheart, we're leaving this airport together whether you like it or not."

She gasped when he pulled her, not letting go. She thought about screaming for security, yelling for help, but the people waiting behind her just looked away, not caring for someone else's problems. Saffron let herself be pulled, wished she was stronger or more determined, but the fight was gone. Extinguished as if it had never existed. Blake would have found her no matter where she was—she'd been kidding herself to think she could run and that he'd forget all about her.

"You can let go of me now," she huffed, pulling back and forcing him to slow down. Blake was impatient, but he did slow, his fingers not gripping her quite so tightly. "And in case you care, you're hurting me."

Blake let go completely then, his hand falling to her back instead, pointing her toward the exit. "Just come with me."

"What about my things?"

"I don't care about your things right now!"

She stopped walking, glared at him. "We're getting my luggage or you can go to hell."

He stared at her for a long moment before marching her back over toward a counter, keeping hold of her as he spoke to someone, flashing a card that she guessed showed he was a priority flyer or something.

"I'm having your things sent. Come on."

Saffron chose to believe him, and within minutes they were seated in a sleek black car, the driver taking off the moment they were buckled in.

"You can't just take me hostage," she managed, forcing the words out as they choked in her throat.

"For the next six months or however long I need to, that's exactly what I intend on doing."

She turned to face him, stared into the eyes that belonged to a stranger right now. Not the handsome, beautiful man she'd slowly fallen for since the night she'd met him. The man she'd been so scared of getting close to, of letting see how broken she was, only to find out that he was broken in just as many ways. Except right now she saw no breaks, not even a crack, just a man calmly and almost silently controlled. This was the first time she'd glimpsed what she presumed was soldier Blake—calm, cool and in control. There was a coolness that was just...*empty*.

"So you want me to have the baby?"

He looked away. "Yes. You can leave as soon as it's born if you like."

"I will not!"

He stared at her, but she wasn't backing down. Not when it came to her baby, and she sure wasn't going to be separated from her child, no matter how much money he had to throw around!

"You used me for my money," he muttered. "You got pregnant, fooled me with your stories of your career aspirations, made me believe that you couldn't ever have a baby. Fool me once, Saffron, shame on you. Fool me twice, and you'll wish you hadn't. I just can't believe I let you close, believed that you were different."

She gulped. "Blake, I'm not going to give you my baby. That's ludicrous!"

"What, you'd prefer just to take my money and raise it alone?" He glared at her. "Not going to happen. You've already done more than enough of that. We're talking about a child here."

"I didn't do this for your money, Blake! You want to investigate me, then go for it. Contact my oncologist, I still have his number in my phone. See my notes, figure out for yourself what a miracle this is that I'm even carrying a child right now," Saffron snapped at him, her confidence seeping back, not about to let him push her around, not now. "No one, not even you, Blake, can act like I haven't worked my butt off for what I've achieved. And that was supposed to be my life, my everything." She fought the tears, wanted to stay strong. "I haven't lied to you, I haven't tricked you, I haven't done anything other than try to deal with this baby on my own so you didn't have to. You've made it more than clear that you don't want a family, and I'm going to make sure my baby feels loved."

He was still just staring at her. "Are you finished?"

She turned away, not about to get into a staring competition. "You can think what you want about me, Blake. But you're wrong."

They didn't speak for the rest of the journey. Saffron wanted so desperately to cry, to just give up, but she couldn't. For the first time since she'd set her mind on being a professional dancer, she had a burning desire within her that no one could dampen. She was going to protect her baby, and no one was going to stand in the way of her being an amazing mom. She might not have wanted to get pregnant; she might not be sure how on earth she was going to do it or what the future held. Except that she had a little baby on the way who needed her more than anything else. Everybody needed a person, and she was her baby's person.

She only wished she had a person herself, someone to look out for her and love her unconditionally.

CHAPTER ELEVEN

Saffron had hidden in the spare room for as long as she could, but it was starting to feel like being left in isolation in the most desolate of prison wards. Besides, if she stayed hidden any longer, she'd probably die of starvation. The little person growing inside her was demanding food all the time—she could hardly keep up.

"Morning," Saffron said as she forced herself to walk through the living space.

Blake looked up from where he was sitting at the dining table, his laptop in front of him and paperwork sprawled. He didn't say a word, just gave her an emotionless kind of stare.

She opened the fridge with a shaky hand, summoning all her strength, not about to let him bully her. She at least wanted to look strong and in control when he was watching her.

"You can't keep me here like a prisoner," she said, continuing what she was doing so she didn't have to look at him.

He ignored her. She hated the silent treatment, would rather he just yell at her and be done with it.

Saffron felt her body temperature rising, just a slow pooling of heat that started deep in her belly and rose slowly up until it flooded her face. She took a deep breath, trying not to explode.

"How dare you," she whispered, forcing her voice as loud as she could make it. "How dare you treat me like some sort of possession, as if you can tell me what to do?"

"You're not leaving, Saffron. That's all there is to it."

"You jerk," she cursed, fingers digging into the counter for support, not scared to stare at him now.

He finally showed something, let her see a flash of anger as he glared at her. "You signed the contract, remember? You were only too happy to live that life, to take my money, hang off my arm and play the doting wife." He sighed loudly. "And let's not forget about that diamond that used to live on your finger."

She swallowed, refusing to cry, to let him see that he'd hurt her. Who was this man? Where was the man she'd fallen for? Who for a moment in time she thought might have felt the same way she did. How had he disappeared so quickly?

"You told me the ring was mine," she choked out.

"And you told me that you didn't need it," he said, voice cold. "Or have you forgotten that already?"

She took her left hand off the counter, her thumb rubbing over the spot where the diamond had once sat. For months, it had been in permanent residence there, fooling her into a sense of…what? Love? She'd never once thought that he'd actually loved her, but she sure had thought she meant something to him. That it hadn't all been make-believe to him. She'd thought they'd leave their fake relationship as friends, maybe even lovers still.

"You know what? You need to leave, give me some space." She was feeling exhausted, didn't have the will or want to fight with Blake.

"And let you just walk out the door? Not a chance."

Hands on hips, she faced him. "I'm not going to run off, Blake, not now that you know. But I do need you to treat me like an actual person instead of some sort of convict."

He pushed back in his seat, eyes on her. "You expect me to believe that you won't run as soon as I turn my back?"

She glared at him. "I'm not going to run." Saffron shrugged. "You know what? Take my wallet so I don't have any money or identification. Is that enough to convince you I won't run?"

Saffron walked out, moving as fast as she could. She only just made it, not even having time to slam the bathroom door shut before she was doubled over the toilet, throwing up so violently she ended up slumped on the floor after. She wriggled down, put her cheek to the cool tiles on the floor.

"Saffron, are you okay?" Blake's deep voice echoed out from the bedroom.

He could probably see her, but she didn't care, didn't have the strength to rise or even look up. The pregnancy was taking everything from her, draining her, making her so ill she could hardly stand it, and the added stress with Blake wasn't helping.

"Go away," she muttered.

There was no other noise, no other words, and she shut her eyes, wishing for sleep but knowing that what she really needed right now was food. Something small and plain to settle her stomach, to give her the strength to face the day. To face Blake.

A door banged shut and still she didn't move, just lay there, wishing things were different, wishing he hadn't found her. Or maybe she should have just faced him, been honest in the first place.

She'd seen the laughter in their eyes, the way they'd enjoyed her pain. She'd been in love, and he'd been sleeping with more women than she could count.

Don't cry. She'd chanted those two words all day, every day. The other dancers were like hyenas, smelling out tears like a predator smelled blood, and she wouldn't give them the satisfaction. They hated her because she was too young, because she'd gotten the lead role too fast, but she didn't care.

"Sticks and stones," she'd muttered, holding her head high, pretending she just didn't care.

But the truth was that Raf's infidelity had almost killed her, because it had drained her of every bit of energy, every bit of confidence she'd had. But she'd survived it, and then she'd never trusted another man again, surrounded herself with a careful little group of friends she could count on.

Blake wasn't going to be the end of her. Blake wasn't going to take anything from her. Blake wasn't going to have the chance to make her feel the way Raf had back then, because she wouldn't let him.

The door banged again, and she forced herself to rise, one foot after another. She splashed water on her face, stared at her reflection in the mirror before braving the living room again. All she needed was something to eat, and she could go hide in bed again, take a long, never-ending shower.

"I put some things on the counter for you," Blake said, zipping his laptop into its Louis Vuitton case as she walked out. "Decaf coffee, a croissant and a bagel. I figured you'd want something."

Saffron could barely hide her surprise. "Thanks."

"Don't even think about leaving," he said, giving her a hard-to-read look. "Just don't."

And with that he was gone, disappearing into his bedroom for a moment before heading out the door.

The apartment was silent, the only noise the barely there hum of the city outside. Saffron took a look inside the bags, the smell sweet but her stomach tender still. She plucked at a piece of croissant, the delicate pastry still warm and tasting like heaven as it dissolved in her mouth.

She hated him. And she loved him.

How could he be so cool one moment then so thoughtful the next? Or maybe he just felt sorry for her. Or maybe she'd honest to God hurt him so bad he couldn't forgive her. For the sake of their unborn child, she sure hoped not.

Blake stayed at work longer than he should have, but it was easier than going home. His assistant had long since packed up and turned everything off except the two matching lamps in his office that were bathing the room in light.

He'd so far fielded calls from his mother wanting them to go out to dinner with her and postponed a business meeting that was supposed to take him out of town, and he was already exhausted with the lies. His life had once been so simple, so easy. He'd worked alongside men he could trust with his life. He'd flown Apaches and extracted teams from live danger areas. His life had been a mixture of adrenaline and fun and passion. And now he was living a life he'd never imagined, a life he'd thought he'd left behind for good. And having to lie about his fake wife who'd thrown him a curveball. He'd been stupid to think a relationship could be anything other than personal, to think he could have lived with a woman like Saffron without getting close, giving part of himself that he'd sworn never to give again. She'd hurt him just when he'd thought he couldn't be hurt by anyone ever again.

Blake poured himself a small shot of whiskey and downed it, wishing the burn of liquor did more for him rather than just temporarily stun his senses. Marrying Saffron was supposed to have made his life easier, supposed to have helped him, given him some breathing space workwise, solved his problems. After a short reprieve, now all it had done was make what was already an existence he didn't want, worse.

What he needed was to fly again, to get up into the sky and see the clouds and feel weightless. To be the rebel he wanted to be, rather than the perfect son forced to conform. His family meant so much to him;

he wanted to care for them and provide for them, but to do that he'd sacrificed his soul. Made a deal with the devil that was his father.

Blake collected his coat and flicked off the lamps. On his way home he collected takeout, choosing Italian since he knew Saffron liked it. He had no idea how he felt about her, what he wanted from her. All he knew was that she was carrying his baby, and that meant he couldn't just kick her to the curb. And he didn't want to.

Saffron had driven him crazy, made him believe in people again, and then she'd gone and betrayed him. Just like Bianca had. Just like his father had.

He steeled his jaw and let himself up to the apartment. At first it took a minute for his eyes to adjust; the lights were on low with lamps illuminating the room. Music played softly from somewhere.

Blake was about to flick the main lights back on, had his hand raised, when he saw her. Saffron had her back to him, arms raised above her head as she stretched then leaped, reaching up, doing something that looked impossible to him on pointed toes before spinning.

He was transfixed, couldn't take his eyes off her.

She dropped forward at the waist, seemed to fall effortlessly down before sweeping back up again and moving side to side. Blake never moved, didn't alert her to the fact he was standing there gaping at her. Because he'd never seen her dance before, and now all he wanted was to watch.

And then she spun in an incredible circle, and he knew he'd been spotted.

"Blake!"

She was breathing heavily, staring at him, eyes wide. It was obvious she'd had no idea he'd been standing there.

"I, ah—" He cleared his throat. "I have dinner. You looked great."

Saffron shrugged, and he noticed how her hand fled protectively to her stomach and stayed there.

"I can't move like I used to, but at least I'm not collapsing into a heap anymore."

Blake set down the food on the table and went to get some utensils and plates.

"You're still wanting to dance?" he asked, wishing he hadn't just asked outright the second the words came out of his mouth. It wasn't exactly something she could just decide to go back to with her stomach rapidly expanding.

"As opposed to having this baby?" she asked, hands on hips.

He hadn't expected her to be so defensive, so protective. She was already like a mama bear, and he admired it, even if he didn't trust her. He liked the flicker of a flame within her, was why he'd been so drawn to her from the beginning.

"You obviously want it," he said, cringing again. For a guy who didn't want to say the wrong thing, he was doing a darn fine job of it. "I just…" He didn't bother trying to finish his sentence or dig himself an even bigger hole.

Saffron blew out a breath, stretching her long limbs out. Her legs were slim but muscled in the way only a dancer's could be, and he dragged his eyes from her.

She was beautiful—that was a given even if he didn't like her anymore. Even if he didn't trust her, didn't want her in his bed, didn't... Who was he kidding? He still wanted her in his bed, only he wanted to yell at her and get everything that was weighing him down off his chest first.

"Yes, I want this baby, Blake. It's the only thing in this world I'm certain about right now." She sat down at the table, opening a container and looking in as he watched. "That and the fact that I'm guaranteed to be doubled over that toilet again at least once before morning, because what I seem to have is all-day sickness. The whole *morning* sickness thing is a lie."

Blake didn't know what to say to her, so he just sat, opening another container and waiting for her to have her first choice. She picked spaghetti Bolognese and he chose the linguine, twirling it around his fork as soon as he'd served himself, beyond hungry. Besides, eating meant he didn't have to make conversation and that he could keep his anger in check. Ever since he'd read Saffron's note it had been bubbling, always on the point of boiling over, and being around her only made it worse. He always stayed in control, was used to remaining calm in the worst situations when he'd been a soldier, but nothing had prepared him for dealing with Saffron.

"Are you worse in the mornings?" Blake asked, setting down his fork.

She looked up at him. "So long as I eat early enough I usually make it through the day. Why?"

He wasn't sure it was the best suggestion, but he was drowning here. With Saffron, without flying, with his mind such a jumble of thoughts he couldn't piece together, he was seriously starting to lose it.

"I want to take you somewhere."

She had a look on her face that told him she no longer trusted his suggestions. "What kind of somewhere?"

"Flying," he told her. "I know we've had a rough— well, whatever we've had has been difficult. But I want you to come flying with me tomorrow. In a helicopter."

If she was shocked she didn't show it. "Fine."

Blake was happy to leave it at that while it felt like a win.

"Have you told anyone?" he asked.

"About the baby?" Saffron was watching him, a forkful of spaghetti hovering in her hand.

When he nodded, she took a visibly big breath. "No. Up until you found out, it was just me and the doctor."

He was pleased to hear that she'd at least seen a doctor, that it wasn't just a home test. Although from how sick she'd been, it wasn't likely to be a mistake. And seeing her dancing, the way she'd touched her stomach… despite the fact that she still looked the same physically, she had looked so instinctively pregnant that he knew without a doubt it was true.

"Saffron, this is a difficult question, but…" He pushed back in his seat, knowing she was going to explode, that he would ruin the sense of calm they were finally experiencing. "You're certain it's mine?"

He'd expected anger, but he hadn't expected the torrent of fury that hit him like a power wave.

"Are you kidding me?" Her words were so low, so quiet, but they hit a mighty punch. She rose, palms flat to the table, leaning forward as she stood, staring him down. "How dare you ask me that?"

When he rose her eyes flashed with such a powerful anger that he should have known to back down rather than try to placate her. Blake reached for her, wanting to tell her that he'd needed to ask, to hear her say it, but the moment he approached her—

"Saffron!" He cursed as her palm made contact with his cheek. It took all his strength not to react, to steel his jaw. But he did grab her wrist; he wasn't about to let her get a swing in again.

"Don't you ever ask me that question again, Blake. Never." She yanked her arm, hard enough to make him release it, her glare like venom.

"It was a fair question," he muttered, annoyed now.

"For an idiot," she snapped.

"Come on, Saffron!" Blake laughed bitterly. "It was a legitimate question! You're asking me to be a father, to parent a child that you know is yours, and I have no idea if…"

"Stop right there," she yelled back. "I never asked you to be a father, Blake. I wanted to give you an out, to raise this child on my own without anything from you, because I knew you didn't want a baby. I wanted to give my child all the love in the world, and I didn't want to back you into a corner, to force you to be someone you didn't want to be."

He sucked in a big lungful of air, calmed down, lowered his voice. "Why? Why give me an out? Why not make me step up? Make me at least reach into my pocket? Isn't that what you wanted?" He shook his head.

"Or was that diamond ring enough money for you?" Blake knew it had been a low blow, but she'd pushed him over the edge and he wanted to hurt her the way she'd hurt him. The pain she'd caused him was real, had pushed him into behaving like someone he wasn't. He knew he was being an idiot, but he couldn't help it.

Saffron had tears swimming in her eyes now, but she didn't back down. Looked so stoic, refusing to show any weakness in front of him, and he had to admire her for that.

"You want the ring back?" she asked, staring at him as she reached into her pocket. "Here it is, Blake. Have it."

She threw it at him and it landed at his feet. He never picked it up, just looked back at her.

"You didn't sell it?"

Saffron laughed, but it was a sad, morose sound. "Maybe it meant more to me than you realized."

She left him in the room alone, with a solitaire in front of his booted feet and a table full of half-eaten Italian.

Blake fisted his hands, clenched his jaw tight and refused to react. He wasn't about to trash his apartment just because he could no longer keep his anger in check.

He bent to collect the ring and stared down at it, remembered the laughter and happiness of that day. Even though it had been a contractual agreement, not love, they'd still had fun. And Blake knew that the way he felt about Saffron wasn't...

He slipped the ring in his back pocket and sat back down at the table.

Betrayal wasn't something he was used to feeling, but he knew there was only one reason it had hit him so hard. Because he felt differently about Saffron. Because he cared about her. Because the feelings he had for her weren't anything to do with a business arrangement.

And that's why what she'd done had hurt so badly.

CHAPTER TWELVE

BLAKE HAD HALF expected Saffron to stay in her room all morning, but when he stepped out of the shower, he heard music playing and knew she was already up. He dressed and headed out, checking his watch for the time. It was a perfect, clear day, and he wanted to get up in the air as soon as they could to make the most of having the chopper for the day. It wasn't often they had one grounded unless it was waiting for maintenance, and he'd instructed his team to keep this one that way even if an urgent booking came through.

"Good morning," he called out.

Saffron was fiddling with her iPod and the music died. She was wearing the same outfit he'd found her in when he'd arrived home the night before, tight black leggings and a skintight top. He wanted to glance at her stomach, see if he could glimpse a hint of roundness there, but she gave him a frosty stare and he changed his mind.

"Are we still going up?"

Blake nodded. Living with Saffron and having so much dislike and distrust between them was like being back in his family home when his mom had been giving his dad the silent treatment. Blake had never asked, but he was certain his father had been unfaithful, knew deep down that was the reason behind why the light in his mother's eyes had slowly faded during his teenage years.

"I don't want it to be like this between us," Blake said.

"Says the man holding me hostage and treating me like a criminal," Saffron said, walking away from him.

He didn't bother answering, let her go and listened to the shower when she turned it on. A quick glance around told him she'd already had breakfast, or at least something to eat. Blake thought about ordering up something for himself but changed his mind. He'd collect some food and coffee on their way past to take up for the day.

Spending the day out with Saffron might not have been his best idea, but they were stuck together regardless of what he wanted, and he was ready to man up and deal with it. Even if catching feral cats sounded a whole lot easier than dealing with Saffron right now.

Saffron forced a smile as she stared at the helicopter in front of her. As a dancer, she was used to plastering on a smile and making herself look happy even when she wasn't. And if she was going to survive Blake, she needed to start thinking positively and acting as if she was happy—maybe one day she'd trick her own brain. She had no idea how long she was going to be stuck with him if he became intent on staying in control where their baby was concerned.

"All set?" Blake asked.

She thought about all the times they'd pretended together—that they were a happy couple, that everything was great between them. Saffron knew why that had worked, though, why it had seemed so natural and easy. She'd loved his company, liked the man he was and everything he believed in. And because they'd both entered into their arrangement with eyes wide-open, everything had seemed transparent.

"Let's do this."

She'd never been up in a helicopter, and her legs were a little wobbly at the thought of being so high in the air. Up front. With Blake as her pilot. Saffron gulped.

"You okay?"

She nodded. "Uh-huh."

"For what it's worth, I'm sorry about last night."

She brushed his apology off, not wanting to engage. The last thing she wanted was to argue with him before they went up in the air, and she wasn't ready to forgive him yet, wasn't sure when she'd ever be.

She followed his lead, keeping her head ducked down even though the rotors were still stationary. She'd been reading up about helicopter safety on her iPhone overnight, so she was fully briefed and didn't have to keep asking Blake questions.

Once they were seated, he leaned over her and helped to buckle her in. She held her breath, glanced away, but when she looked back he was still fumbling, his hand grazing her stomach.

"Sorry," he mumbled.

Saffron instinctively sat back, pulled away from him. "It's fine." Once, she'd loved any excuse to touch him and liked whenever he'd touched her. She still *wanted* to want it, but she doubted it could ever be like that again.

"I've done that a hundred times for other passengers. This is crazy." He finally snapped her safely in and sat back, doing his own safety restraints.

Saffron sat back and listened to the helicopter fire into life. He passed her a headset to wear, and when they were finally rising into the air, she clutched her seat as the ground receded below.

"How you doing, rookie?" he asked, grinning across at her.

Saffron forgot all about the ground disappearing below them when Blake flashed her his big smile. She hadn't seen a smile light up his face like that since before they'd gone out to their last cocktail party, the night she'd ended up in the restroom and found out she was pregnant.

His burst of happiness hit her like a jolt, reminding her of why she'd liked him so much, why she'd wanted to stay with him and why she'd been so afraid of hurting him. Of breaking his trust.

As he expertly maneuvered the chopper, she stared at him, unable to tear her eyes away. He was happy. Genuinely, one hundred percent happy. And it showed her a different side to him.

"You're different when you're flying," she said, still watching him.

He looked at her. "How's that?"

"Everything about you," she told him. "Even when you're just sitting, there's a bit of a smile hovering, there's a lightness in your eyes. You're just…" Saffron frowned. "Different. I can't explain it."

He was looking straight ahead now, and she admired his strong, chiseled jaw, the handsome side profile. She might not like the way he'd treated her, but deep down she got it, understood why he was so hurt by what she'd done. She only wished he'd trusted her enough after spending three months with her as his wife, instead of labeling her a gold digger without at least giving her a chance to explain properly.

"That's because this is the first time you've seen the real me," Blake said, not moving a muscle, staring straight ahead.

Saffron turned away, stared out the window, where everything started to blur a little as they moved fast through the sky. She'd been nervous about going up, but now the helicopter ride was the last thing on her mind.

"Why did you give it up?" she asked. "How could you give what you love up like that? You had a choice, didn't you?"

Blake never answered her, and she never asked again.

They'd been up in the air for what felt like forever, but Saffy still hadn't had enough time to think. She doubted she ever would, not when it came to Blake. Something about him made her crazy, made her feel things she was scared of and had thought would never happen to her.

"Descending," Blake said, loud and clear through the headset.

He hadn't spoken a word to her since just after take-off, and Saffron felt a weird kind of divide between them. There was so much she wanted to ask him, wanted to say. Only nothing felt right when she sounded it out in her head first.

They landed in a field, a ranch from what she could see, and Saffron stayed quiet as Blake did his thing. When he slipped his headset off, she did the same, watching as he exited the helicopter and then opened her door and held up his hand to help her out.

Saffron took it, letting him guide her down. She stretched, taking a look around.

"Let's go," Blake said.

"Where?"

"For a walk over there." He pointed. "We can have lunch under that tree."

Saffron didn't question him, just followed, staying a step or two behind him and looking at their surroundings.

"Where are we?" she asked when he stopped under a pretty oak tree, its branches waving down low and shielding them from the intense sunshine.

"My family used to own this ranch," Blake said. "It was somewhere we came over the summer or just for a weekend getaway. My best childhood memories were spent here."

Saffron listened as she continued to look around. She touched the trunk of the tree, ran her fingers across its gnarled bark. There were indentations in it, markings that she couldn't quite figure out.

"That's me," Blake said, standing close behind her.

She could feel his breath, the warmth of his big body as it cast a deeper shadow over her, making her own body hum even though she tried so darn hard to fight it.

"You?" she managed.

"Yeah." He leaned past her, his arm skimming hers as he traced his fingers across the same spot hers had just trailed over. "I etched my name in here a few times. I used to ride out here on a cute little pony who was always happy to go as fast as I wanted, and when I got older, I landed my first solo here."

Saffron was aware of everything, could feel his body even though he was no longer touching her, her breath loud in her own ears, heart thumping. There was nothing she could do to stop the way she reacted to him.

"My dad saw how much I loved it here, knew how much pleasure I got from flying out here, practicing everything I learned."

"He didn't want that?"

Blake made a grunting noise, and she knew he was stepping away. It gave her breathing space, but she liked having him near, wanted him to stay closer.

"It was around the time we'd started to butt heads a lot. All the time," Blake said. Saffron turned and saw him hit the ground, his big frame sprawled out. He had one leg out straight, the other bent, resting on one arm as the other plucked at a strand of grass. "I started to talk about what I wanted to do with my life, and that didn't tally up with what he wanted. He went from loving my interest in helicopters to despising it, because every time I went up in the air it made me more determined to carve my own path."

Saffron sat down, leaning against the trunk she'd been studying. "I'm sorry."

He laughed and raised an eyebrow. "What for?"

"I'm sorry that you had a dad who couldn't support your dreams. That he had a hold on you that you still haven't been able to shake."

Blake's stare hardened. "I lost that hold, Saffron. I lost it for years, but in the end it was a hidden choke hold that I'd never truly escaped. It started back then, tightened when he paid Bianca off to leave me and then again when he died."

"You need more of this. To remind yourself of what you love."

If she'd been his wife, his real wife, it would be what she'd insist on.

"Anyway, why am I telling you all that stuff?"

She wasn't buying his laugh, knew it was no joke to him. "Because you wanted me to see the real you," Saffron said quietly. "You wanted to show me who you really are."

"You sound so sure about that." Blake opened a bag and pulled out a couple of Cokes, holding one out for her.

"Can I ask you something?" Saffron said, her heart starting its rapid beat again, near thudding from her chest.

"Shoot."

"Did you ever feel anything for me? I mean, anything real?"

Blake had the Coke halfway to his mouth, but he slowly lowered it. "Did you?"

"I asked you first," she insisted, wishing she hadn't asked him but needing, *craving*, the answer.

"You mean did I want you in my bed? Did I want you at my side, on my arm?"

She sucked in a breath. "I know you wanted me in your bed—that's the only thing I'm sure about. But..." Saffron paused. "Was the way we looked at each other real? The way we..."

This time when her voice trailed off she didn't bother to finish her sentence. What was she trying to say?

"Whatever we had was just part of a deal," Blake said matter-of-factly. "Was I attracted to you? Of course. Any hot-blooded man would have been. But we didn't have anything more than sex and a contract."

Saffron had tears burning in her eyes like acid, making her want to scream in pain. But she stayed silent, swallowed them down. She'd thought the feeling had been reciprocated, that he'd felt something real for her, like she had for him, but she'd been wrong.

"Why, did you expect something else?" he asked.

Saffron bravely shook her head. "No. I was just curious." Sobs racked her body, jarred her ribs and her shoulders and every other part of her. But she kept her chin up, sucked back silent gasps to stop herself from giving in, from letting him see how much he could hurt her. *Just like dancing*, she told herself. Crying over real pain, over a real injury, was one thing, but that was the only thing any dancer would ever shed a tear over.

"Do you have anything to eat in there?" she asked instead, desperate to change the subject.

Blake nodded. "Sure. You hungry?"

Saffron nodded. She'd rather eat than talk any more.

Blake had shown her his true colors, how happy he could be in the air, what made his heart sing. Only she'd expected, *hoped*, that there would be more. That he'd say something else, tell her that he felt something, *anything*, for her.

Because even though he'd hurt her and she'd tried to run back home, what she felt for Blake was real. It always had been. She'd slowly started to fall in love with him, a man so beautiful yet damaged by a father and an ex-lover who had done him more harm than good, and a career that he'd loved yet one that had shattered parts of him emotionally, as well.

But that man wasn't hers to take, wasn't hers to love. She was having his baby, and that was it. He didn't love her back—maybe he didn't even care for her beyond what she meant to him on paper.

And that hurt so bad it made her injury seem like a cakewalk.

She touched her hand to her stomach, something she was doing instinctively all the time now. If it wasn't for the baby, she'd be long gone now, and Blake would be a distant memory. *Or would he?*

Maybe without the baby everything would have stayed the same. They'd still be living in their little faux bubble of a marriage.

"Sandwich?" Blake asked, leaning forward and passing it over.

"Sure," she murmured, not bothering to ask what was in it. She didn't care.

"You sure you're okay? You're feeling all right?" Blake asked.

Saffron forced a smile. "I'm fine. Thanks for bringing me here."

"You're the first person I've ever flown out here," he said, taking another sandwich out and holding it in his hands, watching her.

"I thought…" She didn't know what she'd thought. Did that mean something—was it supposed to mean something?

"I want our baby to start flying young," Blake said, surprising her with his smile. "It's all I ever wanted, and if I'm going to share it with anyone, who better than my child?"

Of course. It was the baby. That was the only reason he'd brought her. She'd been fooling herself that maybe he wanted to talk to her, to get away from the city with her for a reason, but now it was all about the baby.

So much for him not wanting to be a dad.

"We need to figure this out, how it's going to work," Saffron said, not seeing any point in putting it off. "You don't have to do this, playing the dad role. It was my choice to keep the baby, and I'm okay with that."

The happy lilt of Blake's mouth disappeared, replaced with a much tighter line. "Oh, yeah? So I could just write a card on birthdays or maybe just Christmas."

Saffron refused to take the bait, didn't want to end up arguing with him when she had no chance of winning.

"What I'm trying to say is that I want custody. I don't want to fight about it, but a child needs to be with its mom," she said, bravely meeting his gaze head-on and refusing to shrink away from him. "You'll always be welcome, I'm not trying to tell you to stay away, I'm just saying that…"

"Oh, I hear what you're saying," Blake muttered. "You're laying it on pretty thick."

"Blake! You don't even want this child! You don't want to be a dad!" Saffron didn't know how to keep her cool, what to say. He was driving her crazy. "We're not a real couple. There is no way for this to work."

Blake stood and stared down at her, his shadow imposing. "I wasn't under any illusion there."

He stormed off, and she didn't bother calling out. She wasn't about to follow him, either. Instead she sat there, picking at her sandwich even though the last thing she felt like was eating.

How had her life turned out like this? She was sitting here all high and mighty about how much she wanted this baby, and she did, but she wasn't *actually* ready to be a mother. All she wanted was to be back on stage, back dancing. Saying yes to performing at Pierre's retirement party. And instead she was growing a big round belly and thinking about names and genders and how on earth she was going to provide for the little future love of her life.

Saffron bit hard on her lower lip. Everything was a mess. She didn't want Blake and his money, but if he didn't let her go back home, then she'd have no other choice but to take whatever he offered. But if he even for a second wanted to take her child from her, take control… She pushed the thoughts away. It wouldn't come to that, because she wouldn't let it.

Suddenly Blake was storming back in her direction, his face like thunder. As she watched, he gathered everything up and marched it back to the helicopter. Saffron stood and reluctantly followed—it wasn't as if she had an alternate ride home.

"We're going," he said.

She shook her head. "Why can't we stay? I think you should blow off some steam before…"

He spun around, only a few feet from her, his hands clenched at his sides, his anger palpable.

"You know why I brought you here?" he asked.

Saffron stayed still, stared at the bulge in his neck where a vein was about to pop out from under his skin.

"I thought we could start fresh, put the past behind us. I brought you here because this place means something to me, and I wanted to show it to you." He ran a hand through his hair, anger still radiating from every part of him. "I wanted to see if you actually cared about me, whether we could at least agree on something to do with this child, *our* child."

"I do care about you, Blake," she said softly, telling him the truth. "You're the one who just acted like what we had meant nothing, that it wasn't real."

"Yeah? You care about *me*?" He laughed, but it sounded forced. "Well, you've got a real strange way of showing it."

"Blake…" she started. He'd just been the one saying there was nothing real between them, yet now suddenly everything was her fault!

"Get in the helicopter, Saffron," he demanded as

he spun back around. "Or find your own way back to the city."

She wanted to believe that he wouldn't actually leave her behind, but given his mood, she wasn't sure about anything right now.

"I'm sorry," she said as she followed him.

"Yeah, me, too," he muttered back.

Saffron took his hand to guide her into her seat, but she never looked at him when he settled beside her and started to flick switches, the engine humming into life. Things had gone from worse to bad to worse again, and there was nothing she could do to change it.

CHAPTER THIRTEEN

THEY'D BEEN SILENT since the ranch. Saffron had goose pimples rippling across her skin whenever she looked at him, but still they never uttered a word. They'd landed, he'd helped her out, driven her home, and now he was about to head out the door for takeout. She knew this because he'd phoned and ordered Thai, and she'd been sitting in the same room as him, snuggled under a mohair blanket while he'd been positioned at the dining table furiously banging away at his keyboard. She was half expecting him to need a new machine in the morning the way he'd been treating it.

"I'll be back soon," Blake said.

When she looked up, he was standing near the door, his eyes still shining with anger. Or at least she was guessing that's what it was.

"Okay." Saffron forced a smile, but he was still staring at her and his gaze was unnerving.

"That's it. That's all you've got to say to me?" His voice was so low, so quiet it was lethal.

Saffron gulped, wished she knew the right thing to say. But the truth was that she'd tried to run from a man with trust issues, and she had no idea what to say to make that situation better.

"I'm sorry. I'm sorry for what I did, Blake, I am," Saffron said, forcing the words out. "But I'm not sorry for what happened, because it's nothing short of a miracle, no matter how scary it is."

He went to turn and she breathed a sigh of relief, but he hadn't moved his body halfway to the door when he was staring at her again. He didn't say anything, just stared, but she could feel the unsaid words hanging between them, knew he was bottling a whole heap of something inside.

"Why can't you just accept that what happened was an innocent mistake? That I never..." She didn't bother finishing. They'd been through all this—there were only so many times she could apologize for what she'd done.

"You want to know why?"

Blake's words sent shivers through her. She was scared of the way he felt, of what he made her feel. The way she felt about him, despite everything.

"Why?" she whispered as he spun around to face her. She'd asked; it wasn't as though she could walk away from him now.

"Because I loved you." He hurled the words at her, and she instantly felt their sting. "I lied before, okay? I fell for you because I thought you were different. I was stupid enough to think that what we had meant more than..."

"Some stupid contract?" she said for him, finding her voice. "I didn't hear you ever offering to rip that up. Not once, during all the times we connected, when I felt like we were something more, did you *ever* make out like you wanted to make what we had real."

It was unfair—she'd agreed to their marriage bargain right from the start to help her stay in New York, but he was hurting her and it was all she had. Because she *had* felt the same, had thought she was falling for him, that something between them was real. That it wasn't all just about their stupid agreement.

"Why didn't you tell me," she finally said when he never spoke. "Why didn't you say something, *anything*? Why couldn't you have just done something to show me?"

"What difference would it have made?" Blake asked, his tone cold, blunt. "What would it have changed between us?"

It would have changed everything. Saffron squared her shoulders. "It would have made a difference," she said, knowing in her heart that it would have. That if she'd just known for sure that he felt about her the same way she was feeling about him…

"What, you would have felt bad about using me? About lying to me?" He laughed. "Would it have changed how guilty you're feeling right now?"

"No," she said simply, tears threatening to spill even though she was trying so hard to fight them. "Because then I would have known that my own feelings were real, that you didn't just think of me like…"

"Like what, Saffron?" he bellowed. "I've treated you with nothing but respect and kindness! I treated you like my real wife, didn't I?"

"I was in love with you, too!" she sobbed. "How could you not have realized how I felt? How could you have been so blind?" Saffron turned away then, couldn't look at him any longer. She was still in love with him, despite everything, and it broke her heart to argue the way they were. "All you had to do was say something, Blake. Instead you hid behind your daddy issues, kept acting like you could never be the man you were so good at pretending to be with me." She shook her head. "You kept saying you couldn't settle down, couldn't ever be a real husband, but in the almost four months I spent with you, I saw a man who could have had whatever he wanted. A man who could have been a darn good *real* husband if he'd wanted to be. You didn't exactly make it look hard."

He stared at her, but she was on a roll now, couldn't stop.

"You're hiding behind your past, not letting yourself live, because you're too scared of change, of what might happen, of being hurt and exposing yourself to that kind of real love. I'm not judging you—heaven knows I'm no different—but things have changed, Blake. Things changed between us long before I took a positive pregnancy test."

"Just go," he finally said, his voice hoarse, unrecognizable. "If you want to go back home to raise our baby that bad, just go."

She hated the emptiness to his tone, the hollowness. It was the same way she felt inside, like a soft toy with all the stuffing knocked from her. "After all that effort to keep me, now you're going to just give up without a fight?" Saffy knew she was being antagonistic, but it was true.

"What do you want from me, Saffron?" he whispered, eyes level with her own.

"I want you to want me, Blake!" she told him, voice shaking. "I want you to fight for me. Show me that I'm not just some asset to you."

"You want me to fight for you?" he muttered, marching toward her, stopping barely an inch away, towering over her, his body almost brushing hers, his gaze fierce. "Consider me in the ring then."

Just as she was about to reply, about to stand her ground, Blake's hand cupped the back of her head, the other snaking around her waist. He pulled her forward, dropped his mouth over hers and kissed her as if it was the final kiss of their lives.

"Stop," she protested, hands to his chest, halfheartedly pushing him away.

Blake didn't let up, kept kissing her. "This is me fighting," he said against her lips. "You want to go, you pull back."

Saffron tried—she wanted to push him away completely. She wanted to forget about him and get on with her life without him, but she couldn't. Because from the moment they'd met, something had ignited between them that she hadn't wanted to admit, and that spark was far from being extinguished. And he'd just told her that he'd loved her. Admitted that what she'd felt between them had been real.

"We can't do this," she whispered, finally parting her mouth from his, dropping her head to his chest, letting him cradle her as she absorbed the warmth from his body.

"You're my wife," he murmured, lips to the top of her head, soft against her hair. "We can do anything we like."

Saffron wanted to give in, wanted to believe him, but... "I can't. We can't." She shook her head, palms to his chest again, forcing some distance between them, needing to look up at him. "We need to talk. Actually talk. Not yell at each other, or make assumptions. I need to talk, and you need to listen. We can't just bury our heads in the sand. Not this time, Blake."

Blake took Saffron's hand and led her to the sofa, sitting down and waiting for her to do the same. He felt as if he'd just stepped off a roller coaster; his body was exhausted and his mind was a jumble. The past few days hadn't exactly been easy, had drained everything from him. And now he had to dig deep and not push his feelings away like he'd been doing for most of his adult life.

"So let's talk."

Her smile was shy as he watched her, and he sat back, glanced away, hoping to make her feel more comfortable. All he'd done since he'd hauled her back from the airport was to tell her what he thought, bully her, throw his weight around. And that wasn't him, wasn't the man he wanted to be. It was the man his father had been. The kind of cold, unfeeling, calculating man his father had shown himself to be time and time again.

Which was exactly why he'd never wanted to be in

this position, to be a dad or a husband. Blake pushed the thoughts away, focused on Saffron. Whether he wanted to be a dad or not was irrelevant now, because he was going to become one regardless. What she'd said had hit home, was true even though he didn't want to admit it. He had been hiding behind his past, living his life with a raft of excuses about what he couldn't do. And that needed to end now. If he wanted to step up and be a parent, not lose the woman who'd finally made him feel, then he needed to be a man.

"I never lied to you, Blake, and we can't move forward unless you believe that."

He nodded. "If I wasn't starting to believe that, we wouldn't be having this conversation." Blake wanted to blame her, but she didn't deserve it.

He watched as she blinked, staring down at her hands. There should be a ring on her finger, a ring to show every other man in the world that she was taken. Their relationship might have been fake to start with, but he was only kidding himself that he didn't want her as his, and he wanted it clear to every man alive that she wasn't available. Suddenly the fact that there wasn't a ring sitting against her skin made him furious.

"I'm scared of being a mom, of holding this baby when it's born and trying to figure out what to do with it, but for the first time I can remember, I want something as bad as I want to dance." She sighed. "And that scares me as much as it excites me."

Blake reached for her hand, squeezed it when he saw a trickle of tears make their way down her cheeks. If she'd wanted to show him what an idiot he'd been, she was doing a fine job. There was no way he could feel worse about his behavior if he tried.

"I'm sorry," he said, clearing his throat, wanting to do better, knowing it might be his only chance after what he'd said. "I'm sorry, Saffron. If I could take back half the things I've said to you, I would."

She nodded, eyes shut as she took a big, shuddery breath. "I want to dance so bad, but I also want this baby, Blake," she said. "I can't explain it, but it's so powerful, so instinctive."

Blake brushed the tears away with his knuckles when she opened her eyes, gentle as he touched her skin. He got how hard it was to open up and be honest, and she looked as though it was hurting her real bad to say how she felt.

"I've been an idiot," he said, finally getting the words off his chest. "I don't exactly find it easy to trust, but you didn't deserve the way I treated you. You deserve an apology."

"You're right," she said, "but I should have told you instead of running away. I made myself look guilty of the crime—you just put the pieces together. And you're not the only one who's said things they regret."

"Why?" he asked. "I still don't understand why you decided to run. I'm not going to lose the plot about it again, but you need to explain it. I need to be on the same page as you, Saffron. Why did you run?"

Her eyes filled with fresh tears as he stared into them, but this time he didn't brush them away, didn't try to comfort her. This time he just needed to listen, and she looked as if she was ready to talk.

"I was terrified you wouldn't want the baby," she whispered, no longer meeting his gaze. "That you wouldn't want anything to do with our child, and I didn't want this baby to feel unwanted."

"What?" He held her hand tighter, fought the anger as it started to bubble within him again. Blake waited a second, not wanting to overreact, needing to calm down before he spoke. He'd wanted her to be honest, and she was, which meant he couldn't judge her for her thoughts. But still, keeping a lid on the way he was feeling wasn't easy.

"I know how strongly you feel about not having a family. How determined you were *not* to be a father, to not ever be put in that position. Not to let your heart be broken by a woman, too."

He took a slow breath, not wanting to snap her head off. "I would never, ever not want my child to be born. And I'd never make a child feel unwanted. Not my own flesh and blood. *Never.*"

"But…"

"I'm terrified of the idea of being a dad, knowing that there is a baby coming into this world with half my DNA," Blake continued, needing to get it all off his chest before it strangled him. "I don't want to be a dad because I had a terrible example from my own father, and I don't want to become that kind of man. To have a child of mine feel such hatred toward me that the moment he finds out his own father has died he feels a sense of relief."

Blake stood, turned away, gulped away an emotion

that he'd never let out before. Something he always extinguished long before it threatened to surface.

"Blake?"

Saffron's hand was on his back, her touch light, her voice kind. But he didn't want her to see him lose it like this, break down when he was usually so strong, so incapable of anything getting under his skin.

"Just give me a sec," he muttered.

"You can't help the way you feel," Saffron whispered, her hand snaking around his waist, slowly, turning him toward her. "Whatever you felt when he died, it's okay. You can't keep all that bottled inside."

Blake shut his eyes, squeezed the tears away. He was not going to cry, not in front of Saffron. Not ever. Tears over anything other than an atrocity weren't for men who'd seen terrifying things, seen what he'd seen when he was serving. There was no way he was shedding tears, not now, not ever. Not over some stupid feelings he'd had for his father.

He opened his eyes and stared into dark eyes that seemed to see straight into his soul. Blake opened his mouth, wanted to tell her she was wrong, but instead a wave of guilt, of emotion and sadness and regret, hit him like a tidal wave. A gulp of tears burst out, the emotion flooring him, his knees buckling as everything he'd held back came pouring from him.

"Shh," he heard Saffron murmur as she held him, cradling his head to her stomach as he stayed on his knees, felled like an oak tree slain at the heart of its trunk in front of her. "Shh."

Her hands were warm, her touch so gentle, but Blake

couldn't stop, the sobs racking his body as the pain slowly washed over him. He didn't try to speak, couldn't get anything out except the grief he'd held so tight for so long.

"Tell me," she said. "Get it all out. You need to share it with someone. Just say the words."

Blake steadied his breathing, felt the rise and fall of Saffron's stomach against his cheek. He had no idea what had come over him, but he couldn't believe what he'd just done. And then he shut his eyes again, tears no longer engulfing him.

His baby was in there. Saffron had been holding him, comforting him, and he hadn't even realized how close he'd been to his little unborn child. It gave Blake the strength to rise and face her again, this woman who'd turned his life upside down and made him feel things, move forward instead of just treading water. If he was going to be a dad, he needed to be honest with himself. And with Saffron.

"I hated him," Blake finally said, keeping hold of her hand and drawing her back onto the sofa with him, keeping her in his arms so he could cradle her warm body against his. "I saw so much while I was serving, realized I was actually living the life I was supposed to live, making a difference in the world and flying the machines that made me feel so amazing. The only stumbling block in my life was my father. And the woman who'd hurt me, made me feel stupid and vulnerable in a way that only my dad had been able to do before."

"Did he ever accept what you did?" she asked, head

to his chest. "Ever give you praise for the career you'd made for yourself?"

Blake didn't want to look at her, just wanted to touch, to feel her there with him. It made it easier for him to say the words he'd only ever said in his head before.

"I grew up around helicopters and planes, and I loved it. I guess that's why Dad thought I was a natural fit for the company, or maybe it was just because I was his firstborn that he felt that way. Before I started to fly myself, at the ranch, I was trailing around after him at the hangars, checking out our stock and soaking up every word he or anyone else in the know said about them. It probably never crossed his mind that I wouldn't do what he wanted me to do."

"But you loved actually flying more than the company, right?"

Blake dropped a kiss into her hair, craving her, suddenly needing to stay connected after so long spent trying to push her away.

"I was addicted to flying from my first flight, and I was a natural in a helicopter, just like I told you today. After he sent my fiancée running for the hills with a pocket full of cash, I knew I had to get away. I hated him so much, and I found my place in the world. I had an amazing job in an industry that needed me, I got to fly every day and I had a new family with my army buddies."

Blake paused, thought back to how he'd felt the day his dad had passed. "He never supported my dreams or wanted to hear anything about my life, not unless I went to work for him. He didn't want to hear about the lives I'd saved, the men I'd flown into dangerous situations to help protect our country that he claimed to love so much. And he sure didn't want to hear about how bad it affected me, that half the time I couldn't sleep for weeks after I returned from a tour."

"You can't help that you hated him, Blake. We feel what we feel, and there's nothing we can do about it," she said.

"Things just got worse and worse, until I couldn't even stand being in the same room as him. Not even at Thanksgiving or Christmas, and I know it broke my mom's heart, which was something I never wanted to do."

Saffron was stroking his shoulder, her face to his chest as she listened to him.

"I have nightmares about what I saw when I was serving, dreams that will haunt me forever, but I'm the type of person who's okay with that because I want to know the realities of our world. I don't want to live in a bubble where rich people have everything and don't care about the world or real people or the next generation." He blew out a breath, amazed how fast the words were falling from his mouth now that he'd started talking, how desperate he suddenly was to share them. "When I heard his helicopter had gone down, that he was presumed dead, it was like a lead weight had been lifted from my chest, a weight I hadn't even known was there. It was a feeling I'll never forget for as long as I live."

Blake stayed silent for a moment, regretted the thoughts he was having, hated the pain he felt at what came next.

"And then I found out that my brother had been fly-ing with him. That it wasn't just my dad, but my brother, too," he murmured. "In that one second, I wished so bad that it was all a mistake, felt so guilty that I'd been relieved about Dad disappearing off the face of the planet."

"You were close to your brother?"

Blake nodded. "My brother was my best friend grow-ing up. We were so different and we fought like crazy sometimes, but I loved him. I'd do anything to have him back, would have traded anything and everything to change places with him and be on the chopper that day. I still would."

"You can't think like that," Saffron said, pushing back and looking up at him. "That's one thing you just can't let yourself think."

"Yeah, I can," he grumbled. "He was with my dad that day for work. If I hadn't been so pigheaded about making my own way in the world, it would have been me with him flying out to meet a new corporate client, not my brother. It would have been me missing, and he'd still be here."

Saffron didn't say anything, just kept stroking his shoulder, her fingers running lightly across his T-shirt.

"It should have been me," he whispered.

"But it wasn't, and I'm glad," Saffron said, her voice soft yet fierce at the same time. "Because then I would never have met you, and we wouldn't have a little baby on the way. This little baby that is an absolute miracle."

Blake touched her stomach, laid his hand flat there, the first time he'd done it, and it calmed him. Made him feel a crazy mix of emotions, protective over the tiny being he'd helped to create that was cradled in her belly.

"I'm scared," he admitted.

"Me, too," she whispered back. "But you're not your father, and I'll never let you turn into him. This baby is going to be whatever he or she wants to be. All we have to do is love and nurture and care for this little person. It's all he or she will need."

"You sound so sure." Blake looked down at her, realizing how stupid he'd been to have almost let her go. She'd been so close to just slipping from his life.

"Being in love and loving is the only thing I am sure about right now."

And just like that, it was Saffron with tears in her eyes and him wanting to be strong for her, and everything else fell away except the woman in his arms.

CHAPTER FOURTEEN

"So what are we going to do?" Saffron asked, closing her eyes and enjoying the sensation of Blake strumming his fingertip across her skin. She snuggled in closer to him, the sheets covering their lower halves, their uppers bare.

"Not much more of that," Blake said with a chuckle. "It can't be good for the baby."

She laughed. "It's fine for the baby. I checked with the doctor."

"I'm glad to hear you had your priorities straight when you were asking questions about our unborn child!" Blake flicked her, his touch no longer so soft and lingering.

Saffron pushed up on her elbows, looking down on Blake. "I'm serious. What *are* we going to do?"

"We're going to get married. For real this time," Blake said, pushing up and pressing a kiss to her lips, his smile serene, a peacefulness on his face that she hadn't seen before. "No registry office this time around."

She giggled when he tickled her. "I can't exactly wear white. I think the tummy will give away my virtue, or lack of."

Blake pulled her closer, rolling them over until she was pinned beneath him, his arms imprisoning her on each side.

"I can't promise that I'm going to be a good dad, but I'm going to try my hardest," Blake said, staring into her eyes. "I don't want to be my father. I don't want to ever be that kind of man, but I want this baby." She smiled, seeing the emotion on his face, the tears welling in his eyes that mirrored hers. "And I want you."

She slipped her arms out and slung them around his neck, needing to hold him, to pull him closer. "I love you, Blake," she whispered.

He dropped a soft, gentle kiss to her lips. "I love you, too."

Saffron smiled so hard, she couldn't have wiped it from her mouth if she'd tried. "I didn't think I'd ever hear you say that. Not to me, not to anyone."

He held her tighter, sighing against her skin. "Me neither, sweetheart. But then I never expected to come across a woman like you. The gloves are off, Saffron. I'm all yours."

"All mine," she murmured as he planted a full kiss to her lips. "And don't you forget it."

EPILOGUE

BLAKE COULDN'T TAKE his eyes off Saffron. *His wife.* His cheeks were sore from smiling so hard, watching as she somehow floated across the stage, twirling and leaping and...he had no idea what any of the moves she was doing were, but whatever it was, she looked incredible. Seeing her like this reminded him again of what he'd been so close to losing, how stubborn he'd been about the only woman who'd ever managed to see the real him.

"Mama."

He glanced down at the little girl sitting in his lap, clapping her pudgy little hands at least every other minute. She'd wriggled to start with, but from the moment her mom had graced the stage, she'd been transfixed, quiet as a mouse as she sat on his knee in the front row.

"Yes, Mama," Blake whispered back to her. "Isn't she amazing?"

"Mama," Isabella said again, clapping and tipping her head back so she was resting against him as she looked up.

Blake focused on Saffron again as she did something else incredible before stopping, her feet no longer moving, her pose perfect as the lights slowly went out. Within minutes the lights were rising again, flooding the theater at the same time that Saffron stood in the center of the stage, the crowd bursting into applause. Then she was joined by the other dancers, but Blake only had eyes for his wife, unable to drag his gaze away for even a second.

He couldn't believe how much she'd changed him, how different he felt from the man he'd been only a few years ago. He held Isabella tight, loving every second of having his little daughter close. She was the best thing that had ever happened to him, even if he was fiercely protective of her, so in love with her that it hurt sometimes.

"Go see Mama," Isabella demanded, wriggling so hard he could barely keep hold of her.

"Come on, let's go then," Blake said, scooping her up in one arm and holding her against his chest. She tapped his head.

"Sho-sho," she said, smiling up at him. Blake never had a chance of saying no to her, not when she looked the spitting image of her mother with her beautiful dark eyes, deepest red hair and angelic smile.

He lifted her up onto his shoulders, which was what she'd been asking for in her own little language, chuckling to himself about the fact he had a tutu all ruffled around the back of his neck. She was just like her mom when it came to ballet, too, and very opinionated about what she liked to wear. Tonight she'd wanted to look like a real ballerina, but she wasn't a pink girl, so it was a dark blue outfit with a tutu and matching shoes covered in bling and she looked impossibly cute.

"Mama!" Isabella squealed when she spotted her mother.

"Hey!" Saffron came running, her face alive as it always was when she was on a high after a performance. Blake hadn't seen her dance live in a show until Isabella was a year old, and now he hated to miss seeing her on stage. Although his daughter was very opinionated about being left home with a sitter, preferring to snuggle up in their bed.

"You were amazing," Blake said, pulling her tight into his arms for a quick kiss before he was pushed out of the way by his daughter, who now only had eyes for her mother.

"Hey, beautiful! Did you enjoy it?" Saffron asked her.

Isabella tucked her face against her mom's chest for a moment before pushing back and touching her mom's cheeks and then patting her hair. Saffron's hair was almost always down when she was home, but when she was performing, it was always pulled up tighter off her face and Isabella seemed transfixed with it.

"You know, if we were normal people, we'd have her with a sitter so we could go out for a late dinner," Blake said, laughing because he knew exactly what kind of reaction he was going to get from his wife.

"Wash your mouth out!" Saffron scolded, pulling Isabella's head tight to her chest and covering one of her ears. It was a constant joke between them, and even though Blake suggested it regularly, they both preferred to take Isabella out with them whenever they could. Especially now that Saffron was back dancing and he was so busy with the company during the day—they juggled as best they could, but after hours they liked to be a tight family unit. Unless his mother begged to have her granddaughter to stay, which usually resulted in a little girl packing her suitcase immediately and demanding to go.

"How about a quick ice cream on the way home instead?" Blake asked, reaching for his daughter and pulling her off Saffron.

"Yay!" Isabella squealed.

Saffron nodded. "Sounds good. Just let me change and say goodbye to everyone."

Blake waited for his wife, chuckling to himself how much his life had changed. Meeting Saffron had changed everything, made him realize how lucky he was in so many ways.

"You know, I took your mommy out for ice cream when I first met her."

"Mommy love ice cream," Isabella said, patting his arm, her beautiful dark eyes looking tired. Not that his daughter would admit to being sleepy for a second, though.

"Mommy was so beautiful then she took my breath away, and she still does," Blake replied without a hint of a lie. "I was a fool once, but when I found out you were in Mommy's tummy, I stopped being so stupid. I asked her to marry me."

"Tell me, story, Daddy."

"What story?" Saffron asked, slipping her arms around him from behind.

Blake grabbed her with his free hand, snaking it around her and pulling her close.

"I'm just telling Bella about when we were first together. Every time we're alone and you're dancing, I tell her how I fell in love with you when she was just a little button in your tummy."

"Oh, really?" Saffron said with a laugh, one eyebrow arched.

Blake laughed and dropped a lingering kiss to her lips when she tilted her head back to stare up at him.

"Really," he replied.

They left the building snuggled up tight, his daughter still in his arms and his wife tucked to his side. They'd never once told another soul the truth about their marriage, how they'd met and the marriage contract they'd once signed. Saffron had even managed to convince her friend Claire that they'd been secretly dating before their fake marriage. Only Blake's lawyer knew the truth, and he paid him enough not to breach attorney-client privilege.

"Our little secret, huh?" Saffron whispered in his ear.

Blake grinned and held her tighter. "Yes, Mrs. Goldsmith," he teased.

He had it all, and nothing would ever be more important to him than caring for his family, fiercely protecting them and doing everything in his power to be everything his father hadn't been.

He'd spent all his life terrified of becoming that man, and in the end nothing could be further from the truth. From the moment he'd accepted how much he loved

Saffron, to seeing his newborn daughter in his arms, he'd known there was no way he could turn into him. Not for a second.

"I love you," she murmured, head to his shoulder.

"I love 'cream," Isabella mumbled in a sleepy voice.

Blake grinned. "And I love Mama *and* ice cream."

They walked out the back exit to avoid any lingering fans, heading for their favorite ice cream parlor. The night air was cool, and he tucked Isabella closer against his chest and Saffron even snugger under his arm, loving the warmth of them.

"Surprise!"

Saffron laughed as her husband stopped midstride, eyes wide as he stared around the room. She ran over to him, throwing her arms around him. He gave her a glare that turned to a sigh and then a smile.

"You fooled me," he muttered.

She shrugged. "Yep, I did."

Saffron had told him it was a simple birthday celebration, just the three of them having dinner with his mother, and instead she'd filled their home with everyone he cared about, including some of his friends and former colleagues that she knew he'd been sorely missing.

"You're crazy," Blake said, holding her tight and kissing her hair.

"It's not only me who gets to live my dream."

He raised an eyebrow and she bit down on her lower lip, watching as his old buddies engulfed him, slapping backs and giving friendly hugs. She'd seen the pain he'd been in at giving that life up, and he'd made her dreams a reality by helping her every step of the way. Not to mention getting a whole lot of flak for rescheduling his days when she was performing to be a stay-at-home dad. It was a role he loved, but she knew it wasn't exactly easy for a company CEO to take time off when all his peers had nannies.

"Saffron, you've got some explaining to do," Blake called out, pushing his friends away and holding out a hand to her, tugging her over.

She couldn't hide her smile, knowing what he was about to say.

"What kind of wife organizes a boys' helicopter weekend for her husband?"

Saffron winked at him, something he often did to her, and it made him chuckle.

"You might not be able to fly for the military again, but it doesn't mean you can't fly with at least some of your old team," she said, standing on tiptoes to kiss him, wanting him to have an amazing birthday. "It's only camping, but I figured it was the closest to replicating what you used to love. There's no use owning a fleet of planes and helicopters if you can't use them, right?"

His smile was impossibly charming, his eyes dancing as he gazed down at her. "You know what I do love right now?"

She tipped her head back. "What would that be?"

Blake swept her up in his arms, lifting her high-heeled feet off the ground and kissing her in front of everyone. His friends clapped and catcalled, but Saffron didn't care that they were putting on a show for them.

"You."

"Just so happens," she said, nipping his bottom lip when he tried to kiss her again, "that I feel the exact same way."

* * * * *

BILLIONAIRE'S BRIDE FOR REVENGE

MICHELLE SMART

This is for Tilly & Eliza.

Follow your dreams. xxx

CHAPTER ONE

BENJAMIN GUILLEM CAST his eye over the heads of the people scattered around the landscaped garden of the Tuscan-style villa in the heart of Madrid, an easy feat considering he was a head taller than most. The only guest there without a plus-one, he was also the only guest in attendance with no intention of celebrating Javier Casillas's engagement.

He snatched a flute of champagne from a passing waitress and drank it in one swallow. The bubbles felt like jagged barbs down his throat, magnifying the hot, knotted feeling that twisted inside him.

Javier and Luis had betrayed him. The Casillas brothers had taken advantage of their lifelong friendship and ripped him off. All the documentary evidence pointed to that inescapable conclusion.

He hoped the evidence was wrong. He hoped his instincts were wrong. They had to be. The alternative was too sickening to contemplate.

He would not leave this party until he knew the truth.

Benjamin took another champagne and stepped over to the elaborate fountain for a better view. He spotted Luis at the far end of the garden surrounded by his usual entourage of sycophants. Javier, Luis's non-identical twin brother and host of the party, was proving far more elusive.

Javier would be hating every minute of this party. He was the most antisocial person Benjamin knew. He'd always been that way, even before their father killed their mother over two decades ago.

Thoughts of the Casillas brothers swiftly evaporated when a dark-haired woman walked out of the summer room, capturing his attention with one graceful step onto the flourishing green lawn. She raised her face to the sky and closed her eyes, holding the pose as if trying to catch the sun's rays on her skin. There was an elegance about her, a poise, a way of holding herself that immediately made him think she was a dancer.

There were a lot of dancers there. Javier's new fiancée was the Principal Dancer at the ballet company the brothers had bought in their mother's memory. Benjamin wondered if the fiancée knew or cared that she was only a trophy to him.

Benjamin had never cared for the ballet or the people who inhabited its world. This dancer though...

The sun caught the red undertones of her hair, which hung in a thick, wavy mass over glimmering pale shoulders. Her features were interesting rather than classically pretty, a strong, determined jaw softened by a wide, generous mouth...

Her eyes suddenly found his, as if she sensed his gaze upon her, two black orbs ringing at him.

A slight frown appeared on her brow as she stared, an unanswerable question in it, a frown that then lessened as her generous mouth curved hesitantly.

His knotted stomach made a most peculiar twisting motion.

No, not classically pretty but striking. Mesmerising.

He couldn't look away.

And she couldn't seem to tear her gaze from him either, a moment in time existing only for them, two eye-locked strangers.

And then a shadow appeared behind her and she blinked, the sun-bound spell woven around them dissolving as quickly as it had formed.

The shadow was Javier emerging from the sunroom to join his own party.

He spotted Benjamin and nodded a greeting while his right hand settled proprietorially on the dancer's waist.

It came to him in an instant that this woman, the slowly forming smile on her face now frozen, was Javier's fiancée.

By the time Javier had steered the dancer to stand before him by the fountain, Benjamin had swallowed the bite of disappointment, shaken off the last of that strange spell and straightened his spine.

He wasn't here to party or for romance. He was here for business.

'Benjamin, it's good to see you,' Javier said. 'I don't think you've met my fiancée, Freya, have you?'

'No.' He looked straight at her. A hint of colour slashed her high cheekbones. 'A pleasure to meet you.'

Under different circumstances it *would* have been a pleasure but now the spell had broken all that remained was a faint distaste that she should have stared so beguilingly at him when engaged to another man.

But that was all the introduction Javier deemed necessary between his oldest friend and new fiancée, saying, 'Have you seen Luis yet?'

'Not yet but I am hoping to rectify that now.' Then, dismissing the striking vision from his consideration, Benjamin added evenly, 'We need to talk. You, me and Luis. In private.'

There was a momentary silence as Javier stared at him, eyes narrowing before he nodded slowly and caught the attention of a passing waiter. 'Find my brother and tell him to meet me and Senor Guillem in my study.' Dropping his hold on his fiancée's waist, he turned and strode back into the summer room without another word.

Two months later...

Smile, Freya, it's a party and all for a worthy cause.
    Smile for the cameras. Smile for your fiancé, still not

here but expecting you to turn on the charm even in his absence.

Smile for the gathered strangers, pretend you know them intimately, let them brush their cheek against yours as you greet each other with the fake air kisses that make your stomach curdle.

Smile, there's another camera. Smile as you nurse your glass of champagne.

Smile at the waiting staff circling the great ballroom with silver trays of delicious-smelling canapés but do not—not—be so gauche as to eat one.

Just. Smile.

And she did. Freya smiled so much her face ached, and then she smiled some more.

Being promoted to Principal Dancer at Compania de Ballet de Casillas came with responsibilities that involved more than pure dance. Freya was now the official face of the ballet company and at this, its most exciting time. The new state-of-the-art theatre the Casillas brothers were building for the company opened in a couple of months and it was her face on all the billboards and advertisements for it. She was the lead in the opening production.

Her, Freya Clements, an East London girl from a family so poor that winters were often a choice between heating and food, a Principal Dancer. It was a dream. She was living her dream. Marriage to Javier Casillas, joint owner of the ballet company, would be the…she almost thought icing on the cake but realised it was the wrong metaphor. Or was it the wrong simile? She couldn't remember, had always struggled to differentiate between them. Either way, she couldn't think of an appropriate metaphor or simile to describe her feelings about marrying Javier.

Javier was rich. Very, very rich. No one knew how much he and his twin Luis were worth but it was rare for their names to be mentioned in the press without the prefix *bil-*

lionaire. He was also handsome. He had chosen her to be, as he had put it, his life partner. When she looked at him she imagined him as her Prince Charming but without the title. Or the charm.

It didn't matter that he was morose and generally unavailable. It was better that way. Marrying him gave her deteriorating mother a fighting chance.

In exactly one week he would be her husband.

The entire ballet company was, as of that day, on a two-week shutdown so the new state-of-the-art training facilities and ballet school that went hand in hand with the new theatre could be completed. Javier had decreed they would fit their nuptials in then so as not to disturb her training routine.

Where was he? He should have been here an hour ago. She'd snuck away to the Ladies to call him but found her phone not working. She couldn't think what was wrong with it but she had no signal and no Internet connection. She would try again as soon as she had a minute to herself.

The media were out in force tonight, ready for their first public glimpse of the couple, beside themselves that Javier, son of the ballet dancers Clara Casillas and Yuri Abramova, a union that had ended in tragedy and infamy, was to marry 'a ballerina with the potential for a career as stratospheric as his mother's had been'. That had been an actual quote in a highbrow Spanish magazine, translated by her best friend, fellow ballerina and flatmate, Sophie, who had mastered the Spanish language with an ease that made Freya ashamed of her own inadequacies. In the two years she had lived and worked in Madrid she had hardly picked up the basics of the language.

Many of the company's *corps de ballet* were in attendance that night, window dressing for the attending patrons of the arts whose money and patronage were wanted. Sophie had begged off with a migraine, something she'd been suffering with more frequently in recent weeks. Freya wished she were there. Just having Sophie in the same room soothed the nauseous panic nibbling in her stomach.

Just smile.

So she stretched her lips as wide and as high as she could and accepted yet another fake air kiss from another of Europe's richest women and tried not to choke on the cloud of perfume she inhaled with it.

A tall figure stepped into the ballroom of the hotel the fundraiser was being held in.

Her stomach swooped.

It was *him*. The man from her engagement party.

Benjamin Guillem.

The name floated in her head before she could stamp it out.

It was a name that she had thought of far too often since the party two months ago. His face had found itself floating into her daydreams too many times for comfort too. And in her night dreams…

Suddenly aware of the danger she was placing herself in, she shifted her stance so he was no longer in her eyeline and smiled at an approaching elderly man.

She must *not* stare at him again. If he came over to speak to her she would smile gracefully exactly as she had to the other guests and this time she would find her tongue to speak in the clear voice she had cultivated through the years; chiselling the East London accent out of herself so no one in this moneyed world ever doubted she belonged.

She'd never been so tongue-tied before as she had the first time she'd seen him. She had literally been unable to say a word, just stared at him like some kind of goofball.

Her senses were on red alert, though, and as hard as she tried to concentrate on what the elderly man was saying— something about his granddaughter being a keen dancer— her skin prickled with electricity.

And then he was there, a step behind the old man, waiting his turn to speak to her.

She didn't look directly at him as she laughed politely at a joke the old man said. She hoped it was a joke. She could barely hear her own words let alone his. Blood pounded hot and hard in her head, a burning where Benjamin's gaze rested on her.

He was well mannered enough to wait for a natural pause in the conversation before stepping forward. 'Mademoiselle Clements?'

To her horror she found her vocal cords frozen again and could only nod her acknowledgement at the simple question.

'We met at your engagement party. I am Benjamin Guillem, an old friend of your fiancé.'

He had the thickest, richest French accent she had ever heard. It felt like set honey to her senses.

Unlike the other guests she'd met that evening he made no effort to pull her into an embrace, just stared at her with the eyes she'd found so unnervingly beautiful at her engagement party. Olive skinned, he had messy thick black hair and thick black eyebrows, a rough scar above the top lip of his firm mouth and a sloping nose. He reminded her of a *film noir* star, his dark handsome features carrying a disturbingly dangerous air. Where the other guests wore traditional tuxedos, Benjamin wore a black suit and black shirt with a skinny silver tie. If he were to produce a black fedora it wouldn't look out of place.

The only spot of colour on him were his eyes. Those devastating eyes. A clear, vivid green, they pierced through the skin. They were eyes that didn't miss a thing.

'I remember,' she said in as light a tone as she could muster, fighting through the thumping beats of her heart. 'You stole him away from me.' She'd been thankful for it.

Javier had put his hand to her waist. His touch, a touch any other woman would no doubt delight in, had left her cold.

She prayed fervently that by the time they exchanged their vows in exactly seven days her feelings for her fiancé would have thawed enough for her to be receptive to his touch. Javier had yet to make a physical move on her but she knew that would change soon.

They both knew what they were getting into, she reminded herself for the hundredth time. Theirs would be a loveless marriage, the only kind of marriage either of them could accept. She would continue to dance and enjoy her flourishing career for as long as she wanted and then, when *she* felt the time was right, give him babies.

She would be Javier's trophy, she accepted that too, but was hopeful that once they got to know each other properly, friendship would blossom.

And even if friendship didn't blossom, marriage to Javier would be worth it. Anything had to be better than the pain of watching helplessly while her mother withered away. Marrying Javier gave her the chance to extend her mother's life and ensure it was a life worth living.

Benjamin inclined his head, those eyes never losing their hold on hers. 'Unfortunate but necessary. We had business that could not wait.'

'Javier said the same.' That was all he'd said when she had tentatively probed him on it when he'd returned to her an hour later. The tone in his voice had implicitly told her to ask no more.

Her fiancé was a book that wasn't merely closed but thickly bound too, impossible to open never mind read.

His disappearance with his brother and friend had only piqued her interest because of the friend. This friend. Benjamin. She'd had to hold herself back from peppering Javier with questions about him, something she'd found disturbing in itself.

It occurred to her that she was lucky she felt nothing for Javier. If her heart beat as rapidly for him as it did for this Frenchman she would have thought twice about accepting his proposal. She knew Javier would have thought twice about proposing if she'd displayed any sort of feelings for him too.

The Frenchman showed no sign of filling her in on their meeting either, raising a shoulder in what she assumed to be an apology.

'I'm sorry if you're looking for Javier but I'm afraid he hasn't arrived yet,' she said when the silence that fell between them stretched like charged elastic. She had to remind herself that people were watching her. 'I don't think Luis is here yet either.'

Benjamin studied her closely, looking for signs that Freya knew about the enmity between him and the Casillas brothers but there were no vibes of suspicion. He hadn't expected Javier to take her into his confidence. Javier did not do confidences.

But there *were* vibes emanating from her, as if her skin were alive with an electricity that sparked onto him, an intensity in her dark eyes he had to stop himself from being pulled into.

He had a job to do and could not afford the distraction of her striking sultriness to delay him at a moment when time was of the essence. He'd planned everything down to the minute.

Tonight, her dark hair had been pulled back into a tight bun circled with tiny round diamonds, her lithe figure draped in a sleeveless deep red crushed velvet dress that flared at the hip to fall mid-calf. Her pale bare shoulders glimmered under the ballroom lights just as they had done under the hot Madrid sun and there was an itch in the pads of his fingers to touch that silky looking skin.

He leaned in a little closer so only she could hear the

words that would next spill from his tongue. The motion sent a little whirl of a sultry yet delicate fragrance darting into his senses. He resisted the urge to breathe it in greedily.

'I already know Javier isn't here. Forgive me, Mademoiselle Clements, but I have news that is only for your ears.'

A groove appeared in her forehead, the black eyes widening.

He turned his head pointedly to the huge swing doors that led out of the ballroom and held his elbow out. 'May I?'

Her throat moved before she nodded, then slipped her hand through the crook of his arm.

Benjamin guided her through the guests socialising magnificently as they waited for their hosts, the Casillas brothers, to arrive and for the fundraising gala to begin in earnest. They would have a long wait. The wheels he'd set in motion should, if all went as planned, delay them both for another hour each. He felt numerous eyes fall upon them and bit back a smile.

When Javier did finally get there, he would learn his fiancée had disappeared with his newly sworn enemy.

He had never wanted it to come to this but Javier and Luis had forced his hand. He'd warned them. After their last acrimonious meeting, he had given them a deadline and warned them failure to pay what was owed would lead to consequences.

Freya was collateral damage in the ugly mess *they* had created, the deceitful, treacherous bastards.

When they were in the hotel's lobby, Benjamin stopped beside a marble pillar to say, 'I am sorry for the subterfuge but Javier has encountered a problem. He does not wish to alarm the other guests but has asked me to bring you to him.'

'Is he hurt?' She had a husky voice that perfectly matched the sultriness of her appearance.

'No, it is not that. He is well. I only know that he has asked me to take you to him.'

He saw the hesitation in her eyes but gave her no chance to act on it, taking the hand still held in the crook of his arm and lacing his fingers through hers.

'Come,' he said, then began moving again, this time towards the exit doors.

Her much shorter, graceful legs kept pace easily.

A sharp pang of guilt punched his gut at her misplaced trust, a pang he dismissed.

This was Javier's fiancée.

Benjamin's sister, Chloe, worked as a seamstress at the ballet company and knew Freya. She had described her as nice if a little aloof. Intelligent. Too intelligent not to know exactly the kind of man she had chosen to marry.

Money and power in the world you inhabited were mighty aphrodisiacs, he thought scathingly.

What he found harder to dismiss were the evocative tingles seeping into his bloodstream from the feel of her hand in his and the movement of her lithe body sweeping along beside him.

His driver was waiting for them as arranged at the front of the hotel.

Benjamin waited until she was sitting in the car before following her in, staring straight into the security camera above the hotel's door as he did so.

'Do you really not know what kind of trouble Javier is in?' she asked with steady composure as the driver pulled away from the hotel.

'Mademoiselle Clements, I am merely your courier for this trip. All will be revealed when we reach our destination.'

'Where is he?'

'In Florence.'

'Still?'

'I understand there was some delay.' An understanding brought about by his own sabotage. Benjamin had paid an aviation official to conduct a spot-check of Javier's private plane with the promise of an extra ten thousand euros if he could delay him by two hours. He'd also paid a contact who worked for a mobile phone network to jam Freya's phone.

As they drove into the remote airfield less than ten minutes later she suddenly straightened. 'I haven't got my passport on me.'

'You don't need it.'

Benjamin's own private plane was ready to board, his crew in place, all ready to get the craft into the air the moment he and Freya were strapped in.

He ignored another wave of guilt as she climbed the metal steps onto his jet, as trusting as a spring lamb.

Within half an hour of leaving the hotel they were airborne.

He inhaled properly for what felt the first time in half an hour.

His plan had worked effortlessly.

Sitting on the reclining leather seat facing her, Benjamin watched Freya. Her features were calm, the only indication anything was worrying her the slight tapping of her fingers on her lap. He would put her out of her misery soon enough.

'Drink?' he asked.

Her eyes found his and held them for the longest time before blinking. 'Do you have tea?'

'I think something stronger.'

'Do I *need* something stronger?'

Not yet she didn't.

'No, but a drink will help you relax, *ma douce*.'

Her throat moved, the generous lips pulling together. Then she loosened her tight shoulders and nodded.

Benjamin summoned a member of his cabin crew. 'Get

Mademoiselle Clements a drink, whatever she wants. I will have a glass of port.'

Soon their drinks had been served and Freya sipped at her gin and tonic. Her forehead was pressed to the window, her gaze fixed on the dark night sky. She covered her mouth and stifled a yawn.

'You are tired?' he asked politely.

A quick, soft shake of her head that turned into a nod that morphed into another yawn. When she met his gaze there was sheepish amusement in her eyes. 'Flying makes me sleepy. I'm the same in cars. Are you *sure* Javier is okay?'

'Very sure. Your seat reclines into a bed. Sleep if you need to.'

'I'll be fine, thank you.' Another yawn. Another sip of her drink.

He observed her fight to keep her eyes open, the lids becoming heavier followed by a round of rapid blinking, then heavying again.

A few minutes later her eyes stayed closed, her chest rising and falling in a gentle rhythm.

He leaned forward and carefully removed the glass from her slackening fingers.

Her eyes opened and stared straight into his.

A shot of something plunged into his heart and twisted.

Her lips curved in the tiniest of smiles before her eyes fluttered back shut.

Benjamin closed his eyes and took a long breath.

There was something about this woman he reacted to in a way he could not comprehend. It unnerved him.

Through all the legal battles he'd been going through these past two months and as the full extent of the Casillas brothers' treachery had become sickeningly clearer, Freya's face had kept hovering into his thoughts.

He stared at it now, watching her sleep through the

dimmed cabin lights, absorbing the features that had played in his mind like a picture implanted into his brain.

It was fortuitous that she should sleep. It would make the difficult conversation they must have easier if they weren't thirty-five thousand feet in the air.

Let her have a little longer of oblivion before she learned she had been effectively kidnapped.

CHAPTER TWO

A BUSTLE OF movement in the cabin woke Freya from her light slumber to find Benjamin's gaze still on her.

A warm flush crept through her veins.

For the first time since infancy, full sleep hadn't taken her into its clutches.

He gave a tight smile. 'I was about to wake you. We will be landing shortly.'

'Sorry.' She smothered a yawn and stretched her legs, flexing her feet before noticing her shoes had slipped off. 'Travel has always had a sedative effect on me.'

It had been the case since she'd been a baby and her parents had taken turns walking her in the pram to get her to sleep. Once she had outgrown the pram the walks had continued with Freya in a buggy, sleeping happily along the same daily walk, which had taken them past a local ballet school. She had always woken up then. Her first concrete memory was pointing at the little girls in their pink tutus and squealing, 'Freya dance too!'

Those early walks had given birth to two things: her love of dance and her unfailing ability to fall asleep in any mode of transport.

Planes, trains, cars, prams, they were all the same; within ten minutes of being in one she would be asleep regardless of any excitement for the destination.

That she had managed almost half an hour before the first signs of sleep grabbed her on Benjamin's jet had more to do with him and the terrifying way her heart beat when she was in his presence than it had about any fears she might have for her fiancé.

She'd had to keep her gaze fixed out of the window to

stop herself from staring at him as her eyes so longed to do. When her brain had started to shut down into sleep it was images of this man flickering behind her eyes that had stopped her brain switching off completely.

Her fingers still tingled from being held in his hand, her heart still to find a normal rhythm.

Rationally, she knew there couldn't be anything too seriously wrong with Javier. Benjamin had told her Javier was unhurt and that there was nothing for her to worry about...

But there was a tension in the Frenchman now that hadn't been there before.

A prickle of unease crawled up her spine and she looked back out of the window.

When she'd last looked out of the window they had been high above the clouds. Now the earth beckoned closer, dark shadows forming shapes that made her think of mountains and thick forests, beyond them twinkling lights, towns and cities bustling with late-evening life.

None of it looked familiar.

The unease deepened the closer to earth they flew and she kept her eyes peeled, searching for a familiar landmark, anything to counteract the tightening of her stomach and the coldness crawling over her skin.

She hardly noticed the smoothness of the landing, too busy straining through the darkness to find something familiar in the airfield they had landed in.

As she whispered words of thanks to the cabin crew and climbed down the metal stairs to the concrete ground, she inhaled deeply. Then she inhaled again.

She had been in Florence as part of her ballet company's European tour only the week before. Florence did not smell like this. Florence did not smell of lavender.

Benjamin had reached the ground before her and stood at a waiting sleek black car, the back passenger door open.

'Where are we?' she asked hesitantly, not at all liking the train of her thoughts.

'Provence.'

It took a beat for that to sink in. 'Provence as in France?'

'Oui.'

'Did I misunderstand something? I thought you said Javier was still in Florence.' Freya knew she hadn't misheard him but told herself her ears were unused to Benjamin's thick accent and therefore she must have misunderstood him.

Slowly, he shook his head. 'You heard correctly.'

Through the panicking spread of her blood she forced herself to think, to keep calm and breathe.

She had only met Benjamin once before but knew he was Javier and Luis's oldest friend. Their mothers had been best friends. They had grown up thinking themselves as family. She knew all this because of a costume fitting she'd had before Compania de Ballet de Casillas had gone on its most recent tour, the one that had taken her to the beautiful city of Florence. A new seamstress had been tasked with measuring Freya, a young, dazzlingly beautiful woman called Chloe Guillem. When Freya had casually asked if she were any relation to Benjamin, she'd learned Chloe was his sister. She should have been glad of the opportunity to speak to someone who knew Javier and taken the opportunity to learn more about her fiancé. It shamed her that she'd had to restrain herself from only asking about Chloe's brother.

'Where is he, then?'

Benjamin looked at his watch before meeting her eye again. The lights shining from his jet, which still had the engine running, made the green darker, made them flicker with a danger that clutched in her chest.

'I think he must now be in Madrid. Very soon he is going to learn you have disappeared with me. He might have already.'

'What are you talking about?' she whispered.

'I regret to tell you, *ma douce*, that I have brought you here under false pretences. Javier did not ask me to bring you to him.'

She laughed. It was a reflex sound brought about by the absurdity of what he'd just said. 'Is this a joke the pair of you have dreamt up together?'

But Javier didn't joke. She had seen no sign whatsoever that her fiancé possessed any kind of sense of humour.

Benjamin's unsmiling features showed he wasn't jesting either. The dark shadows being cast over those same features sent fresh chills racing up her spine.

The chills increased as, pulling her phone out of her bag, she saw it still wasn't working.

There was the slightest flicker in his eyes that made her say, 'Have you got something to do with my phone not working?'

'It will be reconnected tomorrow,' he said steadily. He took a step towards her. 'Get in the car, *ma douce*. I will explain everything.'

Her heart pounding painfully, she took a step back, taking in the darkness surrounding them. High trees edged the perimeter of the huge field they had landed in, the only sound the jet's engine. The vibrant civilisation she'd glimpsed from the window could be anywhere or nowhere.

To the left of the runway sat a small concrete building, its lights on.

When Freya had exited the plane she had seen a couple of figures in high-visibility jackets walking away from them. She had to assume they'd gone into that building. She thought it safe to assume that building contained, at the very least, a working telephone.

'I'm not going anywhere else with you until you tell me what is going on,' she said in the steadiest voice she could manage while sliding her hand back into her small shoul-

der bag. She put her non-functioning phone back into it and
groped for the can of pepper spray.

He must have seen her fear for he raised his hands, palms
facing her. 'I am taking you to my home. You have my as-
surance that you will come to no harm.'

'No. I want to know what's going on *now*. Here. No
more riddles.'

'We have much to talk about. It is better we talk in privacy and comfort.'

'And I prefer to discuss things now, before I get back
on that plane and tell the pilot to take me back to Madrid.'
To get to the plane, though, meant getting past *him*. A lifetime of dance had given her an agility and strength most
other women didn't possess but she didn't kid herself that
she had the strength to match this man, who had to be a
foot taller than her own five foot five and twice her breadth.

She caught a glimmer of pity in those dangerous green
eyes that made her blood chill to the same temperature as
her spine.

Her fingers found the pepper spray.

She might not have the strength to match him but she
would bet her life she was quicker than him.

She pulled the weapon out and aimed it at him, simul-
taneously stepping out of the heels that would hinder any
escape. 'I *am* going back to Madrid and you can't stop me.'

Then, not giving him a chance to respond in any shape
or form, Freya took off, racing barefoot over the runway
and then over the dry grass to the safety that was the concrete building with its welcoming lights. Not once did she
look over her shoulder, her focus solely on the door that
would open and lead her to…

A locked door.

She tugged at it, she pushed it, she pulled it. It didn't
budge.

'This airfield belongs to me.' Benjamin's voice carried

through the still night air that was broken only by the running engine of his jet. 'No one here will help you.'

She turned her head to look back at him, surprised to find herself more angry than fearful.

Surely this was a situation where terror rather than fury should be the primary emotion?

He had lied to her and deliberately taken her to the wrong country.

No one did that unless they had bad intentions.

She should be terrified.

Benjamin hadn't moved. He stood by the car watching her impassively. For the first time she realised the car had a driver in it.

And for the first time she realised his jet's engines were still running for a reason. Not only that but it was moving...

Open-mouthed, fighting back despair, Freya watched it increase in speed down the runway.

A moment later it was in the air.

It soared into the night sky, the roar of its engines decreasing the further it flew until it was nothing but a fleeing star.

And then there was silence.

'Come with me.' This time there was no other sound but Benjamin's voice. 'You will not be touched or harmed in any way. I give you my word.'

'Why should I believe you?' she called back.

He gave what she could only describe as a Gallic shrug. 'When you get to know me, you will learn I am a man of my word.'

She shivered at words that sounded more like a threat than a promise and looked around the airfield for a route that could be her pathway to freedom. As far as she could tell they were in the middle of nowhere.

She could run. She had a good chance of making it to the perimeter before his car could catch her and then she could disappear. But where would she disappear *to*? She had no idea how far she was from civilisation, no money, a phone that didn't work…she didn't even have her shoes on.

She either took her chances and ran off into the unknown or she went with Benjamin into another unknown.

The question was which unknown held the least danger.

Benjamin watched Freya rub her arms as she stared back at him, could see her weighing up her options.

Then her spine straightened and she stepped slowly towards him, holding the spray can outwards, aimed at him.

When she was two metres from him she stopped. 'If you come within arm's reach of me I will spray this in your face. If you make any sudden movements I will spray this in your face.'

He believed her. The fear he had glimpsed before she had run had gone. Now there was nothing on her face but cool, hard resolve.

If he'd believed she was a woman to fall into a crying heap at the first sign of trouble he would never have taken this path.

Everything he had learned about her backed his instinct that Freya had grit. Seeing it first-hand pleased him. It made what had to be done easier.

'I have given you my word that you will come to no harm.'

'You have already proven yourself a liar. Your word means nothing to me.'

He turned to the open car door. 'Are you getting in or do I leave you here?' He didn't like that he'd had to lie and had swallowed back the bile his lies had produced. That bile was a mere fraction of the sourness that had churned in his guts since he'd accepted the extent of the Casillas brothers' betrayal.

She glared at him and backed into the car.

By the time Benjamin had folded himself into the back

next to her, she had twisted herself against the far door, still aiming the spray can at his face.

'Don't come any closer.'

'If I wanted to hurt you I would have done so already.'

Her jaw clenched and her eyes narrowed in thought but she didn't lower her arm or relax her hold on the can. He was quite certain that if she were to spray it at him it would temporarily blind him. It would probably be painful.

'Do you always carry that thing with you?' he asked after a few minutes of loaded silence had passed while his driver navigated the dark narrow roads that led to his chateau.

'Yes.'

'Why?'

She smiled tightly. 'In case some creep tries to abduct me.'

'Have you ever used it?'

'Not in anger but there's a first time for everything.'

'Then I shall do my best not to provoke you to use it on me.'

'You can do that by telling your driver to take me to the nearest airport.'

'And how will you leave France on a commercial flight without your passport?'

Her lips clamped together at this reminder, the loathing firing from her eyes hot enough to scorch.

The car slowed over a cattle grid, the rattling motion created in the car one Benjamin never grew tired of. It was the motion of being home.

After driving a mile through his thick forest, they went over another cattle grid then stopped for the electric gates to open.

For the first time since they'd got into the car, Freya took her eyes off his face, looking over his shoulder at the view from his window.

Her eyes widened before she blinked and looked back at him.

'You can put the spray down,' he informed her nonchalantly. 'We have arrived.'

His elderly butler greeted them in the courtyard, opening Freya's door and extending a hand to help her out.

Benjamin got out of his door in time to hear her politely say, 'Please, can you help me? I've been kidnapped. Can you call the police?'

Pierre smiled regretfully. *'Je ne parle pas anglais, mademoiselle.'*

'Kidnapped! Taken!' She put her wrists together, clearly trying to convey handcuffs, then when Pierre looked blankly at her, she sighed and put a hand to her ear to mimic a telephone. 'Telephone? Police? Help!'

While this delightful mime was going on, Benjamin's driver slowly drove the car out of the courtyard.

'Pierre doesn't speak English, *ma douce*,' Benjamin said. He'd inherited Pierre when he bought the chateau and hadn't had the heart to pension him off just because he spoke no other language as all other butlers seemed to do in this day and age.

She glared at him with baleful eyes. 'I'll find someone who does.'

'Good luck with that.' Only one member of his household staff spoke more than passable English and Freya had just proven she couldn't speak a word of his own language. 'Come, let us go in and get settled before we talk. You must be hungry.'

'I don't want your food.'

Turning his back to her, he walked up the terracotta steps and into the main entrance of his chateau.

'Christabel,' he called, knowing his head housekeeper wouldn't be far.

No sooner had he finished saying her name than she appeared.

'Good evening, sir,' she said in their native tongue with a smile. 'Did you have a good trip?'

'I did, thank you. Is everything well here?'

'Everything is fine and we have prepared the quarters for your guest as instructed.' Christabel's eyes flickered over his shoulder as she said this, which he guessed meant Freya had followed him inside, her bare feet muffling the usual clacking sound that could be heard when people entered the great room.

He had a sudden vision of her black high heels discarded on the runway of his airfield, a sharp pang in his chest accompanying it, which he shrugged off.

He would replace them for her.

'Thank you, Christabel. You can finish for the evening now.' Turning to Pierre, who had also followed him in, he said, 'We require a light supper, anything Chef chooses. Bring me a White Russian and Miss Clements a gin and Slimline tonic.'

When his two members of staff had bustled off, he finally looked at his new houseguest and switched back to English. 'Do you want to talk now or would you like to freshen up first?'

She glared at him. 'I don't want to talk but, if you insist, let's get it over with because I want to go home.'

He held the mutinous black orbs in his. 'Is it not already obvious to you that you will not be going home tonight, *ma douce*?'

CHAPTER THREE

FREYA STARED INTO the green eyes that only a few hours before she had been afraid to stare too deeply at because of the strange heat gazing into them produced. Now, her only desire was to swing her small bag into his face. She'd put the pepper spray back into it and her fingers itched to take it back out and spray the entire contents at him.

'When will I be going home?' she demanded to know.

A single brow rose on his immobile face. 'That will be determined shortly. Come with me.'

'Come where?'

'Somewhere we can talk in comfort.'

He walked off before she could argue. She scowled at his retreating figure but when he went through the huge double doors and disappeared, she quickly got her own legs moving. This chateau…

She had never seen the likes of it before other than on a television screen.

Walking past sculptures and exquisite paintings, she entered another room where the ceiling was at least three times the height of a normal room, with a frescoed ceiling and opulent furniture and more exquisite works of art. She caught sight of Benjamin going through a door to the left and hurried after him. It would be too easy to get lost in this chateau, a thought amplified when she followed him through a third enormous living area, catching sight of a library—a proper, humongous, filled with probably tens of thousands of books library—on the way.

Eventually she caught up with him in yet another living area. It was hard to determine if this living area was indoors or outdoors. What should have been an external wall was missing, the ceiling held up by ornate marble pillars, opening the space to the spectacular view outside.

Her throat caught as she looked out, half in delight at the beauty of it all and half in anguish.

The chateau was high in the hills, surrounded by forests and fields that swept down before them. Far in the distance were the twinkling lights she had seen on the plane. Civilisation. Miles and miles away.

'Are you going to sit?'

She took a long breath before looking at Benjamin.

He'd sat himself on a huge L-shaped soft white sofa with a square glass coffee table in front of him.

Staring at her unsmilingly, he removed his silver tie then undid the top two buttons of his shirt.

The wrinkled old man who'd greeted them on arrival appeared as if from nowhere with two tall drinks. He placed them on the coffee table and indicated one of them to her. Then he left as unobtrusively as he had come.

Benjamin mussed his hair with a grimace then took his glass and had a long drink from it. 'What do you know about my history with the Casillas brothers?'

Surprised at his question, she eyed him warily before answering. 'I know you're old family friends.'

His jaw clenched as he nodded slowly. 'Our mothers were extremely close. They had us only three months apart. We were playmates from the cradle and it's a bond we have shared for thirty-five years. I was raised to think of Javier and Luis as cousins and I did. We have been there for each other our entire lives. You understand?'

'I guess.' She shrugged. 'Is there a point to this story?'

His eyes narrowed. 'The point to this story is the key to it.'

'You're talking in riddles again.'

'Not riddles if you would bother to listen to what I am saying to you.'

She caught the faint scent of juniper. Although only a moderate drinker—very moderate—Freya loved the refreshing coolness of a gin and tonic. Usually she limited herself to only the one. But usually she hadn't been practically abducted. And she'd fallen asleep before she could finish the one on his jet.

And she really needed something to calm the ripples crashing in her stomach.

Giving in, she picked it up then sat on the opposite side of the sofa to him, at the furthest point she could find, using all the training that had been drilled into her from the age of three to hold her core and enable herself to be still.

Never would she betray how greatly this man unnerved her but beneath her outward stillness her pulses soared, her heart completely unable to find its usual rhythm. She wished she could put it down to fear and it unnerved her more than anything to know the only fear she was currently experiencing was of her own terrifying erratic feelings for this man rather than the situation he'd thrown her into.

She took a small sip then forced herself to look at him. 'Okay, so you grew up like cousins.'

Before he could answer the butler reappeared with a tray of food.

The tray was placed on the table and she saw a wooden board with more varieties of cheese than she'd known existed, fresh baguettes, a bowl of fruit and a smaller bowl of nuts.

'*Merci*, Pierre,' Benjamin said with a quick smile.

Pierre nodded and, just as before, disappeared.

Benjamin held a plate out to her.

'No, thank you,' she said stiffly. She would choke if she had to eat her captor's food.

He shrugged and cut himself a wedge of camembert.

'It's not good to eat cheese so late,' she said caustically.

He raised a brow, took a liberal amount of butter and spread it on the opened baguette. 'You must be hungry. I took you from the gala before the food was served. You do not have to eat the cheeses.'

'I don't have to eat anything.' She truly didn't think she could swallow anything solid, doubted her stomach would unclench enough for food until she was far from this beautiful prison.

Staring back out over the thick trees and hills casting such ominous shadows around the chateau, she resigned herself to staying under his roof for the night. As soon as the sun rose she would find something to put on her feet and leave. Sooner or later she would find civilisation and help.

He took a large bite of his baguette and chewed slowly. His impenetrable green eyes didn't move from her face.

'If you will not eat then let us continue. I was telling you about my relationship with Javier and Luis.'

Freya pushed her fears and schemes aside and concentrated. Maybe Benjamin really had gone to all this trouble to bring her here only to talk. Maybe, come the morning, his driver would take her to the airport without any fuss.

And maybe pigs could fly.

If Benjamin wanted nothing more than to talk he would have conducted this chat in Madrid.

Either way, she needed to pay attention and listen hard.

'Like cousins,' she clarified. 'A modern-day tale like *The Three Musketeers*, always there for each other.'

'*Exactemente*. Do you know the Tour Mont Blanc building in Paris?' He took a bite of creamy cheese.

'The skyscraper?' she asked uncertainly. World news was not her forte. Actually, any form of news that wasn't related to the arts passed her by. She had no interest in any of it. She only knew of Tour Mont Blanc because Sophie had been fascinated with it, saying more than once that she would love to live in one of its exclusive apartments and dine in one of its many restaurants run by Michelin-starred chefs and shop in the exclusive shopping arcade.

He swallowed as he nodded. 'You know Javier and Luis built it?'

'Yes, I knew it was theirs.'

'Did you know I invested in it?'

'No.'

'They came to me seven years ago when they were buying the land. They had a cash-flow problem and asked me to go in with them on the project as a sleeping partner. I invested twenty per cent of the asking price. When I made that first investment I was told total profits would be around half a billion euros.'

She blinked. Half a *billion*?

'It took four years for the building work to start—there was a lot of bureaucracy to get through—and a further three years to complete it. Have you been there?'

'No.'

'It is a magnificent building and a credit to the Casillas brothers' vision. Eighty per cent of the apartments were sold off-plan and we had eleven multinational companies signed up to move into the business part before the roof had been put on.'

'So it's a moneymaking factory then,' she said flatly. 'I take it there's a reason you're boring me with all this?'

The piercing look he gave her sent fresh shivers racing up her spine.

'We all knew the initial profit projections were conservative but none of us knew quite *how* conservative. Total profit so far is closer to one and a half billion euros.'

Freya didn't even know how many zeros one and a half billion was. And that was their *profit*? Her bank account barely touched three figures.

'Congratulations,' she said in the same flat tone. It was

a lot of money—more than she could ever comprehend—but it was nothing to do with her and she couldn't see why he thought it relevant to discuss it with her. She assumed he was showing off and letting her know that his wealth rivalled Javier's.

As if this chateau didn't do a good enough job flaunting his wealth!

Did he think she would be impressed?

Money was nothing to brag about. Having an enormous bank account didn't make you a better person than anyone else or mean you were granted automatic reverence by lesser mortals.

Freya had been raised by parents who were permanently on the breadline. They were the kindest, most loving parents a child could wish for and if she could live her childhood again she wouldn't swap them for anyone. Money was no substitute for love.

It was only now, as that awful disease decimated her mother's body, that she wished they'd had the means to build a nest egg for themselves. She wouldn't have felt compelled to marry Javier if they had.

But they had never had the means. They had worked their fingers to the bone to allow their only child to follow her dreams.

'I invested twenty per cent of the land fee,' Benjamin continued, ignoring her sarcasm. 'I have since invested around twenty per cent of the building costs. How much profit would you think that entitles me to?'

'How would I know?' she said stiffly. 'I'm not an accountant.'

'Take a guess.'

'Twenty per cent?'

'*Oui*. Twenty per cent. Twenty per cent investment for a twenty per cent profit. Twenty per cent of one and a half billion equals three hundred million, do you agree?'

'I'm not an accountant,' she repeated, looking away from him, her lips tightening mutinously.

'You do not need to be an accountant to agree that three hundred million euros is a lot of money.'

Her slim shoulders rose but other than a flash of colour on her high cheekbones, the mutinous expression on her face didn't change.

'I have received all of my investment back but only seventy-five million euros of the profit. The equivalent of five per cent.'

Her eyes found his stare again. 'Am I supposed to feel sorry for you?'

'You are not expected to feel anything.' Benjamin stifled his growing anger at her cold indifference. He hadn't expected anything less from the woman engaged to the coldest man in Europe. 'I am laying out the facts of the situation. Javier and Luis have ripped me off. They owe me two hundred and twenty-five million euros.'

He had earmarked that money for a charity that helped traumatised children.

The irony of why he had chosen that charity would be funny if the situation were not so damn serious. The memories of Javier and Luis's traumatisation at the death of their mother at the hands of their father had haunted him for years.

Benjamin had almost bankrupted himself investing in the Tour Mont Blanc project. He'd spent seven years clawing his way back, going higher than he had ever climbed before, investing and expanding his fine food business across the globe until he had reached the point where he didn't owe a cent to anyone. All his assets, his business and subsidiaries were his alone and could never be taken from him. Now he could do some good with the great wealth he had built for himself and Javier and Luis had stolen his first significant act from him, just as they had stolen his money, his trust and all the memories he'd held dear.

'Take it up with your lawyers.'

'I have.' Benjamin remembered the green colour Andre had turned when he'd had to tell his most lucrative client that the Casillas brothers were correct in their assertion that he was only owed five per cent of the profits.

It had been there in black and white on the contract he'd signed seven years ago, hidden in the small print. It could have been written in the largest font available and he doubted he would have noticed it back then. He had signed the contract without getting his lawyer to read it first. That was his own fault, he accepted that. It was the only contract he'd ever signed without poring over every word first. The brothers had been given until midnight to come up with the full asking price or the land would have been sold to another interested party and they would have lost the substantial deposit they'd already paid at that point.

They had come to him for help on the same day Benjamin's mother had been told there was nothing more the medical team could do to stave off the cancer ravaging her body. Although not a shock—she had not responded well to any of the treatment she'd been given—it had been the single biggest blow in his life.

Benjamin had signed with only a cursory glance at the document and transferred the money there and then. If it had been anyone else he would have refused to even contemplate the investment but it had been Javier and Luis asking. Men he regarded as kin. Men his mother had regarded as kin. Men he'd trusted unconditionally. At the time he hadn't cared that it would eat into his own cashflow and that the chateau he'd intended to buy outright for his mother to pass the last of her days in would need him to take a hefty mortgage. It was that knock-on effect that had almost bankrupted him.

'From a legal point of view there is nothing more I can do about it.' The words felt like needles in his throat.

He'd refused to accept Andre's judgement and had fast-tracked the matter to a courtroom. The judge had reluctantly agreed with Andre.

Benjamin's rage at the situation had been enflamed when Javier and Luis successfully applied for an injunction on the reporting of the court case. They didn't want the business world to know their word was worthless or the levels to which they would stoop in the name of profit.

'Have you brought me here to tell me this thinking I will speak to Javier on your behalf?' she asked, her disbelief obvious despite the composed way she held herself.

He laughed mirthlessly and took a paring knife off the tray. He doubted very much that Javier cared for Freya's opinion. She was his beautiful prima ballerina trophy not his partner. Benjamin's hope was that her value as a trophy was greater than two hundred and twenty-five million euros.

Cutting into the peel of a fat, ripe orange, he said, 'I am afraid the situation has gone far past the point where it can be resolved by words alone.'

'Then what do you want from me? Why am I here?'

'Every action has a consequence. Javier and Luis have stolen from me and I am out of legal options.' He cut the last of the peel off the orange and dropped it into a bowl. 'In reality, the money is not important...'

She let out a delicate, disbelieving cough.

He cut into the flesh of his peeled orange. 'I am a very wealthy man, *ma douce...*'

'Well done.'

'And if it was just the money I would write it off,' he continued as if she hadn't interrupted him, cutting the orange into segments. 'But this is about much more than money, more than you could understand. I am not willing to let it go or let them get away with it. You are my last bargaining chip.'

'Me?' For the first time since she had entered his home, her composure made an almost imperceptible slip. 'But I had nothing to do with it. I was still in ballet school when you signed that contract.'

'*Oui.* You.' He looked at his watch and smiled. 'In three minutes it will be midnight. In three minutes Javier will receive a message giving him exactly twenty-four hours to pay the money owed.'

She swallowed. 'Or…?'

'If the Casillas brothers refuse to pay what they have taken from me then by the laws of natural justice I shall take from them, starting with you. If they do not pay then, *ma douce*, the message Javier will receive any moment tells him his engagement to you will be over and that you will marry me instead.'

CHAPTER FOUR

THE BURN THAT had enflamed Freya's brain earlier returned with a vengeance. She gazed into the resolute green eyes that gave nothing away and felt her stomach clench into a pinpoint.

Freya had no illusions about her lack of intellect. Ballet had been her all-consuming passion since she could walk. She couldn't remember a time in her life when she hadn't breathed dance and her education had suffered for it. She had one traditional educational qualification and that was in art.

But this didn't mean she was stupid and she would have to be the dimmest person to walk the earth not to look into those green eyes and recognise that Benjamin was deadly serious.

This was revenge in its purest form and she was his weapon of choice to gain it.

She was his hostage.

Her kidnapper stared at her without an ounce of pity, waiting for her response to his bombshell.

She responded by using the only means she had at her disposal, *her* only weapon. Her body.

Jumping up from the sofa, she swept an arm over the coffee table, scattering the crockery and glasses on it, but didn't hang around to see the damage, already racing through the non-existent wall and out into the warm grounds. Benjamin's surprised curse echoed behind her.

Security lights came on, putting a spotlight on her but she didn't care. She would outrun them. She dived into the thick, high shrubbery that she hoped surrounded the perimeter of the chateau and hoped gave adequate camouflage until she found the driveway they had travelled to reach the chateau and which she would follow until she found the road.

She had run from Benjamin earlier. She had reluctantly gone back to him because she had thought he was the unknown that posed the least danger.

She had made the wrong choice. Her heated responses to his physicality, the strange chemical responses that set off inside her every time she looked into his green eyes had stopped her recognising the very real danger she was in.

How big was this chateau and its grounds? she wondered desperately as she cut her way through the trees and hedges, trusting her sense of direction that she was headed the right way.

It seemed to take for ever before she peered through the shrubbery to find the courtyard Benjamin's driver had dropped them off at. The night was dark but there were enough ground lights for her to see the electric gates they had driven through.

Quickly she looked around it and saw the gate, a high wrought-iron contraption with spikes at the top that linked the high stone wall she would have to scale if she were to get away.

Keeping to the shadows, Freya treaded her way to the wall, her heart sinking the closer she got.

It was at least twice her height.

She stepped cautiously from the high tree she'd hidden behind for a better look. The wall was old. It had plenty of grooves and nooks for her to use to lever herself up. If she kept to the shadows she'd be able to scale it away from the estate lights…but then she wouldn't be able to see what was on the other side if she were in the dark.

Determination filled her. If she didn't climb this wall she would never escape.

She took one deep inhalation for luck then darted forward.

The moment she stepped off the thick, springy ground of the woods and onto the gravelled concrete, it seemed as if a thousand lights suddenly shone on her.

Not prepared to waste a second, she raced to the wall, found her first finger holes and began to climb.

She'd made it only two feet off the ground when she heard shouts. Aware of heavy footsteps nearing her, she sped up. The top of the wall was almost within reach when she stretched to grip a slightly protruding stone and, too late, realised it was loose.

With a terrified scream, she lost her hold entirely and fell back, would have crashed to the ground and almost certainly landed flat on her back had a pair of strong arms not been there to catch her as assuredly as any of her dance partners would have done.

Instinct had her throw her arms around Benjamin's neck while he made one quick shift of position to hold her more securely.

She squeezed her eyes shut and tried her hardest to open her airwaves.

She couldn't breathe. The shock of the fall and the unexpected landing had pushed all the air from her lungs. But her terrified heart was racing at triple time, tremors raging through her body.

How had he reached her so quickly? He must have run at superhuman speed.

'Do you have a death wish?'

His angry words cut through the shock and she opened her eyes to find his face inches from her own, furious green eyes boring into hers.

He was holding her as securely as a groom about to cross the threshold with his new bride but staring at her with all the tenderness of a lion about to bite into the neck of its prey.

Then he muttered something unintelligible under his breath and set off back to the chateau.

'You can put me down now,' she said, then immediately wished she hadn't spoken as now that she could breathe again she could smell again too. Her face was so close to Benjamin's neck she could smell the muskiness of his skin under the spicy cologne.

He shook his head grimly.

She struggled against him. 'I'm quite capable of walking.'

His hold tightened. 'And have you run away and put yourself in danger again?'

'I won't—'

'What were you thinking?' he demanded. His footsteps crunched over the gravel. 'If I hadn't been there to catch you…'

'What did you expect?' Her words came in short, ragged gasps. The feel of his muscular body pressed so tightly against her own made her wish he were made of steel on the outside as well as the inside. Damn him. If he were a robot or machine she could ignore that he was human and that her body was behaving in the opposite manner that it should to be held in his arms like this.

Her lips should not tingle and try to crane closer to the strained tendons on his neck, not to bite but to kiss…

'I expected you to listen, not run into the night. The forests around the chateau are miles deep. You can spend days—weeks—lost in them and not meet a soul.'

'I don't care. You can't kidnap me and hold me to ransom and think I'm going to just accept it.' She squeezed her eyes shut to block his neck from her sight.

If only she could block the rest of him out too.

God, she could hardly breathe for fear and fury and that awful, awful awareness of him.

Pierre had the door open for them. As Benjamin carried Freya over the threshold, the butler saw her feet and winced.

Benjamin sighed inwardly before depositing her onto the

nearest armchair and instructing Pierre, who really should have long gone to bed, to bring him a bowl of warm water and a first-aid kit.

'Telling him to bring handcuffs so you can chain me in your horrible house?' his unwilling guest asked snidely.

'That's a tempting idea, but no.' Tempting for a whole host of reasons he refused to allow himself to think of.

Holding Freya in his arms like that had felt too damn good. The awareness he'd felt for her from that first look had become like an infection inside him.

He must not forget who she was. Javier's fiancée. His only possible means of getting his money back and giving Javier a taste of the betrayal he himself was feeling.

Kneeling before her, he took her left foot in his hand. She made to kick out but his hold was too firm. 'I am not going to hurt you.'

'You said that before,' she snapped.

'The harm you have caused to your feet is self-inflicted. Keep still. I want to look for damage.'

The full lips pulled in on themselves, her black eyes staring at him maleficently before she turned her face to the wall. He took it as tacit agreement for him to examine her feet. The foot in his hands was filthy from walking bare through all the trees and shrubbery but there was no damage he could see. He placed it down more gently than she deserved and picked up her right foot. It hadn't fared so well. Tiny droplets of blood oozed out where she'd trodden on something sharp.

Pierre came into the room with the equipment he'd requested, along with fresh towels.

'Going to do a spot of waterboarding?' she asked with a glare.

He returned it with a glare of his own. 'Stop giving me ideas. I'm going to clean your feet...'

'I can clean my own feet...'

'And make sure you have no thorns or stones stuck in them.'

'You're a doctor?'

'Only a man with a sister who could never remember to put shoes on when she was a child.' And rarely as a teenager either. Chloe had moved out of the chateau a few years ago and he still missed her lively presence in his daily life.

His much younger sister was as furious with the Casillas brothers as he was and had insisted on helping that night. He'd given her the task of delaying Luis from the gala and she had risen to it with aplomb. Now she was safely tucked up in first class flying to the Caribbean to escape the fall-out.

'I'm a dancer,' Freya said obstinately. 'My feet are tough.'

'Tough enough to risk infection? Tough enough to risk your career?'

'Being held hostage is a risk to my career.'

'Stop being so melodramatic. You are not a hostage.' He took a sterile cloth and dipped it in the water, squeezing it first before carefully rubbing it against the sole of her foot.

'If I'm not allowed to leave that makes me a hostage. If I'm being held for ransom that makes me a hostage.'

'Hardly. All I require is twenty-four hours of your time. One day.' He rubbed an antiseptic wipe to the tiny wounds at the sole of her foot, then carefully placed it down on its heel.

'And what happens then? What if Javier says no and refuses to pay?'

'You have doubts?' He lifted her other foot onto his lap. 'Are you afraid his love for you is not worth such a large amount of money?'

She didn't answer.

Raising his gaze from her feet to her face, he noted the strain of her clenched jaw.

'You are the most exciting dancer to have emerged in

Europe since his mother died. You have the potential to be *the* best and Javier is not a man who settles for second best in anything. You are not publicity hungry. You will give him beautiful babies. You tick every box he has made in his list of wants for a wife. Why would he let you go?' As he spoke he cleaned her foot, taking great care in case there were any thorns hidden in the hard soles not visible to the naked eye.

Freya's assessment of her feet being tough was correct, the soles hard and calloused, the big toe on her right foot blackened by bruising.

His heart made a strange tugging motion to imagine the agonies she must go through dancing night after night on toes that must be in perpetual pain. These were feet that had been abused by its owner in a never-ending quest for dance perfection. And what perfection it was...

Benjamin had been dragged across the world in his younger years by his mother, who had been Clara Casillas's personal seamstress as well as her closest friend. His childhood home had been a virtual shrine to the ballet but he'd been oblivious to it all, his interest in ballet less than zero. He'd thought himself immune to any of the supposed beauty the dance had to offer. That had been until he'd watched a clip of Freya dancing as Sleeping Beauty on the Internet the other week.

There had been something in the way she moved when she danced that had made his throat tighten and the hairs on his arms lift. He'd watched only a minute of that clip before turning it off. He'd tried to rid his mind of the images that seemed to have etched themselves in his brain ever since.

Freya belonged to his enemy. He had no business imagining her.

And yet...

As hard as he had tried, he had been completely unable to stop his mind drifting to her or stop the poker-like stabs of jealousy to imagine her in Javier's arms that had engulfed him since he'd first set eyes on her.

'Javier knows I am a man of my word,' he continued, looking beyond the battered soles of her feet to the smooth, almost delicate ankles and calves that were undeniably feminine. A strange itch started in his fingers to stroke the skin to feel if it was as smooth to his touch as to his eye. 'He knows if I say I will marry you then I will marry you.'

'You've rigged everything to fall your way but unless you have something even more nefarious up your sleeve you can't marry me without my permission.' Steel laced her calm voice. 'Besides, you said I only have to stay with you for one day—you've given me your word too. You are lying to one of us. Which is it?'

'I have not lied to either of you. Have you not wondered *why* I had your phone tampered with?'

Clarity rang from her eyes. 'To stop me warning him. You don't want me in a position to scupper your plans by telling him the truth.'

He smiled. She was an astute woman. 'Javier will know by now that we left the gala together. I do not doubt he will hear we left hand in hand. He will know you left willingly with me and will be wondering how deep your involvement goes. If he trusts and loves you he will know you are my pawn and will pay me my money to get you back. If he doesn't trust or love you enough he will refuse to pay and cut you adrift. If he cuts you adrift the ball rolls into your court, *ma douce*. The moment Javier reaches his decision, whatever that decision may be, you will be free to leave my chateau without hindrance. If you choose to leave I will fly you back to Madrid even if your choice is to plead your case with him and throw yourself at his mercy. If, however, you decide to stick with a certainty then you can marry me. I am willing to marry you on the same terms you were going to marry him—I assume there was a pre-nuptial agreement. I am prepared to honour it. Or you can decide to have nothing to do with either of us and get on with your life.'

Benjamin put the towel down by the now cold bowl of water and got to his feet. 'Whatever happens, I cannot lose. Javier will pay for what he has done one way or another.'

While he'd been speaking, Freya's silent fury had grown. He'd seen it vibrate through her clenched fists and shuddering chest, the colour slashing her cheeks deepening.

Finally she spoke, her words strangled. 'How can you be so cruel?'

'A man reaps what he sows.'

'No, I meant how can you be so cruel to *me*? What have *I* done to merit this? You don't even know me.'

'You chose to betroth yourself to a man without a conscience. I notice you have accepted at face value that Javier and Luis stole from me. You know the kind of man he is yet still you chose to marry him. What kind of woman does that make you?'

The colour on her face turned an even deeper shade of red, her stare filled with such loathing it was as if she'd stored and condensed all the hatred in the world to fire at him through eyes that had become obsidian.

She rose from her seat with a grace that took his breath away. 'You don't know anything about me and you never will. You're the most despicable excuse for a human being I have ever met. I hope Javier calls your bluff and calls the police. I hope he gets a SWAT team sent in to rescue me.'

He reached out to brush a thumb against her cheekbone. It was the lightest of touches but enough for a thrill to race through him at the silky fineness of her skin.

He sensed the same thrill race through her too, the tiniest of jolts before the eyes that had been firing at him widened and her frame became so still she could be carved from marble.

'If he were to involve the police the news would leak out and his deception would become public knowledge,' he murmured, fighting the impulse to run his hand over her hair and pull the tight bun out, imagining the effect of that glorious hair spilling over her shoulders like a waterfall. 'But the police would not do anything even if he did go to them because I have not broken any law, just as Javier has not technically broken any law.'

'You kidnapped me.'

'How? You got into my jet and my car of your own free will.'

'Only because you lied to me.'

'That was regrettable but necessary. If lying is a crime then the onus would be on you to prove it.'

'You paid someone to disconnect my phone.'

'Again, the onus would be on you to prove it.'

Her throat moved before her voice dropped so low he had to strain to hear. 'How do you sleep at night?'

'Very well, thank you, because my conscience is clear.' Finally he moved his hand away and took a step back from her lest the urge to taste those tempting lips overcame him. 'I will get a member of staff to show you to your quarters. Sleep well, *ma douce*. I have a feeling tomorrow is going to be a long day for both of us.'

Then he half bowed and walked away.

CHAPTER FIVE

FREYA PACED HER bedroom feeling much like a caged tiger prowling for escape. The only difference between her and the tiger was she hadn't been locked in. She could walk out right now and never look back. Except it was now the early hours of the morning and her feet would rightly kill her if she tried to escape again. Third time lucky, perhaps? A third attempt to escape into the black canopy of Benjamin's thick forest? She might even emerge on the other side alive.

She slumped onto the bed with a loud sigh and propped her chin on her hands. Her feet stung, the corset of her dress dug into her ribs and she was suddenly weary from her lack of food. The pretty pyjamas on her pillow looked increasingly tempting.

A young maid had shown her to her quarters. She hadn't spoken any English but had been perfectly able to convey that the pyjamas were for Freya and that the clothes hanging in the adjoining dressing room were for her too. There were even three pairs of shoes to choose from, all of them worse than ballet slippers for an escape in the forest.

All the clothes were Freya's exact size, right down to the underwear. She guessed Benjamin's sister had passed on her measurements.

The planning he must have undertaken to get her there made her shiver.

He was remorseless. Relentless. He left nothing to chance, going as far as installing a camera outside her bedroom door. She'd seen the flashing red light and known exactly what it was there for. A warning that should she attempt to leave her quarters she would be seen in an instant. If she found a landline phone she would never get the chance to use it.

Without laying a finger on her he'd penned her in his home more effectively than a collie rounding up sheep.

But he *had* touched her.

The shivers turned into tingles that spread up her spine and low in her abdomen as she remembered how it had felt to have his large, warm hands holding her feet so securely, different tingles flushing over her cheek where he had brushed his thumb against it.

She had never met a more unrepentantly cruel person in her life and being part of the ballet world that was saying something.

But he had cleaned and tended to her feet with a gentleness that had taken her breath away. She had expected him to recoil at them—anyone who wasn't a dancer would—but instead she'd detected a glimmer of sympathy. Bruised, aching feet were a fact of her life. Smile through the pain, use it to drive you on to perfection.

She had to give him his due—in that one respect Benjamin had been the perfect gentleman. If she'd allowed any of her straight male colleagues to clean her feet she could only imagine the bawdiness of their comments. The opportunity for a quick grope would have been almost impossible for them to resist. The ballet world was a passionate hotbed, the intimacy of dancing so closely together setting off hormones that most didn't want to deny let alone bother to fight. Freya wasn't immune to it. The passion lived in her blood as it did in everyone else's; the difference was when the music stopped the passion within her stopped too. She had never danced with a man and wanted the romance to continue when the orchestra finished playing. She had never felt a man's touch and experienced a yearning within her for him to touch her some more.

Benjamin had held and touched her feet and she had had

to root her bottom to the chair so as not to betray her own body's betrayal of wanting those long fingers to stop tending and start caressing. She had had to fight her own senses to block out the thickening of her blood at his touch, had fought to keep the detachment she had spent a lifetime developing.

She squeezed her eyes shut, her brain-burn deepening at how she reacted so physically to the man who threatened to ruin *everything*.

She was caught in a feud between two men—three if she counted Luis—but it wasn't Freya who had the potential for the greatest suffering as a consequence of it, it was her mother. Her mother was the only reason she had agreed to Javier's emotionless proposal.

You know the kind of man he is yet still you chose to marry him. What kind of woman does that make you...?

It made her a desperate one.

Dance was all she knew, all she was, her life, her soul, her comfort. She had achieved so much from her humble beginnings but there was still so much to strive for, both for herself and for her parents who had made so many sacrifices to get her where she was today. Imagining the pride on their faces if she were to get top billing at the Royal Opera House or the Bolshoi or the Metropolitan gave her all the boost she needed on the days when her feet and calves seared with such pain that she forgot why she loved what she did so much.

Javier's proposal had given her hope. He would give her all the space she needed to be the very best. Marriage to him meant that if she did make it as far as she dreamed in her career then she would have the means to fly her parents all over the world to watch her perform. Much more importantly, her mother would have the means to be alive and well enough to watch her perform, not be crippled in pain with the morphine barely making a dent in the agony her body was putting her through.

But she *did* know the kind of man Javier was and that was why she had no faith he would pay Benjamin the money he owed. She didn't doubt he and Luis owed Benjamin money, although how they could have got one over the French billionaire she could not begin to guess, and right then she didn't have the strength to care.

Her forthcoming marriage was nothing more than a marriage of convenience. Javier's feelings for her ran no deeper than hers did for him.

If he didn't pay Benjamin then it meant their marriage was off. It meant no more money to pay for her mother's miracle drugs.

If he didn't pay it meant she would have to trust the word of the man who'd stolen her and hope he'd been telling the truth that he would marry her on the same terms.

Because if Javier didn't pay she would have to marry Benjamin. If she didn't her mother would be dead by Christmas.

Benjamin was on his second cup of coffee when a shadow filled the doorway of the breakfast room. He'd drained the cup before Freya finally stepped inside, back straight, chin jutted outwards, dressed in three-quarter-length white jeans and a dusky pink shirt, her glorious hair scraped back in another tight bun.

The simplicity of her clothing, all selected by his sister, did not detract in the least from her graceful bearing, and Benjamin found himself straightening and his heart accelerating as she glided towards him.

She allowed Christabel, who had followed her in, to usher her into the seat opposite his own and made the simple act of sitting down look like an art form.

'Coffee?' his housekeeper asked as she fussed over her.

'Just orange juice, thank you,' she answered quietly.

Only when they were alone did Freya look at him.

He'd thought he'd become accustomed to the dense blackness of her eyes but right then the weight of her stare seemed to pierce through him. He shifted in his seat, unsettled but momentarily trapped in a gaze that seemed to have the ability to reach inside him and touch his soul…

He blinked the unexpected and wholly ridiculous thought away and flashed his teeth at her. 'Did you get any sleep?'

She smiled tightly but made no verbal response.

'You look tired.'

She shrugged and reached for her juice.

'Have some coffee. It will help you wake up.'

'I rarely drink caffeine.'

'More for me then.' He poured himself another cup as the maid brought Freya's breakfast tray in and placed it in front of her.

His houseguest gazed at the bowls before her in surprise then smiled at the maid. It was a smile that made her eyes shine and for a moment Benjamin wished he were the one on the receiving end of it.

'Please thank the chef for me,' she said. 'This is perfect. She must have gone to a great deal of trouble.'

As the maid didn't speak English, Benjamin translated.

The moment they were alone again, Freya said, 'Has Javier been in touch?'

'Not yet.' He'd turned his phone's settings so only Javier, Luis and Chloe could reach him. He didn't want any other distractions.

She closed her eyes and took a long breath. He could see her centring herself in that incredible way he had never seen anyone else do, as if she were swallowing all her emotions down and locking them away. If he hadn't seen those bursts of anger-fuelled adrenaline when she had run away at his airfield and then when she had sent his supper flying before fleeing into the night, he could believe this woman never lost her composure.

And yet for all her stillness there was something about her that made her more vivid than any other woman he had ever met, a glow that drew the eye like a breathing, walking, talking sculpture.

What kind of a lover she would be? Did she burn under the sheets or keep that cloak of composure?

Had her exotic, intoxicating presence turned his old friend's heart as well as his loins? Had he lost himself in her...?

Benjamin shoved the thought away and swallowed back the rancid taste forming in his mouth.

He should be hoping Javier *had* lost himself in her arms as that would make it more likely for him to pay to get her back. He should not feel nauseous at the thought of them together.

That sick feeling only became more violent to think of Freya losing herself in Javier's arms.

How deeply did her feelings for Javier run?

If they had any depth then why did her eyes pulse whenever she looked at *him*?

He inhaled deeply, trying to clear his mind. He needed to concentrate on the forthcoming hours until Javier made his move. Only then could he decide what his own move would be.

In that spirit, he looked pointedly at the varying bowls of food his chef had prepared for her. He'd sent Christabel to check on his unwilling houseguest earlier and see what, if anything, she required for breakfast. He did not deny his relief to learn she'd abandoned her short hunger strike.

'What are you having?' he asked. 'It looks like animal feed.'

'Granola. Your chef has kindly made it fresh for me.'

'Granola?'

'Rolled oats.'

'Animal feed.'

She pulled a face at him and placed a heaped spoonful of berries on her animal feed, following them with a spoonful of almonds. Then she spooned some natural yogurt onto it and stirred it all together. As she raised the spoon to her mouth she paused. 'Do you have to watch?'

The colour staining her cheeks intrigued him. 'It bothers you?'

'You staring at me? Yes.'

'Why?'

'Because…' Freya put the spoon back in the bowl. She could hardly believe how self-conscious she felt sitting before him like this. She spent hours every day with her every move scrutinised by choreographers, fellow dancers, audiences and had long ago learned to tune out the weight of their stares.

Yet sitting here with Benjamin's swirling green eyes fixed upon her she was aware of her body in ways she had never been before, could feel the blood pumping through her, heating with each cycle.

It wasn't merely herself and the components of her own body that she was freshly aware of, it was Benjamin too, this Lucifer in disguise. The vibrating hairs on her nape and arms strained towards him as if seeking his scent and the heat of his skin, her senses more alert than they had ever been before.

'It just does,' she said tightly. 'Why don't you get yourself something to eat and leave me in peace?'

'I rarely eat in the morning,' he informed her.

'Cheese late at night then no breakfast…all the ingredients for health problems when you reach middle age.'

A glimmer came into his eyes. 'I can assure you I am in peak physical health.'

She could see that for herself though she would never admit it to him and felt a pang of envy at a life where you could eat any morsel you liked without scrutiny and without having to weigh up its nutritional value or energy-boosting properties.

Oh, to have the freedom to eat whatever you liked—or not—whenever you liked...

Benjamin's phone suddenly buzzed loudly.

She met his narrowed green eyes the moment before he reached for it.

'It's an email from Javier,' he said matter-of-factly.

Her stomach dropped. 'Already?'

He nodded. 'He has sent a copy to your email too.'

'What does it say?'

He studied it for a long time before sliding the phone to her.

The email contained no text. Javier had sent an attachment of two adjoining photos.

She blinked a number of times before the pictures she was staring at came into focus and their significance made itself clear.

They had been taken by one of the photographers at the gala who had spotted something intriguing about them leaving together and decided to capture it. The first shot caught the moment when they had paused in the hotel lobby for Benjamin to briefly explain the situation, the other had them walking out of the hotel hand in hand.

It was the first picture she found herself unable to look away from and, she knew in the pit of her stomach, it was the reason Javier had sent the pictures to her too.

Benjamin's face had been mostly obscured but her own features were there for all to see, and all could see her black eyes staring intently into his and her body tilting towards him. They looked like a pair of lovers caught in the midst of a most intimate conversation.

The blood whooshed up and into her brain.

That look in her eyes as she'd stared at him...

Had she really looked at Benjamin like that?

She covered her mouth, horrified.

She couldn't even bring herself to say anything when Benjamin's large hand stretched across the table to take his phone back from her.

Freya was so shamed and mortified at the expression captured on her face she feared her vocal cords had been stunned into silence for ever.

Nothing was said between them until another loud buzzing cut through the silence, a continuous buzz signalling a phone call.

Benjamin put it on speakerphone.

His eyes rested on Freya as the gravelly Spanish tones of Javier Casillas filled the room.

'You will not receive a cent from me, you son-of-a-bitch. Keep her. She's all yours.'

Then the line went dead.

This time the silence between them was loud enough for Freya to hear the beats of her thundering heart.

The room began to spin around her, the high ceiling lowering, the wide walls narrowing.

She was going to be sick.

She might very well have *been* sick had the most outrageous sound she'd ever heard not brought her sharply back to herself and the room back into focus.

Benjamin, his eyes not once dropping their hold on hers, was laughing.

'How can you think this is funny?' she asked with a croak, dredging the words from the back of her throat. 'You've lost.'

And she had lost too. Javier had emailed the pictures to her too as a message. Their engagement was over.

'Lost?' Benjamin's face creased with mirth. He threw his head back, his laughter coming in great booms that echoed around her ears. 'No, *ma douce*, I have not lost. I told you last night, I cannot lose.'

It was a struggle to breathe. 'He's not going to pay the money.'

'There was only an evens chance that he would. There were only two end scenarios: Javier would pay or he would not. This result is not my preferred one but I can take satisfaction that he will be burning with humiliation at the photographs of us so it is not a loss by any means.'

'Not a loss for you, maybe, but what about me? He's never going to take me back. You know that, right? These pictures make it look like I was encouraging you…that I was a part of it.'

Oh, God, that look in her eyes as she'd stared into his…

There was not an ounce of penitence to be found in his glittering eyes. 'You don't have to lose anything, *ma douce*. Your career is safe. You are one of the most exciting dancers in the world. If Javier is foolish enough to sack you then I guarantee another company will snatch you up.'

'You think I care only about my career?' she demanded.

His laugh was merciless. 'My sister says you are the most driven dancer she has ever met, but if it is the loss of your fiancé that grieves you then I suggest you have a re-think. If he had feelings for you he would have fought for you. If he'd believed in your love he would have fought for you. You should be thanking me. I am saving you from a lifetime of misery.'

'I can assure you, you are not. I told you last night that you don't know anything about me.'

'If he means that much to you, now is your chance to go to him and plead your case,' he said sardonically. 'He has made his choice, which means you are now free to make yours. Say the word and I will arrange transportation to take you back to Madrid. You can be back there by lunch.'

Rising from her chair, Freya leaned forward to eyeball him. She had never known she could feel such hate for someone. Her heart was beating so frantically against her ribcage she had to fight to get the words out. 'Believe me, my preferred outcome would be to leave this awful excuse for a home and never have to see your hateful face again. Quite frankly, if I were stuck on a desert island with the choice between you and a rat for company, the rodent would win every time.'

Something flickered on his darkly handsome face, the smug satisfaction vanishing.

A charge passed between them, so tangible she felt it pierce into her chest and thump into her erratic heart.

He gazed at her with eyes that swirled and pulsed before his lips curved into a knowing smile and he too leaned forward. 'The way you were looking at me in that photograph proves the lie in that.'

CHAPTER SIX

'I DON'T KNOW what you're talking about.' Freya hated that her burning cheeks contradicted her.

Benjamin rose slowly from his seat and walked around the table to her, that feline grace she had seen before taking a dangerous hue, the panther stalking towards its prey.

She twisted around so her thighs pressed into the hard wood, her usually nimble feet becoming like sludge.

And then he was standing in front of her, that strong neck her lips kept longing to press into right there in her eye line, standing close enough for his fresh spicy scent to seep into her senses.

'I think you know exactly what I'm talking about, *ma douce*.' He placed a hand on the arch of her neck and dropped his voice to a murmur. The feel of his fingers on her skin burned through her, the heat from his breath catching the loose strands of her hair and carrying through it to her scalp and down into her bloodstream. 'The camera never lies. Javier saw the desire you feel for me. I have seen it too and I have *felt* it, when I carried you back into my home and the moonlight shone on us both. You say you hate me but still you long for my kiss.'

Freya found herself too scared to move. Too scared to breathe. Terrified to make the slightest twist in her body lest her lips inch themselves forward to brush against the warm neck so close to her mouth and the rest of her body, aching at the remembrance of being held so securely in his arms, press itself wantonly against him.

Focus, Freya. The next few minutes will determine you and your mother's whole futures.

He moved a little closer so his breath danced over the top

of her ear, electrifying parts inside her she hadn't known were there. 'There is an attraction between us that has been there since we first saw each other in Javier's garden.'

She gave a tiny shake of her head to deny his words but he dragged his hand from her neck and placed a finger on her lips, standing back a little so he could stare straight into her eyes.

'Now you no longer belong to him, we are free to act on it.' Benjamin brushed the finger from her lips to rest lightly on her cheek. She truly had the softest skin he had ever touched, more velvet than flesh.

He'd always known it would be fifty-fifty whether Javier would pay up, which was why he had gone to the lengths he had to make sure that whatever the outcome, he would still win.

He hadn't expected the destruction of Javier and Freya's relationship to feel like a victory that would taste as sweet as if Javier had paid in full.

Never again would he be haunted by thoughts of Freya enjoying herself in his enemy's bed because she had been correct that Javier would never take her back. She could plead with him but Benjamin knew Javier too well. His Spanish foe's reputation and pride were the fuel he needed to get through the day. In one stroke Benjamin had battered them both and soon he would set his sights on Luis too.

Benjamin was well aware the actions he'd taken made him as bad as the men he sought to destroy but he didn't care. Why should he? Who had ever cared for him?

His mother had loved him but when he had discovered the Casillas brothers' treachery the past had come back into sharp focus and he'd been forced to accept that her love for him had always been tied with her love for them. Louise Guillem had loved Javier and Luis as if they were children of her blood because, for his mother, Clara Casillas had been the love of her life. A platonic love, it was true, but with the emotional intensity of the most heightened love affair. Benjamin had been a by-product of that love, a child to raise alongside Clara's, not wanted as a child should be for himself but more as a pet, an accessory.

His father had long gone, leaving the marital home when Louise had fallen pregnant by accident a decade after Benjamin had been born. Already fed up playing second fiddle to the World's Greatest Dancer, his father had refused to hang around and raise a second accessory. Benjamin had never missed him—you had to know someone to miss them and he had never properly known his father—but, again, with the past being brought back into focus, he had realised for the first time that his father hadn't just left his mother but his only son too. He hadn't cared enough to keep their tentative relationship going.

Then there was Javier and Luis. Their betrayal had been the most wrenching of all because it had made him look at the past with new, different eyes and reassess all the relationships he had taken for granted and unbury his head from the truth.

The only relationship he had left was with his sister but she was a free spirit with wounds of her own, a beautiful violin with broken strings.

Every other person he'd trusted and cared for had used or betrayed him.

He was damned if he would trust or care again.

This beautiful woman with eyes a man could fall into was no innocent. He regretted that he'd had to use her but it had been a necessary evil. He would not regret destroying her relationship with Javier. If she had cared an ounce for his foe she would not be staring at him as if she wanted him to devour her.

Dieu, a man really could fall into those eyes and never resurface…

But there was something else breaking free in the heady

depths of those eyes, a fire, a determination that made him drop his hand from her cheek and step back so he could study her carefully without her sultry scent playing under his nose and filtering through into his bloodstream…

The moment he stepped away she folded her arms across her chest and seemed to grow before his eyes.

'The only thing we're going to act on is your word.' Freya's husky voice had the same fiery determination as resonated in her eyes.

'You are ready to be taken back to Madrid?'

This time she was the one to laugh, a short, bitter sound. 'Yes. But not yet. Not until you have married me.'

For a moment it felt as if he had stepped onto quicksand.

He shook his head. 'You want to marry me?'

'No. I would rather marry the rodent on the desert island but you told me I would have three choices once Javier had made his. He won't take me back, not even if I get down on my knees and beg. I need the money set out in our pre-nuptial agreement so going back to Madrid and resuming my single life is not an option either, which leaves just one remaining choice—marrying you. You need to honour the contract Javier and I signed on our engagement as you said you would.'

He stared into her unsmiling face, an unexpected frisson racing up his spine.

Marriage to Freya…?

He had made his threat to Javier with the full intention of acting on it if it came to it but never had he believed she would go along with it, let alone demand it of him.

He tried to envisage Javier's reaction when he heard the news but all he could imagine was Freya naked in his bed, the fantasies he'd been suppressing for two months suddenly springing to life in a riot of erotic colour.

Marriage had never been on his agenda before. He'd spent the past seven years so busy clawing his business back to health and then into the business stratosphere that any thoughts of wedlock had been put on the back burner, something to be considered when his business no longer consumed his every waking thought.

Now the thought of marriage curdled his stomach. Marriage involved love and trust, two things he was no longer capable of and no longer believed in.

'Were you lying to me when you gave me your word?' she challenged into the silence.

'I save the lies for your ex-fiancé. He's the expert at them. And I am thinking you must be good at them too seeing as you fooled him into believing you had feelings for him.'

'I didn't fool or lie to anyone. Javier and I both knew exactly what we were signing up for.'

'You admit you were marrying him for his money?'

'Yes. I need that money.'

'And what did Javier get out of marrying you other than a prima ballerina on his arm?'

Fresh colour stained her cheeks but her gaze didn't flicker. 'The contract we signed spells it out. If you're the man of your word you say you are, you will duplicate it and honour it.'

'You are serious about this?'

'Deadly serious. The ballet company is on a two-week shutdown. I was supposed to marry Javier next Saturday. I presume with all the strings you're able to pull you can arrange for us to marry then instead. Either that or you can pay me now all the money I would have received from Javier, say, for the first ten years of our marriage.' Her eyes brightened, this idea clearly only just occurring to her. 'That can be my compensation for being the unwitting victim in your vindictive game. It comes to...' her brow furrowed as she mentally calculated the sum '...around twenty million. I'll be happy to accept half that. Call it ten million and I go back to my life and we never have to see each other again.'

'You want me to pay you off?' he asked, part in astonishment and part in admiration.

'That would be the best outcome for both of us, don't you think?'

He shook his head slowly, intrigued and not a little aroused at the spirit and fight she was showing. No wonder Javier had chosen her for his wife. She was magnificent. '*Non, ma douce*, the choice was marriage or nothing. If I pay you off, I get nothing from it.'

'Your conscience will thank you.'

'I told you before, my conscience allows me to sleep well. With you in my bed every night I will be able to sleep even more sweetly.' His arousal deepened to imagine that wonderful hair fanned over his pillow, the obsidian eyes currently firing fury at him firing only desire…

'Maybe you should read the contract before assuming I will be in your bed every night. You might find you prefer to pay me off.'

'Unlikely but, even if that is the case, the knowledge Javier will spend the rest of his life knowing it is my ring you wear on your finger and not his will soften the blow.'

'You really are a vindictive monster, aren't you?'

'You insult me and speak of my conscience when you are a self-confessed gold-digger.' He smiled and closed the gap that had formed between them and placed a hand on her slender hip. There was no danger of trusting or caring for this woman, even if he was capable of it and even if she did have eyes he could sink into. 'We don't have to like each other to be good together…and I think we could be *very* good together. Marry me and you have everything you would have had if you had married Javier.'

'And you get continued revenge,' she finished for him, her tone contemptuous.

'*Exactemente.* We *both* get what we want.'

Freya could smell the warmth of his skin beneath the freshness of his cologne...

Benjamin was *not* what she wanted. He provoked her in ways Javier never had. Javier was scary but Benjamin terrified her for all the wrong reasons.

She wouldn't be swapping one rich man for another, she would be swapping ice for fire, safety for danger, all the things she had never wanted, all the things she had shied away from since she had learned sex was the only control she had over her body.

There was not a part of her external body that hadn't been touched or manhandled; a grab of her arm to raise it an inch higher, rough hands on her hips to twist her into the desired shape, a chuck under the chin to lift it, partners holding her intimately in dance... Her external body was not hers; it belonged to dance. Her body was public property but her emotions and everything inside her belonged to herself.

That the control she'd worked so hard for was in danger of slipping for this man, this vindictive, abhorrent...

She clamped her lips together to contain a gasp.

Benjamin had taken another step closer. Their bodies were almost flush.

For the first time in her life someone had hold of her hip and she could *feel* it, inside and out, her blood heating and thickening to treacle.

She closed her eyes and breathed in deeply, trying to block her dancing senses and contain what was happening within her frame.

'You know what this means?' he murmured.

She swallowed and managed a shake of her head.

'It means you and I are now betrothed. Which means we need to seal the deal.'

Before she could guess what he meant, he'd hooked an

arm around her waist and pulled her tight against him. Before she could protest or make any protective move of her own, he'd covered her mouth with his.

Having no preparation or warning, Freya found herself flailing against him, her hands grabbing his arms as her already overloaded senses careered into terrifying yet exciting new directions. She struggled helplessly to keep possession of herself while his lips moved against hers in what she instinctively knew was the final marker in the game he'd been playing, Benjamin claiming her as his in an expert and ruthless manner that...

His tongue swept into her mouth and suddenly she didn't care that it was all a game to him. Her body took possession of her brain for the very first time and she was kissing him back, taking the dark heat of his kisses and revelling in the sensation they were evoking in her. Such glorious, heady sensations, burning her skin beneath her clothes, sensitising flesh that had only come alive before for dance. She loosened her hands to wind them around his neck and press herself closer still while he swept his hands over her back, holding her tightly, possessively, devouring her mouth as if she were the food he needed to sustain himself. When his hand moved down to clasp her bottom and grind their groins together, it was *her* moan that echoed between them.

Her breasts were crushed against his chest, alive and sensitised for the first time in her life, making her want to weep that she had chosen to wear a bra when she so rarely bothered, and as these thoughts flickered in her hazy mind reality crashed back down.

All the clothes she wore, her underwear, her shoes, every item designated as hers under this roof had been bought without her knowledge.

She was a pawn in Benjamin's game of vengeance and she *hated* him.

She would not accept his kisses with anything but contempt.

When Freya suddenly pulled out of his arms and jumped back, seeming to leap backwards through the air yet still making the perfect dancer's landing, Benjamin had to blink rapidly to regain his focus and sense of place.

What the hell had just happened?

Breathing heavily, he stared at her, stunned that one simple kiss could explode like that. He'd known the attraction between them was strong but that…that had blown his mind.

He hadn't experienced such heady, evocative feelings from a kiss since…since ever, not even those illicit teenage kisses when he'd first discovered that the opposite sex was good for something more than merciless teasing.

She stared back, eyes wide and wary, her own breaths coming in shallow gulps, her cheeks flushed. Her hair was still pulled back in that tight bun but there was something dishevelled about her now that made the heavy weight in his loins deepen.

He put a hand on the table, partly to steady himself and partly to stop himself crossing the room to haul her back into his arms. His loins felt as if they had been set on fire, the burn spread throughout him but concentrated there, an ache such as he had never experienced before that threatened to engulf his mind along with the rest of him.

Had she reacted to Javier's kisses with that same intensity…?

The thought deflated the lust riding through him as effectively as a pin in a balloon.

He needed air.

'Your pre-nuptial agreement. Where is it?' he asked roughly.

A flash of confusion flittered over her features before she blinked sharply. 'In Javier's safe but I have a copy of it on an email attachment.'

'*Bien.* I will get your phone unlocked. When it is working again, forward it to me. I will get it redrafted with both our names on it. It will be ready to sign by the end of the day.'

CHAPTER SEVEN

BENJAMIN RAPPED LOUDLY on the door to Freya's quarters, his heart making as much noise in his chest as his knuckles made on the door.

It was incredible to think these would be her permanent quarters.

When he had bought the chateau seven years ago there had been a vague image of a future Madame Guillem to share the vast home and land with but it had been a secondary image. He'd bought it for his mother and, at the time, nursing her through her final months had been his only concern. Not long after her funeral, he'd found himself unable to repay the mortgage and forced to face the reality of his financial situation. Nursing his mother had taken him away from his business. The bills had mounted. Suppliers had threatened court action. He'd been days away from losing everything.

All thoughts of a future Madame Guillem had been buried. He'd dated. He'd had fun. But nothing permanent and definitely nothing serious. He'd had neither the physical time nor the mental space to make a relationship work.

It was only when he'd reached a position in his life where he could take his foot off the accelerator and slow things down enough for a real life of his own that he'd reached the inescapable conclusion that he would never trust anyone enough to pledge his life to them. As much as he'd regretted it would likely mean he would never have children, another of those vague in-the-future notions, he would not put himself through it. If he couldn't trust the people he'd loved all his life how could he trust a stranger?

He didn't have that worry with Freya. Knowing there was no trust to fake made taking this step more palatable.

Reading through the contract she and Javier had signed had made it even more so.

He had read it, shaking his head with incredulity at what it contained.

He could easily see his old friend signing this cold, emotionless contract but for the hot-blooded woman whose kisses had turned him to fire to sign such a thing stretched the realms of credulity.

But then, she was already proving to be far more fiery a woman than he'd thought Javier would commit himself to.

He hadn't seen her since their explosive kiss that morning. He'd been busy in his office organising things. She'd kept herself busy doing her own thing, his staff keeping discreet tabs on her.

He knocked again. After waiting another thirty seconds, he pushed the door open and let himself in.

Her quarters were large and comfortable, a small reception area leading to a bedroom, bathroom and dressing room to the left, and a spacious living area to the right, where the faint trace of music played out through the closed door. He opened it and paused before stepping over the threshold.

All the furniture had been pushed against the far wall to create a large empty space. The music came from her freshly working phone.

Freya had contorted herself into the strangest shape he'd ever seen the human body take right in the centre of the room. Her calves and knees were on the carpet as if she'd knelt to pray but instead of clasping her hands before her and leaning forward, she'd gone backwards into a bridge, her flat stomach arched in the air, her elbows on the floor where her toes rested, her face in the soles of her bare feet with her hands clasping both her heels and her temples.

It looked the most uncomfortable pose a person could

manipulate themselves into but she didn't appear to be in any discomfort. If anything, she seemed at peace, her chest expanding and her stomach softening in long, steady breaths.

He found his own breath stuck in his lungs. He didn't dare make a sound, afraid that to disturb her would cause her to injure herself.

After what felt like hours but in reality was probably less than a minute she uncoiled herself, walking her hands away from her feet then using them to push herself upright.

Kneeling, she finally looked at him. She showed no concern or surprise at his appearance in her quarters.

He'd been so entranced with what he'd seen that it was only when her eyes met his that he noticed all she had on were a black vest and a pair of black knickers.

If she was perturbed that he had walked into her quarters while she had hardly any clothes on she didn't show it.

But then, recalling all the years spent touring with Clara Casillas, he had never met a body-shy ballerina before. He'd seen more naked women in the first ten years of his life than if he'd been raised in a brothel. It was a fact of their life. Freya was a woman who spent her life with her body under a microscope, different hands touching it for different reasons, whether to lift, to shape or to dress.

Desire coiled through his loins to imagine what it would feel like to lift this woman into his arms as a lover...

He would bet she had poise and grace even when she slept and felt a thickening in his loins to know it wouldn't be long before he discovered that for himself.

And, as his imagination suddenly went rampant with heady thoughts of this beautiful, supple woman in his bed, those long, lithe legs wrapped around him, those black eyes currently staring at him without any expression coming alive with desire, the strangest thing of all occurred. Freya blushed.

She must have felt the heat crawling over her face for

her features tightened before she jumped gracefully to her feet, going from kneeling to standing in the time it took a mortal to blink.

'If you'll excuse me, I'll put some clothes on,' she said stiffly.

The lump in his throat prevented him from doing more than stepping aside to let her pass through the door to her bedroom.

Breathing deeply, he took a seat on the armchair while he waited for her to return, keeping his thoughts and imagination far away from sex, trying to quell the ache burning in his loins.

They had business to take care of.

Feeling more together in himself when she came back into the living room, he said, 'What were you doing?'

She'd put her three-quarter-length white jeans back on and covered her chest with an off-the-shoulder navy top. Her battered feet were bare. She sat on the leather sofa nestled next to his and twisted her body round to face him. 'Yoga. That pose was the Kapotasana.'

'It sounds as painful as it looks.'

The glimmer of a smile twitched on her lips. 'It's invigorating and, under the circumstances, necessary.'

'Why?'

'I need to keep fit. I'm used to dancing and working out for a minimum of seven hours a day. I need to keep my fitness levels maintained, I need to stretch and practise regularly or it will be extra hard when I return to the studio. This is all I have available to me...unless you have a secret dance studio tucked away somewhere with a barre?'

'I am afraid not but you are welcome to use my gym and swimming pools and sauna. There's tennis courts too.'

She pulled her lips in together. 'I have to be careful using a gym and swimming. It's what they do to my muscles—they bulk them in all the wrong places. I've never played tennis before and wouldn't want to risk taking it up without advice.'

He looked around again at the space she had created for herself in this room and knew without having to ask that this was not suitable for her to practise dancing in.

'Still, I'm sure you're not here to discuss my fitness regime,' she said, changing the subject and straightening her back before nodding at the file in his hand. 'Is that the contract?'

He'd almost forgotten what he had come here for.

Pulling his mind back to attention, he took the sheets of paper out of the folder. 'I've booked our wedding for Thursday.'

She was silent for beat. 'Thursday?'

'*Oui.*'

'I was supposed to marry Javier on Saturday.'

'At this short notice there are no slots available for Saturday.'

'Couldn't you have bribed or blackmailed someone?'

'I pulled enough strings to bypass the notice period. If it's a Saturday wedding you long for we can always wait a few weeks.' He stared hard at her as he said this. Having now read the terms of the contract he understood why she was keen to marry on the same day she would have married Javier. On the day of their wedding he would transfer two hundred thousand euros into her account, the first recurring monthly payment of that sum. According to the contract, Javier had already paid her two lump sums of one hundred thousand euros.

'No,' she declined so hurriedly he could see the euro signs ringing in her eyes. 'Thursday is fine.'

He gave a tight smile. 'I thought so. I will take you to the town hall tomorrow to meet the mayor and fill out some forms but the arrangements are all in hand. Is your passport in your apartment?'

She nodded. 'I've spoken to my flatmate. She's got it safe.'

'I will send a courier to collect it.'

'I'll go and get it. I need to collect the rest of my stuff.'

'Your possessions can be couriered over with the passport.'

'I want to get them myself.'

The thought of her being in the same city as Javier set his teeth on edge. '*Impossible*. There is too much to arrange here.'

'I need my clothes.'

'I have appointments in Paris after our meeting with the mayor tomorrow. You can fly there with me and buy whatever you need.'

'With what? Fresh air? I can't buy an entire new wardrobe with one hundred and fifty euros, which is all I have in my account.'

His lips curved in distaste. 'You have spent all the money Javier has already given to you?'

'Yes. I had…'

'I have no cares for what you spend your money on. I will give you a credit card. Buy whatever you need with it. Consider it an early wedding present. While you are there you can buy a wedding dress.'

'Something black to match your heart?' she suggested with a touch of bitterness.

'You are hardly in a position to talk of my heart when you were party to a contract like this one.'

There was the slightest flinch. 'Javier and I drew up a marriage agreement that suited us both.'

'It does not suit me.'

'You said you would honour it.'

'And I will. I have only changed one item.'

'I'm not signing unless it's the original with only Javier's name substituted for yours.'

'You will if you still want the fortune and all the assets that come with it.'

'What have you changed?'

'Look for yourself.' He handed the file to her. 'The change is highlighted in red.'

She took it from him with a scowl.

'May I remind you,' he said as she flicked through the papers, 'that it is your choice to marry me. I am not forcing your hand.'

She didn't look up from the papers. 'There was no other choice for me.'

'The lure of all that money too strong to give up?' he mocked.

But she didn't answer, suddenly looking up at him with wide eyes, colour blasting over her cheeks. 'Of all the things you could have changed, you changed *that*?'

'I am not signing away a chunk of my fortune and my freedom to spend only one night a week in a bed with my wife.' He'd read that part of the long, detailed pre-nuptial agreement with his mouth open, shaking his head with disbelief as he'd wondered what kind of a woman would sign such a document.

Scheduled, mandated sex?

And then he had read the next section and his incredulity had grown.

How could the woman who kissed as if she were made of lava agree to such a marriage?

He stared at Freya now and wondered what was going on in that complex brain. She was impossible to fathom, a living contradiction. Scalding hot on the outside but seemingly cold on the inside. Which was the real Freya: the hot or the cold one?

'I will comply in full with the rest of the contract but when we are under the same roof we sleep in the same bed. If it is not something you can live with I suggest you tell me now so I can make the necessary arrangements for your departure from my home.'

Freya stared into eyes as uncompromising as his words and dug her bruised toes into the carpet. Her skin itched with the need for movement, the hour of yoga she had done before he had walked into her quarters nowhere near enough to quell the fears and emotions pummelling her.

Their kiss...

It had frazzled all her nerve endings.

How could she have reacted to his kiss like that? To *him*?

It had been her first proper kiss and it had been everything a first kiss should be and, terrifyingly, so much more.

She had spent the day searching for a way to purge her heightened emotions but her usual method of dancing her fears away was not available to her. She'd taken a long walk through his grounds and explored the vast chateau praying that somewhere within the huge rooms would be one she could use to dance in. It had been like Goldilocks searching for the perfect porridge and bed but without the outcome; not one of the rooms had been right. The majority could work with their proportions but the flooring was all wrong, either too slippery or covered in carpet, neither of which were suitable and could be dangerous.

Meditation and yoga were her fail-safe fall-backs, clearing her mind and keeping her body limber, but they weren't enough, not for here and now when she was as frightened for her future and as terrified of what was happening inside her as she had ever been.

Her brain burned to imagine Benjamin's private reaction when he had read the section that covered intimacy in her pre-nup. Javier had insisted it be put in, just as he had insisted on the majority of all the other clauses, including the one stating they would only have a child at a time of Freya's choosing. He hadn't wanted them to ever get to a point in the future where either could accuse the other of going back on what had been agreed. That agreement would always be there, a guide for them to enter matrimony and ensure a long, harmonious union without any unpleasant arguments or misunderstandings.

The whole document read as cold and passionless, entirely appropriate for a marriage that had nothing to do with love but business and safety.

Javier had been cold but he *had* been safe. There had never been any emotional danger in marrying him.

She had never had to dig her toes into the ground when she was with him. There had been no physical effect whatsoever.

The brain burn deepened as she read the contents again, the only change being Benjamin's name listed as Party One. And the new clause stating they would share a bed when under the same roof.

Her heart thumped wildly, panic rabid and hot inside her.

When she had envisaged making love to Javier it had been with an analytical head, a box to tick in a marriage that would keep her mother alive and ease her suffering for months, hopefully years, to come.

There was nothing analytical about her imaginings of Benjamin. She had felt something move inside her in that first look they had shared, a flare of heat that had warmed her in ways she didn't understand and could never have explained.

Their kiss had done more than warm her. She could still feel the scorch of his lips on hers and his taste on her tongue. Meditation and yoga had done nothing to rid it but it had helped to a small extent, allowing her to control her raging heart and breathing when he had unexpectedly entered her quarters.

And then he had stared at her with the look that suggested he wanted to strip the last of her clothing off.

She had never been shy skimpily dressed in front of anyone before but in that moment and under the weight of that look she had felt naked for the first time in her life.

And she was expected to share his bed and give herself to this man who frightened her far more than her ice-cold fiancé ever had?

He, Benjamin, was her fiancé now...

She could do this, she assured herself, breathing deeply. She had faced far scarier prospects, like when she'd been eleven and had left the safety and comfort of her parents' home to become a boarder at ballet school. That had been truly terrifying even though it had also been everything she'd wanted.

Joining the school and discovering just how different she'd been to all the other girls had almost had her begging to go home. Having been accepted on a full scholarship that included boarding fees, she'd been the only girl there from a poor background. In comparison, all the others had been born with silver spoons in their mouths. They'd spoken beautifully, worn clothes that hadn't come from second-hand stores and had had holiday homes. Freya's parents hadn't even owned the flat they'd lived in.

Somehow she had got through the chronic homesickness and the merciless taunts that nowadays would be considered bullying by burying herself in ballet. She had learned to hide her emotions and express it all through dance, fuelling the talent and love for ballet she had been lucky enough to be born with.

If she could get through that then she was equal to this, equal to Benjamin and the heady, powerful emotions he evoked in her. She could keep them contained. She must.

She could not predict what her future held but she knew what the consequences would be if she allowed this one clause to scupper their marriage plans: a slow, cripplingly painful death for her mother. She would do anything to ease her mother's suffering. Anything. The first message that had popped into her phone when it had come back to life earlier was her father's daily update. Her mother had had 'a relatively comfortable night'. Translated, that meant the pain had only woken her a couple of times.

'If you're allowed to make a change in the contract then I must be allowed to make one too,' she told him, jutting her chin out and refusing to wilt under the swirling green eyes boring into her. She would not let him browbeat her before they had even signed the contract.

'Which is?'

'I was supposed to be moving in with Javier. My flat-mate's already found a new tenant to take my room so I'm not going to have anywhere to live when I'm at work. I want you to buy me an apartment to live in in Madrid. We're on a two-week shutdown so that's plenty of time for a man of your talents to buy one for me.'

She saw the faintest clenching of his jaw before his eyes narrowed.

'I will not have my wife working for my rival.'

'The contract states in black and white that I continue my career for as long as I like and I do what is best for me and my career. You have no say and no influence in it.'

'I can change the terms to include that.'

'You said one change. Or have you forgotten you're a man of your word?'

No, he had not forgotten, Benjamin thought grimly. It had simply not occurred to him that, having agreed to marry him, Freya would want to return to Madrid. She could work anywhere. It didn't have to be there.

'He will make your life a misery,' he warned.

'Javier has nothing to do with the day-to-day running of the company. He's rarely there.'

But Madrid was his home. The thought of Freya living in the same city as *him* set his teeth further on edge.

'There are many fine ballet companies in France who would love to employ you. I will never interfere with your career but in this instance I am going to have to insist.'

'Insist that I quit Compania de Ballet de Casillas?'

'Oui.'

The black eyes shot fire-dipped arrows at him. 'So you want to punish me and an entire ballet company for the sins of its owners, is that what you're saying?'

'Non. I am saying I do not wish for my wife to work for her ex-lover. It is not an unreasonable request.'

Something shone in her eyes that he didn't recognise, a shimmer in the midst of her loathing that disappeared as quickly as it had appeared. 'It's a request now? That's funny because the word *insist* made it sound remarkably like a demand.'

'This will be my only interference.'

Her foot tapped on the carpet but her tone remained calm. 'So I can get a job working in Japan and you won't complain?'

'You can work wherever you like.' As long as it was far from the Spaniard who had captured her long before he'd set eyes on her...

'Just not for Javier.'

'Just not for Javier.'

She sucked in a long draw of breath before inclining her head. 'I will hand my notice in but I will work my notice period. You can add that to the contract and reiterate you are never to interfere with my career.'

'How long is your notice period?'

'Two months. That will allow me to do the opening night of the new theatre. I'm on all the advertising litera-ture for it. I can't pull out. It's the biggest show of my life. I've worked too hard to throw it away.'

'D'accord.' He took in his own breath. Two months was

nothing. He could handle her working for Javier for that period.

He reminded himself that until that morning he had expected her to insist on returning to Madrid.

'You share my bed when we are under the same roof and hand your notice in to Compania de Ballet de Casillas. I buy you a property to live in while you work your notice and guarantee never to interfere with your career again. I believe that is everything unless there was something else you wished to discuss.'

Colour rose up her cheeks, her lips tightening before she gave a sharp nod. 'Just one thing I think it is best to make clear. I may be agreeing to share a bed with you but that does not mean you take ownership of my body. It belongs to me.'

'I think the kiss we shared earlier proves the lie in that, *ma douce*,' he said silkily.

The chemistry between them was real, in the air they both inhaled, a living thing swirling like a cloud, shrouding them.

'Think what you like.' She dropped her gaze. 'I will not be your possession.'

'I am not Javier. I do not expect you to be. But I do expect a wedding night. After that, you can turn your back to me as often as you wish. I do not forget the clause in the contract allowing Javier to take a mistress without question or explanation and, seeing as you have not requested that clause to be removed, it stands for me too. And as you know, I am a man who likes to have all options on the table.'

Her nostrils flared as she jutted her chin back out again, a sign he was starting to recognise meant she was straining to keep her composure.

Let her try and keep it. Come their wedding night he would shatter that composure and discover for himself if her veins ran hot or cold.

CHAPTER EIGHT

'YOU BOUGHT EVERYTHING you need?' Benjamin asked as his helicopter lifted into the air to fly them back to Provence after what had proven to be an extremely long day. 'It doesn't look like much.'

They had sorted out the paperwork for their wedding first thing then flown to Paris. Having work to do, he'd arranged for his PA's assistant who spoke English to take Freya shopping.

He had been so consumed in recent months with his feud with the Casillas brothers that he'd neglected his business. He'd hardly stepped through the headquarters of Guillem Foods in weeks and knew from bitter experience how dangerous it could be to take his eye off the ball. Now that the first part of his revenge had been extracted he needed to concentrate on his business for a while before making his next move. Luis would have to wait.

Yet even though he'd needed his brain to engage with Guillem Foods, he'd had to fight to keep his attention on the job because his mind kept wandering back to the woman who would be his wife in three days' time.

What was it about Freya that consumed his thoughts so much? She'd lodged herself in his mind from that first look, a fascination that had refused to shift that, now she was under his roof, was turning into an obsession.

Things would be better once he'd bedded her. The thrill of the chase and the unknown would be over and she would become mere flesh and bone.

He stared at her now, convinced she was the perfect wife for him. When the desire currently consuming him withered to nothing she would not care. Her own desire for him, unwanted as it was to her, wouldn't last either. Her heart was too cold for lust to turn into anything more. The marriage agreement she had willingly signed giving herself to two separate men proved that.

Freya was a gold-digger in its purest form. A gold-digger who at some point in the future would give him a child…

A sudden picture came into his head of Freya dancing, a miniature Freya at her feet copying her moves; the child they would have together, the child that would make the chateau he had bought for his mother to end her days in a home.

It was a picture he had never imagined with anyone in all his thirty-five years and the strength of it set blood pumping into his head and perspiration breaking out over his skin.

So powerful was his reaction to the image that it took a few moments to realise she was answering his question.

'Sophie's packing my stuff up for me. I've arranged for the courier to collect it later when he gets my passport.'

'Will you not need it for your new apartment in Madrid?' How he hated to think of her returning there but a deal was a deal. The contract had been signed over breakfast.

He'd already instructed an employee to hunt for a suitable home in Madrid for her. The main stipulation was that it be located as far from the district Javier called home as possible.

'I'll decide what to take with me when I go back,' she said. 'It'll be mostly my training stuff I take.'

'Would it not be easier to have separate wardrobes for each home?' He spent the majority of the year in his chateau but had apartments in Paris and London and houses in Australia, Argentina and Chile. Each had its own complete wardrobe, allowing him to travel lightly and spontaneously when the need or mood arose.

She shrugged, not looking at him. 'That would be wasteful.'

Incredulous, he stared at her. 'You're going to have two hundred thousand euros credited to your account every month for the rest of your life on top of your earnings and you are worried about being wasteful?'

The black eyes found his.

His heart thumped in the unnerving way it always seemed to do whenever those eyes captured his.

'I learned not to waste things as a child.'

'You had strict parents?'

'No, I had poor parents.' She said it matter-of-factly but with a hint of defiance and more than a little hint of pride.

'How poor?' Sob-stories of childhoods were everywhere. Some were even genuine.

However much he might despise the Casillas brothers Benjamin would never deny how traumatic their childhood had been. It made his own seem like one of the fairy tales Freya danced to.

'So poor that when I was offered a full scholarship to the ballet school with boarding fees included, they *had* to let me board as they couldn't afford the commuting fees.'

'Did the scholarship not include travelling fees?'

'Only for me, not for them. Commuting would also have meant one of them would have had to give up one of their jobs to get me there and back twice a day and they were on the breadline as it was. They didn't think it was safe for me to travel from one side of London to the other on my own.'

'How old were you when you went to boarding school?'

'Eleven.'

Benjamin winced. That was a horribly young age to leave home. 'Were they those awful pushy parents we read so much about nowadays?'

Her eyes glinted with anger. 'No. They were wonderful. They held down two jobs each and juggled things so one of them was always home with me. They worked their backsides off to pay for my ballet lessons when I was little and then to support me at ballet school because the full scholarship didn't cover everything. They did it because they loved me and wanted me to be happy.'

'Ballet makes you happy?' It might have sounded like a stupid question but he remembered from his early childhood on tour with Clara Casillas the haunted faces of some of the dancers who had definitely not been happy with their lives.

'More than anything else. It's my life.'

He studied her in silence, their gazes fixed on each other.

He had never felt the pull of a woman's eyes the way he did with Freya. It was like staring into a black pool of unimaginable depths.

'Do you want to invite your parents to the wedding?' Their marriage had such a surreal quality to it that the thought she might want the people she loved there had never occurred to him until that moment.

'They don't travel.'

'Were they not going to come to your wedding to Javier?'

She shook her head.

'Have you told them?'

'That I've exchanged fiancés like a child swapping marbles in the playground? Yes, I spoke to my dad about it this morning. I told him you had stolen me.' The faintest smile curved on her lips. 'At least it wasn't a lie. How he interpreted it is up to him.'

'How did he take it?'

'I told you, my parents only want what's best for me. They love me and want me to be happy. Are you going to invite anyone?'

'The only person I would want is my sister but she is away.' Chloe was still in the Caribbean, taking advantage of the ballet company's shutdown for a well-deserved holiday and an escape from the fall-out.

Javier's representatives had issued a short statement that morning saying that his engagement to Freya Clements was over. No details had been provided and the press were in a spasm of speculation, the main question being whether Freya's disappearing act with Benjamin at the gala had been the cause.

'No other family to ask?' she asked.

'You are interested in me?'

'Not in the slightest. I'm merely curious as to what I'm marrying into.'

'My mother died seven years ago. My father and I are not close and never have been.' Not even when they had lived under the same roof. His mother had raised him as if she were a single parent and his father had let her, never suggesting that their only son stay behind with him rather than tour the ballet world. A second unplanned pregnancy ten years after the first had been the final nail in his parents' precarious marriage.

He'd barely noticed when his father left, let alone missed him.

'Are you sure you don't want to have anyone there?' he pressed. 'There is not much time if you do.'

'I would have said Sophie but she told me earlier that she's going to make the most of the shutdown and go off somewhere. I suppose it saves her being put in a compromising position.'

'Because she works for Compania de Ballet de Casillas?'

'Like all ballet companies it's a hotbed of gossip.'

'Then don't go back,' he stated immediately, seizing the advantage.

'Do you really think I could care less what my colleagues think of me?' she asked coolly. 'Sophie is the only one I care about. We've been friends since ballet school.'

'A long friendship then,' he observed. Not many friendships survived childhood. He'd thought those that did were the strongest. He'd learned the hard way how wrong that notion was.

'The only time we've been apart since we were eleven was when I first moved to Madrid.'

'She followed you there?'

She shrugged and turned her face to the window. Soon they would be landing back in Provence, time speeding on. 'There were vacancies for new dancers to join the *corps de ballet*. I put in a good word for her. She's the only dancer I'm close to. The others can say what they like about me, it doesn't matter in the slightest, but I will not have Sophie hurt.'

He stared at her shrewdly, nodding his head slowly. 'I can see why Javier thought you were the ideal woman for him to marry. Neither of you invite closeness. But you seem to have loyalty, which he does not possess. And there is fire in your veins, *ma douce*. There is passion. I have seen it and I have felt it. What I find myself wondering is if *he* ever saw it or if it was something you kept hidden from him.'

'How very poetic.' If not for the quiver in her voice and the tapping of her foot, he could believe the drollness of her tone was genuine.

'It is no matter.' He leaned forward. 'In three nights' time I will discover for myself how deep the fire runs inside you.'

Freya's eyes were just reaching that heavy about-to-fall-asleep stage when the motion of the car driving over the cattle grid pulled her back to alertness. She stared out of the window her forehead was pressed against; the forest that marked Benjamin's territory overhung and surrounded them, the moonlight casting shadows that made her shiver. This was a fairy-tale forest where the nightmares came out at night.

The prickling of her skin told her Benjamin, beside her in the back of the car, was watching her.

He was always watching her. As much as she wished she could claim differently, her eyes always sought his too.

It was the night before their wedding. The intervening days had been relatively easy to handle as he had spent them in Paris or in his office working. She had occupied herself as much as she could, taking long walks in the forest that scared her so much at night but which during the day came alive with wildlife and glorious colours. But there was nowhere to dance, not a single room within the multitude where she could risk putting pointe shoes on and letting her body relax in the movement that had always invigorated and comforted her.

The evenings were the hardest.

They dined together but the dishes they were served were entirely separate. Benjamin favoured dishes like juicy steaks and creamy mashed potato while she ignored the tantalising aromas and concentrated on her super-salads and grilled chicken, the meals punctuated by periodic polite conversation.

It was all the unspoken conversations that had her feet tapping and her limbs aching for movement, when their eyes would lock together and electricity would flow between them, so thick she felt the currents in her veins. She could never finish her meals fast enough to escape to the sanctuary of her quarters where, mercifully, he had not attempted to join her again.

If he did, she was no longer confined to practising yoga in her underwear; all her leotards and practice outfits had been delivered from Madrid with her passport and neatly put away.

She kept her passport on her at all times.

That night he had taken her out to the theatre to watch a play she couldn't remember the plot of, the movements and words on the stage passing her by in a blur, her concentration focused solely on the man sitting in the private box beside her.

'We are home,' he said quietly as the chateau appeared before them, illuminated in its magnificence.

'This is not my home.' Her denial was automatic.

'This will be our main marital house and the base for which we lead our lives. I want it to feel like home for you but you need to be the one to make it that. Do whatever you feel is necessary.'

Unable to help herself, she turned to look at him.

She wanted to deny his words more vehemently. She wanted to throw it all in his face, tell him that she could never make a home in the place he had basically imprisoned her in but she couldn't get the words out. The expression in his eyes had frozen her tongue to the roof of her mouth.

She had seen desire there; it was always there. She had seen loathing, she had even glimpsed pity in those green depths, but this...

This look made her insides melt into liquid and her heart race into a thrum.

This was a look of possession but not the look of a buyer appreciating his chattel. It was the possessive way a man looked at his lover, and the thought made the liquid in her insides *burn* to think that, in only one night, she would *be* his lover.

He was telling her to treat his home as her own and, more than that, he *meant it*. She could see it in the eyes she found herself continually seeking.

She could never imagine Javier saying something like that. Their engagement party had been nothing but an exercise in showing her off to his peers—he didn't have friends, he had acquaintances—and cementing their forthcoming union. She had never felt comfortable in his home and he had never done or said anything to make her feel that she should feel comfortable there. In truth, she had dreaded moving into that villa and living within the cold, emotionless walls.

Yet for all her dread at marrying him, she'd felt safe. He could touch her but he could never hurt her.

Benjamin on the other hand...

'Do you want a drink?' he asked casually as she hurried through the chateau doors. 'A last drink to celebrate the last night of our freedom?'

'No, thank you.' She shook her head for emphasis. 'I'm going up. I need to do some yoga and get some sleep.'

'Yoga at this time of night?'

She took the first step up the cantilevered stairs. 'If I can't dance it's the next best thing.'

And God knew she needed to do something. She would be marrying this man in fourteen hours.

'In that case, *bonne nuit.*'

Not looking back and holding the rail tightly, she skipped up the stairs feeling his stare on her with every step she took.

She had to remember that Benjamin had stolen her. He had *stolen* her.

Nothing he did or said could make up for that.

Marrying him was the only way she could salvage the mess that he had created for her in his ruthless game of revenge.

If she dropped her guard, he had the potential to hurt her in ways she did not have the imagination to imagine.

The wedding ceremony was simple and, best of all, quick.

Two hours after they had been pronounced husband and wife, they sat alone in an exclusive restaurant at the pretty little town they had married in, and all Freya could remember of the ceremony itself was how she'd trembled; her hands, her voice as she'd made her vows, but she could remember nothing of the vows themselves. She remembered how warm her skin had been and how certain she'd been that the mayor, who'd officiated the service, and the witnesses he'd brought in could all hear the hammering of her heart.

She couldn't remember the faces of the witnesses. She couldn't remember the face of the photographer who had taken the official picture of the newly married couple on the steps of the town hall but she could remember the butterflies that had let loose in her stomach as she'd waited for the kiss that would show the world she belonged to Benjamin, striking a further blow to the pride of the man she should have married.

She had held her core tightly in dread and anticipation. Benjamin had stared intently into her eyes but instead of stamping his possession on her mouth, had pulled her to him so her cheek pressed against his chest and his chin rested on the top of her head. She could remember the scent of his cologne and the warmth of his skin through the smart suit he'd married her in, and most vividly she remembered the dive of disappointment that the kiss she'd worked herself up for had never happened.

From that day the world would know her as Freya Guillem. It would be her professional name, just as she had agreed to take Javier's name what now felt a lifetime ago.

She could no longer remember Javier's face. She didn't think she had ever looked at it properly.

But she knew every contour of Benjamin's. His features had been committed to her memory all those months ago in that one, long, lingering look when she should never have noticed him in the first place. Her hungry eyes had soaked in all the little details since she had been living under his roof and now she knew the exact position of the scar above his lip, the differing shades of his eyes depending on the light and his mood, the unruliness of his black eyebrows if he didn't smooth them down, the faint dimple that appeared in his left cheek when he smiled, which wasn't often.

But when he did smile...

His smile had the capacity to make her stomach melt into a puddle.

Trying her hardest to hide the fresh tremors in her hand, she took another drink of her champagne and readily allowed the maître d' to refill it.

'Is the food not to your liking, madam?' he asked, staring with concern at her plate.

'It's delicious,' she replied honestly. 'I'm just not very hungry.'

She'd had to virtually force-feed herself the few bites she'd had of her challans duck with crispy pear and other little morsels of taste sensation artfully displayed on her plate.

The town they'd married in was a beautiful place of old, steep, narrow streets and chic, impeccably dressed men and women. This was rural France but with a modern twist, its eclectic shops and restaurants catering to the filthy rich. The restaurant Benjamin had taken her to to celebrate their nuptials was the plushest of the lot, its chef the recipient of so many awards he was a household name, even to her. Benjamin had hired the whole restaurant for their exclusive use.

'Has anticipation caused you to lose your appetite?' the man she had married only a few hours before asked with a gleam in his eyes, the look of seduction, the unspoken promise that the kiss he had failed to deliver on at the top of the town hall steps would soon be forthcoming.

Whatever had affected her appetite had not had the same effect on him, she thought resentfully, staring at his cleared plate. He had eaten with the same relish he ate all his meals. Apart from breakfast, she remembered. Benjamin had an aversion to breakfast.

'Anticipation about what?' she challenged. 'If you think I'm nervous about sharing a bed with you then I'm afraid I must disappoint you.'

And she wasn't nervous. She was terrified.

The gleam in his eyes only deepened. 'I don't think it is possible that you could disappoint me, *ma douce*.'

You'll be disappointed when you discover my complete lack of experience.

She knew she should tell him. It was something she had told herself repeatedly these past few days but every time she practised in her head what to say, her brain would burn and she'd get a queasy roiling in her belly. Benjamin was expecting to share his bed with an experienced woman, not a virgin.

Would he laugh at her? Or simply disbelieve her? Maybe he would even refuse to sleep with her, a thought that would have sent her into hysterical laughter if her vocal cords hadn't frozen. As if he would care. The man was remorseless.

Whatever his reaction would be she had yet to find the words to tell him and now the time was speeding up and all she could do was drag this meal out for as long as she could to delay what she knew was inevitable.

Yet staring into those green eyes that gazed so blatantly back at her, she couldn't deny there was truth in Benjamin's observation. Anticipation had laced itself within her fear. It had steadily coiled itself through her bloodstream and now she didn't know if it was fear or anticipation that had her clutched in its grip the strongest.

She had to get a hold on herself and keep her head. Keep her control, the only part of herself that would be left for herself when this night was over.

He reached over to take her hand, leaning forward as he rubbed his thumb against her wrist to stare at her with a piercing look that sent fresh tingles racing through her blood. She was certain he must be able to feel the pulse behind the skin of her wrist throbbing madly.

His voice dropped to a sensuous murmur. 'As you are not hungry for food...' He raised her hand and pressed his lips to the very spot on her wrist his thumb had brushed against. 'Time to leave, *ma douce*. Let us see if we can whet and satisfy a different hunger.'

CHAPTER NINE

THE DRIVE BACK through the winding roads of Provence to his secluded chateau seemed to take hours rather than just twenty short minutes.

Benjamin had never known his veins to fizz as wildly as they were doing right then or been so aware of the heat of his skin. Freya stared out of the window beside him, her stillness absolute. Only the erratic rise and fall of her chest showed it to be nothing but a façade.

He could not believe how stunning she looked that day. Freya's striking looks had turned into a beauty that had stolen his breath so many times he was surprised he had any oxygen left in his lungs.

She'd chosen to marry him in a simple white silk dress that floated to her ankles, with a lace bodice that sparkled under the sun's rays held up by delicate spaghetti straps. On her feet were flat white sandals that suited the bohemian effect of the dress, her dark hair loose and falling in waves over her shoulders.

The dress she had chosen had hardly been a traditional wedding dress but it had been perfect for their wedding. It had proven her commitment in the vows she was making.

Benjamin had taken one look at her and wished he'd arranged for them to exchange those vows in his chateau garden under an archway adorned with flowers of all different scents and colours.

They had left the town hall as husband and wife and stood together at the top of the steps, the photographer's lens trained on them exactly as Benjamin had instructed.

The sun's rays had bounced over Freya's skin and he had stared into eyes that were wide with trepidation, and felt that same dazzling punch in the guts he'd experienced the first time he'd set eyes on her. Just like that, the kiss he'd planned for the media's delectation and Javier's continued humiliation had seemed all wrong.

This was their wedding. Whatever the circumstances behind their vows, this was a commitment they were making to each other.

He didn't want to think about his nemesis.

Instead, he had put an arm around her and drawn her to him so her cheek rested against his chest. She had trembled in his arms.

It had come to him then as he inhaled her scent with the photographer's lens flashing at them why he needed their first kiss as husband and wife to be away from prying eyes...his need to possess Freya had become stronger than his thirst for revenge against Javier.

When he kissed her next, he had no intention of stopping.

'The first time we drove this road together in the dark you had a can of pepper spray aimed at my face,' he commented idly as his driver took them through his forest.

They were almost home.

She didn't move her head from the window. 'I wish I had used it.'

'Do you think it would have changed the outcome between us?'

She raised a shoulder in a light shrug. 'If I hadn't left the hotel with you, if I had taken my chances at the airfield, if I had made a successful escape over your wall...any of those things could have changed the outcome.'

He reached a hand out to smooth a lock of her hair behind an ear.

'Do you wish you *had* been able to change it? Do you wish it had been Javier you exchanged your vows with today?'

She stilled, whether at his touch or his question he did not know.

Her throat moved before she said quietly, 'I married you. It is pointless wishing for an alternative reality.'

A stab of something that felt a little like how he imagined jealousy would feel cut into his chest.

That hadn't been a denial.

Freya had never given any indication that she harboured genuine feelings for Javier but nor had she given any indication that she didn't.

She desired him; that had been proven beyond doubt, but that didn't mean she didn't desire Javier too.

Had she spent their wedding day wishing she had married the other man? Was she approaching their wedding night wishing it were Javier's bed she would be sharing instead of his?

He rubbed his finger over the rim of her ear. Freya had such pretty, delicate ears...he had never thought of ears as pretty before. He had never noticed *anyone's* ears before.

He noticed everything about Freya. There was not a part of her face he wasn't now familiar with in a way he had never been familiar with another.

He could hardly wait to discover the parts she kept hidden from view. That time was almost with them and if she was approaching it wishing it were with Javier then he would make damn sure to drive his rival from her mind.

Come the morning her first thought would be him and him alone.

Come the morning and she would never wish she were with Javier or think of him again.

'Drink?'

Freya nodded tightly. Her knees shook so hard they could hardly support her weight. She had been unable to speak since they had walked back into the chateau to a vibrant display of flowers and balloons in the main reception room.

She had no idea where the staff were though. The chateau, normally bustling with unobtrusive life, was silent enough to hear a pin drop.

The silence in Benjamin's bedroom was even more oppressive. She fought the urge to bolt like a frightened colt.

'Take a seat.' He strolled to a dark wood cabinet, gesturing to the cosy armchair in the corner of his bedroom.

She sat and pressed her knees together under the wedding dress she knew wouldn't be covering her for much longer.

As terrified as she was at that moment, there was none of the coldness in her veins fear normally brought about. Instead there was heat, electricity zinging over her skin, dread and desire colliding.

Benjamin's quarters had a similar layout to her own but, where hers were painted in light, muted colours that had a decidedly feminine feel, his was much darker with a rich, masculine hue.

His bed...

She had never known beds that large existed. She had never known beds could be a work of art in their own right. Made of a dark wood she didn't know the name of, it was clearly a bespoke creation, and covered in a beautiful silk-looking slate-grey duvet that must be bespoke too to fit the bed.

Freya breathed in deeply, trying her hardest to keep the trembles threatening to overwhelm her under control, looking everywhere but at that bed.

'Your drink, Madame Guillem.'

She had to hold herself back from snatching the glass from his hand and downing it all in one.

It wasn't the first time she had been addressed by her

new title since the service but it was the first time Benjamin had said it.

She was thankful she hadn't downed her drink when she took the first big sip and tasted its potency. Benjamin had made her a gin and tonic that was definitely more gin than tonic and the one sip was enough to steady her nerves, if only momentarily.

He'd moved away from her again to return to the cabinet, dimming the lights on the way. A moment later, low music filled the room and broke the heavy, stifling silence.

She had never heard the song before but the singer's soulful baritone calmed her that little bit more. It didn't make it any easier for her to breathe though and she took another sip of her drink, her nerves back on tenterhooks as she waited for Benjamin to make his move.

He held a crystal tumbler of what she assumed to be Scotch in his hand and was wafting it gently under his nose while he stared at her, a meditative gleam in his green eyes. His gaze not dropping from hers, he drained his drink in one swallow and placed the empty tumbler on the cabinet.

Then he strode to her with a hand held out.

He didn't speak. He didn't need to.

She stared at the steady hand, so much larger than her own, taking in the masculine elegance of his long fingers before slipping her hand into it and wordlessly allowing him to help her to her feet.

At some point since they'd returned to his chateau, Benjamin had removed his tuxedo jacket and bow tie and undone the top two buttons of his white shirt. Freya had never seen him wear white before, black being his colour of choice, which she had assumed was to match his heart.

The white contrasted against the dark olive hue of his skin and even more starkly against the shadows the collar of his shirt made against his throat.

Her gaze rose with a will of its own to rest on his face

and the eyes that had become as dark as the forests that surrounded his home.

The hand still holding hers tightened and she swayed forward so their faces were close enough for the warmth of his breath to whisper against her lips and suddenly she was taken by that same burst of desperate longing that had overcome her two months before when she had first seen him standing in Javier's garden.

This was the man who had haunted her dreams for two long months, the man she had been unable to stop herself obsessing over, the last man in the world she would have chosen to marry simply because he was the one man in the world who evoked this sick, desperate longing inside her with nothing more than a look and made her heart feel as if it could burst through her ribcage and soar like a songbird to lodge itself in his chest.

Their faces still close enough together that one tiny jolt forward would join their lips together, Benjamin's hold on her hand loosened. His fingers trailed up her arm to her shoulder, burning shivers trailing in their wake.

She closed her eyes to the sensation firing through her, the beats of her heart so loud they drowned out the music playing.

His hand now drew up her neck to burrow into her hair, the other splayed across her lower back. Her lips tingled as his warm breath drew closer, filling her mouth with moisture as his lips finally claimed hers.

The first press of his mouth against hers set off something inside her, a rush of need so powerful that she fought frantically against it, clenching her hands into fists to cling onto the last of her sanity before the desire dragged her down to a place she feared—the greatest of all her fears—she could never come back up from.

Since agreeing to marry him she had imagined herself playing the role of sacrificial virgin, lying on the bed and letting him take what he wanted but giving nothing back. She had known that to remain passive would take the greatest self-control of her life, especially after the kiss they had shared, but it was only as his tongue danced into her mouth that she understood how futile a hope it had been. Her hunger for him...it was too much. With a sigh that could have been a moan, she swayed into the strength of his solid body and welcomed the heat of his hungry kisses.

Her movement set something off in him too. The hands securing her gently tightened and then she was on her toes, crushed against him, breasts against chest, pelvis against abdomen, her hands winding around his neck, her fingers digging into the nape of his neck, her tongue dancing against his. And it was his hands now sweeping over her back and up her sides, brushing the underside of her breasts, the ferocity of their kisses intensifying with every passing second. Every time he touched her bare skin she felt the mark of his skin against hers and her hunger grew.

She was so caught up in their kisses she only realised he'd pulled the zip of her dress down her back when his hand slid into the opened space and dipped down to clasp her bottom.

Her breaths shallow, she moved her face to stare at him, terror making its return.

She had to tell him, she thought wildly. If she didn't...

'Benjamin...'

But he'd taken the skinny straps of her dress and skimmed them down her arms. She had hardly spoken the last syllable of his name before gravity pulled her dress down, her lean body offering it no resistance so it fell into a pool at her feet leaving her naked bar her plain, cotton knickers.

Her arms flailed to cover her breasts, panic now clawing at her.

Nudity was no big deal to her, it couldn't be. She danced

without wearing underwear, as most dancers did. She had never been body-conscious, never been one to torment herself over her shape. She ate the best diet she could and worked hard to keep her body lean and supple so she had every tool she could to be the best dancer she could be.

But she had never been virtually naked in front of a man who wasn't looking at her as a dancer but as a lover.

She hadn't had an hour of meditation and yoga to calm her mind as she had when he'd walked into her quarters the other day.

Never, until that moment, had she felt truly naked.

Her breasts were *tiny*, she thought hopelessly. She didn't have the curves other women had.

Benjamin had stepped back to look at her, and she cringed to see the frown on his face.

Then the frown softened and his hands rested on her arms that still desperately covered her breasts. Gripping them lightly, he slowly pulled them apart to expose her for his scrutiny.

Her mortification grew when he let go of her arms so they hung by her hips, her fingers twitching to cover her breasts again.

He stepped back again then slowly walked around her. She could feel the stare of his eyes penetrating her skin and could do nothing to stop the trembling of her legs.

She was exposing herself in a way she had spent years fighting to keep covered, not her external flesh but what lay beneath it, the sensuality that lay beneath her skin, the only part of herself that was hers alone, never to be given, never to be shared, the only part of herself she'd been able to keep *for* herself.

It was slipping through her fingers and the harder she tried to keep control of it, the more it pulled away from her and into Benjamin's hands...

When he finally stood in front of her again he placed a

finger on her lips and leaned in to nuzzle his lips against her ear. *'Tu es belle, ma douce.'*

She was stunned at the tenderness in his voice even if she didn't understand the words, her breath leaving her again as he moved his finger from her lips to cover her cheeks with the whole of his hands and stare hard into her eyes.

'You are beautiful, Freya.'

His lips brushed against hers before brushing over her jaw to burrow into her neck. Then he sank onto his knees so his face was level with her breasts.

He stared at them before covering them entirely with his hands. He gazed up at her. 'They are perfect. *You* are perfect.'

She couldn't breathe. Her throat had closed, fresh sensation bubbling inside her, the hunger in his eyes driving out the panic.

Then he slid his hands sensuously over her stomach to grip her hips and covered her breasts with his mouth.

At the first flick of his tongue over her nipple she gasped, her hands flailing to rest on his shoulders.

Sensation suffused her, intensifying as he took one breast into his mouth, his obvious delight in them and the thrills shooting through her veins driving the last of her embarrassment and fear clean out of her.

Benjamin felt Freya's sharp nails dig through his shirt and into his skin, the most pleasurable pain of his life.

For two months he had dreamed of this moment; dreamed of Freya coming undone in his arms, imagined her naked and fantasised about all the things he wanted to do with her.

This was beyond anything his feeble imagination could have dreamt up, and they had barely begun.

Her breasts were the smallest he had ever seen but they were the most beautiful. He hadn't been lying when he had called them perfect. Perfectly round, perfectly high and the perfect fit for his mouth.

They had the perfect taste too.

She had the perfect taste.

Slowly he trailed his mouth down her stomach, revelling in the smooth perfection of her skin, thrilling at the quiver of her belly when he licked it and the ragged movement of her chest as she struggled to breathe, knowing it was her response to *him* causing it.

His own breaths had become ragged too. The tightness in his groin was almost intolerable, his need for relief a burn that he willingly ignored, too intent on seducing this beautiful woman—his *wife*—to care for his own needs.

His time would come.

Lower down he went, raining soft kisses over her abdomen to the band of her underwear, the heat inside him rising as he got closer to her womanly heat.

Pinching the elastic of her knickers in his fingers, he gently tugged them down her hips to her supple yet shaking thighs.

He touched his nose to the soft hair between her legs and breathed deeply.

About to nuzzle lower, he became dimly aware that her fingers, which had been digging into his scalp, had stopped moving.

Looking up, he found her staring down at him with what could only be described as terror in her eyes.

It stopped him in his tracks.

'Have you not done this before?' he asked slowly.

She hesitated before giving a jerky shake of her head.

His brain racing, he pressed a tender kiss into the downy hair, inhaled her intoxicating scent one more time and tugged the underwear back up to cover her.

Freya had less experience than he had thought...

Getting back to his feet, he pressed himself close to her

quivering body and gently kissed her, then lifted her into his arms.

There was no resistance. She wound her arms around his neck and gazed into his eyes as he carried her to the bed.

Laying her down, he kissed her again, more deeply, before dipping his face into the elegant arch of her neck and tenderly nipping the skin with his teeth.

'I have too many clothes on,' he said into her neck, then pressed a kiss against the pulse beating wildly at the base of her jawline and sat up.

The obsidian of her eyes seemed to glow with the weight of a thousand emotions. She raised a hand as if to reach out and touch him then swallowed. The hand fell back to her side.

He picked it up and razed a kiss across the knuckles. *'Tu es belle.'*

She *was* beautiful. Mesmerising.

Her lips quirked in the glimmer of a smile and her chest rose as she took a deep breath.

Not taking his gaze from her face, Benjamin proceeded to undress, first his shirt, then getting to his feet to tug his trousers and underwear off until he was fully naked. He'd been so caught up in his seduction of Freya and the headiness of the moment that he hadn't appreciated how constricting his clothes had been until he took them off and his arousal sprang free.

Resisting the urge to take it in his hand, he sat back on the bed. 'Now you are the one with too many clothes on,' he said with a lightness that belied the heavy thuds of his heart, tracing his finger in a line from the dip at the top of her neck, down between her breasts and over the flat plain of her stomach to rest on the band of her knickers.

Dieu, he could devour her whole.

Her hands clenched into fists, her breaths becoming ragged again. He took hold of both her wrists and slowly spread them up to rest either side of her head as he laid himself over her until he covered her, propping his weight up on his elbows to gaze into her pulsating eyes.

Then he kissed her.

As their mouths moved together, fused into one, the passion reigniting and deepening, he loosened his hold on her wrists and laced his fingers through hers. She squeezed in response then dragged them away to wrap her arms around his neck and pull him down so his weight was fully on her.

He groaned at the sensation of her breasts pressed so tightly against his chest and kissed her more deeply. His skin was alive with heat that seeped through his veins and deep into his bones, all thoughts leaving him except one; the one that needed to touch and taste every part of this beautiful woman who had been in his head for so long and now lay in his bed and in his blood.

With his mouth and hands he began his exploration, discovering the parts of her body that made her suck in a breath at his touch, the parts that made her moan, the parts that made her nails dig into his flesh, feeling her relax so much that when he pressed his mouth to her pelvis again, she sighed and her left leg writhed.

Encouraged, Benjamin slowly tugged her knickers down, making a trail with his tongue down her legs in its wake before kissing his way back up and inhaling the scent of her heat without any barrier at all.

She stilled.

For a long time he didn't move, waiting to see what she would do.

Then he felt the whisper of her hand on his head, her fingers threading through his hair...

He traced his tongue between the damp folds and heard her gasp. Her fingers made twisting motions in his hair that pulled when he found her secret nub and her bottom lifted.

Dieu.

With all the languid care in the world, he made love to her with his mouth, relishing the taste of her sweet muskiness on his tongue, letting her responses, which were becoming more overt by the second, guide him as to what was giving her the greatest pleasure, intent only *on* her pleasure, Freya's pleasure, Freya, this beautiful, beautiful woman he ached to make completely his.

Only when he was sure that she was nearing her peak and completely ready for him did he slide his tongue back up her stomach, nipping each of her breasts with his teeth as he went, to reclaim her mouth and gently part her thighs.

Guiding his erection to the warmth of her heat he closed his eyes and gritted his teeth.

This was a moment to savour.

Inhaling deeply through his nose, he covered her mouth with his then could hold on no longer. With one long thrust, he buried himself deep inside her...

Freya felt a momentary sharpness that she would probably have missed if she hadn't been waiting for it, then there was nothing but sensation, every single nerve ending inside her sighing and delighting in the feel of Benjamin finally inside her, filling her completely.

She gazed into the green eyes that were staring at her with such hunger, and touched his face before lifting her head to kiss him.

How she loved his kisses. Loved his tongue taking such rough possession of hers. Loved his touch. Loved the feel of his broad chest covering hers, the dark hairs brushing against her breasts. Loved what he was doing to her right then...

Ohhhhh...

Her head fell back on the pillow as he began to move. He withdrew slowly only to plunge into her again. And then he did it again, and again, over and over, somehow knowing exactly what she wanted and what she needed, all the things about herself she hadn't known.

The last of the fight had left her when he'd carried her to the bed and laid her down so tenderly, almost as if she were precious to him...

And then he had kissed and stroked all her defences and fears away until sanity had ceased to matter. Nothing mattered. Nothing apart from *this*; here, now, them, together.

She'd had no idea that she could feel such things.

And the sensations ravaging her were heightening.

As Benjamin's movements grew wilder, his breath hot on her face, his groans soaking into her skin, the throbbing ache deep within her tightened and burned into a flame. Hotter and hotter it grew, blazing into a peak that came to a crescendo...

And then she was soaring, sparks exploding through her on a riptide of pleasure she had never, never, imagined possible.

Hazily she was aware that Benjamin had let go too, burying his face in her hair with a ragged, drawn-out moan.

She held him tightly as they rocked together, holding on to the pleasure for as long as they could until, finally, they both stilled and all that was left of the explosion were tiny glowing flickers that tingled and buzzed through and over every part of her.

CHAPTER TEN

FREYA LOST ALL semblance of time as she lay there with Benjamin's weight so deliciously compressing on her. They could have lain there for minutes or hours.

She opened her eyes. She felt so profoundly different from when she had walked into this room that she half expected the room to look different too.

The dim lights were still on. The music Benjamin had put on still played, a different song now worming its way through her slowly de-fuzzing head.

'Okay?' His question came as a murmur yet cut through the silence as if he had shouted it.

Her throat closed and she had to breathe deeply to get air into her suddenly constricted lungs.

'Fine,' she managed.

He rolled off her and onto his back, though kept his head turned so he faced her. 'You are sure?'

She wanted to offer a pithy comment, something that would negate the huge whirl of emotions filling her, to deny the wondrousness of what she had just experienced and which she knew, as pathetically inexperienced as she had been, that he had shared too.

But she couldn't. Somehow this man who was still very much a stranger even if he was her husband... He had made her feel beautiful. He had recognised her fear and inexperience and made love to her as if she were someone to cherish.

She would not let fear demean or diminish it.

Slowly she turned her head to look into the eyes that always saw too much, and nodded.

He studied her for long moments before craning his neck

to kiss her gently. 'I'm going to turn the music off. Can I get you a drink?'

'No, thank you.'

He kissed her again then turned over and climbed off the bed.

She watched him stride to the sound system, completely at ease in his skin.

And no wonder. Until that moment she hadn't looked at him properly. She'd gazed at his broad chest and felt it crushed against her, seen his strong, muscular arms and felt them bunch in her hands, the rest of him only glimpsed at, even the long legs she'd wound her own around.

She'd thought of him as having the stalking grace of a panther but only now, seeing him unashamedly naked, all the components that made him Benjamin put together, did she fully appreciate his rugged masculine beauty. It made the breath catch in her throat...

'You like what you see?'

She blinked, suddenly aware she had been staring at him.

Cheeks flaming, she then became aware that she had been staring at him naked, forgetting her own nakedness.

The hazy glow of their lovemaking had gone and with it her confidence to be naked around this man.

He'd cast her in a spell. He must have done.

She had done more than bare herself to him, she had given the essence of herself. She had lost control.

He'd made her forget. Forget what he'd done. Forget who she was and all the reasons she needed to keep an emotional distance from him.

His lovemaking had been incredible...*they* had been incredible. Just as she had feared.

'I like what *I* see,' he murmured, seemingly unfazed by her silence.

She averted her eyes from his gleaming scrutiny and,

keeping her thighs together to protect her modesty as best she could, grabbed the duvet, which their lovemaking had dislodged and managed to heap into a pile, and burrowed low into it.

He laughed lightly. 'I have embarrassed you.'

She sensed him treading back to his side of the bed and wished she could escape to the solitude of her own quarters.

A breeze fluttered against her back, Benjamin lifting the duvet to climb back in beside her. As she waited for the bed to dip, holding the part of the duvet she was wrapped in tightly, she became aware of a silence.

Coldness crept up her spine that had nothing to do with her back being exposed as the silence drew out and she was on the verge of saying something to break it when he finally got into bed.

She held her breath, squeezed her eyes shut and waited for him to turn off the dim lights. If she kept her back to him and played dead he might leave her alone.

Don't touch me, she silently begged. *Your touch is too much. Please, don't make me lose any more of myself than I already have.*

But the question he posed into the silence made her wish he had touched her instead.

'You were a *virgin*?'

What else explained the small, red stain marking the under-sheet of his bed? Benjamin wondered, his mind reeling. He'd seen it as he'd pulled the duvet back and his blood had run from languidly sated to ice cold in an instant.

Freya had been more than merely inexperienced. She'd been a virgin.

His chest tightened.

Why hadn't she told him?

Slowly she rolled over, her black orbs fixing straight onto him.

The tightness in his chest turned into a cramp.

For a long time neither of them spoke.

'You were a virgin.' This time he posed it as a statement.

She gave the briefest, jerkiest of nods.

'Why didn't you tell me?'

She swallowed and blinked rapidly. 'I couldn't.'

'Why not?'

Clenching her jaw, she shrugged.

'If I'd had the slightest idea you were a virgin, I would never...'

'Never have *what*?' she interrupted, suddenly fierce, her neck and face turning the colour of crimson, the obsidian in her eyes spitting at him. 'Stolen me? Blackmailed me? Wrecked my life? Forced me to give up my job in a company I love? Does my being a virgin somehow *improve* me? Does my innocence make me a better, more worthy person?'

The tenderness he'd felt towards her vanished as a flash of lava-like anger coursed through him. At her. At himself.

At himself for blackmailing a virgin into marriage.

At Freya for putting money above her own morals, or whatever it was that had caused her to reach the age of twenty-three years untouched.

'Innocent? You signed a contract exchanging your body for money!'

'No, I signed a contract of *marriage*. You read that contract without any context and made assumptions about me because it suited your agenda. Not once did you ask *why* I chose to sign it. You were determined to punish Javier and to hell with who got hurt while you did it.'

'You wanted the money. You made that very clear.' He leaned forward so his nose almost touched hers, delivering his words with ice-cold precision. 'Paint yourself as a sainted martyr if you must but no one forced you to sign those contracts. No one forced you to marry me. No one forced you into my bed, and no one, *no one*, forced you to enjoy being in it.'

Her face became aflame with colour but she didn't back down. 'Who said I enjoyed it?'

He slid his hand around her neck and rested his cheek against hers, ignoring her attempt to rear out of his hold. Speaking into her ear, he whispered, 'You came undone in my arms, *ma douce*, and that is why you are so angry now. You hate that you desire me and you hate that what we just shared proves the self-control you take such pride in is built on sand. If I were to kiss you now, you would come undone all over again.'

'Get your hands off me,' she said with such venom her words landed like barbs on his skin. 'Do not forget my body belongs to me. I am not your chattel.'

He did more than move away from her, he threw the duvet off and climbed out of the bed to stride to his bathroom. Over his shoulder, as if delivering a throwaway comment, he said, 'I'm going to take a shower. Feel free to use my absence to return to your own quarters.'

He could feel the burn of her stare as he locked the bathroom door.

Alone, he pressed the palms of his hands tightly against the cool white tiles and took a deep breath, then another, and another, fighting the urge to punch the walls until his knuckles bled.

The world had turned itself upside down in a matter of seconds.

Dieu, she had been a virgin.

Stepping into the shower, he turned the temperature up as high as he could bear and scrubbed vigorously at his skin, determined to rid himself of the grubby, scaly feeling cloying in his pores.

When he'd finally rubbed himself raw and returned to the bedroom, Freya had gone.

* * *

'This is where you've been hiding.'

Freya looked up from the bench she was sitting on under the cherry tree, shielding her eyes from the sun with her hand.

Benjamin walked towards her, a bottle of water in his hand, a wary smile on his face.

'I've been looking for you,' he explained with a shrug.

Feigning nonchalance at his unexpected appearance although her heart immediately set off at a canter, she stretched her legs out. On this scorching summer's day, he'd dressed in black jeans and a dark blue shirt, his only concession to the sun his rolled-up sleeves. She couldn't detect an ounce of perspiration on him whereas little beads trickled down her spine even though she wore a cotton summer dress.

'I went for a walk.' She fixed her gaze on the spectacular view surrounding her.

She had woken before the sun, everything that had passed between them that night flashing through her on a reel before she'd been fully conscious, sending her jumping out of the bed and into the shower.

So early had it been that when she'd hurried to the kitchen not a single member of staff had been awake.

She'd found an avocado and a banana that would suffice for her breakfast and forced them down her cramped throat and stomach. And then she had set off, walking the forests and fields of his estate, keeping her legs moving, *needing* to keep them moving, her usual way of expelling her emotions still denied her and would always be denied when she resided under Benjamin's roof.

She had never needed to dance as much as she did then, never felt that the fabric of her being could fray at the seams without the glue she had learned to depend on.

He sat next to her and offered her the water bottle.

'Thank you.' She took it from his hand being careful not to let their fingers brush, instinctively knowing just one touch would be her undoing.

She needed to keep her focus. Had to. She would not let what was happening inside her derail the future she had worked so hard for and which her parents had sacrificed so much for.

But Benjamin awoke her senses so they all tuned into his frequency just with his presence. Her nose begged her to lean closer so she could smell his gorgeous scent better, her fingers itched to slide over and touch those muscular thighs inches from her own...

She didn't want this. Not any of it. When he'd asked after the wedding if she wished she'd married Javier instead, the answer that had screamed through her head had been a resounding *yes*.

And that had been before they had made love.

If she'd married Javier there wouldn't have been any of this angst tormenting her, there would have been only indifference. None of the hate. None of the passion.

None of the joy she had discovered in Benjamin's arms...

Hands trembling, she drank heavily from the water bottle then wiped the rim and handed it back.

Silence fell between them until he broke it by saying, 'This was my mother's favourite spot.'

Freya had discovered this unexpected patch of paradise by accident a few days ago. The bench and its overhanging cherry tree were in a small clearing accessed through a short cut-through in his forest, sitting on the crest of a hill. Fields of all colours sprawled out for miles below them.

It was just a bench under a cherry tree but there was something so calming about the setting she'd sought it out again.

'Was this your family home?' she asked.

'My family home was in a suburb of Paris. My mother

always said she would move to Provence when her children were grown up and Clara retired from the ballet.'

'Clara Casillas?'

He nodded. 'My mother was her seamstress. She worked for the ballet company in Paris where Clara first made her name. Remember I told you of the closeness between them? Clara refused to let anyone else make her costumes. They denied it but I am sure they deliberately got pregnant at the same time so they could raise their babies together.'

'You and the Casillas brothers?' she asked cautiously, afraid to break their tenuous cordiality by saying the names she knew were like a red rag to a bull.

Another nod. 'We saw the world with them.'

'You were lucky. I would have loved to have seen her perform in the flesh.'

'I found the ballet as boring as hell. I wanted to play football, not be stuck in a theatre. But I had Javier and Luis. We would sneak off together and kick drink cans in theatre car parks or try and spy on the dancers undressing. We had the run of the backstage when performances were on and we made the most of it.'

A bubble of laughter burst from her lungs. 'I can't imagine Javier doing any of that.'

He met her eye, a tinge of amusement in his stare. 'He joined in grudgingly—he was always the serious one. Luis and I were always the instigators of any trouble.'

'Did Chloe not join in?'

'We were ten when she was born. By the time she was old enough to get into trouble with us it was over.'

Neither of them needed to say why it had been over. The story of Clara Casillas's death at the hands of her own husband was still a tale rehashed *ad nauseam* by the press and ghoulish television producers. The friendship between Benjamin and the Casillas brothers had endured…until mere weeks ago.

'Did your mother buy the chateau after Clara died?' she asked.

'She was a single mother by then—my parents divorced when she fell pregnant with Chloe. I bought the chateau for her to end her days in when we learned the treatment for her cancer had failed. I would carry her here to sit on this bench when she was too weak to walk any more.' He lifted his head to look up at the branches of the cherry tree hanging sweetly over them. 'We planted this tree when she died seven years ago. Her ashes are buried under it.'

Freya jumped up. 'I'm sorry. I had no idea...'

'Sit back down, *ma douce*. This is not a shrine for her. It is a celebration of her memory, and if there is an afterlife I know my mother will be delighted that you, a dancer she would have loved, were sitting in the spot she loved so much and enjoying the same views that gave her such peace. Please, sit.'

She sat back down gingerly, trying to process what he'd just revealed to her.

Benjamin had said his mother died seven years ago. Hadn't he said before that Javier and Luis had gone to him for the money they'd needed to buy the land for the Tour Mont Blanc building seven years ago too?

These were both things she already knew but only now did she put the two dates together.

Had they gone to him when his mother was dying? Had they taken advantage of the grief he must have been dealing with—and she knew what that felt like, a ticking time-bomb hanging over your head...?

'Javier and Luis were with me when we planted the tree,' he said, breaking into her thoughts with words that made her certain he'd been able to read what she'd been thinking. 'She loved them. I thought they loved her too. The night Clara was killed, it was my mother who comforted them...'

'You were there that night?' That was not something she had known.

He nodded. His jaw had tightened. 'It was after the performance. We were in a hotel across the road from the theatre babysitting Chloe so none of us were there to see or hear what went on between them. My mother woke us to tell the news. She held those boys in her arms the whole night. After they were taken to Spain by their grandparents, my mother made sure they still saw us. They stayed with us many times.' Benjamin swallowed the bile forming in his throat. 'After Clara died, Javier and Luis's visits were the only things that could make her smile. She became like their second mother. They visited her when she was ill. Luis visited so many times the hospital staff assumed he was her son. She never corrected them. She liked them thinking that.'

He had no idea why he was revealing all this to her. These were things he never spoke of.

But the past had become so entwined with the present in recent months that he found it a relief to finally speak of it.

In truth, he owed it to her. Freya deserved to know.

What had she said that first night, about being able to sleep soundly? That his conscience should prevent it?

He understood now what she'd meant. His sleep had been fractured, in and out of wakefulness, his mind a constant whirl.

He still couldn't believe she had been a virgin, did not see how it was possible to reach the age of twenty-three untouched, especially in the hotbed of the ballet world. But the proof had been there, undeniable.

He'd taken her virginity and the more it played on his mind, the worse he felt, sicker in himself.

Her husky voice carried through the humid air. 'When did they ask you for the money?'

'The day she got the terminal diagnosis. They knew I

had the money.' He looked at her, his heart tugging to see the glimmer of compassion ringing in eyes that normally only rang with loathing. 'I knew my mother wasn't going to survive it even before we had it confirmed. I'd already made up my mind to buy the chateau for her.'

He'd known the romance of its architecture and its spectacular views would be a tonic to his mother's cancer-ravaged body and he'd been right. She had spent the last three months of her life there and slipped away peacefully.

He had kept the dire financial situation buying the chateau had left him in from her.

He cleared his throat before continuing. 'I had the cash available to buy it outright. It was a lot of money. The chateau had undergone a complete renovation so was priced high.'

'They knew?'

'Of course they knew.' He didn't hide his bitterness. 'They knew everything. They knew taking my money to finance Tour Mont Blanc meant I would have to take a mortgage to buy the chateau. They knew I overextended myself. They knew when I got into financial trouble over it and was on the verge of bankruptcy. They knew I only gave them that investment because it was them and I trusted them as if they were my own blood. I never blamed them for the situation I got myself in but I gave them that money in good faith and then I learned they had taken it in bad. They knew the terms we agreed verbally were different from the terms on the contract.'

'So your revenge really wasn't about the money then,' she said in the softest tone he had ever heard from her lips. 'They hurt you.'

'They did not hurt me,' he dismissed. 'They betrayed me and kept the lie going for seven years. I was going to donate the profit to a charity that helps traumatised kids. Javier and Luis had to deal with one of the most traumatic things a child could go through but they had been lucky to have family and my mother to help pick up the pieces. Other children aren't so lucky or resilient. They haven't just stolen from me but those children too. I'm fortunate that all the hard work I've put into the business in the past seven years has left me with a sizeable fortune. I'm in the process of liquidating some assets so I can still donate the money but it should never have come to this. They are thieves. They have stolen my money and robbed me of my childhood memories. Everything is tainted now. I think of them carrying my mother's coffin with me into the church and want to rip their heads from their necks.'

He closed his eyes and took a deep breath. Beside him, Freya remained silent but he could feel something new emanating from her that he had never felt before, something that was neither loathing nor desire and flowed into his skin like a balm.

'Do you feel better now you have taken me from Javier?' There was no malice in her voice, just simple, gentle curiosity. 'Do you feel avenged?'

'There is some satisfaction to be had but do I feel avenged…? When I have had my revenge on Luis too, *then* I will feel avenged.'

'What are you planning to do to him?'

'I am still thinking.' *Trying* to think. His thought process had been awry since Freya had been under his roof, her presence even when not in the same room taking all his focus.

'I don't suppose there's any point in saying that sometimes it is better for the soul to let things go,' she said quietly. 'But I will say this—please, for the sake of your soul, don't involve anyone else in it. This is between you and the Casillas brothers. Don't let anyone else suffer for it.'

'I don't want you to suffer.' He took another deep breath and looked up at the cobalt sky, the distant wispy trail of an aeroplane the only thing to cut through the skyscape, then got to his feet. 'Come back to the chateau with me. I have something to show you which, I hope, will make you feel more at home here.'

'What is it?'

'The reason I spent an hour searching for you. Your wedding present from me.'

CHAPTER ELEVEN

FREYA FOLLOWED BENJAMIN into the chateau and up the stairs, apprehension colliding with the ache in her heart at all he had confided in her and which she needed to sit down and think about properly to digest.

She had never thought her heart would ache for him but it did. Badly.

How could Javier treat his oldest friend in that way? And she didn't doubt a word of it. What he and Luis had done was so much worse than merely ripping him off of a fortune. It was a betrayal of biblical proportions.

She shivered to think that was the behaviour of the man she had intended to marry.

When they reached the second floor, Benjamin stopped outside a door that was, she judged, positioned above his own quarters. This was a floor of the chateau she had made a cursory search of on her first day when seeking a dance space and quickly forgotten about. All the rooms up there were laid in thick carpet that would act like a grip on her pointe shoes.

His eyes were on her. 'Open it.'

'It's not a cell, is it?' she asked with a nervous laugh.

He shook his head. 'For once trust me and open the door.'

She stifled the instinctive retort of trust having to be earned.

Benjamin had opened himself up to her. Only a small part, she knew, but it was enough for her to see him with eyes not quite so prejudiced.

He'd made an effort to build a bridge between them and for that she would, this once, place her trust in him and do as he asked.

Holding her breath, Freya opened the door a crack and peered through. The smell of fresh paint hit her immediately.

Then she blinked, certain she was seeing things. But no, she wasn't seeing things. This was a dance studio.

She pushed the door fully open and stared in stunned, disbelieving awe at what had been revealed before her.

Benjamin folded his arms over his chest as he waited for Freya's response. Since opening the door and stepping into the newly revealed room, she hadn't moved a muscle. He didn't think she'd even taken a breath.

'What do you think?' he asked roughly. His heart beat heavily through the tightness in his chest, his stomach twisting.

She shook her head, her throat moving, then slowly turned her head to look at him. Her black eyes were wide and shining. 'You did this...for *me*?'

'You're a professional dancer. You need to practise.'

She needed to dance. Freya was a woman with ballet flowing in her veins, ballet the air she breathed. To deny her the opportunity to dance in the chateau was tantamount to torture.

She raised a hand that had a slight tremor in it to her mouth. 'I don't know what to say.'

'You can say whether you like it or not,' he commented wryly.

She blinked and gave a muffled laugh. 'I can't believe this.'

'Is it suitable for your needs?'

'It's perfect. Beautiful. Just beautiful. And it's so light and high.' She drifted forward into the centre of the huge room, her head now turning in all directions, then stopped when she caught his reflection in the walled mirror. Her forehead creased. 'How did you do it? *When* did you do it?'

'This week. When we agreed to marry.'

'But how?'

'By calling the director of a Parisian ballet company for guidance and employing a top building team.'

'But *how*?' she repeated.

'By paying them ten times their usual rate to stop what they were doing to make it happen. I had hoped it would be completed for our wedding so I could surprise you with it then but there was a delay with the flooring.' Specialist flooring for dancers.

'*How?*' she virtually shrieked, bouncing on her toes and waving her arms in the air. 'From conception to finished product in...what? Five days? How is that even possible? How many rooms were knocked down?'

'Only three.'

'*Only?* You knocked three rooms into...*this*, and I didn't have a clue. I didn't hear anything or see anything, not even a single contractor.'

'They used the tradesman's entrance. The walls were knocked down when you were on your walks.'

'But...'

'No more questions about it. It is done and it is for you. I appreciate you will not spend many nights here once your break is over but this is your home now and when you are here I want you to feel at home.'

The animation that had overtaken her limbs disappeared as she stilled. An emotion he didn't recognise flickered over her face. She chewed at her lip as she stared at him, the intensity of her gaze seeming to cut through the distance between them and burn straight in his chest...

Backing away from her with lungs so tight he could hardly pull air into them, he said, 'I have work to get on with so I shall leave you to enjoy your new dance studio. If there is anything you are not happy with, tell me and we shall change it.'

He left the studio in quick strides and had reached the top of the stairs when she called after him. 'Benjamin?'

It was the first time she'd called him by his name.

'*Oui?*'

'Thank you.'

'*De rien.* Enjoy your dancing. I will see you at dinner.'

Freya sat in the middle of the wonderful dance studio Benjamin had created, just for her, soaking it all in with a heart thumping so madly she was surprised her ribs didn't crack with the force.

This was a studio every little girl who dreamed of being a ballerina dreamed of dancing in. The left wall was a mirror, the rest painted soft white, a barre traversing the entire room, broken only by a huge round window at the far end, a floor-to-ceiling cupboard by the door and a beautiful high table next to it.

Eventually she pulled herself out of her stupor, got to her feet and opened the cupboard.

Inside it lay rows of pointe shoes, rows of ballet slippers all lying below a row of assorted practice outfits. They were all her exact size.

Further exploration revealed the tools needed to soften the pointe shoes and she pounced on them with glee.

Ignoring the cosy armchair placed in the corner, she sat cross-legged on the floor and began to massage the stiff toe cup, then, when she felt it was softened sufficiently, moved on to the shank, the hard sole that supported the arch of her foot, and gently bent it back and forth at the three-quarter mark. When she was happy with both shoes— by now convinced Benjamin had got Compania de Ballet de Casillas own shoemakers to provide them for her, the shoes' response to her well-practised manipulations rendering the alcohol spray and hammer often used to soften them redundant—she stripped her clothes off, pulled on a pair of tights and a leotard, and put the softened pointe shoes on, binding the ribbons securely.

Atop the table next to the cupboard sat a small sound system. Preloaded into it was the music for every ballet that had ever been created.

She found the music to Prokofiev's *Romeo and Juliet*, still her favourite after all these years, and pressed play.

Music filled the room, startling her into spinning round and gazing up at the ceiling where she spotted small, unobtrusive speakers placed at strategic intervals.

She covered her mouth as fresh emotion filled her.

Benjamin had done this, all of this, for her.

She blinked to focus herself and stood by the barre to begin simple stretching exercises that would warm her body and limber her up. A dancer's life was fraught with injury and not doing enough of a warm-up beforehand was a shortcut to a sprain or strain, as was a hard floor that didn't have any buoyancy for the inevitable falls.

Benjamin had had a semi-sprung sub-floor fitted that would be the perfect cushion for her falls.

The exercises she did were moves she had made thousands of times and the familiarity of them and the comfort of the music settled her stomach into an ease she had begun to fear she would never find again.

Her mind began to drift as it always did when doing her barre exercises alone. She imagined herself dancing the balcony scene where Romeo and Juliet danced the *pas de deux*, imagining it as she always did when visualising this scene, with a faceless partner.

But this time the imaginary faceless partner didn't remain faceless for long.

It was Benjamin's face that flowed through her mind, his strong arms around her waist then lifting her into the air, his green eyes burning with longing into hers...

An ache ripped through her, pulling the air from her

lungs with its force, the strength so powerful that she dragged herself from her trance-like state to rush to the sound system and skip to the Dance of the Knights, breathing heavily, fear gripping her.

A knock on the door should have been a welcome distraction but what if it was him, catching her now, at this moment when she couldn't trust herself not to fly into his arms and beg him to make love to her again?

Benjamin had *stolen* her, she reminded herself, again, desperately.

She had insisted on this marriage because there had been no other choice.

But Benjamin had knocked down three rooms in his chateau to create a dance studio any ballerina would want to die in, and he had done that for her. He'd been under no obligation. He got nothing out of it for himself.

This was the man who had almost bankrupted himself so his mother could live the last of her life in beauty.

Her heart heavy though a little calmer, she braced herself before opening the door.

Christabel stood there with a tray and a smile. 'Monsieur Guillem thought you would be hungry. Chef has made you a whole grain tortilla wrap with avocado, chicken, tomato and lettuce. She can make you something else if…'

'This is perfect,' Freya interrupted with a grateful smile. Benjamin's chef had proven herself to be a shining star, keen to provide the resident ballerina with the nutritious meals she depended on and make them as appetising as they could be. Freya had never eaten so well and had not been in the least surprised to learn the chef had once been awarded her own Michelin star.

Once Christabel had gone, Freya poured herself a glass of iced water from the jug delivered with her wrap and ignored the armchair to sit on the curved ledge of the enormous round window.

Chewing slowly, she gazed out. The window overlooked the back garden giving her the perfect view to appreciate the stunning landscape, including the cherubic fountain in the centre that wouldn't have looked out of place in the palace of Versailles.

Slowly but surely she was starting to appreciate the beauty of Benjamin's chateau without angry eyes, like a filter being removed from the lens to reveal it in all its glory.

This was a chateau childish dreams were made of.

And now, with this wonderful studio, she had a place in it that was all her own.

Maybe one day it really would feel like home to her.

When she was about to pop the last bite of her delicious wrap into her mouth, her heart leapt into it instead as she saw Benjamin stroll by talking animatedly on his phone.

Her leaping heart began to beat so hard it became a heavy thrum and she found herself unable to tear her eyes away. Her suddenly greedy eyes soaked in everything about him, from the way his long, muscular legs filled the black jeans he wore and the way his muscles bunched beneath his black T-shirt…he had changed his clothing since he had left her in the studio. Even with her distance she could see how untamed his thick black hair had become and the shadow on his jaw hinting at black stubble about to break free… She had never seen a more rampantly masculine sight and it filled her with a longing that kept her rooted, right until the moment he turned his head.

She pressed her back into the curve of the window quickly before he could look up and see her staring down at him.

'You are happy with your studio?' Benjamin asked that evening as they dined together. This evening he had decided to eat the same meal as Freya, pork tenderloin with a lentil salad that he found, to his utmost surprise, to be extremely tasty. It wasn't quite hitting the spot the way his rich meals usually did but that would be rectified by the cheeses he liked to finish his meals with.

She lifted her eyes from her plate to his and gave a dreamy sigh. 'It's…perfect. I'm still rather overawed, to be honest.'

'As long as you are happy with it that is all that matters.' He reached for his glass of white wine. Freya, as usual, had stuck to water, the wine glass laid out for her as usual remaining empty.

'I am.' She looked, if not happy, then more content than he had ever seen her. Her time spent in her new studio seemed to have freed something inside her, all her hostility towards him gone.

'*Bien*. I hope you are as happy with the houses my employee has found for you. I've had him searching for an apartment in Madrid…' he found himself almost choking at the word '…and a house in London as per the terms of our contract. He has narrowed them down to a choice of five for each. I will forward the email with all the details to you later.'

'Thank you.'

'I assume you will want to view your preferred ones?'

'Just the London ones. The Madrid apartment is only going to be somewhere for me to sleep so don't bother with anything fancy as it will be a waste.'

The relief at this was dimmed by what it represented. If she only intended to use the Madrid apartment as a base to rest her head, what did that mean for the London house?

'I have appointments in Greece on Friday but we can fly over on Saturday. Tell me which ones you like the look of and I will get Giles to book viewings.'

He waited for her to respond, his sharp eyes noting she was rubbing the napkin between her fingers.

'Is something wrong?' he asked when her silence continued.

She pulled her lips in together, colour heightening across her cheekbones, then took a number of deep breaths.

'Freya?'

'Can I have a glass of wine, please?' she said quietly. 'There is something I need to tell you.'

Apprehension filling him, he took the bottle from the ice bucket and filled her glass.

She took a large sip then set the glass on the table, clutching the stem in her hand.

Then she took another deep breath and squared her shoulders before squaring her jaw. 'My mother is ill. The house in London is not for me. It's for her. For both of them.'

Now Benjamin was the one to take a long drink of his wine.

'What is wrong with her?' he asked, already knowing from her tone and the serious hue reflecting from her eyes that it was not good.

He watched the signs of her faltering composure, the fluttering of the hand not clinging to her glass, the rapid rise and fall of her chest, the movement of her throat.

'She has a rare degenerative neurological disease that affects muscle movement. There is no cure.'

Banging immediately set off in his head. 'No cure…?'

'It's terminal,' she supplied matter-of-factly but with the slightest cracking of her voice on the final syllable.

Benjamin swore under his breath, a clammy feeling crawling over his skin.

'I want her to end her days in a home that has space and with a garden she can sit out in and listen to the birds and feel the breeze on her face.'

'I understand that,' he said heavily.

Her smile when she met his eyes was sad. 'I know you do.'

His heart ached in a way it hadn't done in seven years, the beats dense and weighty. 'Is there *nothing* that can be done for her?'

'There has been a medical development in America recently, a treatment that slows it down in some cases and in even rarer cases reverses some of the symptoms. Not permanently though. No one has found a permanent reversal.'

Everything suddenly became clear.

Pushing his unfinished plate to one side, Benjamin rubbed his temples. 'That's why you married me. To pay for the treatment.'

'Yes.' She shuffled her chair back a little and stretched her neck. 'It's not authorised for use in the UK because it's unproven and incredibly expensive. The money I get from our marriage is to pay for her to have a doctor fly to England every month and administer it to her in a private hospital. It won't keep her alive for ever, but it might give us an extra year or two, and they could be good years for her. The money Javier paid after we signed the contract on our engagement has paid for two cycles of it. Her speech and breathing have improved a little and she's got slightly more movement in her hands. It's stopped it getting any worse. For now,' she added with a sigh. 'None of us are stupid enough to think it will hold it off for ever.'

'Miracles do happen.' But his words were automatic. Miracles were something he had stopped believing in during his mother's battle with cancer.

Freya shook her head ruefully. 'Not for my mother. When the treatment is developed more in the future they might be able to fully reverse it and hold the symptoms off permanently but that will come way too late for Mum. We're just grateful that she's receiving *any* benefit from it. She's already proving to be one of the lucky rare ones.'

Lucky to be trapped in a failing body with no hope of lasting longer than a year or two?

'And now I can give them a home too.' She paused and blinked rapidly. 'I never told them. I was scared to jinx it. They've wanted to move for years. They live in a two-bedroom third-floor flat in a building with communal gardens that are used by the local drug addicts. They're basically prisoners in their own home now.'

'We can fly to London tomorrow to look at the houses.'

She blinked again, this time in astonishment. 'Don't you have to work?'

'Some things are more important. We can fly out after breakfast.'

He saw her throat move. 'That is incredibly generous of you. Thank you.'

'If I had known why you wanted a house I would have made it a priority.'

'I didn't think you'd care.'

He winced at her unflinching honesty. 'I cannot say I blame you for that.'

'It wasn't just that I didn't think you'd care,' she said in a softer, more reflective tone. 'I'm not good at opening up in any capacity, especially about such personal matters.'

'Your dance does your talking for you.'

For a moment she just stared at him, eyes glistening before she jerked a nod. 'It's the only way I know how. I find it hard opening up at the best of times. I didn't want to share something so personal with someone I hated.'

He hesitated before asking, 'Does that mean you no longer hate me?'

'I don't know.' She took a sip of her wine. 'You're not the complete monster I thought you were. You had your reasons to do what you did. I feel a certain…kinship, I think the word is. I understand what you were going through when your mother was ill because I'm living it myself. You signed a contract without reading the terms and conditions; I signed a contract pledging my life in exchange for an extension to hers. If that makes me a gold-digger then I can live with that.'

He closed his eyes briefly and breathed heavily. 'You are not a gold-digger. I should never have called you that.'

She shrugged, her shoulders tight. 'It doesn't matter. You could have called me worse.'

He'd thought worse. When he recalled the things he had thought about her he wanted to retch. She had married him to extend her mother's life. He had married her out of vengeance against his oldest friend.

'It does matter. I know what it's like to watch someone you love slowly lose their life. You will do anything to help them and give them more time.'

Their eyes met. Something, a flash of understanding, passed between them that, like a switch being flicked, darkened and deepened.

He blew out a long puff of air and got to his feet. 'We'll make an early start tomorrow. Get some sleep and I will see you in the morning.'

There was a smattering of confusion in her returning stare before she nodded. 'See you in the morning.'

CHAPTER TWELVE

THE FAMILIAR RATTLE of the cattle grid woke Freya from the sleep she had fallen into. Covering a yawn with her hand, she cast a quick glance at Benjamin beside her. His face was glued to his laptop as it had been since they'd got into the car from the heliport. The seductive looks and words were a thing of the past.

She felt as if she had lived a thousand lives in the past two days.

They had spent the day in London as he had promised. He'd organised everything. A stretched Mercedes had met them at the airport with Giles, Benjamin's assistant who had been tasked with house-hunting for her, in attendance, and then driven them to all the shortlisted houses.

She had fallen in love with the second property, which ticked every box she'd wanted and more.

Best of all, it was unoccupied.

Benjamin had made an immediate cash offer and got the wheels put into motion for the quickest of quick sales. Her parents could move in that coming weekend. Benjamin was going to take care of everything for them.

He had then taken her to the tower block her parents lived in but had refused to come in with her.

'This is a home you are providing for them,' he had explained without looking at her. 'It is better they hear it from you. I will only be a distraction.'

'But they will want to meet you,' she had said, surprising herself with her own argument. 'They will want to thank you.'

His nose had wrinkled before he'd looked at the building she had called home for the first eleven years of her life.

'There will be plenty of time for us to meet in the future. I have things to organise. Giles will see you in. Take all the time you need. There is no rush.'

She had then spent a wonderful couple of hours with her parents, finally having the confidence to tell them they were going to be able to move out of the flat that had become their prison into a house of their own, and that her new husband was in the process of getting a team together to help them make the move and would be providing them with an unlimited credit card to furnish their new home to their liking.

Javier had been prepared to buy them a home as part of the contract. He had known about their situation for two whole months.

Benjamin had known about it for less than a day and had already gone above and beyond his contractual obligations.

And yet there was a distance between them that had never been there before. He had hardly looked her in the eye all day. And it had been a long day, dinner eaten in silence on the return flight back to Provence.

'It is late,' he said as the car came to a stop in the courtyard. 'I am going to call it a night.'

'You're going to bed?' she asked, surprised at the stab of disappointment cutting through her stomach.

'I have a few more calls to make and then I will sleep. I'll see you in the morning. *Bonne nuit.*'

And that was that.

The man who had devoured her with his eyes, who had insisted they would sleep together every night they were under the same roof, would be sleeping in his own bed without her for the second night in a row.

Feeling nauseous although she had no idea why, Freya carried her heavy legs up the stairs.

It *was* late. Maybe she should get some sleep too.

But after taking a shower and brushing her teeth she

knew sleep was a long way off. There was a knotted feeling in her stomach that time was only making worse.

All she could think was that Benjamin was bored of her after only one night together.

Or, worse, had her confession about her family background turned him off? Had seeing the place she had been raised tainted her somehow too? Did he see her differently now he knew her polish and poise had been taught and were not inherent in her?

And why did her heart hurt so much to think all this?

She shouldn't care. She should be thankful his desire for her had been turned off. Wasn't that the safety she craved where all her passion and emotions were expressed in her dance?

The knot in her stomach tightened, pulling at her chest, and she paced her room until she could take no more and, uncaring that it was the middle of the night, bolted out of her quarters.

Thoughts and questions crowding her head, her heart throbbing, she hurried up the stairs to her studio and threw her dressing gown on the floor. Not wanting to waste time putting on tights and a leotard, she pulled a black, calf-length floating exercise dress off the rail in the studio cupboard and shrugged it over her head.

The pointe shoes she had softened into reasonable comfort the day before were on the floor where she had left them and still had plenty of wear left. She put them on, tied the ribbons, then put the sound system on shuffle and settled herself by her barre.

Inhaling deeply through her nose, she then exhaled through her mouth and repeated ten times, determined to clear her mind while stretching her limbs and increasing her blood flow.

But as she made the familiar comforting movements, her eyes drifted around the studio.

Everything that had been done to create this had been with one focus in mind—her needs. The light she needed. The height she needed. The space she needed. Nothing had been missed, nothing stinted on.

The music she had been stretching to came to an end and seconds later the opening bars to the Habanera from *Carmen* came on in its stead.

Freya paused as the wonderful score, with its seductive Spanish vibe, filled the studio.

The Habanera was the part where the immoral, wicked Carmen danced with such allure that Don José, the soldier about to arrest her, instead fell for the temptress and bedded her.

It was a most sensual of dances and, though she had danced it many times, Freya had never wriggled her shoulders at the start and imagined a real, flesh and blood man watching her and desiring her for real.

Had Carmen desired Don José when she had danced for him? Freya had always assumed not, thought of the dance as a trap to hook him in—one that obviously backfired considering he killed her at the end for loving another man—but now, as Benjamin's features shone brightly in front of her, the dance moves coming back to her, she wondered if in the heat of the moment Carmen *had* felt desire for the man she used for her own ends.

Maybe that was all it was for her and Benjamin too, a desire born through circumstance that now, in Benjamin's case, was spent.

She wished with all her heart that it were spent in herself too but it had only grown. Benjamin had made love to her and only now, as she made a series of jetés across the perfect floor, did she acknowledge the truth to herself that every part of her body ached for him to touch her and make love to her again.

She wished he were there with her right now, that she could pirouette to him and see that hunger in his eyes again.

Benjamin could hear music.

At first he'd thought he was imagining it but there was an echoing, haunting sound ringing through the chateau's thick walls, usually so still and silent in the dead of night.

He looked up at the ceiling.

Freya's studio was directly above his own quarters.

He closed his eyes.

He hadn't slept well the night before. Two bad nights' sleep had left him exhausted.

Three large Scotches in quick succession meant he should have passed out the moment his head hit the pillow but he couldn't even shut his eyes without forcing them.

He opened them again and stared at the ceiling. The heavy beat of his heart echoed in his ears and he put a hand to his bare chest in an attempt to temper it.

All he wanted was to go to her. All he wanted was to haul her into his arms and make love to her, again and again.

He'd spent the day with her avoiding her gaze, knowing that to look into those black depths would pull him back into a place he needed to keep away from.

His head was a whirl of diverging thoughts but the one that flashed loudest was that he should never have married her. If he had known about her mother and her parents' situation he would have paid her off when she'd suggested it rather than tie her into this.

Wouldn't he...?

Yes, he *would* have paid her off, he told himself forcefully. Freya hadn't pledged herself to Javier for her own greedy benefit as he had assumed. None of it had been for herself.

Why wasn't she sleeping? Her conscience was clear.

There was nothing to stop her sleeping as sweetly as he had always been able to do.

But she was awake and dancing above him.

Freya needed to dance in the same way he needed air. There was still so much to learn about her but on the very essence of who she was he had no doubts.

Dieu, he ached to see her, hold her, kiss her, touch her...

She was all he had wanted since he had seen her that first time with the sunlight pouring onto her skin.

Benjamin had pulled his trousers back on and reached his bedroom door before even realising he was out of his bed.

With long strides he climbed the stairs and opened the door to her studio.

She was at the far side by the window, moving like a graceful blur to the beats of the music.

There was only the merest glint of surprise when she caught his eye in the reflection of the walled mirror but no pause or hesitation in her movements.

She continued to dance, contorting her body and creating shapes out of her legs and arms that appeared completely natural and effortless. She'd left her hair loose and it flew around her, spinning in a perfect wheel when she spun on pointe, all the while her eyes seeming to never leave his.

And he could not tear his eyes from her.

He had never, in his entire life, been witness to anything so beautiful or seductive.

Freya didn't dance, she *was* dance; she was the emotion of the music brought to life. She was incredible.

Closer and closer she came, every fluid motion bringing her nearer to him until she jumped with her left leg fully extended and her right leg bent at the knee, creating the illusion of flight.

She landed a foot before him and sank into a bow.

Slowly she raised herself back up to stare at him with a stillness that was as elegant and stunning as her movement.

She didn't speak.

He didn't speak.

They just gazed at each other.

It felt as if her eyes were piercing right into his soul.

And then she flew at him.

At least that was how it seemed in the moment, that she had taken flight to throw her arms around his neck and her supple legs around his waist, holding and supporting herself around him without any effort.

Benjamin gazed at the perfection of her face for one more moment before all the pent-up desire and emotions inside him burst free.

Wrapping his arms tightly around her back, he crushed his lips to hers and was met with her matching hunger. Like two starving waifs finally being given a meal, they kissed greedily and possessively, his hands splaying and digging into her back, her fingers digging into the nape of his neck, fusing every part of their bodies together they could.

His arousal, a simmering feature of his life he had learned to endure since he'd stolen her out of the hotel and her hand had first slipped into the crook of his arm, burned. Everything in him burned, from the lava in his veins to the swirling molten heat of his skin.

From the heat of Freya's kisses and the tightness of her legs around him, he knew it was the same for her too.

This was a need too great and too explosive to do anything but quench. The sensual music only added to the mixture, creating the most potent chemical cocktail that, now ignited, had only one possible outcome.

With nowhere to lay her down, Benjamin carried her effortlessly to the nearest wall and slammed her against it.

Slipping a hand up the skirt of her dress, which had bunched up against the top of her toned thighs, he found her bottom deliciously bare, and pressed his palm to the damp heat of her pubis.

She gasped into his mouth and pressed against him, unhooking an arm from his neck to drop it down to his waist and the band of his trousers.

Until she dug her hand into the opening, he hadn't realised he hadn't buttoned himself up. Like her, he was naked beneath the only item of clothing he wore. She caressed him, biting into his bottom lip with her teeth before sweeping her tongue back into his mouth and kissing him harder than ever.

He grabbed her hand with his and, together, they pulled him free. With no further restrictions, all that was left was to adjust their forms against the wall until he was there, fully hard and fully ready, and thrusting up into her welcome tightness.

There was no savouring of the moment, not from either of them. The instant he was fully inside her, Freya's hand grabbed his buttocks and she was urging him on with her body and with mumbled, indecipherable words.

Their lovemaking had a primal, almost feral quality to it, he thought dimly as he thrust into her. Her nails now dug into his skin as she matched him, thrust for thrust, stroke for stroke, until the hand still on his neck suddenly grabbed at his hair and she cried out, every part of her clenching around him in a spasm that seemed to go on for ever and pulled him even tighter inside her and then he, too, could hold on no more and he let go as the most powerful climax of his life ripped through him.

Freya stretched out her leg and immediately her foot connected with something solid and warm and very, very human. Benjamin's leg.

Her languid limbs wakened properly as all that had gone

on between them through the night came back to her like a glorious cinematic masterpiece in her head.

The ghost dream had come to life. She had danced to her lover. She had danced *for* her lover.

Her *lover*.

How else could she describe him after they had come together like two people possessed?

After the explosion that had rocked them in his studio, he had carried her down to his bedroom and made love to her all over again.

And she had made love to him too.

The song birds were already singing the dawn chorus when they finally sated their hunger.

Incredibly, the familiar ache in her loins fired up again. The hunger hadn't been sated, merely put to sleep.

She could handle this, she thought as she snuggled closer to him. A huge arm hooked around her and in an instant she was wrapped back in the wonderful comfort of Benjamin's strong body, his warm skin smelling of them and the heat they had created between these sheets.

This was no big deal. This was merely two compatible people who happened to be married unlocking their desire for each other.

It didn't mean anything. It didn't affect anything. The rest of their contract would stay the same.

Nothing else would change because of it.

It couldn't. She wouldn't let it.

She would not let these wonderful feelings erupt into anything more.

The risks were far too great.

'No, no, no, *jeté* to the *left*! Freya, *concentrate*!'

'I'm sorry.' Freya stopped moving and put her hands on her hips, leaning forward and breathing in deeply. She was exhausted. The rehearsal had started off badly and gone downhill from there. And it was all her fault.

Mikael, the dancer she was supposed to be *jeté*-ing to before pirouetting into his arms, glared at her. The four members of the *corps de ballet* merely looked embarrassed.

The harassed choreographer sighed. 'Let's take a fifteen-minute break. Come back with heads screwed on.'

Freya went straight to her dressing room. She drank some water and ate a banana, then went back to the studio determined to get it right.

The rest of the rehearsal was even worse. She couldn't even get the basic footwork right and these were moves she had been doing since she was a small child. It was as if her feet no longer connected to her brain and her arms were made of modelling clay.

She returned to her apartment knowing one more bad rehearsal could mean her understudy being given the role of Vicky.

This was a role she had coveted for so long and she was in danger of losing it. Every dancer had a bad day but this had been a bad week, following on from a week that had been only marginally better.

Her dancing was deteriorating and she could not for the life of her think why.

She had one more day to get through and then she had a day off. If she could get through the next day's rehearsals she would then have time away to recharge and refocus her mind.

She checked her phone as she ran a bath and found a message from her father, his daily update.

She read it and closed her eyes with the first smile to cross her lips all week.

At least here was some good news. Her mother had wiggled all the fingers of her left hand and hummed along to a song on the radio.

Her mood managed to lighten even more before plunging when her phone rang in her hand and Benjamin's name flashed on the screen.

'Bonsoir, ma douce.' The rich seductiveness of his tone sent tingles of sensation curling across her spine.

'Hi.'

'Is everything okay?' he asked.

'Yes. All good.'

She would not admit her body was forgetting the basic dance moves that had been ingrained in her before she'd learned her times tables. As far as Benjamin was concerned, everything was fine.

He hated her being back in Madrid. It was a simple, mostly unspoken truth between them and she knew it was a proprietorial thing for him. Benjamin hated his wife working for his enemy.

And she hated it too. Mercifully, she hadn't seen anything of Javier or Luis since she had arrived back to work but she found herself constantly on alert for them, which she knew was stupid as Javier especially rarely bothered to grace them with his presence.

Mercifully too, the new building the company had moved into, adjacent to the new theatre that was undergoing its finishing touches, meant her fellow dancers had been too busy exploring and comparing to bother with her. Freya jilting Javier for Benjamin was already old news. There had been the odd snide comment, of course, but the kind she had inured herself against over a decade ago. It grieved her deeply that Sophie had unexpectedly quit the company and returned to England but what she hated the most, and which she also would never admit, was that her mind was almost completely occupied with Benjamin.

Freya had known that keeping a lid on her feelings for him would be hard, especially after they had become proper lovers, but she had never imagined the strength it would take to keep that lid on. He called her every night, and she would listen to the rich honeyed tones with an ache in her heart that had slipped into her every pore.

She did *not* miss him, she told herself constantly. And she did *not* count down the hours until she would be with him again.

But the precipice she had seen her mother edging towards if she didn't accept his proposal was now inching towards her. She could feel it with every minute spent with him and every communication between them, a drop of unimaginable depths waiting to swallow her whole if she couldn't keep her feet rooted to the ground and that lid on, even if she needed to pull it down with both hands gripped tightly to it.

The days they had spent together as lovers before she had left for Madrid had been the best days of her life.

They had spent most of them in bed, yes, but they had enjoyed themselves out of it too. He had joined her in her studio while she practised, making calls and sending emails with her pirouetting around him. They had eaten their separate meals together and even shared more of the same meals. They had shared stories of their childhoods, very different but fascinating to the other.

And then they had flown to England together and met her parents in their new house.

He had been welcomed with open arms and even wider hearts.

And then she had gone back to her life and found everything had changed.

She had changed.

'*Bien.* I just want to check you have no late rehearsals tomorrow.' It was only when she heard him speak after days apart that she heard the thickness of his accent when he spoke her language. She never heard it when she was with him any more.

'Not that I've been told.'

'*Excellente*. I will get my driver to collect you at six-thirty.'

A few minutes later, Freya disconnected the call and climbed into the huge bath.

Then she laid herself down until she was fully submerged and held her breath for as long as she could.

CHAPTER THIRTEEN

FREYA RAN A brush through her hair a final time and laid it on her dresser feeling much better in herself. Rehearsals the day before had gone much better. Today, after a night of making love to Benjamin, she had taken herself to her studio to practise her solo dance and found herself foot-perfect. Not a single step or movement had been wrong, and she had dressed for their night out feeling as if a weight had been lifted.

Now she could enjoy a meal out with her husband without any cares.

Selecting a red button-down shirt-dress that fell to her knees, a thick black rope belt hooked around her waist and a pair of high strappy silver sandals, she then dabbed perfume behind her ears and on her wrists, applied a little gloss to her lips and considered herself done.

She found Benjamin in the half-inside, half-outside living room where he had first told her she would have to marry him, talking on his phone.

He got to his feet when he saw her and ended his call.

Tilting his head, he studied her with sparkling eyes.

'Madame Guillem, you look good enough to eat.'

The feeling is entirely mutual, she thought but didn't say.

Charcoal trousers, a shirt only a shade lighter and un-buttoned at his throat, and a Prussian blue jacket gave him a dangerously debonair appearance.

'Where are we going?' she asked.

'I've booked us a table at Le Cheval D'Or.'

'Where's that?'

'A restaurant near Nice. It's about half an hour's drive away.'

When they stepped out in the courtyard Benjamin smiled to see the furrow on Freya's brow at the car waiting for them, a bright yellow convertible with the roof down.

She ran her fingers along the paintwork and then suddenly that striking face was grinning widely. 'What a beautiful car.'

'It's a 1949 Buick Roadmaster Riviera Convertible. I bought it at auction four months ago.'

She stepped all around it, examining it with the same reverence he'd first studied it. When she was done, he opened the passenger door for her.

Her brow furrowed again. 'Where's your driver?'

He grinned. 'Tonight, *ma douce*, *I* am your driver.'

She matched his grin and got in.

Minutes later, they were out of his estate and speeding through the sweeping roads to their destination, Freya's hair sweeping around her.

'This is amazing,' she said, bursting into laughter, a sound he had never heard from her before.

As incredible as it was to believe, he had never heard Freya laugh until that moment.

Her joy was as infectious as it was heart-warming and he laughed with her. 'Isn't it?'

Not much more was said but every time he looked at her she would turn her eyes to him and they would give identical grins.

Benjamin was big enough to admit he was greedy about his time with her. Since she had returned to Madrid he guarded their time together zealously. He wanted her to be happy but seven hours in her studio on her one whole day off?

He'd resented ballet enough for stealing all his mother's attention while she was alive and now he found himself with a wife whose passion for it would more commonly be known as an addiction.

He reflected that next week she had two whole days off. He'd already rearranged his diary to free his time so they didn't have to waste any of it.

Tonight he had deliberately booked a table in a restaurant rather than dine at home as they usually did. Selfishly, he wanted all her attention.

So far his ploy was working.

Ten minutes from the restaurant and the first clear view of the Mediterranean appeared; he looked at her and laughed again to see her head flopping on her shoulder.

'You're falling asleep?' he asked with faux incredulity.

She straightened and gave a yawn that turned into muffled giggles. 'Sorry… Wow! That view is incredible.'

All sleepiness deserted her in an instant as Freya took in the glamorous sight in front of them, so different from the peaceful views that surrounded Benjamin's chateau but equally beautiful in its own right.

But none of those views were a patch on the masculine beauty of the man who sat beside her, driving a car that wouldn't look out of place in one of those glamourous films from the Cary Grant era. It suited Benjamin perfectly, far more than any modern-day Bugatti or Ferrari, cars she knew he had in his underground garage.

The wind whipping through her hair and the feel of the sun soaking into her face had rid her of the last of that godawful tightness that had been compressing her all week.

This was *fun*.

She honestly could not remember the last time she had done anything that constituted fun. Maybe the theme park she and Sophie had visited on one of their days off on their European tour last year? They hadn't gone this year. Sophie had begged off with stomach cramps and Freya hadn't wanted to go without her.

She wished she knew what was wrong with her oldest

and closest friend and why she had quit the company so abruptly, but Sophie had clammed up.

Soon the roads became even narrower and steeper and they drove into a town with medieval architecture, coming to a stop outside a high monastic stone building with a red-tiled roof and pillars.

Immediately a valet appeared, opening the passenger door for her and helping her out, then zipping to Benjamin's side. Benjamin pressed the keys in the valet's hand then turned to Freya with a grin. 'Ready?'

'Ready.'

Stone walls and floors greeted them, along with high stained-glass windows and a high vaulted ceiling. A low buzz of chatter rang out from the other diners, all dressed in their finery, low bursts and high bursts of laughter and the most delicious smells.

They were led to a table under a window, menus presented to them by the self-important maître d' with the same reverence as if they were being presented with a first edition of a masterpiece. He then took hold of their napkins and, in turn, flicked them to open them up, his face grave as if performing an act of live art as he placed them on their laps.

Freya caught the laughter in Benjamin's eye and ducked her head down to study the menu lest she start giggling at the maître d's pomposity.

The second he left their table, they covered their mouths so the laughter they'd both been supressing came out like muffled sniggers.

'Were we supposed to applaud?' she said when she'd caught her breath, dabbing a tear of mirth with the napkin.

'I think he expected a standing ovation.'

By the time they'd ordered their food—thankfully their order was taken by one of the lowly waiters—Freya felt thoroughly relaxed and sipped her champagne with pleasure.

The food they were served was incredible, her starter of artichoke served with caviar in a lime broth possibly the best dish she had ever eaten…until their main courses were set before them and she had her first bite of her clay-cooked chicken that came with white asparagus, a rocket salad and little delicacies she didn't recognise but knew would be delicious.

'I have never seen you enjoy your food so much,' Benjamin commented as he tackled his smoked lobster. 'I must get my chef to recreate these recipes.'

'Your chef is amazing,' she protested. 'I'm just exceptionally hungry.'

'So am I.'

Her heart leapt at the gleam in his eyes and the suggestiveness of his tone, sending a hot surge of blood pumping through her.

Would this desire ever abate?

His sparkling eyes devouring her a little longer, he said, 'It is strange to see you eat a meal out without worrying over every ingredient.'

She laughed. 'I allow myself the occasional splurge. I've only had one non-healthy meal since you kidnapped me and that was on our wedding day.'

'You hardly ate any of that and I didn't kidnap you. I whisked you away with deception.'

'If it looks like a duck, walks like a duck and talks like a duck then it's safe to say it's a duck. You kidnapped me.'

'Ducks can't talk and I didn't kidnap you.'

'Okay, you stole me, then.'

'Only with your consent, and ask yourself this—who would you rather be sitting at this table with? Me or Javier?'

'You want me to answer that?'

He flashed her a grin that didn't quite meet his eyes. 'Only if the answer is me.'

It's you, every time, she almost said but cut herself off.

She couldn't lie to him but nor could she tell him the truth.

Instinct told her that to tell the truth would be to drag her even closer to the precipice that frightened her so much.

She never thought of Javier unless it was to compare him unfavourably to Benjamin.

Her brain burned to remember she had agreed to have children with him. The ball had been entirely in her court as to when it would happen so she had decided that she would wait until her biological clock started ticking, thinking by then she and Javier would have forged a friendly marriage.

She no longer believed anything of the sort. How could she when she now believed the heart she'd thought he kept hidden from view was actually missing? The way he and Luis had treated Benjamin and taken advantage of his mother's cancer for their own ends enraged her.

Benjamin's heart wasn't missing. His heart was as enormous as his ego. He was a man who did everything wholeheartedly, whether it was loving someone or hating them. When he set on a path he was relentless until he reached his destination.

They had never spoken of children. It was there in the contract though. The ball would always be in her court for that.

What kind of a father would he be? A hands-on, nappy-changing, kicking-a-ball-around-the-park dad? Or the kind of father who appointed an army of nannies and left them to it?

And why did her heart ache to imagine it...?

'You and Javier are very different people,' she said quietly, trying to be diplomatic without giving anything of her thoughts away. 'When I agreed to marry him I knew he was a cold fish but I didn't realise what a complete bastard he was. It wouldn't have changed my mind though. His proposal was just too attractive for my mother's sake.'

'And what about your sake?'

'I have dealt with colder and crueller people than Javier Casillas. You want to know real cruelty, put a hidden camera in a girls' boarding school.'

'Did you suffer a lot?'

'The other girls took an instant dislike to me. They hated everything about me. The clothes I wore, the way I spoke... even the way I held my cutlery. They took pleasure in humiliating me. Petty, nasty things. Constant name calling, stealing my stuff, tripping me in the canteen when I had a tray of food in my hand—that one was a particular favourite.'

'They hated that you were a better dancer than them?'

Her brow furrowed in surprise.

He explained his thinking with a grimace. 'You had a full scholarship. The school you went to only gives them rarely, for exceptional talents.'

She pulled a rueful face. 'If that was their reasoning then it worked. My dancing went to pieces. That first term I was the worst dancer there because they got into my head. I was an insecure bag of nerves.'

'How did you get through it?' But he already had a good idea. That iron control had started somewhere.

'At the end of the first term one of the dance teachers pulled me aside. She told me I was in danger of losing my scholarship. She also said she knew I had problems fitting in but that, unless I wanted to lose my dream, I had to rise above it and find a way to tune the noise out otherwise they would win.'

She would have been only eleven, Benjamin thought, sickened at the cruelty of children and the ineffectiveness of the adults meant to protect her.

'I took her words to heart,' Freya continued. 'I taught myself to block the noise from my head and focus only on the dance itself. I no longer sought their approval and in time I no longer wanted or needed it. By taking control of my feelings and learning to be completely single-minded, I learned how to survive.' Her face brightened a touch. 'And I did make a friend eventually. Sophie. She helped ease the loneliness but they were still the worst days of my life. If I could get through that, I can get through anything. If marrying Attila the Hun could have alleviated my mother's pain I would have married him and known I would survive it too.'

Benjamin saw so many emotions flickering in the black depths of her eyes that his heart fisted in on itself.

Their backgrounds might have them poles apart but when it came to those they loved, there was nothing either of them would not do.

Having met her parents for himself, he understood even more.

He had been struck with the warmth of their welcome, their gratitude for the home he had given them so stark it had embarrassed him.

It isn't me you need to thank, he'd wanted to tell them. *It's your daughter. She's the one who contracted herself out to marriage for you.*

He'd thought he'd been prepared for her mother's condition but it had been worse than he'd thought. She could do nothing for herself, was virtually paralysed in her failing body, totally reliant on her doting husband. And Freya said this was an improvement?

But she had that spirit in her eyes his own mother had had, a will to fight, and, he had seen whenever she had looked at her only child, fierce pride in her daughter.

Strangely, meeting Freya's father, a humble man with a huge heart, had set him thinking about his own when he so rarely thought of his own father. The only good thing his father had ever done—apart from helping create himself and his sister, even if he did say so himself—was provide maintenance to his mother once he'd left the family nest. His mother had saved all those payments, giving Benjamin his share in a lump sum when he'd turned twenty-one, money he'd used to purchase an old, run-down food-production facility.

He'd left his in-laws' home with a heavy heart, which he still hadn't shaken off.

'How can you stand working for him?' he asked.

Javier had known about her mother's condition for two months and done nothing about it other than sign promises for the future when he had his ring on Freya's finger.

Yes, he had paid for two rounds of treatment but he should have taken them out of that decrepit flat and given them somewhere decent to live.

'I don't work for him. I work for his company,' she answered. 'And it won't be for much longer.'

'Have you started looking for a new company yet?'

'I've been approached by a couple of companies.'

'You never said.'

'My career is not your concern,' she reminded him with a tight smile that immediately made his hackles rise.

'I spoke to the director of Orchestre National de Paris a few days ago,' he said. 'Their theatre has just been refurbished and the owner is in the process of creating a new ballet company.'

'I am aware of that.'

'They want you to be their Etoile.'

'What?'

'Orchestre National de Paris want you to be the star of their new ballet company. I was going to wait until the proposal was confirmed in writing before telling you but now seems the right time. Salary is negotiable and they are prepared to put a clause in your contract that allows you time off to guest star for other companies.'

Silence filled the space between them. She stared at him, totally still, her black eyes unreadable.

'Who approached who?' she asked slowly. 'You or the director?'

'Does it matter?'

'Yes.'

'The director is an old friend who I know through the Casillas brothers. The Orchestre National de Paris's intention to create its own ballet company is not a secret.'

An edge crept into her voice. 'But who approached who?'

'I called him.'

'Did you call him with the intention of pimping me out?'

Anger, already simmering in his guts, cut through him. He controlled it. Just. 'Having a conversation to get my wife a better deal with a better company is hardly pimping.'

She leaned forward ever so slightly. 'And who are you to say what is a better deal for me? Or which is the better company?'

'You are a dancer whose star is in the ascendancy. This move will help you reach the pinnacle that much more quickly.'

'And how will it look when people find out I only got the job thanks to my husband being part of the old boys' network with the director?'

'I don't know that term but I can guess what it means, and no one is going to think that because it is not true.'

'Did you not listen to a single word I just said? Everything I have achieved has been on my own merits and I have worked my toes into stumps to get where I am, without *any* help. What makes you think I need help with my career now? And who the *hell* do you think you are, interfering like this?'

'Interfering?' He was taken aback at her venom. 'I am your husband. It is my job to look out for you.'

'It is *not*. My career is entirely separate to our marriage and you have overstepped the mark hugely.'

How he kept his temper he would never know. 'I am sorry you feel I have overstepped your invisible mark but I am sick of living in a separate country to my wife. I *am* your husband. You married me and took my name. I have an apartment in Paris. Take the job and we can live there when you are working and have a proper marriage.'

There. His cards were on the table.

He stared hard at her waiting for her to respond.

'It's not an invisible mark. It's in the contract we both signed. No interference in my career.' Her voice contained the slightest of tremors.

'If you want us to stick to the contract then answer this—if I were to take advantage of the clause that said I could take a mistress, how would it make you feel?'

Her face turned the colour of chalk. Her throat moved numerous times before she whispered, 'I wouldn't try to stop you.'

'I didn't ask if you would try to stop me. I asked how it would make you feel.'

'I would accept it.'

'Accept it?' he sneered.

'I signed up for a marriage that allows us both to live an independent life and I don't want to change any of it. If I move to Paris it will be because that's what's right for my career.' She took a long sip of champagne and blew out a long puff of air before saying, 'I *do* appreciate you thinking of me. I will speak to the director of Orchestre National de Paris but I'm not going to make any promises. My career comes first, you already know that.'

Wishing he hadn't chosen to drive, Benjamin jerked a nod.

Why had he thought the outcome of this conversation would be any different?

His own parents had both put him second to their needs. Why should he think his wife would be any different?

The drive back to his chateau was a far more muted affair than the drive to the restaurant, hardly a word exchanged between them.

Twenty minutes after they'd left, right on cue, Freya had fallen asleep. A minute after that, her head fell onto his shoulder and stayed there for the final eight miles.

Benjamin had put the roof back up before setting off and, without the wind to drive it away, her sultry scent filled the enclosed space cocooning them. It was a scent that slowly worked its way into his senses and pushed out the anger that had gripped him at her uncompromising attitude.

As he brought the Buick to a stop, her face made a movement and then she opened her eyes.

She didn't look surprised to find her head resting on his shoulder.

'I fell asleep again,' she whispered, making no attempt to move away from him.

'You did.'

Her black eyes stayed on his, darkening and swirling. And then she did move, shifting slightly to bring her face closer to his and to brush her lips against his...

Much later, naked and replete in her arms, Benjamin reflected that if fantastic sex was the most he got out of this marriage then he would be a luckier man than most.

If Freya wanted to stick to the exact letter of that damned contract, then so be it. From now on he would stick to the damned thing too.

CHAPTER FOURTEEEN

FREYA WANTED TO scream until all the fear and frustration that held her in its grip was ripped from her.

She settled on crawling into a ball in the corner of the living room and rocking.

She'd thought she'd cracked the role of Vicky.

That afternoon she had walked into the practice room to overhear a seething Mikael shouting at the choreographer that he would not 'partner someone who cares so little for the dance'.

'We can't replace her,' the choreographer had replied with the exasperation of someone who had already had that conversation. 'Her face is *everywhere*. The opening night is a sell-out because of her.'

'She is a terrible dancer.'

'Usually she is the best…'

And then they had noticed her standing at the door, aghast at what she had just heard.

'Freya…' the choreographer had begun, but Mikael had cut him off to barge past her saying loudly for anyone passing to hear, 'You find your dancing feet or you find a new partner. I will not be associated with this crap.'

She couldn't even blame him. She would feel the same if she were lumbered with a partner who had lost all co-ordination and couldn't remember the simplest moves in their dances.

In her studio at the chateau she was foot-perfect.

She *did* know the dances. She knew the whole choreography for the whole production. She just could not translate what was in her head to her feet.

So frightened had she become about it that she'd paid a

private doctor to test her for the cruel disease slowly killing her mother.

The fast-tracked results had come back negative.

Whatever was wrong with her was psychological not physiological.

The problem was in her head.

Impulse had her leaping to her feet and flying to her phone.

She would call Benjamin,

Since she had virtually ruined their evening out together by reminding him of the terms of their contract, his daily calls when she was in Madrid had reduced to nothing.

She hadn't meant to anger him but he was breaking the terms of their contract, interfering when he had no business to.

That interference had terrified her but not half as much as his reasons for it had.

He *knew* she couldn't give him a marriage of true spouses. He'd never wanted a true marriage either. This was a marriage he had backed her into a corner to wed herself to and now he was trying to change all the rules. She had given him her name. She had given him her body when she had never thought she would give that to *anyone*. Hadn't he taken enough already?

Why did he have to push things when the career she kept such tight control of was already spinning away from her faster than she could pirouette? And to threaten to take a mistress…?

She would not think about that.

But he *had* called her the other morning as she'd been locking her apartment door to go to work, checking if she would be available to accompany him to a business dinner on her next days off.

She'd found the mere sound of his beautiful voice soothing and that morning's practice had been the best of the whole week.

'Is something the matter?' he asked without preamble when he answered.

'No,' she denied automatically. 'What makes you ask?'

'You have never called me before.'

'Oh. I just wanted…' *To hear your voice*. 'To check what I should wear to your business dinner.'

'I would never presume to tell you what to wear, *ma douce*. Come dressed as Carabosse if you want.'

She disconnected the call with ice in her veins.

Carabosse was the wicked fairy godmother in *The Sleeping Beauty*.

The faint sound of music seeped through the ceiling and into Benjamin's office.

It was a sound that wrenched at him, the sound of his wife under his roof but hidden away from him.

On the nights they were together she made love to him with abandon but the days they were apart she treated him with indifference. She never called him or messaged him or made any effort to keep in touch. Her one call to him had been for advice on an outfit. As if he knew anything about women's fashion.

He knew his reaction had been harsh but when he'd seen her name flash up on his phone for the first time in almost seven weeks of marriage, he'd been gripped by fear for her.

Why else would she call unless there was something wrong?

His wife wanted him for two things. Money for her family and sex for herself. As a husband he was surplus to requirements, a fact he was finding harder to deal with as time passed rather than easier.

Come the morning she would be up and showered by

six, ready to return to her life in Madrid, the life she refused to include him in.

It should not smart. This was what he'd signed up for. Two separate lives.

But it did.

There was a tap on his office door.

Immediately he straightened in his chair and pressed a key on his computer to spring the unused screen back to life.

'Entrez.'

To his surprise, it was his wife who stepped inside.

'Do you have a minute?' she asked quietly.

She was wearing the black practice dress she'd worn when he had made love to her in her studio for the first time. Hair had sprung free from the loose bun she had pulled it back into, her whole appearance more dishevelled than he had ever seen her be.

The usual stab of lust filled his loins to know that beneath her dress she was completely naked...

He gritted his teeth and turned his attention to his computer screen. 'One moment.'

He used the time to compose himself.

Freya had never graced his office with her presence before.

'What can I do for you?' he asked after making her wait a little longer than was strictly necessary.

She had taken the opportunity to perch herself on his leather sofa, leaning forward with her elbows on her thighs and her hands clasped together.

'I want to ask you a favour.'

'Then ask.'

The black eyes held his before her shoulders dropped and she said, 'I know this is a big ask but will you come to the opening performance on Saturday?'

'I would rather swim with sharks than set foot in a theatre owned by those two bastards.'

'I know you would. I'm not asking this lightly but I could really do with the support.'

He made sure to keep his tone amiable. 'Show me where in the contract it says I have to support you in any way that isn't financial and I will abide by it.'

'I didn't have to go to your business dinner last week.'

'That is hardly the same thing.'

'Please. Benjamin, this is the biggest night of my life.'

'If it is support you require, Javier will be there. I am sure he will be glad to lend his support to you.'

'I would rather swim with sharks than have his support,' she said with a shaky laugh, her words clearly intended as a joke to defuse the tension filling the office.

It had the opposite effect.

'And how would I know that?' he asked silkily.

Her brow furrowed. 'Know what?'

He drummed his fingers on his desk. 'That you wouldn't want his support. I know nothing of your life outside this chateau. I know nothing of what you do in Madrid. You keep me excluded from it.'

'There's nothing to tell. I go to work, I come home. That's it. That's my life in Madrid.'

'I only have your word for that.'

The furrow turned into grooves. 'What are you implying?'

'You're a clever woman. You can work it out.'

Comprehension glinted in her eyes. 'You're being ridiculous. Do I cross-examine you about your life when we're apart?'

'I spent weeks hoping you would and now I find I do not care that you don't. You are happy to take my money and share my bed but God forbid I want to spend time with you outside our contracted hours or deviate from that contract in any form whatsoever. I had few expectations of what our marriage would be like and the reality is beyond the lowest of them. You are uncompromising and selfish.'

Her mouth dropped open, angry colour staining her face and neck. 'You have the nerve to call me selfish when you *stole* me from another man out of revenge?'

'That *man* and his brother stole over two hundred million euros from me.' The reins of his temper he'd been clinging to finally snapped and he got to his feet, put his hands on his desk and glowered at her. 'You know exactly what they did and now you want me to spend a night under the same roof as them?'

Her entire frame shook, her fingers grasping the material of her dress as if she would rip it to pieces. 'No, I want you to support me. I want you to put *your* selfish, vindictive nature to one side for one night and be there for me.'

'Why do you want my support?' he sneered. 'You don't even want my company. When you're here on your days off you hide yourself away in that damned studio for hours on end.'

'I'm spending hours in there because right now it's the only place I can dance in and remember what I'm supposed to be doing!' Her voice had risen in pitch and she dropped her hold on her dress to clutch at the bundle of hair on the back of her head. 'My dance has gone to pot. My partner hates me, the choreographer is about to have a nervous breakdown and for some reason this chateau is the only place I find my body doing what it's supposed to do. I'm not hiding away from you up there. I'm trying to turn off the noise in my head. I'm terrified that on Saturday night I'm going to step onto the stage and find my feet turned to lead. I'm fighting for my career and you're calling me selfish when all I'm asking is for you to put your vendetta to one side for one night and be there for me. You *owe* me, Benjamin.'

'I do not owe you anything. How long has your dance been suffering?'

'Since I went back to Madrid.'

He stared at her, his heart hardening to stone. 'That's over six weeks. You didn't bother to share any of your worries with me before so why should I care now?'

The coil that had been stretching and stretching the longer this awful conversation had gone on finally snapped and with it the last of Freya's dignity.

Jumping to her feet, she yanked the ruffle holding her bun in place and threw it onto the floor.

'You should care because this is all your fault!' she shouted. '*You've* done this to me. You!'

'How am I responsible for your failure to remember your moves?'

'Because you are! You wanted to know why I was a virgin? Well, this is why! It was the last thing of myself that I could keep for myself, the only thing that wasn't public property. I saw how passion and sex worked, the jealousy and the bitterness, how some dancers threw away their careers because they became blinded and I was scared to open myself up to that. I've worked too hard and my family have made too many sacrifices for me to allow emotions into my life that would distract me from my dance but I had no *idea* how bad it could be. You've got in my head and I can't get you out and it's affecting *everything*! I can only remember the moves properly when I'm here in the chateau with you. If I'm going to have any chance of getting through the performance on Saturday I need…'

'Ask someone else,' he cut in coldly.

'There is no one else!' Fat tears sprang out of her eyes. 'I'm scared, Benjamin. I know you think I'm uncompromising but I don't know how to be any other way. It's the only way I've been able to survive this life. I'm not good at asking for help but I'm asking you because...'

Freya took a deep breath and finally spoke the truth of what lived in her heart, a truth that no amount of denial or putting her fingers in her ears to drown out the noise could deny any longer. 'I need you, Benjamin. I need you. Just you. Even if Mum and Dad and Sophie could all be there I would still need you. So please, I am begging you, for one night, please, put your vendetta aside and be there for me.'

The tightness of his jaw softened, the tight white line he'd pulled his lips into loosening.

And then Freya looked into his eyes and found nothing but enmity.

'*Non.*'

'No?'

'*Non.* I will not be used as an emotional crutch. If it is physical support to retain the dance moves you require I suggest you speak to your choreographer about getting help. If it is emotional support you need then you will have the entire audience on your side and willing you to do well, but I will not be there and I will not be a part of it.'

He spoke as if discussing how to repair a broken car.

The tears that had leaked out of her eyes dried up as comprehension struck home.

Just as she had finally accepted her feelings for him had gone way beyond her control came the stark truth. She had only ever been a tool for him to hurt Javier with.

He didn't care about her.

Her heart splintering into a thousand pieces, fury suddenly cut through the agony and she was filled with the need to hurt him back, to see those stony features flinch and make him feel a fraction of her pain; pain that *he'd* caused.

Right then she hated him more than she'd thought it was possible to hate a living being.

'How many times have you asked me if I would have preferred to have married Javier? I can tell you the answer now. I wish I *had* married him. At least I knew he was a cold emotionless bastard from the off.'

But he didn't flinch. There was not a flicker of emotion to be seen in the icy eyes staring back at her.

He lowered himself back into his seat and folded his arms across his chest.

'Get out.'

She stormed to the door. 'With pleasure.'

'No, I mean get out for good. Pack your things and leave.'

'Are you serious?'

'*Oui, ma douce*, more serious than you could ever comprehend. You are not welcome in my home any more. I should have left you alone to marry Javier. That would have been the best revenge on him, to let him spend his life with Carabosse.'

For an age they stared at each other, all the loathing that had been there at the beginning of their relationship brought back to life for its dying gasps.

'You need to let it go,' she said in as hard a tone as she could muster. 'This vendetta is not going to destroy the Casillas brothers, it's going to destroy you. It's already destroyed your soul.'

Then she walked out of the office, slamming the door behind her.

She was opening the door to her quarters when she heard the most enormous crash ring out from his.

She didn't pause to worry what it could be.

By the time she'd shoved as much of her possessions as she could into her cases, a car and driver were waiting for her in the courtyard.

As she was driven out of the estate she didn't look back.

* * *

Only through iron will did Freya make it through the dress rehearsal.

Her performance was not perfect, not by any stretch of the imagination, but Mikael had only screamed in her face once so the improvement was there.

But she wasn't feeling it. She heard the music but it didn't find her soul the way it always used to do.

Had she lost her soul?

That was a question she had asked herself countless times the last few days.

She had accused Benjamin of having lost his. Had the deal she'd made with the devil caused her to lose hers too?

If he really were the devil then why had he transferred ten million euros into her account the day after he'd thrown her out of his chateau?

Her instinct had been to transfer it straight back but she'd resisted, having the frame of mind to remember her mother.

She had been who he'd transferred the money for. Not Freya.

Benjamin would never let her mother suffer out of spite for Freya because, fundamentally, he was a decent man.

A decent man who had been crossed by his closest friends.

She had asked him to sit in the theatre owned by the men who had caused so much damage to him, when she knew how much he hated them.

She lay back on the huge bed he had never seen let alone shared with her and put a hand to her chest to still her racing heart, her thought drifting to Vicky Page, the role she would perform to the public for the first time tomorrow night. *The Red Shoes* was a fabulous, iconic production but Freya had spent so long learning the choreography and then frantically working to retain it that the storyline itself had passed her by.

Or had she wilfully blocked it out because of the parallels with her own life…?

The story, in its essence, was about ambition. In it, Vicky, a ballerina starring in her first lead role, finds herself torn, forced to choose between love and her career.

Freya had chosen career over everything since before she had developed breasts.

Vicky chose love.

Vicky made the wrong choice.

Freya feared she had made the wrong choice too.

She had fought against letting Benjamin into her heart from the beginning because the danger had been there right from the very first look between them in Javier's garden. She had pushed against it and fought and fought but all that fight had been for nothing.

Everything she had feared about marrying Benjamin had come to bear. That pull she had felt towards him from that very first glance had grown too strong. Without him she had become untethered, as if her anchor had been sliced away and she were drifting out to sea without a way of steering herself back to land.

If it looked like a duck, talked like a duck and walked like a duck then it was a duck. That was what she had said to him.

'Ducks can't talk,' he'd retorted.

No, ducks couldn't talk, but fools could fall in love even when it was the very worst thing they should do, and she was the biggest fool of all.

Benjamin hadn't just stolen her body, he'd stolen her heart.

She didn't just need him. She loved him.

She'd fallen in love with every vengeful, cruel, generous, thoughtful part of him and to deny it any longer would be like denying the duck its existence.

And now her greatest fear about falling in love had come to bear too. Her dancing had gone to pieces. That was why the music no longer worked its magic in her soul, she realised. She'd given her heart and soul to Benjamin.

The music no longer worked its magic without the man who thought she was the reincarnation of the wicked Carabosse.

CHAPTER FIFTEEN

BENJAMIN CLICKED HIS pen moodily. He'd read the news article spread out on the table before him so many times he could recite it.

A burst of something suddenly pummelled him and he grabbed the offending newspaper, scrunched it into a tight ball and threw it on the floor at the exact moment one of his maids appeared to clear away his breakfast coffee.

She looked at him for a moment then walked straight back out again.

He didn't blame her. He hadn't been in the best of moods lately and was aware of it affecting his entire household.

That didn't stop him getting up from his seat and kicking the ball of paper.

He would tell Pierre he no longer needed to send someone into town to collect him a newspaper any more. Who even read their news in this old-fashioned format any more anyway? It was all there on the Internet, news from all corners of the globe available at his fingertips.

If he stopped getting it he could avoid all news about the arts. There would be no danger of him turning a page and seeing a news article about the grand opening of Compania de Ballet de Casillas's new theatre that night. There would be no danger of him turning the page to be greeted with his estranged wife's striking face staring at him, *the* face of Compania de Ballet de Casillas.

The face of the ballet company owned by the two men he hated. The face he could not expel from his mind even though he refused to think about her. He'd had every last trace of her removed from the chateau and her studio door locked.

How dared she ask such a thing of him? She wanted him to put his vendetta aside when she didn't spare two thoughts for him outside their contracted hours?

I need you.

Of course she did. Just as his mother and his two closest friends had needed him, all of whom had only ever wanted him for what he represented or could give them and not for himself. He didn't add his father to that list. He had never pretended he needed him.

And then to say she'd wished she'd married Javier?

If that comment had been designed to cut through him it had…

Suddenly he found his legs no longer supported him and he sat back down with a thud.

Freya was used to doing everything on her own and being single-minded. She'd *had* to dedicate her life to get where she was, turning her body black and blue in the process.

She had lost control in his office.

He had only ever seen her lose control before in the bedroom.

The rest of the time she was fully in command of herself and her actions. She never did or said anything without thought.

She *had* wanted to hurt him with that comment.

Because he had hurt her, he realised with a rapidly thumping heart.

She had come to him for help. She had *begged* him.

Freya had never asked for anything from him before but his jealousy over her love and commitment to her job, his automatic disbelief that she should need him, added to his fury at what she had asked of him, had all done the talking for him. And the thinking.

She was going to star in the most important performance of her life that night and she was terrified.

His beautiful, fiercely independent wife was terrified.

But how could she need *him*?

And after everything he had done to her.

He had called her selfish but that was far from the truth. *He* was the selfish one.

He'd been wrong to think she should change habits formed over a lifetime just to suit his ego in a marriage she had never wanted to a man she had never wanted.

And he was wrong to allow his vendetta to destroy her life.

Slumping forward, he rubbed at his temples and willed the drums and cymbals crashing in his head to abate.

He willed the throbbing ache in his heart to abate too. He had been willing that since he had watched her be driven out of his life.

The press would be out in force that night and the spotlight would be on her, the heir to Clara Casillas's throne.

She would see Javier that night too. Everyone would be watching them both to see how the mercurial Javier Casillas dealt with the dancer who had dumped him for his oldest friend.

No one knew their marriage was already over.

Over…

He had thrown her out.

The banging in his head got louder, his chest tightening so hard he could no longer draw breath.

Dear God, what had he done?

Freya would have to deal with all the press attention and Javier on her own while trying to find a way to get her unwilling body to do the performance of its life.

How could he let her go through that alone?

She *did* need him.

She needed him to fix the damage he had caused with his bitter selfishness and untrammelled jealousy.

Freya sat at her dressing table applying colour to her whitened cheeks. She liked to do her own hair and make-up before a performance, liked that she had a private dressing room in which she could concentrate on nothing but her breathing. She was fully warmed up, her costume had been fitted and in two minutes she would join her fellow dancers in the wings. From the apprehension she found whenever she looked in anyone's eyes, they were as terrified about her performance as she was.

Strangely, admitting her feelings for Benjamin had had a positive effect on her psyche. It had been like removing the weights that had turned her limbs to lead. She felt sicker in her stomach but freer in her arms and legs. She could only pray it translated to the stage.

She blinked rapidly and dragged her thoughts away from Benjamin before the tears started up again.

No tears tonight, Freya, she told herself sternly.

A short knock on the door was followed by one of the stagehands poking her face into the room. 'More flowers for you.'

Her dressing room was already filled with enough bouquets to open her own florist's and this was the largest bunch by a clear margin.

Accepting them with a forced smile, she was about to put them on her dressing table when she caught the scent of lavender.

She put her nose into the bunch, closed her eyes and inhaled deeply, memories of Provence and Benjamin flooding her.

Lavender was the scent she would always associate with him. If she made it to old bones she already knew it was a scent that would still hurt her.

Her hands shook as she sniffed again and looked at the bunch properly.

Flowers of all different colours and varieties were in the beautiful bouquet but overwhelming it all were purple lavender flowers.

Placing the bouquet on her lap, she fought her fingers to open the envelope they had come with.

You are a shining star, ma douce. *Every heart will belong to you tonight but mine will beat the strongest.*

Her heart thumping, she stared around the small dressing room as if he would suddenly appear.

Did that mean he was here?

'Who gave you these?' she asked the stagehand, who was still at her door.

'A tall man in a tuxedo.'

'That narrows it down,' she said with a spurt of laughter that wasn't the least bit humorous. Every person there would be dressed in their finest clothes. 'Can you be more specific?'

The stagehand's face scrunched up in thought. 'Black hair. Thick eyebrows. Scary-looking.'

It *was* him!

Benjamin was here!

She could hardly believe it.

Joy and dread converged together to set off a new kaleidoscope of butterflies in her belly.

He was here! Here to support her. Under the same roof as the two men who had caused him such harm for *her*.

The stagehand looked at her watch. 'They're waiting for you.'

With a start, Freya realised she was in danger of missing her cue.

She ran to the wings, whispering her apologies to everyone she passed.

The orchestra played the opening beats and then it was time for the performance to begin.

From the private box Benjamin, who had paid an extortionate amount of money to procure it from a richly dressed couple in the theatre lobby, large glass of Scotch in hand, watched Freya dance on the stage with more pride than he had ever known he possessed.

Seeing her in her studio practising alone and clips on the Internet were no substitute for what he witnessed now, beauty expressed in its purest form, a witty portrayal of ambition and a heart-wrenching portrayal of love.

Freya flew as if she had wings. No one else watching would believe the pain she put her feet and limbs through to create something so magical and here, seeing it with his own eyes, he understood for the first time why she put herself through the torture.

She captivated him and, from the faces in the rows below him, she had captivated everyone else too. When the tragedy at the end occurred he doubted there was a dry eye around.

He sipped the last of his Scotch to burn away the lump that had formed in his throat.

If anything were to happen to Freya for real…

It would kill him.

She wouldn't give him a second chance, he knew that. He didn't deserve it and wouldn't ask for it. But as long as he knew she was living the life she had worked so hard for and creating the magic he had witnessed that night, he could live his own life with some form of peace.

It was only as he left the box to search for her and caught sight of Javier and Luis that he realised he hadn't thought about either of them once that evening. His entire focus had been on Freya.

This could be his moment, he thought, heart thumping, blood pumping. The opportunity to punch them both in their treacherous faces, to show his utter contempt for them with the world's press there to witness it in all its glory…

He turned on his heel and walked in the other direction.

* * *

Freya accepted the warm embraces from her colleagues and told them, one after the other, that no she wouldn't be attending the after-show party but yes, of course she would keep in touch.

The best embrace had come from Mikael, who had thrown her in the air before planting a massive kiss on her lips. 'I knew you could do it!' he had said in his thick Slavic accent. 'You were magnificent!'

And then she had set off to the privacy of her dressing room reflecting that this would be the last time she would walk these corridors. There was none of the sadness she'd expected that this chapter of her life was over.

She still didn't know what her future held dance-wise. She'd put everything on hold to get through that performance.

And she had done it!

She felt giddy. And sick.

Because the other part of her future was also an unknown.

Now the euphoria of the performance was dissipating, the relief at having Benjamin there somewhere within the packed theatre was leaving her too.

If there was any chance he had feelings for her, and her gut told her he did, she knew it wasn't enough for them. How could it be when they both wanted and needed such different things?

Their ending had been fated from their beginning. How could any union forged on hate ever end in anything but disaster?

But still she longed to see him.

Where was he?

Would he seek her out?

She had no idea how she would react or what she would say if he did.

Her heart sank to find her dressing room empty of everything but the dozens and dozens of bunches of flowers. They would be forwarded to her apartment in the morning.

By the time she'd stripped her costume and make-up off and donned a pair of skinny jeans and a black shirt her heart had fallen to her feet.

He hadn't sought her out.

Unnoticed by anyone, she slipped out of the theatre and hailed a taxi.

The short journey to her apartment took for ever.

Had she imagined the note from Benjamin? If she hadn't then where was he? Why had he not come to find her?

So lost in her desolate thoughts was she that when she stepped out of the elevator across from her apartment, she almost didn't register the figure sitting on the floor by her door.

The keys she had in her hand ready to let herself in almost slipped through her fingers.

Benjamin lifted his head and stared at the woman he had been waiting for.

He got to his feet while she walked slowly towards him. Her face didn't give anything away but her eyes…they were filled with a thousand different emotions.

'I apologise for leaving the theatre without seeing you,' he said, breaking the silence. 'Javier and Luis were there. I didn't want to create a scene so thought it best to leave before anything could happen. Please, can I come in?'

She inhaled then nodded and unlocked the door with a shaking hand.

'Can I get you a drink?' she asked politely, no longer looking at him.

Grateful that her first words to him weren't of the *get the hell out* variety, he answered with equal politeness. 'If it isn't too much trouble.'

'Wine?'

'You have alcohol?'

Her gaze darted to his. The glimmer of a smile quirked on her lips. 'I had a glass last night. There's three quarters of the bottle left.'

'You will have a glass with me?'

'Do I need it?'

'Probably. I know I do.'

A sound like a muted laugh came from her lips but the way she tore her eyes from him and blinked frantically negated it.

In the kitchen, she opened the tall fridge and pulled out a bottle of white. She took two glasses out of a cupboard, filled them both virtually to the rim and took a large drink from one. She gestured for him to take the other.

So she didn't want to risk touching him. He could not blame her for that.

'You were wonderful tonight,' he said softly. 'I could not take my eyes off you.'

A hesitant smile played on her lips. 'Thank you. It helped knowing you were there. I know it must have taken a lot.'

'Do not dare thank me,' he said darkly. He did not want her gratitude. He downed the rest of his wine and put the glass down on the counter.

Her eyes had become wary. 'Benjamin…?'

He held out a hand to stop her. 'First, let me apologise unreservedly for the way I spoke to you and for throwing you out of my home.'

'You hardly threw me out. You got your driver to take me to the airport.'

'Do not make excuses for me.' He glared at her. 'I do not deserve excuses and I will not accept them. My behaviour, everything I have done to you has been abhorrent. I will not make excuses to myself any more. I *did* steal you from Javier. I have been a jealous fool. I saw you in Javier's garden and have not been the same since.'

'What do you mean?' she asked in a far softer tone than he deserved.

'Something happened to me when I first set eyes on you. I could not get you from my mind. I was obsessed with you. I wanted you for myself because I am a selfish, greedy man. I chose you as leverage against Javier, not because I thought it was the most effective way to get my money back but to destroy your engagement.'

'You wanted to destroy us?'

He gave a tight nod. Since making the decision to go to Madrid to support her, he had done nothing but think. It had not been a pleasant awakening.

'I could not bear to think of you in his bed or him touching you,' he told her. 'I salved my conscience by telling myself you were better off without him, but you were right that time when you asked me who I thought I was deciding what was right for you. And you were right that everything I did was to serve my own agenda. *You* were my agenda. If you weren't I would have paid you off when you suggested it. I would have done anything to have you and make you mine. And now I would do anything to make amends. I don't deserve or expect your forgiveness. I have ruined your life. Javier would have been the better man for you to marry, and I do not say that lightly. He would never have tried to control you or influence where you worked.'

'Only because he wouldn't have cared,' she interjected with a whisper.

'But that is what you need, is it not? The freedom to live your life for what is best for you and your career without anything else fighting for space in a life already full with your dance and your parents? I took that away from you. I made what should have been the greatest night of your life a nightmare. When you reached out to me about your troubles I pushed you away because I didn't believe an independent woman like you, who has never needed anyone, could need me when no one has ever needed me before. I was jealous too, of you living under the same skies as Javier, and jealous you had a passion that didn't involve me.'

'You were jealous of me dancing?'

'*Oui*. Your dance. It is who you are, *ma douce*. It is one of the reasons I fell in love with you.' Her eyes widened at his casual admission but he carried on, wanting to get everything off his chest while he had the chance. 'When you commit to something you do not do it lightly. I cannot tell you how much I admire the dedication and commitment it must have taken you to become the woman you are today or how envious I am of the childhood you had.'

'You're jealous of my childhood? What on earth for? We were dirt poor.'

'But rich with love. My father left when he couldn't take playing second fiddle to Clara Casillas any longer—and to think I am anything like him just destroys me—and my mother...' He breathed heavily. This was an admittance he had barely acknowledged to himself. 'She loved me in the way an owner loves its pet. I was an accessory, conceived as a playmate for the children Clara would have. When Clara died she transferred her love to Clara's sons. I could never make her smile the way they did. When my father left he didn't give me a second thought and I didn't give him one either. That's what I mean about never being needed before.

'Your parents love you. Whatever career path you chose they would have done anything they could to support and encourage you whatever the cost to themselves. And you are the same. When you love someone you give them your whole heart and I will never forgive myself for making you a pawn in my vengeance.'

He paused to get some air into his lungs.

Freya was staring at him, eyes wide, her mouth half open but no sound coming out.

'You will have seen the deposit I made into your account. It's the sum I should have paid you to begin with rather than force you into a marriage you did not want. Anything you want, for you or for your parents, message me—I don't expect you to call. I know I can't make things better by throwing money at it but, for the sake of my conscience, promise you will always come to me. I need to be able to sleep again, *ma douce*, and abandoning my plans for revenge on Luis isn't enough.'

She smiled weakly. 'You're going to leave Luis alone?'

'I have done enough damage to spend eternity in hell. I will let his own conscience punish him.'

Her chin wobbled. 'I'm glad. And I'm proud of you.'

'I do not deserve that,' he said with a grimace.

'You could have made a scene tonight but you didn't. You walked away. Your soul isn't a lost cause, whatever you believe.'

'I only walked away because of you. You are more important to me than anything. More important than my hate for them. I can only apologise again and again that it was nearly too late for your performance before I realised it.'

'But it wasn't too late, was it? You were there. You came. That means the world.'

He managed the semblance of a smile. 'You have a beautiful heart, *ma douce*. I hope one day you find a man deserving of it.' He took one more deep breath and gave a sharp nod. 'And now I shall leave you to your rest.'

Stepping over to her, he put his hands lightly on her shoulders, breathing in the scent he had missed so badly for the last time. Brushing his lips to her forehead, he whispered. *'Au revoir, mon amour.'*

He took comfort that she didn't flinch away from his touch.

Holding his frame together by the skin of his teeth, he walked to the door.

He would fall apart when he was in the privacy of his

home. There was a whole bar full of Scotch for him to drown his sorrows in.

'So that's it?' she called after him, stopping him in his tracks. 'You come here to pour your heart out and tell me you love me and then *leave*? What about all the things I need to say to you?'

He closed his eyes. 'Whatever you need to say, I will listen.'

'You can start by turning around and facing me.'

Slowly he turned, expecting to see anger, preparing for the full-scale verbal attack he deserved.

Instead…

Instead he was greeted by the softest, gentlest expression he had ever seen.

She treaded over to him and placed a hand on his cheek. 'I took one look at you in Javier's garden and I fell in love with you. I was obsessed with you. I couldn't stop thinking about you even though they were thoughts I knew I shouldn't have. When you stole me away…' She sighed. 'I have tried my hardest to hate you. There have been times when I *have* hated you but running beneath it all has been my heart beating harder than it has ever beaten before because it is beating for two. It is beating for you. I lost my ability to dance because my heart and soul became yours without my knowing. I could only dance in the chateau because that's where you were. I needed to be near you. I still need to be near you. I can dance again now, I found a way through it, but without you in my life the passion is lost. I do need you, Benjamin. Like a fish needs water. I can't breathe properly without you.'

Her lips found his to press the most tender of kisses to them.

She sighed again. 'I love you. When I dance it is your face I see before me and it lifts me higher than I have ever jumped before. You make me want a life that's more than dance. You bring all the different colours and flavours of life out in me.'

He didn't dare allow joy anywhere near him. 'But can you forgive me? Can you ever trust me?'

'I *do* trust you. As for forgiveness, I can promise to forgive you if you can promise to forgive yourself.'

'I don't know how,' he answered honestly. He would never lie to her.

'By drawing a line in the sand on the past. What's done is done and we can't change it. All we can do is look to the future and the only future I want is with you.'

'The only future I want is with *you*. Without you I am nothing. I will follow you anywhere. To the ends of the earth. You can dance in China for all I care, I will be there with you.'

She kissed him again. 'Then prove it to me.'

'How?'

'By loving me for ever.'

Suddenly feeling as if his heart would burst, Benjamin finally allowed himself to believe...

She loved him! This incredible woman who could move his heart with the tilt of her head loved him.

In his wildest fantasies he had never allowed himself to think that.

But she did. And he loved her.

Parting his lips, he kissed her back with all the love and passion she had filled his heart with, thanking all the deities in the skies for giving him this second chance to be a better man with this woman who completed him.

And he would love her for ever.

EPILOGUE

TERROR CLUTCHED AT Benjamin's heart.

That was his wife, waiting in the wings, ready to come on stage and dazzle the packed theatre of families at the Orchestre National de Paris in her role as the Sugar Plum Fairy for this one-off Christmas production of *The Nutcracker*.

And this was their year-old son asleep on his lap, blissfully unaware his mother was about to perform for the first time since his birth. And in such a monumental, iconic role too.

It would also be her first performance since her mother had died peacefully in her sleep that summer. Freya and her father had consoled themselves that they had been given another two years with her, good years with months in which she'd been well enough to travel to Russia and New York and watch her only daughter guest star with some of the most famous ballet companies in the world and meet her first grandchild.

Benjamin had no idea how Freya was going to pull it off. His darling wife had had a roller-coaster year with tears and laughter, sadness and joy. All the ups and downs had only brought them closer together.

Freya was his world. Christopher, the dark-haired bundle of mischief in his arms, had completed them.

Gasps from the children in the audience brought him back to the present, and he blinked to see the vision in a glittering white tutu take to the stage.

Then the familiar tinkling music began and his wife transformed into the Sugar Plum Fairy.

With subtlety, charm and grace, she moved over the

stage, that illusion of flight she did so perfectly enthralling the whole spellbound theatre.

'She's wonderful,' whispered his father-in-law, sitting beside him in Benjamin's private box.

Benjamin nodded his agreement, too choked to speak. He didn't have to look to know Freya's loving father had tears rolling down his face.

When the orchestra played its final note in the dance, the theatre erupted. Cheers and bellows rang out, a sound so different from what had played before that Christopher woke up.

Bouncing in excitement, he pointed to the stage. 'Mama!'

'*Oui*, that's your mama,' Benjamin whispered into his son's ear. 'And your grandfather is right—she is wonderful.'

* * * * *